Story of the Hutchinsons (tribe of Jesse) Volume 2

Hutchinson, John Wallace, 1821-1908

Nabu Public Domain Reprints:

You are holding a reproduction of an original work published before 1923 that is in the public domain in the United States of America, and possibly other countries. You may freely copy and distribute this work as no entity (individual or corporate) has a copyright on the body of the work. This book may contain prior copyright references, and library stamps (as most of these works were scanned from library copies). These have been scanned and retained as part of the historical artifact.

This book may have occasional imperfections such as missing or blurred pages, poor pictures, errant marks, etc. that were either part of the original artifact, or were introduced by the scanning process. We believe this work is culturally important, and despite the imperfections, have elected to bring it back into print as part of our continuing commitment to the preservation of printed works worldwide. We appreciate your understanding of the imperfections in the preservation process, and hope you enjoy this valuable book.

JOHN W. HUTCHINSON, 1895 — (p. 1)

STORY

OF

THE HUTCHINSONS

(TRIBE OF JESSE)

BY

JOHN WALLACE HUTCHINSON

Compiled and Edited by
CHARLES E. MANN

With an Introduction by
FREDERICK DOUGLASS

VOLUME II

BOSTON
LEE AND SHEPARD, PUBLISHERS
No. 10 Milk Street
1896

Copyright, 1896, by Lee and Shepard

All rights reserved

Story of the Hutchinsons

TYPOGRAPHY AND PRESSWORK
BY S J PARKHILL & CO
BOSTON

CONTENTS OF VOL II.

CHAPTER I — Crusading for Temperance, 1870–1876   Page 1

Cooper Institute meetings — Horace Greeley speaks — Wm H Burleigh — Stephen Merritt — Matthew Hale Smith — Abby goes to Florida — Dining with General Howard — A trip South — "Don't Stay Away" — An unreconstructed planter — Experience with General Lee — Southern cities do not take kindly to the Hutchinsons — "John Brown's Body" — C F P Bancroft — Henry's peculiar photograph — The Fisk University singers — John suggests that they take the road — Rev D H Pratt — Rev. Thomas K Beecher and his cider — Chaplain Yard again — The unique Talmage — Concert advertised at a funeral — Viola sings "Your Mission" — Antoinette Sterling — Henry Ward Beecher and Nast — Carpenter's great painting — "Give us (hic) suthin lively" — Daisy Cottage going up — Rev J Hyatt Smith — Two concerts in legislative chambers — Kate Hutchinson — Rev Wm Morely Punshon — General Butler talking for temperance — Zerah C. Whipple — Charles W. Sohier — Susan B. Anthony eulogizes the Hutchinsons — Henry Wilson and woman suffrage — A talk with President Grant — Chase's prophecy — At Barbara Fietchie's home — Singing the "Star-Spangled Banner" over Francis Scott Key's grave — An evening with General Sherman — Washington's temperance crusade — Entertained by Grace Greenwood — Visiting Vinnie Ream — "The Blue and the Gray" — Singing the song to Alexander H Stephens — Dr Mary Walker — Concerts at Richmond — Abby in Europe — Gough raising chickens — At John P. Hale's home — Life in New York — 'Where is Heaven?" — Two temperance societies formed — A great anti-slavery anniversary at Philadelphia — Vice-President Wilson and reconstruction — Judge Jonas Hutchinson — Henry with the Camilla Urso troupe — At the Centennial — All the family sing — John Wanamaker — Singing for Bishop Newman — The Hayes election — John's proposition for settlement — At the White House

CHAPTER II.—ACROSS THE CONTINENT, 1877-1888 . . . 68
Singing in Chicago — Rufus Blanchard — Lillie C Phillips — The Hughes Brothers — Henry rejoins the company — Great successes — A mishap in Jersey City — Trans-continental experiences — In San Francisco — A tribute to Jesse — Rev I N Kalloch — Ada C Bowles — Henry's son, Jack, born — Joseph Cook — The Yosemite chapel — At San Diego — Judson seriously ill — Bound for Oregon — A touch of sea-sickness — General Howard's welcome — John takes the "shingles" — Over the California mountains — General Grant's great banquet — Rev L D Mansfield — Gen John Bidwell — A call from Denis Kearney — Hayward Hutchinson — "Under the Ice" — Back to Lynn — Jesse Harriman — Rev Samuel Everett — Asa sells John his interest in High Rock — Shall the rock be a public park? — A ghost story — The Hawkes family — Henry appointed a signal officer — In "Purgatory" — David gets a present — The McGibeney family — "Which Way is Your Musket A-p'intin' To-day?" — Abby foretells Garfield's election — Death of David — Death of Rhoda — At Emerson's funeral — Little Jesse dies — Joshua's death — A trip to Santa Fé — Among the cliff dwellings — In Hutchinson once more — Abby, Asa's daughter, dies — At Wendell Phillips's funeral — Death of Henry — Terrace Lodge built — Asa dies — A landlord's perplexities — At Asa's grave — At Beecher's funeral — Emma Sheridan Frye — Rebecca Moore's visit — Fanny's death

CHAPTER III — LOOKING TOWARDS SUNSET, 1888-1894   152
A reunion of pioneer Abolitionists — Harrison's inauguration — Guest of Fred Douglass — "Are you Harrison's grandfather?" — Getting a housekeeper — S F Smith — Story of "America" — A visit to Whittier — Lynn's great fire — "The People's Advent" — Felicitations to "Susan" — The seventieth birthday party — Dr Miner and his bald head — At the Republican national convention — Hale's statue dedicated — Death of Whittier — Abby and John's last song at the funeral — Abby's death — Singing at Whittier's memorial services — At General Butler's funeral — The Danvers anti-slavery meeting — Off to the World's Fair — Depew's tribute to John — "Ho, for California" — General Miles — With Douglass in the Hayti building — New Hampshire Day — Facing 500,000 people — Mrs Isabella Beecher Hooker — Rev Mr Morgan's gospel wagon — A visit to Helen M Gougar — Reunion of Forty-niners — "Chicago Day" — Minnesota Day — Manhattan Day — Ringing the

Page

Columbia liberty bell — Carter Harrison's last speech — John's tribute to his memory — Scaring an Indian with war-whoops — The last song on the grounds — "Old Hutch" — Introducing Latimer to a Boston audience — The Milford centennial — Birthday of author of "Kathleen Mavourneen" — The Bryant centennial — "After All" — A reception to Neal Dow

CHAPTER IV — AN OLD-TIME YANKEE FAMILY . 234
Garrison's tribute to the "Tribe of Jesse" — Little Jesse — His death — David — "Noise is not music" — David's family — Noah — Mary — Andrew — Baptised by father — Zephaniah, an early pioneer — Caleb and Joshua, twin songsters — "Wake up!" — The twin buglers — A country music-teacher — Joshua's many concerts — Jesse, the Bard of High Rock — A happy printer boy — "In perfect *dis*-order" — Jesse's anti-slavery songs — Rogers writes of Jesse — A circular letter from California — "Brothers, I hear your voices sweet" — Benjamin, a member of the "home guard" — Judson — His wonderful voice — His ventriloquial powers — A master of satire — Tributes to his memory — Asa, the youngest son — A heavy bass — Notices of his death — Rhoda, the sister of the "Home Branch" — Elizabeth — Abby, the sixteenth child — Her wonderful conceit experience — Frank B. Carpenter's sketch of her life — Her literary instinct — A friend of reform — Some impromptu lines — Other literary work

CHAPTER V — AMERICAN SONGS AND THEIR INTERPRETATION 286
This a record of the public, not private life of the Hutchinsons — Their industry, devotion and hopefulness — "American singers" — What is the true "American folk-song?" — The Hutchinsons' songs as examples — President Emerson's view — How the family programmes were made up — "Topsy" — The family rehearsals — Judson knew when he had enough — John's motto "Spero Meliora" — Accompaniments — John's celebrated melodeon — Abby cannot sing with it — "The Maniac" — The family forced to compose its own music — How the "Old Granite State" was written and brought out — Joint composition — Judson's songs — Asa a composer, but not a poet — Caleb's "Millennium" — John's songs — Abby's music

APPENDIX . . 311
The Hutchinsons in Europe — Notice from the *Birmingham Journal* — The *London Morning Chronicle* — Singing of the "Home Branch" in 1846 — At Sing Sing as told in the *Tribune*

Page

— The Henry Clay incident, 1846 — Comments by Garrison in the *Liberator* — Another comment — Brother Jesse replies — Garrison's response — The "Hutchinsons' repentance" — Henry Clapp, Jr., in the *Pioneer* — The *Chronotype's* strictures on the "She Kinah" — The *Pioneer* again — The bull-frogs and the sun — The *Freeman's* views — *Newark Reformer* takes a hand — Garrison's final shot — Douglass pours oil on the waters — Letters and reminiscences — John G. Whittier — General Sherman — Thurlow Weed — General Howard — Gerritt Smith — Parker Pillsbury — Rev. Brooke Herford — Dickens's comment on the "Bridge of Sighs" — Rebecca Moore — Rev. R. H. Howard — Frederick Douglass — Ex-Governor Root — William Lloyd Garrison — W. Augustus Fonda — J. S. Bliss — Rev. J. B. Davis — J. N. Stearns — George W. Latimer — C. G. Foster — George M. Dutcher — Brother Joshua — Seventieth Birthday Letters — A. P. Putnam — Parker Pillsbury — Rev. M. J. Savage — John H. Hunt — John J. Wallace — E. R. Brown — Grace Greenwood — Wendell Phillips Garrison — Frank B. Carpenter — John Mills — Frances E. Willard — E. E. Johnson — S. F. Smith — Charles Buffum — Edward Bellamy — J. Q. A. Brackett — Wm. M. Springer — Rev. S. B. Stewart — Rev. Charles G. Ames — Sister Abby's letters — The Portland riot — Abby in Naples — Abby's poems

LIST OF ILLUSTRATIONS.

VOL II.

	Page
John W Hutchinson, 1895	Frontispiece
Tent at Martha's Vineyard	14
The Hutchinsons in 1872	25
Tower Cottage, High Rock	46
Judson Whittier Hutchinson	71
The Tribe of John, 1878	72
John, Henry and Judson Hutchinson	109
At the Cliff Dwellings	114
Camping in Chapulio Canon	117
The Hutchinson Pioneers	122
Henry J Hutchinson	127
John and his Grandchildren	132
Henry D Campbell	166
Kate Hutchinson Campbell	200
Cleveland J Campbell	210
The Dearborn Quartet, Tribe of Judson	219
William Lloyd Garrison	234
The Tribe of Noah	238
Judson J. Hutchinson	255
John and Family	262
Asa and Family	263
Abby Hutchinson Patton, 1892	270
Ludlow Patton	274
Mother of the Hutchinsons	277
The Original Quartet (old cut)	294

HISTORY OF THE HUTCHINSON FAMILY

CHAPTER I.

CRUSADING FOR TEMPERANCE.

"Unite, unite, to battle for right,
　　The war has just begun,
Through all the land let the cry go out,
　　'We've need of more earnest ones'
Brave hearts and stout,
King Alcohol we have to rout,
　　Come, join the temperance band."

WE opened 1870 with many important engagements on our books. On the 23d of January I carried through a monster temperance meeting in the Cooper Institute, New York. It was followed by another on the following Sabbath in the same place. Horace Greeley agreed to speak at the first, but was unable to be there. There were thirty-five hundred people present. Wm. H. Burleigh repeated his great poem, "Delirium Tremens." He became so excited that he never got over it. Not long after, I sang at his funeral. Rev. Stephen Merritt spoke, and I gave a twenty-minute address. On the following Sunday the Institute was jammed again. Greeley spoke. One of the leading Sons of Temperance took the matter up, and continued the meetings afterwards. Matthew Hale Smith, "Burleigh," of the *Boston Journal*, said to me, "John, don't you let them cheat you out of the credit of this, for you were the original designer of these meetings." But I could not stay in the city, and was glad to have any person take them up who would continue them as free temperance meetings. It needed some organization to back the movement up. Following is the *New York Times'* report of the meeting on the 23d.

"A goodly audience assembled in the large hall of the Cooper Institute last evening, to listen to the advocates of the temperance cause. Every seat was taken before the meeting opened.

"The meeting opened with an 'invocation' by the Hutchinson Family. A prayer was then offered by Rev. Stephen Merritt, Jr., who presided, after which Mr. E. Z. C. Judson (Ned Buntline), was introduced. He said that a soldier, who was for a long time on the wrong side of the question, must never shrink from standing up for the right. He has noticed a convention of rumsellers, called to meet on this day, to devise means to secure a repeal of the excise law. The temperance movement meant mercy to humanity and justice to God. The excise law would be repealed because the temperance men of New York folded their arms during the last campaign. The time has come for every Christian man to come out for prohibition. He had never written a line for woman's rights or in favor of woman's wearing anything but crinoline, but knowing how much women were sufferers from alcohol and its influences, he wished every woman could have a vote and sweep it from the country.

"After a temperance song by the Hutchinsons, Mr Wm. H. Burleigh recited an original poem entitled 'Delirium Tremens.' He explained that his sketch was drawn from actual life. The poem portrayed the sufferings of a man under the influence of an attack of delirium tremens.

"The Hutchinson Family sang 'Marching On,' the audience joining in the chorus. Mr. John W. Hutchinson then read an address. He said among other things that the number of crimes committed under the influence of drink in New York was 36,114; the sheriff of Albany said the proportion of crimes traceable to intoxication was five-tenths; the sheriff of Niagara County said three-fourths; the police justice of Buffalo said nine-tenths. Connecticut reports 90 out of every 100 crimes committed under the influence of liquor. Massachusetts had in one year committed 12,000 criminals to her prisons, and reported 9,000 made such by intemperance. The address was largely made up of personal observations. In Egypt Ill. the candidate for office enhanced his chances of election by being found drunk in the streets. The speaker alluded to the inauguration in 1865 as an instance of drunkenness in high places. He spoke of Johnson and his 'tipsy retinue' as he 'swung around the circle.' He then dwelt on the woman's rights question, and demanded the ballot for woman, and thought she would purify it. [Faint applause and hisses.] Every woman would vote to close the dram shops. God grant that she may obtain the right to do so! Voting would be done in a well-carpeted hall or church, and men and women would approach, arm-in-arm, with heads uncovered, and deposit the sacred ballot. He read an original poem entitled 'Speed the Temperance Cause,' and mentioned that his mother's three sisters were blessed with sots for husbands. One of them was a brother to Theodore Parker, and was said to excel him in brilliancy of intellect. He then read another poem for prohibition and opposing 'license.'

"Rev. Mr. Merritt wanted every one to unite in banishing the rum power from the land. A collection of forty-seven dollars was taken up. Rev. T. T. Kendrick read an essay on the rise and progress of intemperance, dwelling particularly on the way it affected women."

The following week the report of Mr. Greeley's address said that he reviewed the past fifty years of struggle for temperance and summed up what had been accomplished in that time. His judgment was that the so-called "permissive liquor law" was the right thing for present needs. The best part of the country will always be able to do away with the liquor traffic. Let the people vote on the question whether they want liquor or not. He did not expect that the temperance cause would be triumphant immediately. No law will stop men's drinking, but it will remove temptation from the face and eyes of a great many. New York averaged more than three hundred murders in every year, and not more than one-tenth of them are committed by men who do not drink. Liquor should be treated just as a poison. Temperance, in its effects, is the best argument for temperance as a principle.

On the first of January, 1870, Sister Abby left New York for Florida. After singing a month longer for the

Literary Bureau in New York State, we made a short tour in Vermont, and one even shorter in Rhode Island. Then we received a pressing invitation from Abby to come to Florida, and early in March the trio, Henry, Spinning and I, started for Jacksonville. We stopped in Washington, and while there I dined with General Oliver O. Howard, then in charge of the Freedmen's Bureau, and he kindly gave me many letters of introduction to various people in the South. We reached Savannah on the 22d, and Jacksonville on the 25th. Passing through Charleston, S. C., I called on the mayor, Gilbert P. Pillsbury. He was a Northern man, in other words, a "Carpet-Bagger," and told me that since his appointment he had received no courtesies from the aristocracy in the city. He was an ostracized man, and felt it necessary to keep his body-servant with him all the time. He had had his first invitation to be present at a society event in an official capacity for that very evening. "But," said he, "I shall take my body-servant with me."

Abby was at Magnolia, and the day following our arrival at Jacksonville, we set out for that delightful place, passing by the orange grove of Harriet Beecher Stowe on our way. The next few weeks were passed in singing in the towns along St. John's River, at Jacksonville, St. Augustine and other points. We went to picnics and other social gatherings, had oranges in abundance, and enjoyed the society of every one we saw. Abby had become very much interested in the colored people and took us to their meetings, where we found much to delight us in their songs. Some of them we learned and brought back with us and they so pleased our audiences that we published them. Notably among these was "My Jesus Says there's Room Enough:

"My Jesus says there's room enough,
My Jesus says there's room enough,
My Jesus says there's room enough,
　　Don't stay away

"My brother, don't stay away,
My sister, don't stay away,
My elder, don't stay away,
　　Until the judgment day

"There's a starry crown in Heaven for you, etc.,
　　Don't stay away

"There's a robe of white in heaven for you, etc.,
　　Don't stay away"

This song set to one of the simple and pathetic melodies of the freedmen, became very popular, was taken up after being heard in our concerts and is still often sung in gospel meetings and similar services in the North.

We were very much interested in the great cathedral at St. Augustine. Here we met an old friend, Mr. Atwood. We first met him in London, and found him a man of strong character, able and agreeable. In 1849 he chartered a large vessel, filled it with goods, and shipped for California. He was wrecked, and his family and all on board perished except himself. He was landed on a strange island, with everything he possessed gone except a cat. By the aid of the consul he was sent to New York. There we met him at Dr. Wellington's hydropathic establishment. Next we met him at Washington at the opening of the war, and he aided us in getting up a great concert in the Smithsonian Institution. At this meeting in St. Augustine we found him married again, with a pleasant wife and family. With his characteristic friendliness he had interested himself in getting out a large audience to our concert, and it was so successful that we went again and gave another.

We had quite an idea of buying an orange grove, but after investigating, found it would be an unnecessary care, and gave it up. Before our coming, Abby had made the acquaintance of an old gentleman, Captain May, whose son had been on the staff of General Lee. He invited us to his plantation, and accompanied by Abby, we went. It was a desolate-looking place, having been stormed by Union gunboats during the war. A cannon-ball could be seen, partly embedded in the frame of the house. The fiery old gentleman would not let it be removed. He was quite unreconstructed, and very wrathy against the North. He, with his wife, told me the story of their experiences during the war. We saw a dozen or more of his former slaves about the premises, trying to eke out a miserable existence. The only income from the place was from his orange grove. I referred to the foolishness of war. The old man at once roused up against the North. Thinking a reference to religious things might subdue his strong feeling, I remarked that my father and mother were both Baptists. They smiled. They were Baptists, too, and the conversation took a pleasanter turn.

Many years before I had attended, in Portland, Me., an exhibition by graduates of a female seminary. Among the pupils was a young lady with a peculiar swelling on her face. When she spoke, her recitation was Poe's "Bells." What might have been called her disfigurement seemed to vanish from the mind, she repeated her lines with so much spirit and soul. While on this trip we were invited to a sail, by a Maine man who had come to Florida in his yacht. On board I foun

seminary exhibition. I was pleased enough to meet her. She soon after attended a concert we gave. During the evening I announced that I would recite Poe's "Raven." At one point in the recitation a line dropped out of my mind, and I paused in dismay. Instantly the lady spoke the word I had forgotten.

At Green Cove, Fla., we were giving a concert, and I was singing "The Fatherhood of God and the Brotherhood of Man." When I sung the lines,

"Columbia's sons must lead the way, raise high the lofty standard
Of equal rights they now maintain, though once to slavery pandered,"

two settees' full of Southerners arose and indignantly brushed their way out. Our equanimity survived this shock.

While in Magnolia we made a habit of going to the steamboat landing and welcoming coming and speeding parting guests with song. Therefore it did not seem strange when we took our departure for the North from Jacksonville to see a large concourse of friends at the landing. We soon found that there were two sets of people in the gathering, and that one of them came not to bid farewell to us, but to General Robert E. Lee, who was also a passenger of the steamer *Nick King*. Several of his former retinue of army officers were with him. He stood on the deck, apparently preoccupied. We sang "Uncle Sam's Farm," "Come, let us part with lightsome heart," and "Good-by, brothers, good-by sisters." Soon one of General Lee's staff introduced me to him. He smilingly remarked that our honors in the farewell were equal. Finally amid hearty cheers, we left the pier. We sailed North by the inland route. Soon we gathered at the dining table. Lee sat at the head of the table, I at the other end. During the meal, he courteously sent me his wine. This embarrassed me. It was against my convictions of right to drink, and I did not, but I was afraid he would think I declined because I would not drink with a rebel. The General was ill, and kept so close to his cabin that I was unable to have the familiar chat with him that I desired. I was hopeful the report of such an interview might get into the papers and so aid in a small way in promoting a better feeling between North and South, besides making our reception pleasanter at such Southern towns as we visited. He was a handsome man, and notwithstanding my disappointment in the particular matter of which I have spoken, I had several conversations with him on general topics. At one point on our journey we came to a landing where there was a mixture of Northern and Southern people, gathered out of curiosity to see Lee. We struck up a song on deck. They cheered us. Then some one called for three cheers for Lee. They were given. Immediately Henry shouted "Three cheers for General Grant!" These, too, were given with a will, but from different voices. Then we sang a mournful good-by and went on our way.

We were landed at Savannah. I had sent ahead an announcement of our intention to give a concert. The result was a "blow" in the *Savannah Republican*. We always loved to have a "blow" when we knew the source from which it came, for often our enemies did us the greatest service. The *Republican's* remarks were as follows:

"'AND LAST OF ALL CAME,' etc.—Among the many public exhibitions now travelling through the South to amuse the people and put money in their own pockets, we notice the Hutchinson Family. They are, perhaps, the only company of public performers who have been thoroughly identified politically with the Abolition ultra-Radical party of the North, and sharing fully in all its hate and denunciation of the Southern people. They have, for years, been indispensible adjuncts to radical political meetings in the New England States, with appropriate songs catering to the popular prejudice against the South, and doing what they could to help on the work of our mis-government and humiliation. With the effrontery indigenous to their section, they now come South, we suppose, to receive their reward out of the hard earnings of our people. Their modesty is certainly refreshing. In a free country every man has a right to his own opinion and to express it freely, and moreover, to be respected in all his rights as a citizen, while Southern hospitality would frown upon any breach of decorum toward a stranger, let him be whom he may; but, we submit, when the Southern people are called upon to pay a premium on hate and persecution, it is a little more than we would advise them to grant."

When we arrived at Savannah, my attention was at once called, at the hotel, to this scurrilous article. At once I went to the office of the paper, boldly stepped in and walked up to the counter, behind which the "staff" were busy at work at their desks. I addressed one of the editors, "Sir, can you tell me who wrote the notice of the Hutchinsons which appeared in your paper?" Not a word was spoken, but the man turned to his assistant and looked at him. I had one hand behind me, in what I suppose might have been termed in the South at that time, a threatening attitude. He sprang up, put his hand behind him also, and savagely said, "I wrote it." "Well," said I, "I'm complimented; yet it may injure us here. I came not to bring a sword, but peace. I brought an olive branch, hoping to assist in securing a more cordial feeling between North and South. I did not desire to prejudice the people." Then he began to talk. "You have whipped us," he said, "but we are not conquered. Nothing will bring good feeling but fighting a common enemy like England. Did you ever sing 'John Brown's Body?'" I admitted that we sometimes did. "Did you sing 'Hang Jeff

Davis to a sour apple tree?'" "That was a verse of the song," I said, "and I presume we did." "Our Northern regiments also sang it together," I remarked.

At the hour appointed for the concert, I took my melodeon and went to the opera house, gloomy, sad and uncertain. Both sidewalks, as I walked along, were packed with people, pointing at me. I reached the hall a few minutes before the concert should have commenced. It was dark and closed, not a soul inside and evidently not a soul coming, but all on the sidewalks, ready to do me bodily harm, and perhaps kill me. I returned to my hotel, taking the darkey's advice, to "keep in de middle ob de road," for I preferred death by shooting to dirking.

The next day the *Constitutionalist*, another paper said:

"DID NOT DRAW.— The Hutchinson Family concert advertised for last night did not seem to draw well, and the performance was severely let alone by audience and players alike. 'John Brown's soul goes marching on,' and 'We'll hang Jeff Davis to a sour apple tree,' have elevated the reputation of this company several degrees *beyond* the appreciation of the section which they took particular pleasure in singing into contempt and disregard during the war. The cotton crop of the past season was infinitely too small to justify the Southern people in hiring minstrels of that ilk to pipe to them, now that 'grim-visaged war has smoothed his wrinkled front.' Perhaps when a thorough reconstruction of the tastes, spirit and preferences of our white people has been brought to that perfect 'loilty' contemplated, the Hutchinsons will be welcomed. As an experiment, they might try again — in about thirty years."

The *Republican* said:

"WISE.— The agent of the abolition war singers, the Hutchinson Family, was here a few days ago, to provide for a performance, but, after taking the bearings, concluded to try his luck in some other quarter than Savannah. He patronized us to the amount of a few spare numbers of the *Republican*, containing a notice of this troupe, which he thought could be used as political capital at the North."

Sister Abby had accompanied us to this point, but took the train for home. Our hotel accommodations at Savannah cost us each five dollars a day. The fare furnished was execrable. I do not wonder people revolted who ate such food. From there we went to Aiken, a quiet little village where there were several hundred boarders. We gave a successful concert to them. At Augusta, Ga., we had an experience similar to that at Savannah. But few appeared at the hour our concert was advertised, and we were sadly out of pocket. Years before, we had made the acquaintance of a Yankee, formerly an overseer in the mills at Chicopee, Mass. He always showed a great friendliness for the Hutchinsons. Being of a speculative nature, he had assisted in building a cotton factory in Augusta. We wrote to him, suggesting concerts. His answer was, "If you approve of the present course of Congress and its attitude toward Georgia, I advise you not to come." When we arrived, we found him reluctant about assisting us, but he consented to come to the concert. Two ladies and three gentlemen comprised the audience. We sang a few selections and postponed it indefinitely. Evidently the notices in the Savannah papers had reached Augusta and the people were indignant. We were grieved at this show of sectional feeling. We might have sung "Hang Jeff Davis" in the excitement of war times, but had no such sentiments in our hearts at this time. We took the night train for Atlanta and spent the next day advertising a concert. But slanderous stories were again circulated against us, and there were so few at the hall that we had to give it up. The disappointment made me sick. All through Georgia we could see the signs of the ravages of war — and marks of Sherman's march to the sea were everywhere.

Leaving Atlanta we visited Chattanooga, Tenn., and Lookout Mountain. On the mountain was a college, the president being C. F. P. Bancroft, formerly principal of the academy at Mont Vernon, N. H., where Henry and Viola were educated. Of late years he has been at Andover, Mass. We walked five miles from Chattanooga, Henry assisting my feeble steps up the mountain to the institution.

Professor Bancroft received us very cordially, and invited us to stay a week. All his retinue of servants were colored people. One by the name of Jackman was very kind to me. I loved him for his thoughtful attentions. One day he said, "I can sing some." "Can you?" said I. I told him I would be glad to hear him as soon as I was able to get to the dining-room, for I was still far from well. When I heard him I found he had good powers as a singer. I asked him if he would like to go to the North. He said he would like to go first rate, and I said I would send for him after my return. Later he was a chorus singer with the Fisk Jubilee people. I was quite feeble. However, I was thankful I was able to go to the top of the mountain, where the famous "Battle of the Clouds" was fought. Henry sought fame in a curious way. A photographer on the summit desired to take our pictures, and we consented. Henry, to have his name associated with the mountain in a special manner, struck an attitude on the edge of the precipice, on his head, with his feet in the air, and the artist took him. I still have the picture. Finally we bid an affectionate farewell to my Yankee friend and his school. We met my old and cherished friend T. C. Severance in Chattanooga. He then held a government position there. He got us up a concert. When we reached Nashville, we found the Southern prejudice still against us. We advertised a concert, but the audience was so meagre that we postponed it, announcing that it would be given the next evening, and that the proceeds would be devoted to the sufferers from a great catastrophe that had just occurred in Richmond by the falling of the floor of the court house. The result of the announcement was that the best citizens took hold of the ticket selling, and we had an audience. Professor White, of Fisk University, invited us to go to the school and sing to his colored pupils. We gave them some of our best pieces. At the conclusion he said, "I wish you to hear some of my singers." We said we would be most happy, and resigned the platform to them. I was delighted by their wonderful harmony. The whole world has heard it since. I suggested to the professor that he bring a choir of his freedmen to the North, for I was sure it would prove a great financial as well as musical success. The result of the suggestion was a tour of the Fisk University Jubilee Singers, which so soon followed.

From Nashville we went to Bowling Green, Ky., where we lost money on our concert, and from there to Louisville, where the prospects were so poor that we gave up, took the boat, and had a beautiful sail up the Ohio River to Cincinnati. Here we made arrangements to sing in concerts for the Y. M. C. A., and stayed several days. While there my wife and son Judson came from Toledo. They arrived on a Sunday, and that evening we sung at a vesper service in one of the churches, where the crush for admittance was so great that at least five hundred were unable to get in. After giving a few concerts in Ohio, we spent a few days in Toledo with Viola, whose second son, Harry, I saw for the first time, and then went to Buffalo, whence, after some concerts we kept on through New York State until we reached New Jersey, where we gave several concerts at Newark and other places.

Then followed a rest at Lynn. In July I went to Martha's Vineyard and made arrangements to erect a tent later. A Providence man, Mr. Clark, gave me the

use of a lot adjoining his own, within a stone's throw of the preacher's stand. On my return to Lynn we had a good time making the tent, and in August we went down and put it up. It was a merry company there that season. Abby came and also Nellie MacKay Hutchinson, who was one of the editorial staff of *The Revolution*, the suffrage paper in New York, and subsequently on the *Tribune*. We sang often to the people, and had a good time all around.

At the close of the camp-meeting, we hired a man to take us in a boat to Falmouth. With our baggage and the company we made a full boat load. There came up a squall, with thunder, lightning and rain. Even the skipper thought we must surely go down. However, we passed safely into the harbor of Edgartown, singing "Drop the anchor; we are safe within the veil." After that we went to Nantucket in the same sail-boat. When we reached there, the people said, "Don't do it again." We took their advice, and went home by steamer.

During the autumn of 1870 we filled engagements made by the American Literary Bureau in towns and cities within a hundred miles of New York, and sung in many temperance meetings in Rhode Island and Connecticut, with no unusual incidents.

We opened 1871 with a big Sunday temperance meeting at the Morning Star Sunday-school in New York City, George W. Bungay being one of the speakers. On the evening of the 3d of January a happy company gathered at the home of Mrs. Washburn, on Union Square — Sister Abby, the Carpenters, Glovers, Graziella Ridgway, Henry, Spinning and I. The clock struck twelve and we were still there. I then announced to them that I had reached my fiftieth birthday since coming in, and was now a half-century old. On the 12th of January there was a big meeting to favor Italian unity in the Academy of Music. Beecher made one of the most powerful addresses I ever heard.

Through January and February most of our time was spent in temperance work in Connecticut, with Rev. E. H. Pratt, agent of the State Temperance Society. We were paid thirty dollars a day. In the afternoon there would usually be a prayer service, followed by a free temperance meeting for the children, to which they would march with banners, etc., and we would sing to them. In the evening there would be a paid concert, the receipts going into the treasury of the society. We also sang under the same arrangement with Rev. H. W. Conant, of the Rhode Island society. Of course, our expenses were paid, and our entertainment was usually at the house of some sympathizer. Meanwhile, we had occasional engagements from the Bureau, and whenever I was out of Rhode Island or Connecticut on the Sabbath, I usually managed to get the pastors of the different churches to advertise and speak at a union temperance meeting at the largest hall.

On Sunday, the 5th of March, we were in Elmira, N. Y. We had given a concert the night before in the Opera House, and during that day I had been arranging a mass temperance meeting in the same hall. It was necessary to have the meeting in the afternoon, I found, for Rev. Thomas K. Beecher, the youngest of the celebrated family, although he preached in his own church in the morning, preached in the Opera House in the evening, and usually filled it to repletion. When I had secured the sympathy of all the other pastors of the city, I sought out Mr. Beecher. I knew him years before. He was pastor to a relative, E. P. Hutchinson. He was stopping at a water-cure, near the city. I found him out when I called. On my way back, I saw a man walking abstractedly in the gutter, whom I recognized as Beecher. "Mr. Beecher," said I, "we are to have a big temperance meeting in the Opera House to-morrow afternoon; won't you honor us by your presence?" He looked at me mischievously, and answered, "I've got some nice cider at the house. If you'll come up, I'll give you some, and talk it over." I did not go. He was the only pastor absent from the meeting.

On March 19th we were in a temperance meeting in Washington, N. J., at which the speakers were Rev. R. B. Yard, the chaplain of our Potomac days, and John W. Hutchinson.

On the 21st of the same month the funeral of Wm. H. Burleigh, one of another famous "band of brothers," occurred at Brooklyn. We sang "Beyond the Smiling and the Weeping." He married Mrs. Burr, formerly the wife of the man I mentioned as figuring in an antebellum episode at Concord, N. H. Later I met her in Brookline, Conn., where she had become a settled Unitarian minister. After that she went into a decline, and the last time I saw her she remarked, "O John, it doesn't pay! This is a hard life."

On Sunday, April 2d, we had another big temperance meeting in the Opera House at Elmira.

On the 6th we sang in the Brooklyn Tabernacle, Talmage's church. There were two thousand people at the concert. The organist, Mr. Loretz, played on the big Boston Peace Jubilee organ, which had become the property of the church. It was a pleasure to be with Talmage. He is Talmage; nobody is like him. He does not strive to be odd. He has a large share of oddities and peculiarities, but is sincere. He never was either as smart, brilliant or agreeable a speaker as Beecher, though Beecher himself had peculiarities. I have sometimes questioned his full belief of the doctrines he preached. He was a man who would entertain doubts, and had periods of scanning the creed carefully.

Early in May we spent a few days in Lynn, and then were off again to the vicinity of the Hudson. We made our headquarters at Chaplain Yard's in Washington, N. J., during much of June, meanwhile filling engagements in that State. There was great interest in the no-license question, and we had a splendid chance to do good educational work for temperance.

After a few weeks' rest at High Rock, in August I went to Martha's Vineyard, put up my tent, and prepared for service. I secured the privilege of using the grove and grand-stand for some temperance meetings. One was held on Sunday, August 20. It was the day before the opening of the camp-meeting proper, and the meeting and the conditions surrounding it were thus described in the *Boston Journal* correspondence of that date:

"The rustic cottages and dainty tents, of which some thousands are now located on the camp ground and Oak Bluffs, are nearly filled with their summer tenants, and the piazzas, shaded walks and promenades assume the loveliest aspect. Nearly eight thousand people are already on the grounds, and the first gathering of the eight days of religious service, which takes place to-morrow evening, will call together a large number of additional visitors. For the last two days, concerts and other entertainments have furnished the means for passing the evenings pleasantly. A large number of distinguished vocalists are upon the grounds, including the well-known Hutchinson Family, and the choir of the Park Church of Hartford, Conn. The Foxboro Brass Band is also upon the grounds, and their music signalizes the arrival and departure of the steamboats from the Oak Bluffs landing. These steamers appear to be one of the greatest attractions, for at the hour of their arrival thousands of people congregate upon the wharf, and the seats which line the walks in either direction are filled with those who expect the arrival of friends or have the curiosity to get the first peep of the inflowing tide of visitors. Saturday evening, being the last opportunity for gaiety before the people must be toned down to a proper camp-meeting sobriety, was the occasion for an overflow of jollity which resulted in quite a pleasant celebration. The band discoursed music from the grand-stand in the park, and a large number of the streets and private cottages were finely illuminated and decorated with Chinese lanterns. The sweet voices of talented musicians added harmonious and familiar melodies to the other attractions of the evening.

"The temperance meetings have been mainly sustained and carried forward by the magnetic melody of the Hutchinsons. The meeting last evening opened with a prayer by Rev. D. C. Babcock of Nashua, N. H. after which the president of the day Rev. J. W. Willett, of Providence, made an address upon the hopeful progress of the cause, and considered the chief element of the power of the liquor traffic to be the profits which accrue to the dealer. Rev. O. H. Tiffany, of Newark, N. J., made a very eloquent and stirring address, in which he contrasted the drinking usages of society in this country with those in vogue across the water. The custom of treating was essentially American, and in Germany it would be considered an insult to offer to pay for the drinks. Other brief addresses were made by Hon. Rodney French, and Hon. John W. Berry of Lynn, and at the close of the meeting a Vineyard Temperance Association was formed, to meet on the grounds each year. The beautifully rendered songs of the Hutchinsons were frequently applauded. This evening another meeting will be held, addressed by several of the speakers already mentioned."

I struck a slight snag in carrying on these meetings, in the conviction of many people that they were of a political nature. This was not true, and finally this was seen to be so, and the trustees cordially invited me to freely use the grounds for similar meetings the following year. Judge Berry was my guest during the meetings.

At the last meeting of the series, a love-feast, we sang and at the close I gave away several hundred copies of my "Fatherhood of God" song.

On Monday, the 28th, we gave a farewell concert at the chapel, which netted us one hundred and twenty dollars, and afterward attended a reception to Governor Claflin, of Massachusetts.

On September 5th there was a great temperance meeting at Rocky Point, R. I., with which a clam-bake was combined. We sang, and Rev. Q. H. Tiffany, Rev. H. W. Conant, Rev. Edwin Thompson and John W. Berry were speakers. On the following day, at Putnam, Conn., we commenced our fall campaign with Rev. E. H. Pratt. In October we went to campaigning with Rev. Mr. Conant, in Rhode Island. This was followed by a short series of temperance meetings in

New Jersey, and then we went back to Connecticut, where we stayed until the middle of December. Then our faces were turned westward, and after singing through Pennsylvania, where we were given fine audiences and most flattering newspaper notices, we reached Toledo, and spent part of the Christmas holidays with my daughter Viola.

The temperance meetings of which I have spoken were satisfactory to us, and remunerative to the associations for which I sung. During this period I had rather a trying experience in Worcester. I engaged Mechanics Hall for temperance meetings on the plan of those in Connecticut, with a children's meeting in the afternoon. The response to our invitation was appalling. The immense hall was swarming with children. They came by thousands, and it was two hours before sufficient quiet was secured to call them to order. Then speaking was practically impossible, and we could only sing to them. Stephen S. Foster assisted me and spoke in the meeting.

In one place, which I will not name, we had another unusual experience. A pastor of the place who was a seventh-day Baptist, and so did double work, preaching for a church of his denomination on Saturday, and for a regular Baptist church on the Sabbath, hearing we were in town, asked us to come to his church and sing at a funeral. We consented, and he sent a hack for us at the appointed hour. At the door of the church he came out, grabbed the melodeon from the carriage, carried it to the choir loft himself, and said, "I will give you a signal when I desire you to sing." Then he started in on his sermon in which he impressed the thought that death was the common lot; that it was nothing strange that people were dying. Then he made a motion, and I sang "A Brother is Dead." "Hark, what is the note so mournful and low ?" There was the corpse, there the mourners. The hush that succeeded the song was followed by the preacher: "The Hutchinson Family will give a concert this evening in the town hall." I was astonished. Soon the sexton mounted the platform and remarked, "If there is anybody that desires to examine the corpse, they can do so." Later in the day Henry went to the hall to take tickets and the sexton referred to spied him, met him with enthusiasm and said, "You're going to have one of the greatest crowds to-night. Your father lapped the song on to that dead man in such a style, that everybody is coming." I judge he was right by the audience which appeared.

Of course my daughter, with her two bouncing baby boys, had little time for singing, but I have before me a copy of the *Akron* (Ohio) *Beacon*, printed in 1871, containing an account of the 21st anniversary of the Ohio Christian Missionary Society, at which General Garfield, a member of the denomination, was present, in which her part in the exercises — singing "Your Mission" — is referred to as follows:

"The president [Rev. Isaac Errett, editor of the *Christian Standard*], after making a few preparatory remarks, in which he said that in the decade preceding the late war great moral ideas had been *sung* into the hearts of the people by a noted family of singers, said that one of the young nightingales from that nest of singers was present as delegate from the church at Toledo, and at his earnest solicitation had consented to sing a piece which herself and other members of the Hutchinson Family often sung at the request of the great Lincoln, and which was sung at the Capitol on the occasion of the 'mustering out' of the Christian Commission at the close of the war. The audience was enchanted with the sweetness of the singing, and the sentiment and burden of the song, which was 'Work, work, work, work.' Rev. William Baxter of New Lisbon, a poet-author, alluded to Mr. Errett's promise of a song from a *nightingale*, but behold the fair lady had proved rather to be a *mocking bird*, for she had caught up the refrain of all the great discourses of the convention, and sang in sweet notes 'Work! work! work!'"

After several days in Toledo, we commenced our work for 1871 by concerts in Wellsville, Hornellsville, and Norwich, N. Y. On Sunday, January 7th, we were in Elmira, and had another big temperance meeting in the Opera House. Two nights later we sang in Rhinebeck, drawing out this newspaper tribute, from the pen of Prof. James M. Degarmon of the Classical Institute in that place:

"The Hutchinsons have been here. These sweetest singers of the land have become endeared to the people, just as the bards and skalds and troubadours of old were dear to those they loved and sang for. They sing because they loved to sing, because music and melody is their natural atmosphere; and the people will crowd to hear them because their music meets a want that the public feels. To praise them would be superfluous. We remember that troupe quite well when they came to the front in the anti-slavery movement, and sang their songs of emancipation. With always a sad undertone, they still sang hopefully and full of faith. How completely has that faith been justified! How triumphantly can they sing of the fruition of liberty now! We always go to hear them sing, for it is good for us. Even their saddest songs seem ever the sweetest. Why is it that the music of sadness is always the best? Their rollicking fun makes us laugh, but these sweet, sad songs, for which they seem to be peculiarly adapted, move us as no others can. 'The New Year comes to-night, Mamma,' fading away into the death song of the boy. 'Those good old days of yore,' reminding us of the pleasant countenance of Asa, and closing with the grand song of hope and heaven and immortality, 'at our Heavenly Father's door,' these with the thrilling song of the 'Nineteenth Illinois' are of themselves a complete concert. 'I work and sing,' said John Hutchinson after the concert in Rhinebeck, 'for the good of the world, and I would draw that human world, "Nearer my God to Thee, nearer to Thee."' One thing more. The Hutchinsons are peculiarly American — they belong to their country, for whose liberty they wooed the bride of song, and made her their own. At their feet the people cast their garlands of praise, and wreathe their brows with the garlands of song worn only by 'The sweetest singers of the Fatherland.'"

At about this time we became quite interested in the idea of going to England again. Miss Antoinette Sterling was then and had for a long time been the leading singer in the choir of Plymouth Church, Brooklyn Beecher and all his church thought a great deal of her She had a separate canopied chair built for her in the choir, and in various ways the interest in her and her singing was shown. We became quite well acquainted with her, and we had many discussions of a plan to go to Europe together. Finally she went without us. Had we gone we should have had great success. She has been there over twenty years, singing before the queen and being a great favorite. She married, and has a family of children, but is now a widow. At the Unitarian Assembly in this year, 1872, she sang the "Star-Spangled Banner" with us.

We spent some time about New York in January. On the 19th of that month, the Fisk University Jubilee singers appeared in concert. I went to the door of their ante-room before the hour of commencing. They remembered me, and greeted me with the greatest delight, insisting that I should go upon the stage and sing. I told them I would go on and sing "John Brown" if they would join in the chorus. They had never heard it. They gathered around me and in a few minutes I had taught them the simple melody, and we went on the stage together and sang it.

For a while we boarded with our friend Roberts, in Brooklyn, next door to Beecher's church. I remember one evening we went into the church, to attend a lecture by Thomas Nast, the great caricaturist. Towards the close, he said he would draw a portrait of a man they all knew. He commenced at the feet, then drew the body. At last came the head, all blind until one finishing stroke and there was Beecher. The perfect likeness struck everybody "It don't look a bit like me," said Beecher, from his place in the middle of the house, rising and stepping into the aisle. This caused a laugh, as no one had said who it was, though the likeness was clearly obvious to the original, and everybody else.

Our temperance meetings continued, varied by an occasional miscellaneous concert engagement. March 15th, we were to sing at a peace convention at Poughkeepsie, N. Y.

There were three sessions, all slimly attended. The papers next day expressed regret that there was no larger attendance to hear the Hutchinsons. A laughable incident occurred in the evening. A shabbily dressed individual with his pants tucked into his boots, apparently a little intoxicated, arose from his seat and advancing to the footlights beckoned to one of the Hutchinsons, who came forward to meet him, when he said in a low tone: "Say (hic), I got (hic) five dollars. Give us (hic) suthin' lively, you (hic), you know." The movement brought down the house.

We continued our work well into the summer. Finally Spinning left me, to continue work with the Rhode Island society. Then I settled down at High Rock. On May 29 we, Henry and I, sang in the Labor Reform Convention in Boston. While the meeting was in progress, I wrote out new verses to "Get Off the Track." Henry, being accustomed to my writing, read them off easily and sung them with me.

I had resolved to raise Daisy Cottage, and put a basement under it. I came home from New York and saw Mr. Lowe, the building mover. He offered to do the job for two hundred dollars. Then I struck a bargain. He agreed to work by the day for thirty-five dollars.

THE HUTCHINSONS IN 1872 — (p. 25)

Then I went off again. When I came back, I notified Mr. Lowe one morning at seven o'clock that I was ready to begin, and would let him work by the day. He went at work to put the timbers under. I told him I wanted to work with the rest. As soon as the jack-screws were under I took my station at the middle one. The house began to go up. I put in as though I was singing. Soon Mr. Lowe saw it was going up at too fast a rate to bring in the two hundred dollars he had counted upon, and began to palaver. "Up she goes!" I shouted. At the end of the first day the cottage was more than half up. I pitched in the next day the same way. The sequel was that the foreman became frantic, because the work was being done so quickly, and when he got it where it was to go, it tipped to the east. I called his attention to it, and he put some screws under. The result was that he broke the ell apart, cracking the ceiling. When he left the job, the house pitched to the northeast. My only recourse was to make calculation so that when it was let down on the permanent foundation it would be level, but that was not quite successful.

The second, or "World's" peace jubilee, occurred at Boston in June. We enjoyed it with the rest of humanity.

On July 23d there was a Presbyterian Temperance Convention at Saratoga, at which Henry and I sung. On the way back we met General Burnside at North Adams. He made a speech, but it was not very successful.

At some previous time during the year, we had sung with Dr. Van Meter, a clerical acquaintance of the Baptist persuasion, at a meeting in New York City in which he spoke. He charged us, if he came to Boston to speak, to be sure and come up from Lynn and sing with him. Hearing he was to be at a Baptist convention in Tremont Temple, we went. Rev. J. Hyatt Smith saw us, and at once asked us to the collation in the vestry, and also to sing when the convention reassembled, before Mr. Van Meter spoke. Henry, therefore, took our melodeon to the platform, and at the proper time we were conducted thither by Mr. Smith.

As we took our places the audience stared at us in apparent surprise at our appearance in such a gathering. Mr. Smith seated himself by a "hard-shell" brother, who remarked, "What'd you bring them here for?" "Because I had a mind to," Mr. Smith replied. "They're not Baptists," returned the good brother. "Neither is a robin," said Smith, "but he can sing." On this the objector subsided.

That summer Henry left me, and went into business at Toledo with my son-in-law, Lewis A. Campbell. After a pleasant season at Lynn and Martha's Vineyard, I spent part of the autumn making arrangements for a company for the winter. I was anxious for a quartet, and at last secured it by getting Brother Joshua and Kate, my Brother Judson's only daughter, with Henry. Kate had a good alto voice, and the result of the combination of voices was an effect very much like that of the old original quartet. We sang for nearly two months under engagement with the New York State Temperance Society, all over that Commonwealth, and then went into Ohio and Illinois.

The year 1873 was not as eventful as some others. The quartet gave concerts through Indiana and Ohio until February 7th, when Joshua left us, at Greenfield, Ind. He had the heart disease, and was much frightened. It happened that some days before, Henry and he were skylarking in the caboose of a freight train, when Henry gave him a boost in the air, and he hit his head against a bolt. He was not only hurt, but frightened, and though his injury was entirely accidental, he was as sober as death about it, began to think of home, and finally could stand it no longer. So we were compelled to go on without him.

Before Joshua left us, we had given two concerts before the Legislatures of Indiana and Ohio. Of the latter event we retained an interesting souvenir in the form of a "blow" by some would-be funny man of Columbus. It was printed in the *Columbus Dispatch,* and read as follows:

"TO THE EDITORS OF THE DISPATCH Last night I dropped into the State House, and hearing music gushing from the hall of the House of Representatives, repaired to that locality instanter, thinking that, perhaps, Charley Babcock was tuning up on his favorite song, entitled 'Move your family West', but, lo and behold, instead I found a free concert in full blast. Being somewhat acquainted with such shows in Gotham, curiosity prompted me to remain and see the thing out. Upon inquiry I learned that the singists were the 'Hutchinson Family' from the far-off State of New Hampshire, and the home of Crédit Mobilier Patterson, President of the Ohio Agricultural College. This fact, I presume, gave the entertainment character and zest, hence the throwing wide open of the doors to the halls of legislation

"The show went on, and as the 'official reporter' of the House may not furnish you with 'copy' I will rush to the rescue, and give you the benefit of my observation. A few temperance songs were trotted out, and 'spheeled' to good effect, which brought down hearty cheers from the friends of the Adair liquor law Some sacrilegious cuss went so far as to declare it was the sole object of the 'reform' free concert troupe to forcibly remind the members of the General Assembly that it was their duty to be 'a little more abstemious, my boy' Well, after singing some, talking more, and making a general spread, the whole concern wound up by a return of thanks to the members of the House for the use of the hall.

"At this critical stage of the game, up popped the chaplain of the Ohio Penitentiary, and moved that a collection be taken for the benefit of the temperate Hutchinson Family And right here I rise to explain that as the reverend gentleman is prohibited from passing the 'sasser' around among his convict congregation, and the propensity for that amusement being large, he is excusable for his sudden and very unexpected outburst of liberality. I am credibly informed that nearly one hundred dollars was scooped into the Hutchinson coffers, and not one d — mented cent for expenses.

"After this Dr. Curtiss, of Cuyahoga, he of the flowing mane and much hair, rose in his dignity, and folding his official robes around his manly form, proceeded to read a few well penned 'whereases,' topped off with a resolution of thanks to the temperate Hutchinson Family — in the name of the General Assembly — for having deigned to drop upon them like a meteor strayed from its course, and edifying the benighted and wicked members. Speaker Van Vorhes, like the good little boy he is, mounted the platform at one graceful jump, put the motion, and it went through quicker than you could say 'scat.' This wound up the programme, all the actors playing their several parts with remarkable precision.

"Now, Mr. Editor, as we have had a free concert, can't the House of Representatives next be let for the noble purpose of negro minstrelsy; then let the concern be run as a variety theatre, and wind up by converting the whole thing into a lager beer shop."

My niece, Kate Hutchinson, who sang with us at this concert, was formerly a teacher in the schools of Columbus. Judge Hutchinson, of Chicago, her uncle, was a principal of the school in which she taught.

Perhaps the reader will be interested also in a notice of John, Joshua, Henry and Kate and their singing which appeared in the Fort Wayne, Ind., *Gazette:*

"We believe in the Hutchinsons. It is good for both body and soul to hear them, for they are not only full of thrilling music but of patriotism, temperance and hearty good humor. To attempt to describe their singing is useless. As well attempt to describe the eloquence of a great orator. But if one word will describe it, it is eloquent. It sends an electric thrill through the heart to hear them. They are singing reformers on the side of temperance, liberty, Christianity and every good cause, with a heartiness and joyous good sense worthy of the Old Granite State, whence they came. Mr. John Hutchinson is a natural actor as well as singer, and his manner is full of eloquence. In short, we would go farther to hear a duet from Mr. John Hutchinson and his son than to hear forty Rubinsteins. We hope they will give Fort Wayne another call ere long, when they may expect a crowded house."

On Saturday, March 1, we sang at a great temperance meeting in Pittsburgh, Penn. The result of the appearance was an engagement to return and sing for thirty-five days in the local option campaign in the city and its environs. On Sunday, March 2d, we sang at a large temperance meeting in the Y. M. C. A. rooms in Washington. It was under the auspices of the Congressional Temperance Society, and Vice-President Wilson presided. During the week that followed we attended many receptions and generally enjoyed ourselves.

On Sunday, March 9th, the great English preacher, Rev. William Morley Punshon, occupied Dr. Tiffany's pulpit at the Metropolitan Methodist-Episcopal church, in Washington. His subject was "Let your light shine." The audience overflowed the vast edifice, and listened with hushed attention to the thrilling periods of "The English Beecher." President Grant sat in his pew, evidently as interested as any auditor. At the close of the sermon, Henry and I, at Dr. Tiffany's request, sang the chant all religious gatherings loved to hear, "Mary at the Cross."

As we came out of the meeting, I had a few words with President Grant on the subject of finance. He said he wanted to have our bills represent a clean, whole dollar.

On the following evening we gave a concert in the same church. Of it one of the Washington papers said:

"Those old favorites, the Hutchinsons, gave one of their characteristic concerts to a brilliant audience, which nearly filled the Metropolitan church, last evening. We say old favorites, but this is to be taken with a reservation, for, though not quite like the boy's new jack-knife, which first received a new blade, and then a new handle, the only member of the present troupe who preserves his identity with the 'band of brothers' which delighted and edified us in our youthful days with their reform melodies is Mr. John Hutchinson, the father But the character of the music, some of the songs, and peculiar style of execution which gave the troupe prestige, are the same, even the quality of the voices has been in a measure transmitted, and hence, the difference is not so great, after all. We are truly glad to see that the children seem, both by their voices and their skill in using them, so well able to perpetuate and enhance the fame of the family who have come to be an American institution Mr Henry J Hutchinson has a baritone of wonderful power and sweetness, while Miss Katie, daughter of Judson, the brother who died, his a rich contralto of good compass, though she evidently labored under a slight hoarseness last evening. John, *paterfamilias*, with the broad Byron collar, long hair and beard, as of old, both now sprinkled with gray, seems to have preserved his ringing and melodious tenor, as well as his youthful vivacity and *esprit* unimpaired"

After this we returned to Pittsburgh, and for over a month sung for local option. We did our best, but it was of no use. The friends of unlimited license won in the election, and to add to our disappointment the temperance people refused to pay us for our five weeks' work. Ole Bull gave some concerts in Pittsburgh at the time. He had Graziella Ridgway with him.

After a few weeks of concerting in New York State, we returned to Lynn. On May 30th, during the anniversaries we sung at the meetings of the Free Religious Association at Tremont Temple, Boston Rev O. B. Frothingham presided. Among the speakers were Rev. Samuel Johnson, Rev. Samuel Longfellow, Rev. John Weiss, Francis Ellingwood Abbott, Lucretia Mott, and others. There was a donation festival in the evening, at which Col. Thomas Wentworth Higginson presided. In introducing us to sing he slyly insinuated that we really had no place in the gathering, as we had latterly affiliated with the Methodists, at Martha's Vineyard and elsewhere. He was equally happy in his introduction of Miss Sterling and others I am compelled to acknowledge that throughout the long experience of the Hutchinsons they never were able to draw theological lines in their singing. The fact that a religious gathering desired our presence, whatever its creed, always fully satisfied us, and we sung songs that awakened Christian sympathy, regardless of denominational leanings.

On July 4th there was a mass temperance meeting at Lakeview, Framingham. By some accident both Henry and Kate were late. I was embarrassed and troubled. Henry was coming from New York, Kate from Milford. Colonel Little, a singer and a cripple, assisted me until the rest of my company came. General Butler, strange though it may seem, was the principal speaker. In the afternoon we went to the State Reform School at Westboro. It was at this time under the superintendency of Colonel A. G. Shepherd, so long a tenant of Bird's Nest Cottage on High Rock.

On the 21st of August we were at the Mystic Peace Convention, in Connecticut. We went by the invitation of Zerah C. Whipple. This was in the early days of the conventions at Mystic, which continue to be of great annual interest, drawing large numbers to the grounds. We sung "O Listen to the Spirit's Call," an original song. Whipple I recall as one of the noble, natural sons of progress and peace. For conscience sake he refused to pay his tax at one time, and was imprisoned for a long period. My son Judson was with me on this trip, singing and speaking pieces.

This was the year of the great panic, "Black Friday," in New York. Henry was in Wall Street at the time, representing his Toledo firm. The date was September 19th. He telegraphed me for help, and I at once telegraphed him the sum he desired to meet his obligations.

Soon after this there was an exhibition of tableaux in the First Methodist-Episcopal church in Lynn. They were projected by John Q. Maynard, formerly of Brooklyn, but at this time superintendent of the Sunday-school of the church mentioned, and residing in the Stone Cottage on High Rock. Maynard was for years with Philip Phillips, the singing evangelist, in his panoramic exhibitions of the "Pilgrim's Progress," and had quite an idea of how tableaux should be conducted. Many of the staid members of the church, the first of the denomination in Massachusetts, were shocked at such an exhibition in its sacred precincts, but it was an artistic success. The affair was in the immediate charge of "Charles Sullivan" as he was professionally known. His real name was Charles W. Sohier, and after the show was over he came to High Rock for the night. I found him an agreeable, talented man, with an endless store of fun, and the result of our acquaintance was an engagement, and he travelled with us all the winter and the following spring.

On October 3d, Frederick C. Hutchinson, Asa's oldest son, died. From the time of the "swarming" he travelled a good deal in his father's company, and his demise was a deep sorrow to us all.

In November we took a short trip into the Essex County towns and villages, especially about Cape Ann. In December we went to New York, and with Sohier commenced a series of engagements in and about the city. January 1, 1874, found us still there.

On New Year's Day, 1874, I had the pleasure of making many calls with Frank B. Carpenter. A few days later found us all in Washington, and we stayed there with the exception of occasional short trips away, for three months. Our first experience of importance was at the National Convention of the Woman Suffrage Association, which lasted two days. Susan B. Anthony presided and there was speaking by many prominent defenders of the reform. One of the subjects discussed was the petition of "Susan" to be relieved from the sentence of the court for voting for Grant and Wilson. Wilson was in the convention, and Susan took occasion to say that no act of her life gave her more pleasure than voting for him. She called on Wilson for remarks, and he, while refusing to speak at length by his physician's orders, remarked that twenty years before he came to the conclusion that his wife, mother and sisters were as much entitled to the right of suffrage as himself, and that he had never changed his mind since. Susan predicted that the next president would be in favor of woman suffrage. Time showed she was right Hayes was the next president. Among the speakers of that day were Mrs. Stanton, Belva A. Lockwood, Phebe Cozzens, and many others. When we sung, Susan gave a history of our work in Kansas, remarking that we moved hearts where heads were too dull to be convinced by argument.

The following Sunday evening we participated in a meeting of the Congressional Temperance Society, Senator Buckingham presiding. Edward Young, A M. Powell, Rev. B. I. Ives, and Hon. Wm. E. Dodge were the speakers. A week later we sung at another, at the Masonic Temple. Two nights later we sung in a concert in Baltimore We went often to the home of Hayward Hutchinson while in Washington. Hayward was a son of my brother David, and a very successful business man. Hayward, with his wife, gave a reception and musicale in our honor. Among those present were Mr. and Mrs. Hastings, Mr. and Mrs. John O.

Evans, Attorney-General and Mrs. Williams, Governor and Mrs Shepherd, Judge Miller, Mrs. Stocking, Mr. S. G. Young, Mrs. Neagle, Mr. James R. Young, Mr. Flagg, Dr. and Mrs. McDonald, Mr. John M. Young, and several others. Prof Carl Richter acted as accompanist. We sung in Baltimore the same evening, returning in time to spend three hours at the reception.

On Monday, February 9th, we were in Toledo, at a great temperance meeting in St. Paul's Church. A few days later we were back in Washington. In the course of our stay we gave many concerts in the capital, a large number in Dr. Tiffany's Metropolitan M. E. Church. F. Widdows, whom I have spoken of as agent for Ole Bull, usually had some connection with these concerts. He at this time played the chime of bells in the Metropolitan Church, and as he was very friendly to us would often play on the bells some of our melodies, "The Old Granite State" and others. We were somewhat restricted in our selections when singing in this church, as the trustees objected to anything of a secular nature. Our entertainments were therefore sacred concerts President Grant often came to these concerts. One night at the close, when talking with him, I told him the story of Chase's prophecy that he would be president for a third term. I was very much in favor of the Chief Justice, always, and during Grant's first term, when the forces were at work that finally culminated in the Liberal Republican movement, said to him that it seemed to me that here was the long-hoped-for opportunity to elevate him to the presidency. Raising his finger emphatically, Mr. Chase said: "Grant will be his own successor as president, mark that." Not long before Chase's decease I called upon him, and reminded him of the fulfilment of his prophecy. He said, "I will prophesy again — Grant will be president for a third term." "What" I said, "are we to revolutionize things and make him a perpetual incumbent?" "No," said Chase, "but there is nothing in the Constitution to prevent his re-election." When I told him this, Grant shrugged his shoulders, as if he might say something, but wouldn't. I repeated to him a portion of the Sermon on the Mount, "Blessed are the meek, for they shall inherit the earth."

On February 25th I sung at a concert in a colored church on L Street. Only a few years since I again sung at a civil rights meeting in the same church at which Douglass spoke. I went to the concert with Mrs. Douglass, but soon after my arrival a colored man politely came and said, "Your place is on the platform." I went up, and took my seat immediately behind the orator. He turned, just as he was rising to speak, and asked me if I would sing. I told him that if I sung at all it would be simply a verse of "America," and I should ask the audience to join in with me. To my surprise, Douglass, in the course of the evening introduced me, first giving the Hutchinsons and their work one of the finest tributes we had ever received. I listened to this with all the equanimity possible, and in responding, made some reference to the national emblem, and drew from my pocket an American flag. There was no other in the edifice, and the act aroused the gathering to the highest pitch of enthusiasm. I told the story of Douglass at the hotel with me, in 1847, when the waiter refused to serve him. They were much interested.

At one time during our stay in Washington I was invited to visit several of the schools, and asked Douglass to go with me. In some of them they would gather large numbers of the pupils in the halls of the schoolhouses, and I would sing and Douglass speak to them.

On Sunday, February 28th, we attended a great meeting in the assembly-rooms at Baltimore. Hon. William Daniel acted as president of the occasion, and then followed many temperance addresses. Hon. R. B. Vance, of North Carolina, Hon. A. M. Powell, Judge Lawrence, of Ohio, and others spoke. We stayed several days at Baltimore and sung at temperance and other gatherings. A few days later we made a trip to Frederick, Md., visiting the graves of Barbara Fritchie and Francis Scott Key, the author of the "Star-Spangled Banner." Henry told the story, in the *Washington Graphic*, his first bit of newspaper correspondence, as follows:

"On a branch of the Baltimore and Ohio Railroad, about equal distance from Baltimore and Washington, on a pleasant slope among the green hills of Maryland, lies the quaint old town of Frederick: a place of some ten thousand inhabitants. While sojourning there last week we were invited by some of the citizens to visit the cemetery. On our way thither we passed the old camping ground of General Lafayette and his army, on the site of which is now erected the State Deaf and Dumb Asylum, at an expense of nearly a half-million dollars. Several of the stone buildings erected by Lafayette, now nearly a hundred years ago, are still substantial looking fortresses.

"We drove on a half-mile to the cemetery, and alighted from our carriage at the grave of Barbara Fritchie, that heroic old lady who, at the age of ninety-six, displayed a patriotism that thrilled the hearts of the whole country, North and South. We plucked a few sprigs of myrtle, breathed a silent farewell, and passed to the other side of the grounds, where in a bleak and apparently unfrequented portion we found a small, humble-looking stone with this inscription:

> FRANCIS SCOTT KEY,
> BORN AUGUST 9, 1780.
> DIED JANUARY 11, 1843.

—reminding us that we were at the grave of the author of the 'Star Spangled Banner.' We were a little surprised not to find a more impressive monument marking the resting place of one of America's greatest bards We could not refrain from singing the old song in honor of its author lying cold beneath the sod The Hutchinson Family sang the solos, while the whole party joined in the chorus

' We were next shown into one of the tombs, where we found a curiosity worthy of mention There were but two coffins in this vault, and in them were the bodies of a man and wife, who died and were placed there in 1838 About ten years after some of the relatives wished to have the bodies replaced in new caskets. When the coffins were opened both the bodies were found to be in a perfect state of preservation. It is now thirty-six years since they were buried, and still they show no signs of decay The body of the woman especially seemed to be most perfect, showing no change except in the color of the skin, which was about the color of leather It is certainly a most remarkable case, as they never were embalmed They simply died and were buried the same as any other people, and they are much better preserved than any Egyptian mummy I have ever seen "

While we were singing at the grave of Key, Charles Sumner died at Washington. Two days later we saw his body lie in state in the rotunda of the Capitol, the very place where a few months before I had noticed him critically examining the Carpenter painting. I never was personally acquainted with him, but remembered seeing him on many notable occasions. One was in war times, when I sat in the Senate gallery with Douglass and heard his great diplomatic speech in favor of delivering up Mason and Slidell.

On Monday, the 23d of March, the Woman's Christian Association began a week of prayer in Washington. The great temperance crusade, which resulted in the formation of the Woman's Christian Temperance Union had been inaugurated in Ohio the preceding year, by Dr. Dio Lewis. At this time the movement reached Washington in full flame. The pastors of the churches held meetings at which practically all the Protestant clergy were present. A committee of the whole was appointed to wait upon Congress to urge bills increasing the power of the Metropolitan Board of Police for the city, and providing a civil damage law against liquor dealers. A thousand ladies held a woman's prayer and conference meeting the first day. There was a grand demonstration in the evening in the Foundry Methodist Episcopal Church, among those participating being Dr. Dio Lewis, Rev. Dr. Butler, Rev. Mr. Baker, F. M Bradley, Commissioner of Patents M. D. Leggett, and others. We interspersed the speaking with our songs.

On March 28th, we all spent the evening at the home of General W. T. Sherman. The great soldier was a firm friend in those days, and his hearty invitations to always visit him when in the city were much like the cordiality shown us by Chief Justice Chase. On the visit referred to I recall we had a discussion on the peace question, lasting a half-hour. The great soldier said — a remark discouraging to me — that although he had passed through four years of war, with its attendant carnage and misery, he believed human nature was such that the climax of discussion would always be a bloody conflict, until there should be a complete revolution in the policy of nations. The selfishness of nations, he said, and the desire to maintain a leading position was always an incentive to foreign war that was hard to control. It seemed to me his words discounted a great principle of Jesus, " Render unto Cæsar the things that are Cæsar's and unto God the things that are God's " His wife was an attentive listener to the conversation. I remember I said, " Whatever is good and grand and heavenly in our religion should be engrafted into our politics." I had heard that Mrs. Sherman was a devoted Catholic, but I did not discover that the general was especially a partisan or a professor of that creed. I spoke of my hope in the triumph of the principle of the fatherhood of God and the brotherhood of man, and said we hoped for better things. Sherman was born on the Connecticut Reserve, in Ohio. Years before, I met his sister at the White Mountains, and through her I made the acquaintance of the general.

At about this time we sang in the Foundry Methodist Episcopal Church, with Mrs. Lippincott (Grace Greenwood), she giving authors' readings during the evening March 29th we went to Washington's home, Mount Vernon, and the same evening were entertained by Grace Greenwood at the Lincoln. Mrs. Mary Clemmer Ames and Colonel John Hay assisted.

On April 2d we visited Vinnie Ream, the sculptor who designed the General Thomas monument. Among the guests were three ex-Rebel generals. At her request I sang. I selected "The Blue and the Gray," a song commemorating the act of the women of Columbus, Miss., who on Memorial Day strewed flowers alike on the graves of Confederate and National soldiers:

> "By the flow of the inland river
> Whence the fleets of iron have fled,
> Where the blades of the grave-grass quiver,
> Asleep are the ranks of the dead;
> Under the sod and the dew,
> Waiting the Judgment Day—
> Under the one, the Blue,
> Under the other, the Gray.
>
> "These in the robings of glory,
> Those in the gloom of defeat,
> All with the battle-blood gory,
> In the dusk of eternity meet;
> Under the sod and the dew,
> Waiting the Judgment Day—
> Under the laurel, the Blue,
> Under the willow, the Gray.
>
> "From the silence of sorrowful hours
> The desolate mourners go,
> Lovingly laden with flowers
> Alike for the friend and the foe;

Under the sod and the dew,
 Waiting the Judgment Day —
Under the roses, the Blue,
 Under the lilies, the Gray.

"Sadly, but not upbraiding,
 The generous deed was done;
In the storm of the years that are fading,
 No braver battle was won;
Under the sod and the dew,
 Waiting the Judgment Day —
Under the blossoms, the Blue,
 Under the garlands, the Gray.

"No more shall the war-cry sever,
 Or the winding rivers be red;
They banish our anger forever
 When they laurel the graves of our dead!
Under the sod and the dew,
 Waiting the Judgment Day —
Love and tears for the Blue,
 Tears and love for the Gray."

When I had finished singing the song the three Confederates rose simultaneously and shook my hand heartily. "Mr. Hutchinson," they remarked, "that song is a passport for you anywhere in the South." I did not specially test this statement, except in Richmond, where the effect of singing it was precisely as they had predicted. Later, by a special request, I went to his hotel and sang "The Blue and the Gray" to Alexander H. Stephens, the ex-Vice-President of the Confederacy. He was wheeled into the room in his invalid chair to hear me. He was not as enthusiastic as the officers, but remarked that under reconstruction, the country was safe. Francis M. Finch was the author of the words of this song; I wrote the music.

A correspondent of the *St. Louis Globe*, after remarking that woman suffrage is the solution of the problem of the dram-shop, made this kindly reference to our visit in Washington:

"We have the Hutchinson Family here, busy in this cause. Grand old John Hutchinson! the very embodiment of lofty enthusiasm in the right. How his clarion notes rang, down the long years of slavery, and sounded out the jubilate when the thousands of victorious soldiers stood before him on the battle-field! Nor do the notes wax weak and faltering; he has seen the freedom of the slave and still in this cause of temperance he sings on and on, the prophetic burden of his song, as of old 'It is coming! the good time coming.'

"I think I never saw a more beautiful face than that of this old man. The features, regularly moulded, are large and tender, his eyes luminous with expression, as of one who dreams ever, prophetically, of the future; his mouth is sympathetic, hiding its quiver of pathos and smile of love beneath a patriarchal beard, which time has generously touched with gray. He has a broad, white, earnest brow, above which a crown of silvery hair lies softly and falls down in long curling masses over the wide, picturesque collar he invariably wears. Brawny shoulders, grand chest and a sturdy frame have carried him safely through long years of exposure and song in the cause for which Christ died — love of the race. John Hutchinson is the friend of woman in the broadest and best sense, and is with us, heart and soul, in all that looks toward emancipation from the evils and misfortunes of life. One cannot listen to the singing of this well-known family without thinking regretfully of the one sister, Abby, 'the little sister in the nest of brothers.' Her health has been delicate for some time and she is now in Florida, writing home glowing letters from beneath the blooming magnolias. She is still a beautiful woman, with that soul beauty which lights up her great shining eyes, and flushes her pale cheeks at times into something far more attractive than mere rose and lily flesh and blood can give. Her tiny frame vibrates with every emotion when she sings, and I can well believe that the soldiers almost fell before her in adoration when upon the field she sang before them her ringing song of liberty. That her voice should be silent during this crusade is much to be regretted."

Abby did not sing before the soldiers. If she had done so the effect would have doubtless been as imagined by Marie LeBaron, the correspondent quoted above, for Abby's singing and presence always secured for her an enthusiastic devotion little short of adoration. It may be said here that the experience in the camps of three members — John, Henry and Viola — of the Hutchinson family always redounded to the the credit of the whole, and was undoubtedly a help, professionally and financially, to each of the singing bands that travelled under that name. The Legislature of Missouri, at the close of the war, sent a most cordial invitation to my brother Asa with his family to come to the State and give concerts and when he went to St. Louis in response to the call, the city officials and the public vied with one another in their efforts to do him honor, in partial atonement for the expulsion of the brothers from the city in antebellum times. When I visited the city I was received with equal honor. Jesse, Judson and I were refused a hall to sing in in St. Louis. Asa was not with us at the time.

One of those most active in the suffrage movement at the time of which I am writing was Dr. Mary E. Walker. We became well acquainted with her. She was a sincere, honest, capable, independent woman, expressing her convictions freely in public, on railroad cars, before assemblies of different kinds, at reform meetings and elsewhere, always keeping herself eminently respectable. Through thick and thin of the reform battle, despite criticisms and sneers, she wore male attire.

As has been hinted, we made a trip to Richmond, giving a concert in the Opera House. The affair was an artistic failure from the fact that there was a tin roof on the building, and as a storm was raging, the rain made such a rattle that we could not be heard. We visited Libby Prison, and cold chills came over us as we recalled the sufferings of the brave boys in blue incarcerated there. We spent an evening with Colonel Daniels, a Yankee, who had established himself in Richmond. The *Despatch*, in speaking of our concert, said:

"The Hutchinson Family gave their first concert in this city at the Virginia Opera House last night. The first part of the programme was executed with smoothness and some success; several songs were rendered with smoothness and satisfaction. The last hour of the concert was, however, made miserable to the singers and laughable to their hearers by the falling of the rain upon the tin roof of the opera house, making a clatter which effectually drowned all vocal efforts. Mr. Hutchinson, when the rain was at its height, appealed to the audience to say whether he should stop or go on. A gentleman in the audience suggested that as it was impossible for the people to go home he had just as well proceed. And he did; but the 'rain upon the roof' won most of the triumphs of the evening. The audience dispersed in fine humor, and received at the door tickets for to-night to assuage their disappointment."

The *Whig* said:

"There were some vacant seats last night, but those present had the self-gratulation of being privileged to hear and enjoy some magnificent, soul-reaching vocalism. The concert was of the humanizing order. It lifted the men and women who were present above the plane of every-day life. There is much we would like to say about this entertainment, but it must remain unsaid. Let us not omit to commend 'The Blue and the Gray' as an approach to the sublime in vocal music lately vouchsafed."

The woman suffrage and temperance movement in Washington brought to us F. W. Root, of Wyandotte, Kan., with whom we had labored when there. He was a Spiritualist and a great believer in the efficacy of prayer. He was lieutenant-governor with Governor Robinson, before the war.

We planned to be in New York during the May meetings. Just before that we went to Nyack and spent a Sabbath with Rev. Stephen Merritt, the indefatigable temperance worker. He was one of the best of men and at the time of our great Cooper Institute meetings acted as presiding officer. At this time Henry and Sohier left me. Early in May my brother Joshua came down to New York with Nellie Gray, daughter of my sister Rhoda. He was confident of success, and had a right to be, for Nellie had a beautiful voice, which simply astonished me by its sweetness. It indicated that there was to be no deterioration in the quality of tone in the next generation of the Tribe of Jesse. These two joined my wife and me in several concerts. On May 11th, in company with Henry, we sang at the ninth anniversary of the National Temperance Society in Steinway Hall, New York. A few days later Sister Abby, with her husband and her father-in-law, Rev. Dr. William Patton, sailed for Europe. She stayed several years, visiting every country in Europe except Portugal and Lapland, remaining quite a while in Italy, and also making tours of Egypt and the Holy Land. Henry and I stood on the pier as the *Adriatic* steamed away. It seemed as if we were never to see her again. Abby was very fond of Henry and wrote him frequently. He had a special bag in which he kept all her letters. This was stolen in Boston, the accident being most unfortunate, for they constituted a history of her tour. Many of her experiences were published, however, in the *Portland Transcript* and other papers, and some letters to Henry and myself are still preserved.

On May 25th, we sung at the anniversary of the Congregational Club in Faneuil Hall, Boston. John B. Gough was the principal speaker. Then, like Gough, we went home and devoted ourselves to raising chickens. At this time Gough was making anywhere from ten thousand to fifteen thousand dollars a season from his lectures, and yet as soon as he could get a respite would hasten to his Worcester County home and soon be engrossed with his poultry-yard. In his eyes a chicken was almost a priceless possession, and any one who would purloin one was a miscreant indeed. My diary, as I have hinted, shows that at this time I, too, had the hen fever.

July 4th we went to Lakeview, Framingham, to sing at a great woman-suffrage meeting. There was a good attendance of the best friends of the cause. Among the speakers were William Lloyd Garrison, Lucy Stone Blackwell, Mrs. Livermore, S. S. Foster and his wife, Abby Kelley Foster, the Smith Sisters, of Glastonbury, Conn., Mrs. Severance and others. On the following day we again visited Colonel Shepherd's charges at the Westboro reform school. When I spoke, I said, 'Will the boys from Lynn who may be present please rise?'" To my astonishment boys began to stand in all parts of the room, and I began to fear the whole school was of Lynn antecedents.

Then followed weeks of rest at home, succeeded by a short visit to Milford, and a trip among the White Hills with Brother Joshua and Walter Kittredge, the author of "Tenting To-night." On September 6th we were guests, at Lancaster, of Mr. Benton, son-in-law of General Neal Dow. We conducted a big temperance meeting. A little later, with my wife, I went to New York, and with Henry we sung at the annual meeting of the Grand Lodge of Good Templars. Returning, I joined Kittredge and Joshua in a tour of several weeks in southern New Hampshire, Vermont and Massachusetts. After a trip to New York, early in November, Henry joined us, and we made a short engagement with J. W. Caverly, a Lynn manager for concerts about Essex County. This brought us near Portsmouth and Portland, and other places where we had not sung for many a year, though they were scenes of our earlier successes, and we gave several concerts in those places. At Dover I took a mournful satisfaction in calling on the widow of my old friend, John P. Hale, and his daughter, Mrs. Wm. E. Chandler. We saw the old year out, and 1875 in, at New York City.

The year 1875 was not as eventful as its predecessor. I secured three connecting parlors in a house on Union Square. These were made our headquarters and home. We formed two temperance organizations, the Manhattan Temperance Society, and the American Temperance Union. One of these met at the parlors on Sunday afternoon and the other Sunday evening. To make the rooms pay a little we permitted a man who sold stereoscopic views to occupy them during week-days. I soon found that the name "American Temperance Union" was not new, though it was as far as I was concerned. Mr. J. N. Stearns of the Temperance Publication Society informed me that it was the name of one of his old societies which had become obsolete.

We did a little singing of a general nature, but largely confined ourselves to temperance work. We found time to help a little in the Morning Star Sunday-school, for which we had sung in concert a few years before. This school was a mission in charge of an old friend, Dr Perry, a dentist of the city. At the time we gave our concerts through New England for the school Rev. Mr. Davis, a superannuated preacher, volunteered to go with us and act as business agent. He had been a Free Baptist clergyman and was my wife's pastor, in Lowell, before her marriage. He was with us at the first concert, given in one of the Methodist churches of Lynn. He was troubled with heart complaint, but took the money at the door all night, and was addressing the audience when he was seized with a faint He went into a pew and laid down. Going to him, he suggested that we go on, so I finished his speech and the concert.

TOWER COTTAGE, HIGH ROCK — (p. 97)

The next night were in Mechanics Hall, Salem. He made his appeal, and took a collection. Then he went to a chair at one side of the platform, and as we were singing, began to count his money. It annoyed us, and Henry looked at him. Instantly putting his money in another chair, he arose, and stepping up to Henry, remarked in an audible tone. "What do you want?" Henry whispered his request that he count his money later, and the old gentleman retired to his chair. Just as he seated himself, a leg of the chair gave way, and as he kicked out in a vain effort to save himself, he hit the chair in which the money lay, and the contributions rolled all over the stage. The concert closed and the work of picking up the money went on. As the people came up to shake hands and congratulate us, they said: "Mr. Hutchinson, do come to Salem as often as you can, but be sure and bring that interesting man, Mr. Davis, with you!"

One day while at this house in New York, I went skating in Central Park with Judson. Between the time of getting my skates on and going upon the ice I lost Juddie. That ended the skating. There were thousands of people there. After searching about for some hours, I went home in despair, and found him there all right. He got on a horse-car, after becoming separated from me. The conductor asked where he was going. "Going home," was his laconic response. He was turned over to a policeman, but could give the whereabouts of his home no more definitely than to say it was near the museum. The officer therefore took him to Barnum's, and at once he led him from that point home. The policeman said he had never met a boy who interested him so much.

It was while at Union Square that we became interested in the theories of a certain Mr. Brewster. This intelligent man came to our temperance meetings, and one night seemed loth to leave. I was mending the fires in the open grates after the company had gone. He stood near one, apparently lost in contemplation. I spoke to him kindly, and he responded in a very sweet tone. He said he had become so entranced with one of our songs, that he felt that he must stop and speak to me in reference to his belief. He said he had become convinced that the centre of the earth was inhabited by the elect. These choice spirits were permitted to make a safe home there. The entrance to this paradise he conceived to be at the poles, and it was lighted not by the direct rays of the blazing sun, but by reflected light, which entered also at the poles. He believed the flow of the Gulf Stream furnished evidence to support his theory. To his mind it was the most beautiful place that thought could conceive. There flowers bloomed perennially, and there was no night there. He asked me to call at his office, where he had a small hollow globe, illustrating his views. I went. I found him to be a manufacturer of very musical tin fifes. He detailed the matter in a very lucid manner and I became enthusiastic. I invited him to give a lecture in my parlors. He did so, and so much interested his auditors that he was asked to go to other places and speak on the subject. Among those in our parlors to hear him were Mrs. Thompson, the philanthropist, and Steele MacKaye, the dramatist. Mrs. Thompson invited him to her rooms, to meet the newspaper men of the city. He went there and spoke to them. Before he had removed his model from the house after the lecture, he was seized with the small-pox, and a short time later was taken to his long home.

The temperance societies formed during this stay in New York, are, so far as I am informed, in existence yet. In later years I visited the city, attended the meetings, and was introduced as the father of the enterprise. The American Temperance Union gave me a reception on my seventy-fifth birthday, January, 1896.

On the 14th of April we went to Philadelphia to attend the one hundredth anniversary of the "Pennsylvania Society for Promoting the Abolition of Slavery, the Relief of Free Negroes unlawfully Held in Bondage, and for Improving the Condition of the African Race." This was the first anti-slavery society, and had Benjamin Franklin for its first president and Dr. Benjamin Rush for its first secretary. The meeting was called not only as a centennial observance but to see what it could do under the last provision of its title. The sessions were held at Concert Hall during the day and at the Bethel Church in the evening. Vice-President Wilson presided at the day meeting and Bishop Campbell at night. Upon the platform with him were Frederick Douglass, Robert Purvis (his rival as an orator), Lucretia Mott, Abby Kelley Foster, Mrs. F. E. W. Harper, Charles C. Burleigh, Bishop D. A. Payne, of the A. M. E Church, Prof. J. M. Langston, Elizur Wright, William Still, ex-Governor Curtin, Passmore Williamson and many others identified with the cause. Henry Wilson was introduced by Mr. Still, and invited Rev. Dr. Wm H. Furness to lead in prayer. After Wilson's opening address we sang one of our songs. Then Purvis read letters from the great pioneer, Garrison, President Grant, Wendell Phillips, General Butler, Rev. Samuel May, John G Whittier and others. The historical oration was delivered by Dr. William Elder. At the close of this we sang Whittier's "Furnace

Blast," it being received with great applause. Vice-President Wilson remarked as we closed, "The words of the Quaker poet, to which you have just listened, could not be sung in the early days of 1862 in the Army of the Potomac without causing military interference. I thank God these words can be sung to-day on every square mile of the republic." He then introduced Frederick Douglass, who followed out the idea of the meeting in presenting in eloquent periods the misery suffered by the Freedmen even under the supposably improved conditions secured by emancipation and the ballot. Lucretia Mott made a few remarks, and then we sung:

> " 'Tis coming up the steep of time,
> And this old world is growing brighter."

Charles C. Burleigh and Robert Purvis closed the speaking of the day session and in the evening the speakers were practically the same. It was an interesting and notable event. The attendants were largely Friends, the noticeable garb of the Quaker women being prominent everywhere. Through it all I could not help a feeling of sorrow and disappointment. I had resolved when I got to Philadelphia to have a good talk with Henry Wilson, and make a suggestion. I had sung with him under many varying conditions. Before the war, in Free-Soil and anti-slavery gatherings, and since at the meetings of the Congressional Temperance Society. In the anteroom, before going on the stage, I put my hand on his shoulder, and said to him it seemed to me that the time was opportune to introduce an issue that would bring about reconciliation and reconstruction in a reasonable way, and ameliorate the condition of the South, by uniting the sections in a war against alcohol. The negro had the ballot; why was it not possible to turn this anniversary meeting into a great temperance gathering? Wilson actually shook all over. I saw that my suggestion was not accepted. "What does this mean?" he exclaimed. He went on the platform and opened the meeting without further comment. I thought, "Henry Wilson, if you neglect to declare the whole counsel of God, your success will be short-lived." Wilson's speech was a disappointment to the audience, which had gathered to rejoice that at the close of a century of the life of the society, emancipation had come and the slave had the ballot. The effort to turn the tide into a channel of complaint that the franchise in the hands of a people waking from centuries of enforced ignorance was not a full success, seemed like a wet blanket. Wilson, temperance man though he undoubtedly was, was a man of ambition; he was already Vice-President, and the presidency seemed not far away. The plaint of this meeting was but the prelude of the campaign that was to come, though Wilson, alas! bore no part in it. I still think the great man, so soon to pass away, missed a signal opportunity to speak a ringing note of temperance into sympathetic ears, sound the keynote of a new crusade that would have united North and South and even have added to the almost universal acclaim and honor paid him at the time of his swift taking-away, but a few months later.

In addition to the selections named, we sang during the meeting "Behold the Day of Promise comes," and "The Millenium," Brother Caleb's song:

> "What do I see? Ah! look, behold,
> That glorious day, by prophets told,
> Has dawned, and now is near

Methinks I hear from yonder plain
The shouts of gladness loud proclaim
 'The Millennium is here!'

"See Freedom's star that shines so bright!
It sheds its rays of truth and light
 O'er mountain, rock and sea,
And, like the mighty march of mind,
Has sought and blessed all human kind,
 And set the bondman free

"Salvation to our God proclaim!
This is a glorious peaceful reign,
 The nations now shall know
The kingdoms of this world are given
To Christ, the Lord of earth and heaven,
 Predicted long ago "

The next day we sung at a temperance meeting in Orange, N. J., with J. Gibbs, who kept a large eating-house on Nassau Street, New York, as the speaker Mr Gibbs's place was quite a home for reformers. He took charge of the Manhattan temperance society after we left New York.

Then we went back to Lynn, and spent a week in putting Daisy Cottage and its environs to rights. Returning to New York, we continued our temperance work a little longer and also participated in the Peace meeting and other anniversaries. On the first of June Henry and I went to Chicago as Massachusetts delegates to the National Convention of the Sons of Temperance. Asa and Dennett came down from Hutchinson, and we sung together in the convention, though much of our singing consisted of duets, as we had not practised together for some time. The convention was a great occasion, and much interest was aroused by it. It was held in Farwell Hall. Asa and his son came with us on our return home, and spent part of the summer on

High Rock. In August we visited the camp-meetings at Old Orchard and Martha's Vineyard. Following this we gave concerts with Asa and his son in many New England cities and towns. In September we sang at the New England Fair at Manchester, N. H., making our headquarters with W. H. Whitmore, next door, by the way, to Maud Porter Wilson, who sang with Viola and myself in our successful tour through the West, a few years before. On the last day of the fair, Henry Ward Beecher spoke, and we sung. In October we travelled in Maine, where Asa left Dennett at the academy in Kent's Hill. Joshua had joined us, and so we had a male quartet in our concerts back through Maine, New Hampshire and Massachusetts. In December we made a plan to go to the Pacific slope, Asa, Henry and myself in the company. Going to Painesville, Ohio, we found E. E. Johnson, our agent when my brother Judson was with us during the '50's, and he agreed to take up the work again. Asa's wife had died a few months before. When we reached Chicago, he received news of the death of his little granddaughter, Frederica, and at once hastened to Hutchinson. He returned and met us at Faribault, and in a few days we had sung our way to Hutchinson, where we gave one very successful concert, and I spent a few days attending to my affairs. Asa's daughter, Mrs. Anderson, joined us, and in January, 1876, we made another start, singing at Litchfield, St. Paul, Winona, Red Wing, Lake City and other points. It was soon evident that Mrs. Anderson was too much of an invalid to sing, and this fact had a most depressing effect on Asa. His wife and granddaughter were dead, and his daughter Abby seriously sick. At Faribault he threw up his engagement, and our cherished plan of going to California had to be given up. I was sadly disappointed, but had long before adopted "There's no such word as fail" for my motto, and so kept at it.

Some of the newspaper notices we received during this brief trip of a "Hutchinson Family Quartet" are of interest. The *Faribault Republican* said:

"'Tis sweet to be remembered.'
"Twenty years have elapsed since these 'sons of song' first came to this village. During the winter of 1855 a few families from the East had clustered in this valley, to establish themselves homes. General Shields, Dr. Jewett and the Nuttings had interested themselves in the settlement and by their notoriety as public men had induced many of their admirers to follow them to this beautiful spot. At that time they numbered all told about one hundred and fifty men, women and children.

"The Hutchinson Family — Judson, John and Asa — Tribe of Jesse, from the old Granite State, had been induced to visit the Territories and in their perambulations came to Faribault. They entered the place singing 'I come, I come, ye have called me long.' During their sojourn with Dr. Jewett, arrangements were made for a concert which was given in the dining-room of the Nutting House, to a thoroughly interested audience. This was the first concert given in the Cannon Valley since the voice of the red man was hushed for aye. Since that period the family have been more or less interested in the growth of our State. The town of Hutchinson established by them, though once sacked and burned by the wild men, now has the advantages of modern civilization.

"They have returned to Faribault to find her educational institutions, public buildings and private residences surpassed by none in the State. An invitation has been extended to them to be present at the old settlers' meeting, but prior engagements will prevent their return so soon."

The *St. Paul Pioneer-Press* said:

"A quartette of this talented family, including John and Asa, of the original troupe, and Abby and Henry, two gifted offshoots, gave a concert at the Opera House last evening to an audience of fair proportions. It is unnecessary to say that the entertainment was peculiar, for its very charm was its peculiarity. A miscellaneous audience, may, in a degree, enjoy a concert given by highly educated singers, that perform the highest class of music, but to truly delight them, give them the pure, simple harmonies of the Hutchinsons. It is a class of music they can understand. The melodies are pure and the part singing is given *con amore*, with not an attempt at display or flourish. There is an originality about the family which has lasted for over a third of a century, and it is a fact that the two older members of the family that appeared last night were as full of life and fun as they could possibly have been when they made their *debut* on the concert platform, thus showing that their adhesion to the temperance doctrine, which they so eloquently sing, has proved a wonderful preservative in their case. The programme last evening was made up of an excellent variety of songs, descriptive, pathetic and humorous, and it afforded a fine entertainment. Henry, who made his first appearance in this city, is really a cultivated singer and he rendered an elaborate buffo song in Italian in splendid style, showing that he is capable of maintaining a position of more than ordinary pretensions among the best singers of the day. At the request of a large number of citizens, it has been decided to give another entertainment to-night."

We spent several weeks in Chicago; a good deal of the time with Jonas Hutchinson, now one of the judges there, and for a long time corporation counsel of the city. He was a brother to Jerusha, Judson's wife. We also visited Hattie Hutchinson Dow, Zephaniah's daughter. While making this stay in Chicago I commenced definite work on the history of the family. In March, Camilla Urso gave concerts in the city, and Henry made a contract to sing with her as basso. On the 5th Henry and I gave a concert together in Chicago and at half-past ten that night he left me to join the company. After that my diary contains two entries, each day, one giving my own whereabouts, and the other his. Madam Urso took a great liking to Henry, at once made him her confidential adviser as to her professional plans, requesting him to make the announcements in the concerts, and the time he spent travelling with her he heartily enjoyed.

The company consisted of Madam Camilla Urso-Lein, Miss Eugenie De Roode, Miss Clara J. Poole, J. C. Bartlett, Auguste Sauret and Henry. The great violinist astonished and delighted all her audiences, and the company received fine notices wherever they appeared. The *Red Wing Republican* spoke of Henry as possessing a "magnificent bass voice, firm, hearty, manageable, and of great compass. He sung with taste and genuine feeling. He had the mental resources to become a truly great artist."

Of Henry, another paper said: "His fine voice and animated style found ample scope in the spirited 'Mariner's Song', and his rendition of the cavitina, 'Femina, Femina,' shows that he is an accomplished buffo singer. His voice had a large range, and is even and full throughout, having great sustaining power, even in the higher tones." A Wild Western sheet in Sioux City said of Camilla, "She fiddles like an angel," which is a reminder of Camilla's remark concerning the quartet's singing of "O hush thee, my babie," "If you were angels you couldn't have done it better." The *Topeka Commonwealth* said: "Mr. Henry Hutchinson was well received on his own merits, and also because he was supposed, whether correctly or incorrectly we do not know, to be a member of the 'Hutchinson Family,' always favorites in this anti-slavery country." The *Terre Haute Express* said he "sung gloriously."

After Henry left me I made a trip to Hutchinson, transacting some matters of business, then returning to Chicago I spent several weeks on my book, and finally went to New York, where I found Henry, he having simultaneously finished his tour with Camilla Urso, she and Frederick Leur, her husband, sailing for Europe. Henry at once entered into partnership with Jesse L. Hutchinson, his cousin, in a foundry business in Baltimore. Meanwhile I began to think of the possibility of our doing some business in Philadelphia, at the Centennial Exposition. I had sent Joshua there to spy out the ground, and ascertain the advantages and privileges that would be allowed us. On May 26th I went down myself. We desired to make ourselves acquainted with the leading spirits of the enterprise, and signify our willingness to be utilized in any way most conducive to the interests of the great exposition.

On my return I went to Lynn for a few days, and made arrangements to celebrate the Centennial year by building a handsome stone wall on the Highland Square front of my premises, also terracing up the slope in front and building what is now known as "John's Avenue." A man named Bisbee agreed to do the job for three hundred dollars, with fifty dollars additional for contingent expenses. His bid proved to be wofully out of the way, for eventually I had to take the job off his hands and superintend it myself, at an expense of about one thousand dollars.

On the 8th of June Sister Abby sailed for home from Liverpool, after an absence of several years. We all went to welcome her; and on June 17th Fanny, Henry, Viola and I stood on the pier at New York to give her greeting. As the steamer went past us in the channel and came about we could see her with Ludlow on the deck, by her side, and sent out a song of welcome. Then we heard her voice, with that of her husband, responding:

> "We come, we come, from a foreign land,
> To welcome again our singing band."

Of course they had made many friends during the passage over, and there was great interest in the greeting.

On the 19th all the party went to Philadelphia. I secured quarters for myself and family in the Atlas

Hotel, but a stone's throw from the Centennial grounds. It was a suite of rooms, and we took meals during our stay just as we chose. I went out for a walk very soon, and found a cow feeding not far from the grounds, and ascertained that we could get a quart or two of her pure, fresh milk a day. It was easy to procure plenty of fruits and other supplies, and so we lived quite comfortably. Besides Fanny, my daughter Viola and her eldest child, "Cleve," was with me. Harry and Kate were left behind.

We made pilgrimages to and from the Centennial grounds and buildings, day in and day out; would grow weary and fly to our rest: then be up and ready to make new discoveries, pleased with all the display, the fine bands of music, the accommodating railroad trains conveying sight-seers to any part of the grounds, shouting and singing as occasion would offer, congratulating everybody that we were mutually privileged to celebrate with the great American people the centennial of the birth of the nation; occasionally giving concerts in the halls and churches of the city; gathering the people in the rotunda of our hotel almost every night, and giving them a programme lasting nearly an hour. We were privileged to invite many speakers of note to address our audiences on subjects vital to the welfare of humanity. Friends and acquaintances from every quarter of the Union grasped our hands in congratulation, and thus the days passed merrily, with little except the heat and dry weather to mar the festivities. Here we stayed until the natal day of the Republic, July Fourth, and witnessed the matchless pyrotechnic display. Then we began to long for the cool breezes of the sea-coast and once more sought dear old High Rock.

I found my Centennial wall had not progressed as I had expected. I therefore took the responsibility on my own shoulders, and in time the substantial piece of masonry was completed. It was the work of weeks to build it; but we were meeting, all the while, the approbation of our best citizens as we proceeded. We had been successful in quarrying the purple porphery with which it is constructed from the grounds adjacent, and with it erected a structure which has stood as a retaining wall for eighteen years without the rupture of a seam or the moving of a stone. No wall in Lynn had ever been built like it. For the benefit of future generations I will describe its construction. A trench four feet wide, sunk to a depth of earth beyond the contingency of frost, was first made, and into this was tumbled the old wall, built a decade before, and other waste material, until it reached the level of the surrounding ground. On this foundation the wall was placed. It was three feet wide at the base, and battened next to the bank, retreating slightly on the front. The porphery was so trimmed to a proper size and shape that the full benefit of the color was retained. This was carried to about five feet in height, the wall being eighteen inches wide at the top. On the bank side, the surface was first covered with the best of cement, to a thickness of about an inch, leaving the exterior perfectly smooth, to prevent water from entering any portion of the fabric. This cement also covered the top, and made a bed to receive the cap-stone, it being laid so thick that no rain could ever penetrate it. The wall was then pointed on the face, and the work was complete. Ever since it was built, the city of Lynn has copied it in building retaining walls. While the work was going on, I had a number of workmen, nearly all from Erin, and they were a jolly set indeed. For convenience, I called them each by some marked feature or characteristic, and they seemed to like it. One had a whiskey bottle concealed somewhere in the bushes, and would occasionally disappear, returning with a tell-tale odor of alcohol about him. I called him "Rum," and he didn't object. The man who was always polishing his spade was called "Shovel;" "Long Neck," was another; "Strap," was another; and so on. I had antiquity and the classics to vindicate me in this course.

In September of this year, I made my annual visit to the old homestead at Milford. Asa and Dennett, with Sister Abby, were there also, and together the family gave a concert. The *Farmer's Cabinet* noticed us as follows:

"THE HUTCHINSON CONCERT.— The ill-success of concert troupes in Milford during the past four years was quite suggestive of a failure on the part of the Hutchinsons to secure a good audience, when they advertised one of their unique concerts for Monday evening,— but a well-filled house greeted them. We have attended all the concerts that have been held in our halls for three years, and can unhesitatingly say we have never seen a more enthusiastic audience in Milford for years than that which greeted the Hutchinson Family. As a general thing, Milford people look down on local talent and prefer something unknown and untried. 'The prophet is not without honor,' etc., applies very snugly to Milford people—but even this was forgotten on Monday evening, and for once, Milford did not go back on her own. The Hutchinson Family, as far as music is concerned, is a marvel, and every one of them is running over with melody. John, Asa, Joshua, Oliver Dennett, Abby Hutchinson Patton, and Nellie H. Gray were the members of the family that greeted us with song; when one wearied at the organ, another was ready to ably fill the vacant place, making a charming variety throughout. Every song was applauded, and the house rang again and again with enthusiastic approbation.

"Nellie Gray, the bright, rising star of this family, never shone brighter than on this occasion, and she received a rapturous encore. Asa, with master hand made the viol speak with almost human tones. Joshua excelled especially in his favorite song, 'There's no time like the old time,' and Oliver Dennett in the song 'Mother says I mustn't.' Dennett appeared several times during the evening and received most complimentary favor from those present. John presided throughout the evening, infusing spirit and humor into the concert, and as the company warmed up in the old but not wornout emancipation song, 'Get off the track,' Mrs. Patton's voice rose clear, sweet and above them all, and to her was due much of the applause that followed. In the freedmen hymn was exhibited that wonderful voice harmony for which the family are so noted, and the audience would have heard it again and again and not wearied."

When the wall was done, we returned to Philadelphia. Resuming our quarters at the Atlas, we were soon busy in singing and sight-seeing once more. Asa and Miss Ella F. Ramsdell, with whom he had been singing, and his children, Abby and Dennett, were there, with Joshua and others who had sung with the family in bygone years. On November 1st there was a great concert in the rotunda of the central building, the Handel and Haydn Society and other noted musical organizations participating. We were invited to a place on the programme, and sung "The Old Granite State," "Uncle Sam's Farm," and "The Fatherhood of God, and the Brotherhood of Man." The chorus consisted of the united tribes: Asa and his new wife, Miss Ramsdell, Abby Anderson, Dennett, Joshua, John, Fanny, Henry, Viola, Walter Kittredge, and Charles Sohier. The same combination gave several concerts in Horticultural Hall.

Then we sung at different State-buildings, for several days. On New Hampshire Day the Governor asked me to sing, and I invited Abby and Ludlow to join me. We sung the "Old Granite State," of course, and "One Hundred Years Hence." The latter seemed to be the very thing for the occasion. At its close, the Governor said, "Mr. Hutchinson, you have saved the day."

On one Sunday, Joshua, Asa, Dennett and I, with Miss Ramsdell, sang at Bethany Sunday-school, where John Wanamaker, afterwards Postmaster-General under Harrison, was superintendent. He never forgot us after that.

As soon as the exposition was over, Asa, with his company, began to give concerts about Philadelphia. He gave fifty before going elsewhere. I, too, would have liked to have given some concerts there, but disliked to have the tribes clashing in their work, so went in another direction. At the Centennial I had met two Welsh boys, or young men, named Hughes. At the time they were not in excellent financial circumstances, but they had good voices, and as I had temporarily lost Henry, they consented to an engagement.

Meanwhile, I bought a new organ. My melodeon had done good service, and made itself famous, but the time seemed ripe for a change. I went to George Woods, the veteran Cambridge organ manufacturer, and told him to make me to order as good an instrument as could be designed for concert work. He went enthusiastically at it, and designed new registers and reeds, and in course of time freighted the instrument to Lynn. My heart went down when the massive box containing it was carted to the door of Daisy Cottage. It was evidently far too large for convenient transportation over our routes. "Is that to be my melodeon?" thought I. Procuring the services of two or three men, it was lifted up the steps, and removed from the box. I placed my fingers on the keys. The sound seemed wooden. I struck another chord. More wood. It was evident that we could never transport this three hundred and fifty pounds in our concert tours. It was placed in the parlor and never saw the concert platform, except in a few instances, near Boston. The old melodeon was repaired, and continued to do service.

With the Hughes brothers I went to Baltimore. On December 17th, we, with Henry, sang at four different churches and temperance meetings. We had an experience which again demonstrated Henry's courage, while in Baltimore. We were in a hack. The driver was drunk, and his horses ran away. Henry crawled out of the side window, climbed on the box, seized the reins, and stopped the runaways. This was but one sample of his bravery. At one time we were singing in Gloucester, on Cape Ann. The concert was in the town hall, and a large assembly was listening. There was a noise in the rear gallery. Some twelve or more fishermen roughs were there. I remarked: "If it is possible to preserve order we will go on." A clergyman of influence in the audience arose and said: "I propose to have order here." Just then Henry leaped from the stage, crossed the hall and went into the balcony. Grasping the ringleader of the party by the collar, he pulled him across the gallery and out through the rear door. I heard them rolling down the stairs together. He put him out of the door and came back a conqueror. The audience roared with delight.

After giving several concerts in Baltimore, we went to Washington. Here we had quite a remarkable experience. We gave some thirty concerts in different halls and churches. On the night of December 31st, by invitation of Rev. John P. Newman, D. D., now bishop of the Methodist-Episcopal church, then President Grant's pastor, I attended the watch-night service in the Metropolitan Church. At Dr. Newman's request,

I had agreed to sing just before midnight, "No Night There":

> "There's no night there,
> But one endless day,
> In that beautiful land,
> Away, far away
> Just beyond the river
> That land I see;
> Loved ones are waiting
> To welcome me."

I had agreed with the organist to arrange the stops of the pipe organ for pianissimo effects. The church was packed. The time arrived. I went to the organ, in the dim light, and placed my hands on the keys. The only response was a far-off squeak. The organist had gone. I sung the best I could, but it seemed as though I was singing very poorly indeed. I did not stay to join in the New Year congratulations, and went home feeling some disappointment. The next day, however, as I was passing along the street, Dr. Newman crossed, grasped me by the hand, and said: "Mr. Hutchinson, I cannot thank you enough for your singing. It was very well received." This rather lifted me up.

We found Washington, as well as the country at large, completely stirred up over the question of who had been elected, Hayes or Tilden. The reader is familiar with the story of those stormy times. The election was close. For weeks the result in South Carolina, Florida and Louisiana was in doubt. General Hayes wrote to John Sherman his conviction that if the vote in the Southern States was correctly counted and returned he would have forty electoral votes, to spare, but that he preferred to be counted out rather than have any suspicion of fraud about the matter. Committees of Congress were sent into each of the three States to investigate the reports regarding the intimidation and suppression of the negro vote. Finally, the governors of the three doubtful States returned the vote as for Hayes in each instance. This gave him 185 votes to 184 for Tilden. Then came the question of whether this return should be accepted by the House of Representatives, or whether it should "go behind the returns." On December 18, 1876, Representative McCrary put in a resolution for a joint committee to report some measure of relief. After the usual reference and amendments, this bill was passed and concurred in by the Senate, and seven senators and seven representatives were appointed on the committee.

Meanwhile the excitement continued, and anarchy seemed to stare the country in the face. I had no sympathy with anarchy, but my course seemed to awaken suspicion of something of that nature, nevertheless. Early in January the conviction came to me that it was my duty as a good citizen to take some action. I listened to the talk in the capital, and was wrought up to a high pitch of excitement by it. Fears were entertained that a civil war was imminent which would be far more bloody than the Southern revolt. On all the trains coming toward the city military officers could be seen hurrying thence, which lent color to the idea. The suspicion was that Grant would effect a military rule, seize the government, and preside beyond the time allotted to him. I sung at a musicale in the three large parlors I had secured, soon after New Year's, and during the evening addressed the audience, speaking of my suspicions, and the necessity of immediate action to change existing conditions. I then asked a vote on the subject of a convention to discuss the matter. A gentleman arose, and said, "Mr Hutchinson, appoint your time." Then I said I had already secured a large room and suggested that the meeting be held two days later. This was January 13th. On the evening of that day there assembled at the appointed place a large gathering of men of every party, drawn by interest or curiosity. I was selected as temporary, and later permanent, chairman. I told them what I had thus far done and expressed my conviction that something must be done to stay the crisis. Many radical speeches were made. Some said, "Let the country go to the wall. If republicanism is a failure, let us have a new order of things." I had suggested that we ought to make a proposition to the disputing factions that one or the other party should carry out certain demands of the people and go in with their endorsement. It was a time to make an advance movement, and gain something for the people at large. The question was, What candidate will consent to carry out their demands. Resolutions were passed, and a committee, of which I was one, was appointed to draw up a memorial. We sung, "The Good Time Coming," and then the meeting adjourned. At its close, a gentleman came to me and said, "There have been two detectives here. They are from the White House." Then I reflected that it was a question whether the meeting was allowable. It was neither Republican nor Democratic, but revolutionary. The "memorial" was never completed, as events that occurred rendered it unnecessary.

On the same day, Senator Edmunds, chairman of the committee to which I have referred, reported the bill for an electoral commission, five senators, five representatives, and five members of the Supreme Court. This commission, it will be remembered, by a vote of eight to seven, refused to go behind the returns in any State; and so Hayes was declared President, being quietly inaugurated March 5th. Through all the excitement, I had been to both Republican and Democratic meetings. The former were much less communicative concerning their plans than the latter. We judged that Grant would consent to remain as President until his successor was chosen; that the Democracy would claim that Tilden was elected, and inaugurate him either in Washington or New York, and that each would appeal to the country for vindication. In that case, the demand of the people, voiced through a memorial, would be conceded by one or the other, and an almost unanimous endorsement would follow. This I believed would be a distinct gain in the condition of the country at large. These demands were outlined in my resolutions, which were submitted at the preliminary meeting, before the congressional committee reported. When it was all over, one man said to me, "John, I made up my mind that if civil war came, three Democrats, at least, would be dead men."

On March 4th, by invitation of the new magistrate, we visited the White House, and sung to President and Mrs. Hayes and their friends.

CHAPTER II.

ACROSS THE CONTINENT.

" Ho, brothers, come hither and list to my story;
   Merry and brief will the narrative be
Here like a monarch I reign in my glory,
   Master am I boys of all that I see

" Where once frowned a forest a garden is smiling,
   The meadow and moorland are marshes no more,
And there curls the smoke of my cottage, beguiling
   The children who cluster like grapes at my door
     Then enter boys, cheerily boys, enter and rest,
     The land of the heart is the land of the West "

" We have formed our band, and are all well manned,
   To journey afar to the promised land,
Where the golden ore is rich in store,
On the banks of the Sacramento's shore "

At the close of our engagement in Washington, in 1877, we made a trip to Chicago, where we spent several weeks. I sent for Fanny, my wife, to come on, and she joined us in our concerts. My son Judson came with her. H. L. Slayton, who ran a lecture bureau, made our engagements. During May we spent quite a time at the home of Rufus Blanchard, in Wheaton, Ill., twenty-five miles from Chicago. He was born in Lyndeboro, N. H., and his father refreshed me with a quart of milk on that Sabbath morning of long-ago when my hopes had been so sadly blighted by the maiden to whom I referred in an early chapter. Lyndeboro was but a short distance from Milford, and as boys we were almost neighbors. Mrs. Blanchard was very hospitable, and careful of our comfort. During the World's Fair I was a guest of Blanchard's again, for quite a long period. Another Mr. Blanchard, well known as an anti-Masonic lecturer, was in 1877 principal of the seminary at Wheaton. He invited us to sing at the institution on two occasions. I remember we spent an evening discussing his particular theories, and were quite agreed, except that I did not attack the secret-order system from behind the bulwark of Presbyterianism.

On one occasion, with Slayton, I went to the church in Chicago in which Lillie C. Phillips was singing. She was a vocalist of considerable note, with culture and experience, having appeared in concert with Annie Louise Cary and other celebrated people. I had learned of her through the Hughes brothers, who heard her sing as a child in her native town. Her voice and manner pleased me so much that with Fanny I called at her home, Millard Avenue. She came after that by invitation and sang at one of our concerts. I then began to consider the feasibility of securing her as a member of my company, and after our return from Chicago my wife kept in correspondence with her. On our way home we stopped, among other places, at Wheeling, W. Va. In the morning, in order to reach a certain train, we crossed a railroad bridge over the river on the ties. Judson, always a frail boy, was taken with a sudden illness when we were about halfway over. He dropped a bag full of valuable papers and falling, fortunately went across the ties instead of between them. The bag also lodged between the ties, and so still continues in service in my travels. We feared the oncoming train, but to our joy he recovered, and we were out of danger before it crossed.

We went to Baltimore and spent a day and night

with Henry. Thence we made our way to High Rock. Quarters were provided for the two young men of the company in another building, and life went on in Daisy Cottage much as usual, except that we missed Henry. A good deal of my attention was engrossed by articles that appeared in print concerning a sale to the city of High Rock. For years the title to some six acres of our property had been in dispute. Jesse bought it, and the brothers had improved it, in entire good faith; but after Jesse's death it had also been claimed by James N. Buffum and others. At this time Buffum was making negotiations to sell the land to the city for a public park. There was no dispute regarding the crest of the rock, and some five acres in front During my absence the subject had been under discussion by the city government and in the papers. The public had begun to see that in making the purchase of High Rock from Buffum it would have "Hamlet" with Hamlet left out, as we still owned the portion of the eminence resorted to by the citizens, which we had kept open to all visitors for nearly forty years. The title to the property was so cloudy that there was no purchase.

In June I went to Milford for a day or two, visited David, Joshua and Rhoda, and had a day's haying with the former, then seventy-four years old.

In July Abby and Ludlow visited me. We spent one day in Boston during their stay, meeting Asa and his wife. On another day we climbed Bunker Hill Monument together On the 25th of July, Ludlow and Abby accompanied Asa and his family to Bangor, Me. As the boat sailed by Lynn, we saluted them from High Rock with a sheet, swung in the air.

In August I received a letter from Chicago, signifying Lillie Phillips's willingness to come on and sing with us.

JUDSON WHITTIER HUTCHINSON — (p. 71)

At once I sent a dispatch for her, and soon went to the White Mountains to make arrangements to sing August 20th. President Hayes, with Mrs. Hayes and others, came to Fabyan's, and I began to wish the boys had come with me. However, I sang to the distinguished guests, without assistance. The next day I turned homeward. Two days later Lillie came. On the 27th we gave our first concert with her at Plymouth, N. H. Concerts followed at the Kearsage, North Conway, the Crawford House, Fabyan's, at the Weirs, where John B. Gough spoke, and other points. It was evident that we had a prize in Lillie; and we were much cheered by our wonderful success, rejoicing at the prospect of many engagements ahead. But the Hughes boys were jealous of her. We commenced a series of engagements around Boston. The Hughes brothers were by this time well acquainted with our songs, and feeling independent. They had put their heads together, and concluded that I desired to sing all the solos. One night in East Bridgewater, I announced a song in which they were to sing also. They sat still in their places, and I scented trouble. Begging the indulgence of the audience, I changed the song and went on. We were particular to sing no song after that which needed their voices. When we reached the "Old Granite State," Judson, who saw that something was wrong, came out from the wings and joined us. In a few days I went to the boys, and suggested that I would give them one more trial. Soon after they tried the same thing again. Then I let them go. They later went to Wales, where they sang my songs to delighted audiences and made money. They are now established in a successful music store in one of the Southern cities.

Then I sought a bass singer. A Boston man joined us, named Frank L. Young. The Philadelphia agent who had cared for Asa's interests the season before, John H. Pilley, had written me that there was a great demand for concerts by the Tribe of John, and we had allowed him to make some fifty dates ahead for us. Mr. Young sung bass for a while and also acted as a violinist to play Lillie's accompaniments, while she would in return play his. After that I met a good bass singer, J. P. Hayes, who is now a resident of Lynn. He sang with us a little. But all this while there was but one bass singer who really met my ideas. No one could sing with me like my own son. On Thanksgiving Day I sent for him to come from Baltimore and attend our concert, in Association Hall. He came, and sang one song. He had never met Lillie before, but at once recognized his fate. It was comparatively easy work after that concert to persuade him that it was for his advantage to drop his business engagements and join us.

Henry began to sing with us again December 10th. After that everything was easy. We began a series of successes lasting for years. Lillie was versed in the more modern methods of concert singing. Henry had had an experience which gave him command of more heavy solos, as well as of the simpler songs of humanity which he had always sung with Fanny and myself. We sought to retain the old favorites in our programmes, while giving a representation also to the best modern concert selections. The combination seemed to take our audiences by storm. We were received with great *éclat* wherever we appeared. When we had filled the engagements for which we had come to Philadelphia, Mr. Pilley gave us many more. Since

LILLIE   HENRY   FANNY   JOHN

THE TRIBE OF JOHN, 1878 — p. 72

the days when the brothers with Abby first won success in the large cities, we had seen nothing more marked in the way of success than this. We were singing practically every night. On Sunday we went to such places as Wanamaker's Sunday-school. We also gave a concert in the Bethany Church. We sang in all the large halls. Musical Fund Hall, where we sang in the 40's, was no longer closed against us, and there was no question of the right of any colored man or woman who chose coming also. Our engagements were a series of ovations.

I remember one Monday morning we sang at the Baptist ministers' meeting. The question of eternal punishment in a material abode for the wicked was under discussion. The gathering seemed to be composed of both "hard shells" and soft shells, for as the old lines of belief were again laid down by the elder element among the dominies, we observed that from one-half to two-thirds of the younger members one by one departed. For myself, I rather leaned toward the views of Beecher, and concluded the younger men were studying philosophy.

While in Philadelphia we concluded to make a trip across the continent to the Pacific coast. This, as the reader knows, had been our cherished ambition for years. When we finished our engagements there, Fanny and I started for New York. We reached Jersey City, and as we were entering the depot, each of the passengers busied himself in preparations to leave the train. I was in the aisle, getting my baggage together. Fanny also was in the aisle. I observed that the train, though in the station, did not stop. Suddenly, crash! went the forward car against the bumper. The recoil sent everybody off their feet, and there we were, piled in a demoralized tangle. Sadly bewildered, and bruised and lamed so that we were unable to tell whether we were really seriously hurt or not, we were led from the car. A woman who had been standing in front of the mirror found her face plunging through it before she knew anything was up. It was frightfully cut and bleeding badly as she was taken from the car. We descended simultaneously, and a reporter, recognizing me and seeing her, instantly assumed her to be one of the Hutchinsons. At once he sent the news of our assumed injury to his paper and it was telegraphed to Philadelphia and everywhere. Henry and Lillie were greatly distressed by the intelligence, and at once hastened to us. We were conducted into the depot, so shaken up and bewildered that we were glad to accept all courtesies. I confess I was curious to ascertain how badly I was hurt. A physician examined us, and found us intact, barring bruises. A carriage was placed at our disposal and we were driven to a boarding-place. I soon concluded that I should have no further use for the turnout, and said to the driver: "I guess I won't keep you any longer. If anything serious turns up, we will notify the directors."

We had previously left our son Judson in good hands, in Lakeville, Conn. We visited him, and found him well and happy. We went to Lynn, found a tenant who would take our house for a year or two, and then returned to New York. Then we sang for six weeks in the towns on the line of the Harlem Railroad. Toward the last of June, I left the party and came home to Lynn, to attend to matters of business. I found the man living in my house had kept everything in fine condition, and that his care of the strawberry bed made it as handsome as I had ever seen one. Picking four or five quarts, I took them to New York, and my company had a feast. On my way, I stopped at Lakeville for Judson

Then we took the New York Central road and went westward, stopping at all large towns for concerts. At Shortsville we found Wm. L. Brown, who offered to take an engagement to go ahead and make dates for us. He kept on through western New York, Ohio, Illinois and Michigan When we got to Toledo, we left Judson with Viola. We filled many engagements in Chicago, with magnificent audiences. We sang one night in the Baptist church at Lillie's home.

Then we bid good-by to Mr. Brown, and turned our faces toward sunset, fully aware as we did so that there was likely to be as much money for us if we spent a year near Chicago as there would be where we were going. Our scrap-books show that our tour was the cause of the publication of a voluminous amount of literature. Histories of the family, interviews with us, incidents concerning our experiences, and reviews of our concerts make quite a volume in themselves. At Council Bluffs we made the acquaintance of the Superintendent of the Union Pacific road, and through him we obtained special rates on four round-trip tickets to the Golden Gate, with all needful stop-over privileges. At Omaha we sung in temperance meetings and heard John B. Finch speak. We were glad to meet him. He asked us to come to his reform meetings, and we gladly did so Rev. Mr. Fisher, the man who was done up in a carpet at Lawrence, Kan, by his wife, to save him from the border ruffians, was preaching in the First Methodist-Episcopal Church at Omaha, and we gave several concerts in that edifice.

We then gave concerts in Lincoln, Crete, Fremont, Cheyenne, Denver, Greeley, Laramie, Salt Lake City (where we sung in the Temple and the Theatre, and made the acquaintance of the leading men among the Mormons who spoke of their system of life unblushingly, claiming it was patriarchal), Ogden, Eureka, Carson, Virginia City, Gold Hill (where we went and sung to the miners, hundreds of feet below the surface, and saw the ore in its primitive condition, though it is said most of the money made out of the mine was in selling stock, everybody, even to the hired girls, having the fever), Sacramento, and so on to San Francisco.

Perhaps I should pause here, and give a brief review of some of the notices we received on our trip from ocean to ocean and during this year, 1878, which closes with our arrival in San Francisco. A notice of our thirty-sixth concert in Philadelphia may well lead the way. The writer says:

"The secret of their attraction is still what it always was. Not only are they good singers, but unrivalled entertainers. Paterfamilias, the *actor* of the family, is an able tragedian. He froze our young blood in the year — never mind — with 'The Maniac,' and so scared its owner, Russell, that that great vocalist, when Hutchinson sang the song in England, got out an injunction and stopped him. He is also, we believe, the only man living who can sing a comic song without losing his dignity. Henry J. Hutchinson is a fine baritone singer, and Mrs. Hutchinson recites and renders such character songs as 'John Anderson' and her part in 'Tommy, don't go,' with excellent effect. This song, by the way, was one of the main features of the concert at Olivet Church. Tommy, a young farmer, is entreated by his aged parents not to leave them to join a gay party, and finally yields to their prayers. The little musical vaudeville was admirably acted, but Miss Phillips, who played the accompaniment, took all the merit out of Tommy's sacrifice by joining in the chorus with her fresh young voice. 'Don't go, Tommy!' sang she, and Tommy stayed. Who wouldn't? The young lady gave Topliff's 'Consider the Lilies' so beautifully that the least emotional audience we ever lost patience with burst into raptures. The audience was not large, but Mr. H., in thanking them, said he ought to feel very much encouraged at seeing such an attendance when he reflected that at one time there were not so many people on the globe as he then saw before him. This joke was heightened by being taken in perfectly good faith by many of the audience."

The writer might have said that I added — "during the rainy season."

A Council Bluffs paper spoke of our singing as "soul stirring." Another said, "Each one fills his part to perfection." An Omaha publication said, "Their art is as soul-compelling as their music is ear-compelling." It also said, "This modern 'Tribe of Jesse' is a living link between all that was sweet and inspiring in the impassioned voice of struggling freedom a generation ago, and all that is high and noble in this glad era of its triumph, in the arts and the amenities of the intellectual, social and art-life of a thinking, earnest and progressive people." "It is rarely that a Lincoln audience has been more completely carried away by the power of vocal music," said another paper. A Cheyenne paper called us "Pioneers of Song," while a Fremont, Neb., paper, speaking of Lillie, said, "This lady has a very fine soprano, broad in compass, remarkably full, sweet and pure in tone, highly cultivated and completely under control." Within a week, another paper had indulged in a rhapsody over her as "A contralto of remarkable quality and range," the two indicating something of the compass of her voice. In Fremont, "Tommy, don't go," moved the audience to tears. The *Denver Tribune* said: "These concerts are unlike any other form of musical entertainment, and would seem to be 'the good' in music. They are plain, and yet all the modern graces and the accomplishments of the age are discernible, in the make-up of the programme." The *Laramie Sentinel* said: "John and Fannie are getting old, but have the consolation, in their declining years, that the high order of musical ability manifested by them through life has not suffered in transmission to their children, and as pure voices as theirs will sing requiems over their graves, when they have gone to join the members of their tribe now singing new songs in that beautiful land of the blue.[1] A Virginia City paper

[1] The expression, "Beautiful Land of the Blue" in the notice above quoted, impressed the compiler of this volume so much when he read it, that within a few days he wrote a song which was published and copied freely in the press. At the request of Mr. Hutchinson, it is inserted here

"'Tis a weary world, and a dreary world
   We pilgrims are journeying through;
But a country bright, with no cloud or night
   Is the land beyond the blue.

"And souls that are sad shall be evermore glad
   With a joy that is perfect and true,
When they reach the strand of that beautiful land;
   The land beyond the blue.

"And there, we are told, is the city of gold,
   Bathed in glory eternally new,
And its streets are trod by the angels of God
   In the land beyond the blue.

"To the fever and strife of this hurrying life,
   To its sorrows we'll bid adieu —
When we stretch our wings and each spirit sings
   In the land beyond the blue.

"O, brothers that mourn, with hearts that are torn,
   There is solace for me and for you;
For no sickness and pain shall grieve us again
   In the land beyond the blue.

"And the spirits we love in those mansions above
   Prepared for the faithful and true,
Are dwelling for aye, in immortal day,
   In the land beyond the blue.

"Oh, sometimes I long, 'mid the evil and wrong
   Of this life, though its days are few,
To be taking my flight to that city of light
   In the land beyond the blue."

said, "The singing of this family is of the good home kind that everybody can understand and feel.' The Sacramento papers praised us for charging only fifty cents admission, half the sum asked by even amateurs.

At Virginia City we were met by Charles R. Bacon, whom we engaged as agent. He went ahead, and made dates for us in San Francisco and elsewhere in California. We gave our opening concert in San Francisco in the Metropolitan Temple, its pastor being Rev. I. S. Kalloch, whom we had met in Kansas, when he was our leading opponent in the suffrage campaign. In his paper, the *Metropolitan Banner*, he said of us:

"The Hutchinsons have won their way into public favor in San Francisco, as we knew they would. We wish every person on the coast could hear them. The emotions awakened are simply indescribable. The harmony of voices is wonderful, the rendering of every tone is faultless. Art contributes to nature in their singing, and does not chill it. Thoughts, sentiments, emotions, glowing with life, flow to enchanted listeners through the poetry of song. Old memories are awakened. The scenes of our childhood, almost forgotten, are brought so vividly to mind that we think, and laugh, and cry, and clap our hands, and are carried, in spite of our struggles to resist, outside of ourselves. We wish all the children could hear them. Happy, sunny childhood has a right to enjoy the benediction of these sweet songsters."

On January 15, 1879, J. M. Buffington, an old friend of Brother Jesse, engaged us to come to his Sunday-school, in the Howard Methodist Episcopal Church, San Francisco, at a later date. We went on the 24th. Addressing the children, Mr. Buffington told a story of his experience in coming to the State in the early days of the gold excitement. He came over the Isthmus, and boarded a ship bound for San Diego. It was crowded with adventurers in pursuit of fortune. They had been on board but a short time when, owing to the crowded condition of the boat, poor food, foul air and fatigue, disease broke out in the vessel. Men were attacked, would be sick but a short time, and die. It seemed like cholera. Then there came to the front a man of spirit, soul and determination, full of strength and magnetism, who went from one to another with words of solace and encouragement. He went to the cook's galley, made soups and porridges and in this way restored hundreds to health, joy and happiness. He was, like Florence Nightingale, an angel of mercy. He was a benefactor, full of words of healing. When they reached San Diego, the ship came to anchor. The man was blessed by both crew and passengers — by everybody on board. "The man who will sing to you," concluded he, "brings that benefactor vividly to my mind. He is his brother." I was as much surprised by this glowing tribute to my Brother Jesse as any one there. In response to the speech we sung "Good Old Days of Yore."

As a prelude to one of our concerts in the Metropolitan Temple, Rev. Mr. Kalloch spoke in part as follows:

"My excellent friend, John Hutchinson, whom we have the pleasure of honoring to-night by this magnificent assembly — the thirteenth child of the "Tribe of Jesse" — has presided over more than ten thousand concerts in person. Who can estimate, much less measure, the moral impressions produced and moral energies stimulated by this protracted and blessed itinerancy? Especially when it is remembered that never in a single song have they stooped to the utterance of a vulgar or debasing word. Their music has been pitched to the tune of humanity. They have sung on the side of human rights. They have given a voice to the wants of weary, wayside hearts. They have chanted the gospel of universal emancipation.

"The first time I heard them was thirty years ago by the side of one who has kept by my side ever since, but, alas! not to be moved and melted as we were then by the mountain melodies of the old Granite State! The first time I knew them was when they were singing and I was shouting the name of Fremont in the memorial campaign of which he was leader. Whatever you may think of the campaign or of the man, there is one thing you will not successfully deny, and that is that it inspired some of the grandest music, poetry and eloquence that ever graced a political campaign. If that campaign had left but one memorial, it would have been enough to immortalize it. I refer to the song which Whittier contributed to its progress. It is called 'The Pathfinder,' and has a double interest for Californians."

We gave fifty concerts in San Francisco during three months. On February 5th we sung at Mills Seminary, an institution of high literary taste and culture. On the following day we sung at the First Universalist Church, its pastor being Rev. Ada C. Bowles, a lady of culture and ability, born on Cape Ann, and a friend of many years standing.

In June, after a series of triumphs in an artistic sense, Fanny and I with Henry and his wife, went to the beautiful Yosemite Valley. Here we stayed many weeks, enjoying with all travelling America, the magnificent scenery and making ourselves happy with hundreds of the tourists there gathered. While there Jack, Henry's first boy was born. Mr. Leidig, at the hotel, proposed that he be named "Frederick El Capitan," but instead he was named Henry John. A little later there was a Sunday-school assembly and the first Sunday-school in the valley was organized, numbering some one hundred and sixteen pupils and eight teachers, the enrolment representing sixteen States. Rev. Dr. John H. Vincent, now a bishop, conducted the exercises. There were lectures every day by some such eminent men as Rev. Thomas Guard, Dr. Sheldon Jackson, Dr. John Muir and Joseph Cook. The first church in the valley, a Methodist, was dedicated during our stay, and for this service Joseph Cook wrote a doxology, which we sung:

"The hills of God support the skies,
To God let adoration rise,
Let hills and skies and heavenly host
Praise Father, Son and Holy Ghost."

Mr. Cook made the speech of presentation of a Bible secured by subscriptions among the tourists. As appropriate to the incident we sang "My Mother's Bible."

The papers published the birth of Jack with various comments. One added to the notice this stanza:

"I was born in the Yo Semite Valley,
    I am healthy and jolly and fat,
They will call me a Yo Semite baby,
    But I'm a Green Mountain boy for all that."

Late in the spring we made a trip to San Diego and gave five successful concerts in the vicinity of the Mexican border. People brought us beautiful flowers by the tubful. We visited the border line and saw the great stone monument between the two countries established after the Mexican war. We went to the great Kimball farm, thousands of acres overlooking the bay, and extending back for a long distance. They gave us a banquet at which we feasted on the olive in its ripened state. Mr. Kimball said he would sometimes eat a pint of olives at one time, taking nothing else for his food.

Just before leaving San Diego we were saddened by the distressing intelligence from Viola at Toledo that the physician said Judson could not live twenty-four hours. We thought, with breaking hearts, of our sweet-souled boy, who had always been gifted with a peculiar charm in expressing his affection. On the morning we left Toledo he placed each arm simultaneously around the necks of his mother and father and said, "Let us sing 'Our days are gliding swiftly by!'" I immediately wired to Toledo, "Embalm and entomb, preparatory for later burial in Lynn." Happily, however, the physician was wrong, and in a few days news of Judson's recovery came to gladden our hearts.

On June 26th we took the boat at San Francisco for

Portland, Ore. It was the steamer *George W. Elder*, and the wife of the captain, whom I met in the city, gave me an excellent recipe for sea-sickness. She recommended that if I felt the malady coming on, I should eat a raw onion, which she guaranteed to be a cure. I said, "I'm not going to be sick." So when the vessel steamed away from the dock in San Francisco, I bravely took a place on the upper deck and rapturously gazed on the scenery as we sailed past the Golden Gate. Then we struck a ground swell and I began to feel premonitory symptoms of something awful. Slowly and sadly I arose and went below. The table in the cabin was set for lunch. "Look here," said I to myself, "I must sit down and eat with these who have preceded me. I'm not going to be sick." I sat down, and at once suffered another peculiar sensation. Just then I noticed a tumbler, full of green onions on the table, and recalled the advice of the captain's wife. Nervously grasping one, I took quite a large bite. As I swallowed it, the fact that it was decayed flashed across my mind. This reflection made me sick. Hastening to our stateroom, I met Fanny at the door. She said, "I feel strangely." "Get out of the way, Fanny," said I, desperately, as I sprang into the upper berth. Just as I lay down, two tin buckets caught my eye, suspended over the berth. "Why do they put those suggestive pails where they will make people sick," said I, savagely, and swung them down under the lower berth. Then I sought a recumbent posture. A minute later I said, in soft but imperative tones, "Fanny, reach me a bucket, quick!" She stooped to do so and I leaned over the edge of the berth anxiously. Just then I suffered the precise sensations experienced by the big fish when he discovered he had no further use for Jonah.

Fanny's errand had not been completed and she sincerely regretted the fact. "Help!" "Murder!" she cried, as she rushed out of the stateroom in a condition that words need not describe. The stewardess came to her rescue, but Fanny's nerves had received a serious shock. Probably this was the reason that she kept her berth for five days until we reached the still water in the Columbia River. I kept her company. Finally we reached Astoria. John W. Cochran had agreed to act as our advance agent. He was a newspaper correspondent and writer, whom I had met at Chicago three years before. We found that he had thoroughly advertised us, and we were warmly welcomed.

Our valued friend General O. O. Howard was at that time in command on the Pacific coast. He came to our concerts in Portland, and invited us to come to his headquarters at Vancouver for a few days. We did so, and had a happy time. I remember we held a great temperance meeting together, he speaking and we singing. Going on the boat to Vancouver, I got my first view of Mount Ranier — or Tacoma — thirty miles away, its snow-capped summit looming up like a sentinel watching over the surrounding country. It was grandeur itself:

> "And there, forever firm and clear,
> His lofty turret upward springs;
> He owns no rival summit near,
> No sovereign but the King of kings."

General Howard stood by my side as I gazed in rapture at the splendid mountain, evidently pleased at my enthusiasm.

We found Abby and Ludlow at Portland, Oregon, preparing to embark on the steamer *California* for a month's trip to Alaska. Before we left that region, they had returned, with most glowing descriptions of what they had seen. They had previously visited Europe, Asia and Africa, but asseverated that they had seen more real beauty on this trip than ever before.

We gave concerts in Portland, Seattle, Port Gamble and Port Townsend, and then crossed the line to Victoria, B. C., where we stayed several days. We attended a Caledonian picnic, among other pleasures. Then came concerts at Olympia, East Portland, Salem, Walla Walla, and other points. Then we went down to the seaside for a few days. Coming back in a carriage, we got into trouble crossing the tidewater. Our horses almost went out of sight, the water rose so fast. Henry jumped to the rescue, and succeeded in keeping the carriage at the correct poise. We were drenched through when we reached dry land. We stopped at a little store, where a clothes-line was suspended in the breeze, and asked the privilege of hanging our garments up to dry. It was given, and by the time the boat to Astoria came along, we had dried most of them.

During this trip I caught the shingles. This is a strange disease. It is said it proves fatal if the eruption surrounds the body, but I have never heard of a case where it did. My case was as extreme as it dared to be. When at the Dalls, we were lodged in a boarding-house, where there was good service, and fair food, but coming in through the open window was a stench, doubtless due to imperfect sewerage. The same trouble was noticeable at the church where we sung. The town had been burned the year before, and the difficulty probably begun then. We gave two concerts, and after the second we at once took the boat for Portland. After retiring, I felt uneasy and uncomfortable. Suddenly something bit me. It was a large spider. This was the beginning of the shingles, brought on, apparently, by the poison of the sewer gas combined with the bite of the spider. I took the advice of every experienced person I saw, but nothing relieved me. It was fully two months before I got that poison eradicated from my system. One day we went to ride in a wagon of the western type. Henry and the rest were on the two front seats, while I sat on a chair in the rear, suffering poignantly from my disease, and taking no particular note of where we were going. Suddenly the carriage gave a lurch. The rear wheel went into a deep rut some eighteen inches, but those ahead did not lose their equilibrium. With me it was different. Engrossed as I was in my suffering, I was off my guard, and therefore pitched headlong, down between the wheels. My shoe caught in the seat in front, as I fell, and was torn, but I was saved a severe blow, though stunned. Henry tenderly lifted me back into the carriage, and we went on our way to Portland.

We met many Indians near the Columbia River. The stream seemed to be simply swarming with salmon.

When we returned to Portland, a little more than a month had elapsed since we said goodby to Ludlow and Abby. They returned to us full of enthusiasm, and we had many happy hours of sweet converse together. It is one of the pleasant reflections of my life that though distance has sometimes prevented our being together in hours of mourning, the migrating habits of the brothers and sisters made the country seem a small place after all, and we met in far-away places almost as a matter of course. While here we had a reception. One of the ladies present turned out to be Mrs. Gildersleeve Longstreet, author of "Mrs. Lofty and I," the ballad which my brother Judson and Abby immortalized, one by setting it to music, and the other by singing it.

We were entertained at the house of a physician while in Oregon, Dr. Eaton, who was evidently a man of influence and standing in the community. We learned that he was once our fellow-townsman and neighbor, born in Milford in the same district as ourselves. He was one of a large family who were poor, and very early in life he was put out at farming with my brother David. He told me that the first money he earned David gave him. It was twenty-five cents for his first month's work, and he considered that he did well to get his board and this money besides. When we met him here, we found him to be a son-in-law of a wealthy gold-miner.

We had a notion that September would be a favorable time to make an overland trip to San Francisco. This we found to be a mistake. It was still disagreeably hot, and at least one hundred thousand people who would naturally have come to our concerts were still at the seaside watering places. However, we were compelled to learn by experience, and so late in August started on our trip over the mountains of Oregon and California. On September 3d we reached Jacksonville by train, and there chartered a stage with four horses to go one hundred and eighty miles for one hundred dollars. Then on we went, creeping over hills and through valleys, the most fatiguing journey we ever took, cramped, jolted, jostled, day and night for several days, pausing for concerts at Ashland, Eureka, Etna, Shasta and Reading, where, very much exhausted, we rejoiced at our release from that style of travelling. It was a ride fraught with exigencies and dangers which its picturesque features did little to relieve. We were in constant danger of being "held up" and robbed, especially in crossing the mountains, and for two days of our ride we endured an agony of expectation on that account.

On September 21st we were once more in San Francisco, and on the next day had the privilege of again taking General Grant by the hand. He was on his return from his trip round the world, having just crossed the Pacific. A grand banquet was tendered him at the Palace Hotel. We accepted an invitation to be present, but only one representative of the family, the writer, could well make his appearance, the tickets being placed at the modest sum of fifteen dollars per plate. I found a seat by Rev. L. D. Mansfield, who had assisted me in literary work at Chicago a year or two before, and partook of the entire *menu*, even venturing to begin with raw oysters, a delicacy that sometimes filled me with regrets. The plates were changed some twenty times

Gen. John Bidwell was in San Francisco at the time. He afterwards ran for President on the Prohibitory ticket. He was quite an effective temperance speaker, and we sung with him several times. We gave a number of concerts in San Francisco, Sacramento and vicinity, and had good success. At one concert there was an intermission of thirty-five minutes for ice cream. On October 16th I had a call from no less a distinguished person than Denis Kearney, the Sand Lots orator I talked Communism to him. He did not seem to understand the philosophy of brotherly love. My nephew, Hayward Hutchinson, of Washington, D C, was there He reminded me that when he was four or five years old, I taught him to go up a ladder. He said he had never been afraid of anything since. The circumstances were these: David, my oldest brother, had been very sick, almost at death's door. I was deputized to go and look after his stock. Noticing the small children as I went through the yard, the thought came to me that if my brother died we should have to be looking after and training them. This led me to ask Hayward's assistance. I requested him to mount the ladder to the hay-loft of the barn and throw off the hay for the creatures. He hesitated, and I encouraged him to go up. Catching hold of the ladder with determination, he went up, threw off the hay, and came down. Ever after he could climb a roof or other high place without being affected by dizziness. He had come on to California to receive his dividends on his immense Alaska interests. His two daughters came with him. He took a suite of rooms at the Palace Hotel, and his travelling expenses, coming and going, in a special car, were six thousand dollars. But then, the dividend he received was fifty thousand dollars. On October 18th we sung in Dashaway Hall, San Francisco, for the benefit of woman suffrage, Rev. Ada C. Bowles speaking.

Before we left San Francisco, we sung at the reception to Dr. Kalloch in celebration of his recovery from his wounds caused by his shooting by DeYoung. The reception was in the Metropolitan Temple, and was an enthusiastic affair. The shooting had occurred during our trip to Portland. Kalloch, in his campaign circulars when a candidate for mayor, to which office he was elected, had uttered disparaging words concerning the DeYoungs. One day he was sitting in his study in the church when DeYoung drove up in a coupé. He sent a boy to the study door to tell the doctor that a lady parishioner desired to see him at her carriage. Dr. Kalloch, with characteristic eagerness and politeness, hastened to the carriage door, bareheaded. DeYoung immediately fired at him, and he fell, supposably mortally wounded. It may well be supposed that the reception at the time of his recovery was an enthusiastic affair. I prepared a special song for the occasion. I also sung, "Under the Ice," words by my friend Clark.

"Under the ice the waters run,
  Under the ice our spirits lie;
The genial rays of the summer sun
  Will loosen the fetters by and by
Moan and groan in your prison cold,
  River of life, river of love,
The night grows short, the days grow long,
Weaker and weaker the bands of wrong,
  And the sun shines bright above

"Under the ice, under the snow,
  Our lives are bound in a crystal ring
By and by will the south winds blow,
  And roses bloom on the bank of spring

"Under the ice our souls are hid,
  Under the ice our good deeds grow;
Men but credit the wrong we did,
  Never the motives that lie below
Moan and groan in your prison cold,
  River of life, river of love,
The winter is growing worn and old,
Frost is leaving the melting mould,
  And the sun shines bright above.

"Under the ice we hide our wrong,
  Under the ice that has chilled us through;
Oh, that the friends that have known us long
  Dare to doubt we are good and true
Moan and groan in your prison cold,
  River of life, river of love,
The winter is growing worn and old,
Roses stir in the melting mould,
  We shall be known above."

This was our last interview with Kalloch. It was after our return East that his son, assistant pastor of the Temple, went to DeYoung's office and shot him dead.

On Monday, October 27th, we gave our farewell concert in Rev. Dr. A. L. Stone's Congregational Church, in San Francisco, shaking hands at the close with many friends we had made. The next night we gave our farewell in Sacramento. Thence we went to Ogden, giving two concerts, and on to Salt Lake City where again we met Rev. H. D. Fisher, formerly of Lawrence, Kan. We sung in his church on Sunday night. We made a number of stops for return concerts at Cheyenne, Omaha, Council Bluffs and elsewhere, and arrived at Des Moines November 15th. Here we left Henry, Lillie and Jack. Fanny and I went on to Toledo, where we had a royal welcome from Viola, Judson, and the rest. Immediately on arrival, I took cold, and with fatigue and all the rest, nearly came down with a fever.

We spent Thanksgiving Day at Toledo, and then with Juddie, proceeded East as far as Shortsville, N. Y., where I left both him and his mother with our friends, W. L. Brown and his wife, and kept on to Lynn alone. High Rock was still there, but there was plenty of work for me to do, after an absence of nearly eighteen months.

I found a good deal to worry me at High Rock. In the first place, Mr. Gay, who had been making a resurvey of Asa's portion of the property, the easterly half, had discovered that Alonzo Lewis when he originally made the plans for the division, for some reason left a strip of several feet, running through the middle, which he allowed to neither brother. That meant trouble in adjustment. Then I found the periodical talk concerning the use of the summit of the rock for a park was going on, and moreover, the city government had taken a hand in the matter. So I busied myself in finding some way of bringing about the purchase without sacrificing our rights or the comfort of our tenants, a difficult task.

Fanny came home during December, and was ready to start with me on a return trip West, January 1, 1880. A day in New York City, another in Shortsville, and a few hours in Toledo, were all the stops we allowed ourselves until we reached Des Moines, January 8th. During our absence Henry had formed a quartet, and had been giving concerts in and about the city. He also appeared, as did Lillie, as a soloist in "Ruth the Moabitess," a cantata. On the next night we gave a concert — our first in eight weeks — in Indianola. The next few weeks we devoted to concerts in Iowa and Illinois. On the 26th we were in Red Oak, Ia., and visited Mrs. Rose Hasty, a sister of "Cousin Maud" Porter. While at Missouri Valley Junction, on the 30th, I had a conference with a man named Chase, and laid plans that were never realized for the founding of a county seat in Nebraska.

On February 5th we rode fifty miles across country in a sleigh, and were almost frozen to death. On the 11th, at Le Mars, we met the notable Robert Morris, Masonic lecturer. He told us that George Baker had died from apoplexy. Baker was the basso profundo of the well-known family of musicians. I remember he came to Chicago at one time and wanted to go singing with me. I took him out to Kankakee, and let him sing one piece. His voice did not harmonize with mine, and we gave it up. It seemed that he had finished a rehearsal with his company at the opera house in a town where they were to exhibit. The company returned to the hotel for dinner. He remained. His chair was turned up at the table. After a while his prolonged absence was noticed, the party returned to the hall, found it locked, crawled through the transom over the door, and discovered him dead.

On March 5th, in Independence, Ia., we met Jesse Harriman, an old anti-slavery friend, then seventy-five years of age. I first knew him in Danvers, thirty-seven years before. On March 8th we received word that Viola and all her family were to start immediately for New Mexico. The next night Asa met me, at Marion, and we talked until two o'clock in the morning on High Rock matters. On the 16th, in Iowa City, I met Robert Hutchinson. In my boyhood, he sung with me in the choir at Milford. He pre-empted Iowa City, which was the capital for a while. Here I also met Samuel Everett, who preached in my youth in the Baptist church in Milford. He baptized me at the age of ten, after a notable revival in 1831. We had a familiar talk on theological matters. In the experience of years, he said he had made up his mind that character was everything. He believed God was a benevolent, reasonable being, and that in his economy, everybody worth saving would be saved. All the rest he thought would be annihilated, burned up as chaff, but not be the subjects of an unforgiving wrath, to suffer eternal torture. It was a sweet interview, in which we talked over old days in Milford, and it was our last. He had given up preaching, but was a strong believer in liberty, brotherly love and patriotism.

On the 27th we were in Elmwood, Ill., with our good friends, Edwin R. Brown and family. On the next night we gave a concert at the house of Mr. Brown. Three generations of the family were represented by the father, eighty-two, son, fifty-six, and grandson, twenty-nine years old. On April 12th we made another visit with our friends President John Blanchard and Rufus Blanchard at Wheaton. At West Liberty, on the 19th I had a very pleasant visit with the poet, Don Piatt.

During all this time I was very much worried concerning home affairs. Asa, when he left me in Iowa, had gone immediately to Lynn, and I had promised to follow him in April. I arrived on the 22d. Meanwhile, he had ordered a surveyor to make a plat of his half of the property, and had cut it up into house-lots and offered it for sale. This was not at all in accordance with my ideas, for it spoiled the apple orchard which Jesse set out, besides disfiguring the entire estate, and spoiling the original design, which had thus far been treated as a whole. I considered the situation with all the judgment I possessed, and finally concluded to buy the lots when the sale occurred. The Stone Cottage, and the pinnacle of High Rock, with contiguous land were owned by us in common. He insisted, against my desire, in selling the cottage. After much reflection, I concluded to sign a bond with him to sell High Rock Cottage, and started for Boston to do so. At the railway station I met Wm. G. S. Keene, a prominent citizen of Lynn, with a reputation for public spirit. He said, "John, can't you sell us an approach to High Rock from Essex Street, thirty feet wide? I can get you $10,000 within a short time." "You would like the rock too?" I ventured. "Yes,' said he. I told him the errand I was on. "You buy Asa out," was his advice, and he expatiated still further on the opportunity presented, his idea being to raise the money by thousand-dollar subscriptions from prominent men, and present the property to the city. I telegraphed the fact of a possible customer to Asa. He answered that he had rather sell the whole thing out in house-lots. Then Keene again suggested that I buy him out. I knew that Asa had offered his share in the property not long before for $11,000; he offered it to me in Iowa for $17,000. He now demanded $20,000. With the prospect of getting $10,000 back through Keene, I thought it wise to close the bargain, and did so. After making the purchase, I went back to Keene. "You'll want the Rock, won't you?" I inquired. "Oh, yes!" was his answer. I told him I would put the price of the Rock and approaches at $15,000. I would contribute $1,000 toward the project myself, Henry would give $1,000 more, I would give $1,000 for improvements and $1,000 for streets, so that all he would have to raise would be $11,000. To this he agreed. He had a plan of the park drawn, and secured a large picture of the Rock, which he framed and hung up in his office. Meanwhile, negotiations were pending for the purchase of the portion of the Rock claimed by James N. Buffum. These went so far that the deed was drawn and awaited in a lawyer's office the signature of the supposed owner. He went in and borrowed it, took it home, and destroyed it. Had he carried out his part of the bargain, Keene could have raised the money, and the city would have had a fine park. The only result of the agitation was, however, to make me the owner of my brother's half. Half the Stone Cottage, Bird's Nest Cottage and the land, cost me $20,000 cash. The same property cost *him* in 1855 $5,350. The failure of the park purchase made it necessary to sacrifice some valuable railroad and other stocks, and of course my taxes immediately doubled. It was several years before houses enough were erected upon it to make it profitable; but I saved the apple orchard, which is still as Jesse left it, forming a semi-park, around which are several dwellings, including my own. With the exception of a small strip, no land has been sold from the estate. There are now twelve dwellings upon it, several of them in flats; so that some forty families enjoy the sightliness and airiness of a home on High Rock. Meanwhile, the best lots are still reserved, forming lawns, outlooks and similar open spaces.

Does my reader believe in ghosts? When I came home from the West, I preceded my family a few days Arriving in Lynn, I went to the home of my friend David J. Lord, to get a small trunk of securities. Safe deposit vaults were not as common then as now; and Lord, then a bank cashier — he is now president of one of Boston's biggest banks — had kept my trunk for a year and a half under his bed. With the trunk, I went to Daisy Cottage. It was cold and dreary, after having been unoccupied so long. It was night, and thinking it would be chilly in my chamber, I made a fire in the kitchen, intending to camp on the lounge there until morning Then I drew my chair up to the kitchen table, and opened my trunk, to look over my papers. Time passed on; the hour grew late, and the chills, despite the fire, crept over me. Suddenly I heard a sound. I glanced nervously at the forty thousand dollars' worth of securities spread out on the table, thought of burglars, and listened. A dead silence prevailed. Resuming my work, I soon heard it again. Thoroughly aroused and suspicious, I resolved that if I heard that sound a third time I would immediately investigate it, and began to pack up my papers. Again it came I arose, and following the direction from which it seemed to proceed, went to a closet under the back-stairs Opening the door, I saw a clothes-basket, and spread over it, the old calico apron of Hannah, the cook, just as she left it many months before. As I gazed critically at it, it rose in the air several inches. "Rats!" thought I, and seizing a broom that stood by, I jammed it into the basket with sufficient force to take the ambition out of any venturesome rodent who might have concealed himself in the receptacle. After a moment or two I raised the broom carefully. The apron followed. Horrors! Just as I was about to cry "Murder!" I saw a string. The key to the situation at once flashed across my mind. I had gone to the closet, earlier in the evening, and put on an old pair of slippers. This string was somehow attached to a slipper. The other end of it was wound on a bobbin, and the bobbin was in the clothes-basket. As I sat at the table, I moved my foot, and the result was a noise in the basket. The string became entangled in the table leg, and in consequence caused the violent agitation in the basket when I walked to the closet. I rested easy for the remainder of the night after that. This illustrates the ancient axiom, "Prove all things."

We gave a few concerts after our return from the West, and then settled down for the summer. On the 29th of July the Hawkes family held a reunion on a picturesque farm in North Saugus. Some two centuries ago, a member of the tribe of Hutchinson was married in this country and moved with her husband to England. Her husband died, and she returned. In a few years Adam Hawkes, a thrifty and land-loving farmer, wooed and won her for the second time. They went to live upon her farm in Lynn, a section now a part of Saugus. From this marriage sprung the Hawkes family. While I was in California a lady who is a descendant of this worthy couple told me the story while we were on a visit to her ranch. She also said there was to be a gathering of the family at the old farm the next year, and invited me to come. During the summer we met her again in Lynn, and she once more invited us, claiming me as a relative. So on the day appointed I said to Lillie, "Let's go up." We went by train to Saugus, and thence by barge to the farm. They had just closed a morning meeting, at which Hon. Nathan Mortimer Hawkes of Lynn, had presided. It had been very interesting. Most of the people — there were one hundred present — were partaking of the collation. We entered a tent, which stood on the site of the home of the aged progenitors of the gathering, and saw an organ. We stepped up to it, I touched the keys, and we sung. Some member of the committee invited us to the collation. Word was soon noised about, "The Hutchinsons are here." "What are they here for?" "Who invited them?" and similar questions were asked. Even the chairman did not know. Our friend from California came to the rescue at this point. She told the story, and proved that I was a descendant of the same ancestry as themselves. Then we had an ovation. We sung to them, and had a pleasant day adding to our list of acquaintances, one of whom was Colonel B. F. Hawkes of Washington, with whom I have been on intimate terms ever since.

At about this time we conceived the plan of putting a weather signal on High Rock. Henry was the first to think of it, and I at once went to work to get it put up. Hon. N. M. Hawkes, referred to above, Captain John G. B. Adams, then postmaster of Lynn, Hon. John B. Alley and others interested themselves in the project. I also wrote to my friend, General Sherman, who as the head of the army, might well be supposed to have influence with its signal-service department. Finally Captain Adams notified me that the material had arrived, in his care. Then a funny thing happened. Henry, of course, hoped to be made signal-officer, more for the name than for the salary. But Captain Earp, one of our neighbors, thought as a veteran of the war he should be preferred before a youth whose only service was singing in the camp. He set up so strong a claim for the place that he carried everything before him. When he learned that the salary was twenty-five cents a day his ardor suddenly cooled, and Henry was appointed. Captain Earp would have to make quite a trip from his house to the top of the rock. Henry worked the halliards from the window of the Stone Cottage. The signals were interesting to Lynn people, but the hope that they would be of use to mariners was not well-founded. The rock was too far removed from the track of vessels to be seen in thick weather. Henry served two years, setting the signals night and morning, and telephoning the weather to the Lynn papers daily, to Boston and elsewhere. I tried to get the appropriation increased, but was unsuccessful. The station was finally given up. But meanwhile, the Government placed a sightly flag-pole on the rock, which long remained — though another has been lately substituted — and put up the convenient flight of steps and gallery, which scale the face of the rock. These were built by Henry, as engineer and mechanic.

In July I visited Milford, in company with Sister Abby. One day, together with Abby and Rhoda, Ludlow, Ettie and Marion, Rhoda's daughter and granddaughter, I visited New Boston. On other days I visited Joshua and David, and Kate Dearborn, Judson's daughter. On the 26th of August there was a picnic at "Purgatory," in Mont Vernon, N. H. Hutchinson's Grove, at this place, has for years been the scene of an annual picnic, where the people of the surrounding country have a good time. It is owned by H. Appleton Hutchinson, a son of Noah, and as many of the family as can get there usually go. I went on this occasion. After spending the night at Brother Noah's old home, I drove down to Milford the next morning. As I passed David's, I could not help noting the contrast between his thrifty fields, and the dilapidated hop-houses standing near the road. Driving up into the yard, I met him, and dismounting and shaking hands, I said: "David, I've come to make you a present." His face lighted up with a smile of gratification. Solemnly placing my fingers in my pocket, I drew forth a match. "Here is the testimonial," said I, "with it you will do well to set fire to those old buildings down by the highway." "Thank you," he remarked, grimly, making no other comment. In a few minutes I was down in the field, mowing, as was my habit when visiting my farmer brothers.

On October 21st the famous McGibeney Family of performers and vocalists came to High Rock. Before McGibeney married he attended my concerts in Bucks County, Pennsylvania. After that he moved to Minneapolis. He was a man of culture, and fine address. He resided in Minneapolis some five years. Subsequently he went to Winona, and became professor of music in the institution there. All the while he was giving training to his increasing family of children, nearly as large as the Tribe of Jesse. Their success in concert is well known. He now has a home in western Massachusetts. On the day mentioned, I brought out a half-bushel of pears, and it was a sight to look upon to see those children devour them. In a few minutes every one had disappeared into the pockets or stomachs of the party.

The remainder of 1880 passed quietly, Henry being busy with his signal-service improvements, and I arranging for occasional concerts. On New Year's Day, 1881, I went to the banquet of the Massachusetts Club at Young's Hotel, Boston, dining with Governor Claflin, Hon. John B. Alley, and other worthies. On the same day Walter Kittredge came down from Reed's Ferry to join me in a campaign, he reading and I singing. He had written a poem-lecture, which he read. The next day we had a temperance meeting, it being Sunday. James N. Buffum was present and spoke. On the 10th we sang in North Saugus; on the following night at Rockport, with Rev. R. B. Howard, the great peace agitator, secretary of the American Peace Society and brother of General O. O. Howard. On the 15th of February I composed the music for a new song, "Which way is your musket a-p'intin' to-day?"

> "In a little log church, in the State of Virginia,
>   Some negroes had gathered to worship the Lord;
> And after the service they had a class-meeting,
>   That each for the Master might utter a word
> The leader exhorted, and spoke of the warfare
>   That Christians should wage against error alway,
> And finished by asking the following question
>   'Which way is your musket a-p'intin' to-day?
>   Which way, which way,
>   Which way is your musket a-p'intin' to-day?'
>
> "One after another gave their experience
>   Some brothers were happy, some lukewarm, some cold;
> One saw his way clear to the portals of glory,
>   Another had strayed, like a lamb, from the fold.

At last Brother Barcus, a renegade member,
    And Satan's companion for many a day,
Arose, cleared his throat, though visibly nervous,
    He folded his arms and proceeded to say

"'Dear brudders and sisters, I once was a Christian,
    I once was as happy as any one here,
I fit for de church, like a battle-scarred soldier,
    And stood by her banners when traitors were near.'
'Hold on dar!' the leader excitedly shouted,
    'Please answer the question I ax you, I say,
I'se given you credit for all you fit den, sir —
    Which way is your musket a-p'intin' to-day?'

"Some people now boast of the glory of temperance,
    And boast of their teetotal record and all —
Of clubs, lodges and unions, their all-active members —
    Take *big rents from tenants* who sell alcohol!
I'd liken their boast to the boast of old Barcus,
    And then, with the class-leader, earnestly say
'Hold on dar, my brudder, just stick to de question,
    Which way is your musket a-p'intin' to-day?'

"The question, my friends, is of vital importance,
    The nation is waiting in anxious suspense;
Each voter can wield a *political musket*,
    Then wield it, I ask, in your country's defence!
The issue before us is plain and unclouded —
    Shall our nation be ruled by King Alcohol's sway?
I candidly ask every qualified voter
    'Which way is your musket a-p'intin' to-day?'"

On March 4th I went to Washington to view the inauguration ceremonies, in company with Abby and Ludlow. It was the gossip about Washington society circles that Abby was the first to predict the nomination and election of Garfield. During her stay in the capital early in the previous year there was a reception at which she was present. General Garfield came in, and as he shook hands with Abby, she remarked, "We are going to make you our president." Time proved her to be right.

The fall of that year was notable for a short trip through Maine as far as Bangor, with my wife, Henry and Lillie, Jenniebelle Neale, reader, and others. The winter and spring of 1882 passed quietly.

During the summer of 1881 I established a *café* in the Stone Cottage, which was in Henry's charge. In May, a man was teaming a load of lumber up John's Avenue, along the Essex Street front of my property. The land pitches off abruptly at this point, and therefore it was very unfortunate that the horse should become balky, and begin to back. The wheels went over the edge of the avenue, and soon the load of lumber, wagon and all, was rolling merrily down the terrace, the horse backing hastily after it, as he could not well do otherwise. The driver saw the peril his turnout was in, and yelled like mad. I arrived on the scene just as the lumber went over my cherished Centennial wall and scattered promiscuously over Highland Square. Fortunately the front wheel of the wagon caught on the capstone of the wall, which stood the strain finely, and the transom bolt, for a wonder, did not break. The result was that the horse remained on the bank, and was saved any injury.

On August 29th, David, my eldest brother, died, at the age of seventy-seven. A short time previous, I had received a dispatch saying that if I desired to see him alive I must hasten to Milford. Responding at once, I arrived late in the evening, and took quarters at the hotel. In the morning I stood on the piazza, when I descried a farmer's wagon coming up the street, with another wagon attached, behind. Sitting erect in the vehicle, driving, was a form that I knew could be none else than my brother. With some agitation, but joyfully, I rushed out to intercept him, remarking,

"David, I came up to bury you!" "Get right in here," he said, cheerily, and then drove on to the blacksmith's, leaving his extra wagon for repairs. Then we drove together to several of the old places, called at Noah's, at the farm where Caleb used to live, and to see Sister Rhoda, then on her death-bed. Up to this time David had never seen his way clear to give up his claim to his share in the old homestead, where Rhoda lived. All the others had released their claims to her years before. Now he said, "Rhoda, all things will be well when I go away." When his will was read it was found to be true. He had released it. I sang to them with tearful voice:

> 'Where is now the merry party,
>   I remember long ago —
> Gathered round the Christmas fire
>   Brightened by its ruddy glow?
> Or in summer's balmy evening,
>   In the fields upon the hay?
> They have all dispersed and wandered,
>   Far away, far away.'

Then they tried to unite with me in singing our family song, the "Old Granite State." After this I bade Rhoda a long adieu, and went home with David. After a hearty dinner I went to the home of Kate Dearborn, Judson's daughter, and after tea to Joshua's, where I spent the night. A few weeks later, and word came that David was dead. At his funeral Joshua and John, with Ludlow and Abby, sang "No Tear in Heaven," and "The Shining Shore." A newspaper clipping of the time says:

"PEACEFULLY ASLEEP.—David Hutchinson, the chieftain of the 'Tribe of Jesse,' of the well-known Hutchinson Family, went peacefully to sleep on the evening of August 29th, at Milford, N. H., having reached the ripe age of seventy-seven years. He was the second son in a family of sixteen children, all singers. Though he had a fine bass voice, he rarely sang in public. His life was spent on a New Hampshire farm, and by untiring energy and industry he had amassed a handsome property. He leaves eight children."

David's sons, Hayward and Jesse, came on from Washington and Baltimore to the funeral. Busy men though they were, they stayed over long enough to go and see their Aunt Rhoda for the last time. In three weeks she, too, passed away. The same quartet sang the same songs at her funeral. The *Farmer's Cabinet* said:

"DEATH OF ANOTHER OF THE HUTCHINSON FAMILY.—We regret to chronicle the fact that the Hutchinson Family have been called to mourn the loss of two of their number within the short space of three weeks. David, who died August 29th, was buried on that beautiful autumnal day, September 1st. He was the first-born of the family but one—who died in early youth—being in the seventy-eighth year of his age. He was a well-to-do farmer, of indomitable will, always having lived upon and tilled the soil of his native town. His sister Mrs. Rhoda Gray, who had been suffering for a long time from spinal difficulty, soon followed him, she dying on Sunday, the 18th instant, in the sixty-third year of her age. Funeral services were held at the house on the following Tuesday, Rev. W. P. Lamb speaking words of comfort to the family and neighbors who had gathered to pay the last respect which the living may minister to the dead. Rare and fragrant flowers adorned the casket of the one beloved, who in life so well sustained all domestic relations. The pall-bearers were Joshua and John, brothers of the deceased, Ludlow Patton, brother-in-law, John, Bruce and Appleton Hutchinson, nephews, with Levi Curtis as conductor. Appropriate quartet music was rendered by the Messrs. Hamblett and Rideout. After the services at the house, the remains were conveyed to the family burying ground on the north side of the Souhegan River, and laid at rest beneath the greensward of the valley. As the family gathered around the grave, 'Our days are gliding swiftly by,' was beautifully sung by Joshua, John and Abby, assisted by others of the family.

"Mrs. Gray was the oldest sister of the world-renowned Hutchinson Family. She was possessed of a rich, high soprano voice, and in her younger days travelled with the 'home branch' of the family while the quartet proper was in England. She was twice married, and leaves two children—by her first husband Isaac A. Bartlett, Mrs. Marietta, wife of Henry Loveridge, of Orange, N. J., by her second, Matthew

Gray, Mrs. Nellie, wife of Charles Webster, who resides at the old (Hutchinson) homestead, where Mrs. Gray has always lived, and where she passed her last days. Of the numerous family of sixteen children but four now remain, Joshua, John, Asa and Abby."

On April 30, 1882, I attended the funeral of Ralph Waldo Emerson, at Concord. I felt well acquainted with the Concord philosopher, for I had often met him at woman suffrage and similar gatherings. During this spring I did little but worry. However, I managed to get in a few concerts and temperance meetings. On July 4th there was a great temperance demonstration at Lake Walden, Concord. We sung ten times during the meeting. Henry Ward Beecher, Mary A. Livermore, Rev. W. W. Downs, and Miss Minnie F. Mosher were the speakers. James H. Roberts, of Cambridge, a noted temperance worker, was in charge of the affair.

A while before this I visited Mount Auburn Cemetery, at Cambridge, with my son Judson. Longfellow had died but a short time before. By his will, he had directed that all ornaments be removed from his burial lot. The workmen were removing the stonework, and one of them gave me the cap-stone from one of the posts.

In August we made a trip down to Martha's Vineyard, and gave some concerts.

In September Lucy Stone and Henry B. Blackwell went campaigning in Nebraska, preaching woman suffrage. I planned to go with them, and even went so far as to secure my ticket, but just as I was about to start, received word that little Jesse, Henry's second son, was dangerously sick, and returned to High Rock. On September 13th, dear little Jesse died. The next day he was buried. One of the most touching things at the funeral was his brother Jack, three years old, singing

"The Sweet By and By." Jack has the musical and general characteristics of the family to a very marked degree, combined with his mother's lovable and engaging qualities

In October and November we gave concerts in Springfield, Fitchburg, Attleboro, Schnectady (N. Y.), Albany, and other points. The latter part of December I spent in New York, having an enjoyable visit with Sister Abby.

The closing hours of the year were spent at the Academy of Music, Brooklyn, in company with my nephew, David J. Hutchinson, whose guest I was. The great hall was crowded with an audience of three thousand earnest souls, attending a watch-night service. Dr. Pentecost spoke. I sung, "No Night There." Mr. and Mrs. George C. Stebbins were also present, and sung, "O turn ye, O turn ye, for why will ye die." I remained with David several days. My sixty-second birthday, January 4th, I spent at Frank B. Carpenter's with Sister Abby. On the 6th I visited my old temperance society, the Manhattan, conducted by my friend Gibbs, and sung to them. On the 9th I went to Warren, Mass., and sung at a concert in the Methodist Episcopal Church, of which Rev. Alonzo Sanderson was pastor. My kind friend, Laura E. Dainty, elocutionist, assisted in giving the entertainment. Mr. Sanderson was a man who had often secured my services. He is one of the most successful church-builders in the Bay State. A few years before this he had built the beautiful Trinity Church in Lynn, enlisting the hearty co-operation of people of all denominations in the enterprise, by his infectious enthusiasm. He was wont to quaintly remark that when he died, he hoped his epitaph would be : "And the beggar died."

In my diary for this period, I find this original expression of my condition of thought:

> Many cares beset my mind,
>   And cause me wakeful hours,
> Yet I will calm my selfish fears
>   And gather naught but flowers
> So, finding rest in quiet thought,
>   I sleep at proper times,
> And joyfully on this blank sheet
>   I improvise my rhymes

The Lynn Assembly was very active at this time. It was one of the most successful debating societies the city ever saw. Many men who have since gained political distinction were members. Henry and I joined, and spent many happy hours as listeners to or participators in the debates. We were in the habit of putting in songs at effective places in the discussions.

On January 21st Joshua died at Milford, at the age of seventy-one years, two months. He had been practically deprived of his singing-voice for six years. The funeral occurred in the chapel of the Congregational Church on the 25th. The services lasted two hours. Among the mourners with me, were Sister Abby and Ludlow, Henry Loveridge, husband of Etta, Rhoda's daughter, Fanny and Henry, John W., 2d, Appleton, and others of the family. The Milford quartet sung, and the family sung three times. A fuller account of the service appears elsewhere.

During this year the custom of having Sunday afternoon temperance meetings in Tremont Temple, Boston, was in vogue. The assistance of the Hutchinson Family was often requested and freely given. On Thursday, February 22d, Washington's Birthday was celebrated by a great temperance gathering of children in the Mechanics' Institute, Boston. John B. Gough, Gov-

JOHN, HENRY AND JUDSON HUTCHINSON

ernor St. John, of Kansas, Rev. Dr. A. A. Miner and James S. Grinnell were the speakers. We sang two songs.

In the spring the perennial question of the purchase of High Rock came before the city government, but nothing came of it.

On April 18th I visited Pine Grove Cemetery in Lynn with Henry, and in the tomb we saw the remains of Wm. A. Lerow. He was a friend of ours who had been killed by the premature discharge of an explosive for which he was an agent. He was a great admirer of our song "The People's Advent," and at one time I remember sent me a five-dollar bill to secure a copy of it, it not then being in print. His funeral occurred in Cambridge, but the interment was in Lynn. Henry received a letter from a friend, enclosing a paper covered with the scribblings of Lerow's little child, with the request that he put it in the coffin. He did so. One year from the date of that sad visit, Henry died.

On May 12th I went to Washington to attend the funeral of Hayward Hutchinson, who had died of Bright's disease. Among those in attendance were James G. Blaine, Judge Miller of the Supreme Court, Colonel R. G. Ingersoll, and other noted men. The funeral was on Saturday. I had agreed to sing at Tremont Temple in Boston on Sunday afternoon, and so thought I would not go to the grave with the mourners. Elias, Hayward's brother, assured me that I would be back in full season to take the train, so I stayed. The ceremonies at the tomb were long and the horses slow in returning, so that I missed the train after all. I went to the W. C. T. U. headquarters and was at once invited to sing in the temperance meeting on Sunday afternoon. Going to the meeting, I sang until the time arrived to take the train north. Meanwhile, Henry and Lillie, with my wife, had proceeded to Boston and filled the engagement there.

On May 19th Fanny and I attended the funeral of Lydia Pinkham, a woman of fine character and lovable disposition, whom we had known over half a century. She was quite an admirer of the Hutchinsons, and all these years had invited us to visit her. Once, on a trip from the White Mountains she with her husband called at our house in Milford, renewing her invitation. I said, "Yes, Lydia, we'll try and come to see you, though we visit but little in Lynn." Thirty years passed, and through her medicines she had become famous, but still our promise was unfulfilled. Four weeks before she died, I met her near the old family homestead on Esther Street. She said, "You haven't filled your engagement yet." I said, "Lydia, I will come." Then a few days elapsed, and taking up a paper, I read that she was dead. "Now," said I, "I will surely go." It was late when Fanny and I arrived at the funeral, but two seats remained vacant, though many people were standing, one at the head and the other at the foot of the remains. These we took. I sat so that I could look at the calm, bright countenance. She was a Spiritualist. The spirit discourses at the funeral were beautiful. By invitation we rode to the cemetery, and at the grave sang "Almost Home," the setting sun streaming over the casket as we chanted the sad but hopeful refrain.

On July 9th I started on a trip to Santa Fé, N. M., where my daughter Viola was then living. Henry was out of health, and I felt it would be much better for him to go, but he seemed loth to leave home. I arrived at Santa Fé on the 15th, meeting Lewis with Kate and Harry at the depot. The Tertio-Millennial Exposition was in progress at the time, and during my stay of several weeks we made excursions to the caves of the cliff-dwellers and other interesting points. Much descriptive matter concerning the journey was published in the papers at the time and some of it I will quote. The first is from the *Lynn Union*, dated Santa Fé, July 20, 1883.

MR. EDITOR. — I have "seen, fought and conquered," and here I am in the ancient city of Santa Fe (Holy Faith) and subsequent civilizations and witness to-day the conglomeration of the retreating tribes, mingling in our grand Tertio-Millennial Celebration directed by the indefatigable aggressors, Anglo-Saxon Yankees, who are predominating in this region and are likely to shape the destiny of these declining people, and lead, we trust, a remnant out of the darkness of superstition and bigotry into the sunlight of progress. But before I elaborate on the possibilities of this country, I design first to give you a word of my success on the route from Lynn, that others may be as fortunate in the undertaking.

My excursion ticket purchased at a Boston office, took me over the Fitchburg Railroad through Hoosac Tunnel. Not being able to secure a sleeper, I took Hobson's choice in the regular passenger car and luckily obtained a whole seat by day and two by night. Being made comfortable by a supply of shawls and blankets, I had my usual amount of sleep. We passed by Troy, Schenectady, Utica, Syracuse and most of the places on the New York Central Railroad the first night. Morning came, and Rochester and the Genesee River, with its Sam Patch Falls in full view. We lingered a short time in the grand depot, learning of its relative situation to the city. "All aboard," and soon the City of Buffalo was reached. From this point we took the Lake Shore Railroad to Cleveland, thence to Indianapolis, Ind. From there to St. Louis, arriving on the morning of the third day, only forty hours from Boston. Passing on through Missouri in the daytime, we arrived at Kansas City, where some exchanging of order for coupon tickets made it necessary to remain a short time. Here all trains coming from every direction, north, east, south, west, exchange freight and passengers, and one needs to watch to secure the right train, or in the hurly-burly he will make a mistake. We passed the places in Kansas lying on the route to Topeka in the night. Sixteen years ago I had visited professionally these new towns and cities, and held campaign meetings, agitating the political waters on the subject of woman suffrage and temperance. They say all these intervening places have flourished. The morning dawned, finding us two hundred miles from Kansas City, driving on through a beautiful, fertile country — all crops growing except the already harvested wheat. This sight, with the cheerful, abundant, contented citizenship manifested in the countenance of the inhabitants, filled my heart with joy and gratitude that these homes were secured to freedom. And a few years of trial and care had produced such a result.

While in this joyful mood, contemplating the struggle with border ruffians in the early settling of the country and more recent contact with drought and the grasshopper scourge and of victory, the brakeman shouted out "Hutchinson!" For the first time I now beheld this town or city, of four thousand inhabitants, situated on the Arkansas River, in the midst of a very promising agricultural district. This town had sprung into existence through the instrumentality of a relative of mine. Acting in harmony with the impulse, he had accomplished what sixteen years before I had suggested — to have a Hutchinson in Kansas, as we had years before settled one in Minnesota. Here and in the two counties along the railroad are embraced the garden lands of southwestern Kansas. I felt I could content myself and go to farming. All kinds of grains, vegetables and fruits can be produced in abundance. The cattle flourish on the green grass in summer, and browse for a living in the winter, with very little feeding or expense to the owners. By some slight irrigation, crops are certain. Flourishing towns at proper distances are springing up along the route and fertile valleys spread out to cheer the tourist. These inhabitants along the way are sons and daughters of New England, and contentment with prosperity marks this civilization.

Crossing the line, we pass through a part of Colorado, where a variety of tablelands and mountain cañons is in view. For the convenience of the traveller a saloon dining-car was switched on and attached to our long train and those who desired to partake on the wing were notified that dinner was ready.

"No Caliph of Bagdad e'er saw such display."

Swiftly we journeyed on, but leisurely partaking as we had fifty miles to eat in. Catching glimpses of the glorious country we were doubly fed, and abundantly satisfied with modern improvements. "Spero meliora" we hope to travel the air yet and believe our dream of flying will be realized. For did not Darius try his best to fly and only found his approach to the ground a failure?

"What now with science and electric aid
We'll soar aloft on ethereal grade;
Our flying car will sweep the sky,
All dangerous casualties passing by;
And lighting down where'er we please,
On any ground with greatest ease."

The heavy train dragged slowly up the grade, and stopped. Passengers inquired, and learned a steam-pipe had burst. This circumstance delayed the train, so that we arrived in La Junta in the night. Sleeping soundly, we left to go on towards Denver instead of Santa Fé. Being startled from my sleep, I found I was at Pueblo, sixty-five miles away. This caused a delay of twenty-four hours, otherwise I should have arrived from Boston in four and a quarter days.

Friends welcomed me to a pleasant home on the north side, where I command a fine view of the "City of Holy Faith," and the mountains and valleys in the environs. I find I have to sleep and eat more in this altitude than in the East. I made an early visit to the grand "Tertio-Millennial" Exhibit, which had already been fifteen days open to the public.

A man said to me before leaving Lynn, "Mr. Hutchinson, are you not running a great risk in going from Lynn to that far-off Southern latitude?" I feel now that I can answer the question in the negative. Thus far I have had exposures which, if made in New England, might have proved fatal to me. Of course, I am not laboring as hard out in the sun as when at High Rock. The sun is quite hot, mercury ranging from 80° to 90° in the shade; still an invigorating, cool mountain air almost constantly bracing the frame, and at night cool enough for sleeping under two good blankets, with windows and doors open; sleep well and awake refreshed.

Many celebrated men have visited the Tertio. General John A. Logan, whose prospects for the presidency seem so favorable, has paid a visit to his daughter, whose husband is stationed here as paymaster in the army. He has graciously received the congratulations of the public and taken his departure. Stopping with my daughter is Hon. William M. Springer, M. C., from Illinois, with whom I am proud to say I am acquainted, and I trust his prospect for the speakership in the next Congress will prove most satisfactory. He is a gentleman and scholar, while Mrs. S. is a rare lady of a most sympathizing Christian heart. I met Governor Glick, of Kansas, who stepped into Governor St. John's shoes. I did not discover him to be a Butler man, but found him to be so much of a temperance man as this: he would punish to the extent of the law the drunkard. The retailer or trafficker would stop selling if there were no patrons. Of course no one would expect the Tertio to compare in any way with the Centennial, yet the mineral display is far superior to any ever made from any one State or Territory in the Union. Some other features excel in novelty; and considering that but recently have the tribes of Indians been antagonistic to the interests of the white man, and are now sending chiefs from all parts of this territory and Arizona to join in the jubilee, it seems this millennial will prove a success. The subdued red man, the Spaniard or Mexican, with the white Yankee, all parading under the grand old "stars and stripes," has been to me a spectacle worthy of the faithful and indicates to me that "peace on earth and good-will to men" is pervading this continent. Such music the management has provided! Two bands, both of this town, discoursing all the best music of the masters each day and night at stated intervals till the closing. A classical concert came off in the large exhibition hall which would do honor to any city, even Boston. Fine piano playing, violin and lady artists. Being invited, I sang the song, "One Hundred Years Hence," and answering to an encore, gave our "Uncle Sam's Farm," to good acceptance.

The grand display of minerals, gold, silver, iron, lead and copper is very creditable to so young a State, and considering how long the prospectors have been kept at bay by the contending factions and tribes of Indians, who have made it unsafe for working the mines until within a short time. Now these same remnants of tribes are represented here with all their paraphernalia, and are entertained inside the grounds, amusing the thousands of visitors with their antics, war dances, etc., while their monotonous music is kept up, the sound of which reminds one of Chinese music.

The grandest of all the experiences I have had in this country was our visit to the cliff dwellings, situated about thirty-five miles from Santa Fé. The party consisted of men, though one boy was along, the son of our captain, it being admitted that ladies would not be pleased to endure the fatigue of the journey over rough roads, among the cañons, ravines and mountains, camping out on the ground, or the length of time required to make the journey. The company numbered with drivers and guides, sixteen persons, and in our absence from Monday morning to Thursday evening a jollier party never passed over this wild country. The showers of rain encountered and the general fatigues of the journey, heightened the pleasure of the occasion. We all bathed in the Rio Grande River and basked like children in the sunlight on the pebbly beach, in the presence of the grand old cliff and a range of mountains, and a beautiful valley known as the "Council Ground," where the several tribes of Indians in olden times came to consult and arbitrate for peace. While in the freedom of the free breeze, reflecting on the past usages of the races and inroads of the white man, I was seized with the inspiration, and sang Eliza Cook's grand words

"Why does the white man follow my path
Like the hound on the hunter's track?"

While closing with the refrain, the "Ya-ha, ya-ha," I discovered two Indians coming toward the river in course from their village, who, receiving signs of welcome approached and shook our hands warmly. I soon had them singing with me in monotones. So we danced and en-

AT THE CLIFF DWELLINGS—(p. 114)

joyed the interview. I suggested that some one should try the fleetness of the younger Indian, and a twenty-five cent piece was offered to the victor. One of our party was soon on the line made in the sand, toe to toe, when at the signal, the dropping of the hat, and the words, "Ready, aim, fire!" the two racers in fierce competition spread their limbs and leaped forth into the fray. The race was an exciting one, but the red-skin proved the winner, as he came to the stand several feet in advance of his competitor and received the quarter.

In the letter above I refer to the cliff-dwellings. I consider my trip to them among the most important and interesting experiences of my life. The ancient cities of the Southwest are in an area of several thousand square miles, embracing the adjoining corners of Colorado, Utah, Arizona and New Mexico. They are remains of far more interest than those of the mound-builders and their pueblos and houses, high up among the cliffs that tower above the valleys and river-beds, still contain inscriptions and fragments of pottery and implements which show a far higher grade of civilization than that of the mound-builders. Ruins of buildings of three and four stories in height are in existence, containing sometimes as many as five hundred rooms. It is believed that the Pueblo Indians of this region are the remnant of these cliff-dwellers. They worship the sun and fire as their ancestors evidently did. It is a curious fact that these ruins, discovered within two decades, were reported by the Spaniards who conquered the territory, but for centuries their stories had been regarded as fabulous. The descriptions then given of the ruins tally exactly with them as they now appear.

In some parts of the wide territory I have mentioned the walls of the cañons rise for thousands of feet, and on the terraces of the more open cañons are multitudes of picturesque ruins. Sometimes the width of the shelf permitted clusters of cave houses, making a village. These houses were reached, evidently, by ladders. Some of them are so high that the eye distinguishes them as mere specks. The overhanging rock prevents access to them from above, and there seems to be no way of reaching them from below. The cliffs are of limestone or sandstone, with alternating strata of shales or clay. The action of the weather wore out the softer layers, leaving caves, the solid stone serving as floors and roofs for the houses. The front of the cave was neatly walled, so that often it is almost impossible to distinguish the artificial work. In some sections ruins of ancient circular watch-towers remain on the top of the cliff. These cliff-dwellers, those who have made a study of the subject tell us, were not a warlike people, and evidently sought these homes for security from tribes which were. When their workshops are found, there are stone axes and saws, but no spear or arrow-heads, which appear so plentifully in other prehistoric ruins all over the country. Wherever arrow-heads are found among the cliff-dwellings, they are always with points toward the houses, showing that they were fired by an attacking party from without.

What a story these remains tell! As a writer has recently said, we call this the New World, but the name is a misnomer. These red men, worshipping the sun and living as free as the birds of the air, had no means of writing history but by pictures in the stone, and these are usually only of trophies of the chase, or some such simple subject. They have left no traditions even, behind them, but yet we can see in these cave homes all the evidences of domesticity. Here are household utensils, and low down on the walls the impressions of chubby baby hands, made in the soft

CAMPING IN CHAPELLO CANON — (p. 16)
(CLIFF DWELLINGS IN DISTANCE)

material when the house was new and the honeymoon but a short time over, but now hardened into an eternal record.

The *Santa Fé Review* of July 17th told this story of our trip:

"The excursion party to the ancient pueblos and cave dwellings of Chapullo, Questacito Blanca and Pajarito returned late Thursday evening. A scribe called upon Professor Ladd yesterday and plied him with interrogations about the expedition, and learned many things of interest alike to the citizens and tourist. Their four days' trip was in the highest degree satisfactory to all. The party numbered with the drivers sixteen persons. A Studebaker wagon with four mules carried thirteen and the provisions, the rest went on horseback. Among the excursionists were Revs. J. B. Gregg, J. W. Stark, G. N. Kellogg, Dr. E. F. Little, Mr. John W. Hutchinson, Messrs. Handy and Waldon, photographers, F. W. Carter and Means, and Professors Howard S. Bliss and Cragin, of Washburn College, President H. O. Ladd, of the University, and his son. Professor Ladd was the conductor of the excursion, having become familiar with the region on the previous trip. There were many new discoveries made on this visit of great interest to travellers, scholars and citizens of Santa Fe. On the road to the Rio Grande, sixteen miles out, is Red Rock cañon, which was explored and photographed. From its summit a magnificent view is obtained. The entrance to the gorge is grand—far surpassing anything in Santa Fé cañon. A fine spring was found about one quarter of a mile from the entrance. The drive from the city, the views and grandeur of this gorge make it a most desirable destination for a picnic party. The road most of the way is fit for a boulevard. Ten miles farther brought the party to the fords of the Rio Grande. The scenery after the river is reached excels that of the famous Crawford notch of the White Mountains.

"The first camp in the Chapullo cañon was made about nine o'clock. The road from the Rio Grande to this camp runs up an *arroyo* on either side of which are castellated cliffs with strata of varied colors and commanding height. A magnificent sky above and soft beds of sand below gave to this place, with the unanimous consent of the party, the name of Camp Comfort. Even the long, steep and rugged hill above this camp was easily traversed by the heavy wagon, and the second camp was made under Chapullo cliff. Here is one of the finest views in this region, and the wonderful fissure here in lava rocks two miles long and two hundred or three hundred feet deep which the party explored is a sight worthy of the whole trip. It is the remains of a subaqueous crater, and has within it a water-fall of one hundred and fifty feet. A beautiful pool like a silver mirror lies in a round, narrow basin at its foot, inaccessible from above, except by a rope forty or fifty feet long. The descent is even then dangerous. Farther down is a spring of the coldest water and very abundant. A grove of large cotton-wood trees rises from the banks, and black currants in large quantities cover the bushes, though the chasm is not twenty feet wide.

"The cliff-dwellers' homes on Chapillo were also explored on the second day. Professor Ladd's recent articles in the *Chicago Advance* have fully described these, and also those at Questacito Blanca. Among a hundred others there were several caves discovered by this party with three or four rooms, and two and even three stories high. A soaking rain greeted the party on the return to the camp that evening, but the darkness and discomforts of the night were forgotten while listening to the singing, which made the cliffs re-echo with melodies of every description, as five gifted singers sat around a brilliant camp-fire, led by Mr. Hutchinson, who sang with such rare inspiration and sweetness that the spirits of the cliffs seemed to gather and take up the soft strains that were dying on the night air.

"An early start shortly after sunrise of the third morning carried the happy company to Pajarito by ten o'clock. This great pueblo with its surrounding caves gave new objects for study. Its dimensions are indeed surprising, and its walls in better preservation than the other pueblos. There are many strange inscriptions and carvings on the faces of the rocks about the cave dwellings. These were carefully copied by one of the party for future study. Similar ones were found and sketched next day on the rocks above the falls in the Chapillo gorge, already described. They would tell stories of wonderful interest if they could be interpreted. After another evening of rain, the Rio Grande was reached, and the party made their bivouac under piles of lumber like common tramps."

On August 6th, I sent another letter from Santa Fé to the *Union*, which was as follows:

Mr. Editor:—If you are not weary of my long epistle on matters and manners connected with the visit to the city of 'Holy Faith,' and my experience since arriving, I will renew my effort and endeavor to be brief in my description of country, climate, people, industries, advantages and possibilities of this territory of New Mexico. In the first place the country is decidedly mountainous, and from the adobe, and from Yankee house as an annex, built by a former resident of good old Lynn, who went west sixteen years ago, and at whose hospitable board I am made welcome and comfortable, the finest view of the town and surrounding mountains is obtained. The house is situated on the side of a hill, facing the town on the south, and about a quarter of a mile from the plaza and overlooking the "Tertio Millenial" grounds. Looking in any direction from the portal of this house, the eye is met by lofty mountains, peak on peak rising thousands of feet until we come to old "Baldy," which is said to be between nine and ten thousand feet above the sea-level, down the sides of all of which canons and gorges can be seen with the naked eye leading to the rich valleys at their base. The sides of these mountains are covered with a stunted growth of cedar and piñon timber while on some of the mesas very heavy timber is found. We must bear in mind that the inhabitants have for hundreds of years indiscriminately cut this timber for fuel, and now the natives bring in the supply for the town on the back of the burro or jackass, and it is no uncommon sight to see twenty or thirty of these patient animals loaded down with from two hundred to three hundred pounds of wood cut into stove size wending their way down the sides of the hills to market. These loads contain from four to five cubic feet, and sell for from twenty-five to fifty cents each, varying in price with quality and season of the year.

Some Eastern parties have just returned from Taos County, about eighty miles north of here, where they had been to examine a cattle ranch containing about twenty thousand acres. This is now offered for sale at seventy-five cents an acre, title being perfect. They report abundance of water with grama and altalfa grass two feet high. This grass makes the finest kind of feed for stock, as it cures on the stalk, and affords feed through the winter equal in nutrition to corn or oats, and stock can feed all winter without shelter. They also report thousands of acres covered with the finest timber, mostly mountain pine, some trees yielding four cuts ten or twelve feet long from two to three feet in diameter. There are similar tracts scattered all through the territory which can be bought on just as good terms and just as well adapted for stock-raising and lumbering.

The surface of the country when I arrived seemed rather barren, and I missed the showers and green grass covering the earth. My friends said, "You will see all this;" and now, after waiting, I have witnessed the beginning of the rainy season, and vegetation springing up as a result. All the corn-fields seem refreshed, and vegetables are springing forth at the call of the all-important visitor, and one can almost see them grow. The rains descend with so much force and quantity that very little of it soaks into the ground on the hillsides, but fills up the channels opened for the floods and in torrents rushes down in waves several feet high. Swiftly they rush through the *arroyos* in their course, sweeping away all debris that has accumulated in their beds, and the bridges, if not built high above this flood, must go with the current towards the sea.

The climate is wonderful for its purity. Though the sun shines all the day and the mercury ranges from eighty to one hundred, yet a cool breeze may be experienced at any time out of the direct rays of the sun. At night the sleepers, if not provided with sufficient covering, must awake and draw up the extra quilt or suffer with cold. Yet the dryness of the atmosphere prevents any miasma from poisoning the breath. Invalids may come here at any season of the year with perfect immunity, being benefited, if not entirely restored to health. Here in Santa Fé about two thirds of the inhabitants are Mexicans in a total population of about ten thousand, while there are many Indians living in their pueblos in the vicinity who come to this town to buy or sell what they may want or have. Of course the white man is increasing rapidly, and since the advent of the railroad three years ago, the American population has increased from about two hundred to its present number. All trades and industries are being established. The natives all live in their adobe houses, which are very comfortable, one-story high with flat roof, having just pitch enough to shed water, walls from eighteen to thirty inches thick, and dry within, they are made habitable at all seasons of the year, being cool in summer and warm in winter, really pleasanter than our brick and stone, and the cost is slight. Shovel up the earth anywhere, moisten and mix with straw, mould it in frames about four by eight by eighteen inches, dry in the sun and lay up in the wall, with the same material for mortar. The roof is made by laying across large, round rafters, or vegas, putting boards over these, then covering with earth to the depth of twelve or eighteen inches. These structures, with little repair, will last for centuries. Different tribes of Indians are scattered up and down the whole country, are now all peaceable, and through the fatherly interposition of Uncle Sam, when his behests and mandates are not trifled with by rascally agents, will preserve order and peace *ad infinitum.* This "Ter Show" will conduce to a good understanding among the tribes, all of which have been represented by their chiefs, principal men, squaws and pappooses.

The natives pursue agriculture as a livelihood, and by irrigation make sure of crops, and with the latter rains which come most surely in July or August, make crops in the harvest season abundant. A German who is gardening here told me he raised last year cabbages, some of which weighed sixty-four pounds each head. All vegetables are large, fine flavored and quite tender; onions very pleasant, large as a saucer, cauliflower, etc., as good as any country can afford. The Yankees who are here have mostly honorable callings. Some, I am sorry to say, do not resist the temptation to follow the low Dutchman and foreigner in the disreputable business of retailing alcohol and encouraging vice.

All industries are springing up. The heavy business is, and will be for a number of years, cattle and sheep raising. The boom is on now. Stock has risen fifty per cent in eight months. Foreign capital is flooding the country, buying up the large ranches, and giants of millions of acres, and it seems to me the best chances for small capitalists are fast disappearing. Beef is as high here as in Massachusetts, and the general market for groceries about the same. Butter is high, cheese double what I pay for it in Lynn, fruit scarce and high, as the present supply comes from California. But when the Yankees get agoing here, they will show the soil to be adapted to all fruits, vegetables and grains, in great variety and abundance.

Last, but not by any means the least, comes the mining interests. They are moving fast, and the most sanguine are being surprised at the rapid discoveries and developments, and the increase in the output of bullion.

All the excursion parties *en route* to California stop here. The novelty of the adobe city, with a run through the Tertio Millennial Exposition, gratifies their curiosity, and the satisfaction of reading in the morning paper their names, addresses, and calling in life, pleases the tourists' vanity, knits closer in sympathy their association with the place, and sends them off on their way rejoicing, towards the Golden Gate and Yosemite Valley, remembering this with other courtesies and hospitalities, as they are rolled on their retreat over the Central Pacific Railroad homeward to the Eastern States, by the Lakes to the Atlantic.

Among the arrivals last week came our good lady reformer, Mrs. Leavitt, who is travelling under the auspices of the W. C. T. U. She was very pleasantly entertained by Mrs. Campbell, under whose hospitable roof she obtained a much needed rest, and was made at home. She was invited to hold a public temperance meeting in the Presbyterian church, and it came off Sunday evening, and although the hackneyed subject would tire most people, yet with her large experience and knowledge she interested the audience much. Of course the Hutchinsons had to sing, as they always have sung for any honest radical reform. I passed the hat, and the large collection showed that there must have been some Methodism in the assembly. A concert was announced, and on Thursday following came off, and we had the satisfaction of helping to build a fence round the church lot. Our home songs are a pleasant reminder to these far-away citizens of their early days, when the "Hutchinson Family" singing was the first they heard. The song, "Forty Years Ago," caused many a moistened eye when the sentiment of early associations was enumerated in the lines the native farm by the village town, the old school-house, the master, the river flowing by, the bubbling spring, the old elm, with the name of the sweetheart cut in the bark, the flowers scattered over the graves of the loved ones,—all, all with the hope of meeting again those pure spirits in the near future, after the uncertain is passed,—awakened such aspirations as we count the soul's best treasure, and tears were in the eyes of the refined audience who honored us with their presence. With the "God Bless You," and shaking of the hand, we bid farewell.

On August 16th I left Santa Fé, taking Viola and Kate with me. That night we gave a concert at Montezuma Hot Springs, Viola singing, and Kate, who had already begun to display good elocutionary powers, reciting "The New Church Organ," which I had taught her. We also gave a concert in Hutchinson, Kansas, and then went on to Glencoe, Minn., where I had a good deal of business connected with my property to transact, and finally reached Hutchinson, Minn., on August 28th. The next day was Sister Abby's birthday, and Asa's family joined with mine in celebrating it in a grove by the Hassan River. The citizens gathered *en masse* to hear us sing and play. The old settlers, while here, were photographed with us in a group. Three days later, on Sunday, we had a big praise meeting in the same grove. One day, with Asa, Abby, his daughter and Kate, I went out to see my one-hundred-and-sixty-acre farm. We saw a wolf while there. A little later we gave a concert in the Vineyard Methodist Episcopal Church, Asa, Dennett and his wife, John and Viola, with speaking by Kate, my only granddaughter. During our stay in Hutchinson we went down to St. Paul and witnessed the opening of the Northern Pacific road. On October 4th Abby (Anderson), Asa, Viola and John gave a concert in Brownton. Then Viola and Kate went on toward Chicago, where I overtook them later, and Asa and I threw ourselves into the project of getting a railroad to Hutchinson. We held meetings in

THE HUTCHINSON PIONEERS — p. 125

Hutchinson and towns along the proposed route, sung to the people and talked to them. Our efforts seemed likely to be fruitless at one time, but the railroad magnates of the Northwest took the matter up, and the transportation facilities of the town are now first-class.

On October 25th I left Hutchinson, feeling a good deal of solicitude for Abby Anderson, Asa's daughter. It was well grounded, for a short time later Asa took her to New York, to Sister Abby's home, and she never left her bed after her arrival. I reached Lynn on the 30th, to find a number of engagements to sing waiting for me. On the following night I sung in the North Avenue Methodist Episcopal Church, Cambridge, with Henry, Lillie and Viola. During my absence Henry had been hard at work getting in the foundation for my great apartment-house, Terrace Lodge, containing twelve suites of rooms. The happiness and sorrow of the year that followed was mingled with the care of its erection. Henry's cough was getting very bad, and although he sung with us several times through the autumn and early winter, he was unable to do much. It was a great grief to him that I felt it necessary to have others do the work of assisting me about the premises that he had done so long.

On December 19th I participated in an entertainment at the Y. M. C. A hall, with many old Lynn friends. There were thirty numbers on the programme; and all —readings, songs and instrumental music— were by Lynn authors. The united singers gave old "Waterhill," fugue tune composed a century before by a Lynn musician. Among the readers of their own selections were Cyrus M. Tracy, J. Warren Newhall and George E Emery. Representatives of the Barker Family sung Nathan Barker's setting of "Sweet Alice, Ben Bolt."

In company with Viola, Lillie, Jud, Kate and Jack, I sung Brother Jesse's "Old Granite State," our family song.

The year 1884 was in many respects a sad one for me. A year of partings with old friends, and dearest relatives,—saddest of all because of the parting from my noble son, my firstborn. On the 5th day of January a dispatch came from Asa that his daughter Abby was dead. That last wave of the handkerchief at Hutchinson was her adieu to me forever. A few days later Asa came to me with Beth, Abby Anderson's daughter. It was my brother's last visit to High Rock. We went together to view old scenes and old friends, sung, played and talked together. On January 7th, I bid him farewell in Boston, and he went to Milford.

The 15th of January was marked by two narrow escapes. Judson was taken ill while in Terrace Lodge, and I caught him just as he was falling out of a fourth-story window. Within fifteen minutes little Jack, my grandson, fell down the well-room from one of the stairways, two stories, but was unhurt.

A few days later I went to New York and spent a short time with Asa and Abby, my last remaining brother and sister. Together we made a trip to Washington. We three, with Judson and Zephaniah, enjoyed our first impressions of the capital together exactly forty years before, and we felt a sweet satisfaction in renewing these experiences, and noting the changes that four decades had wrought. The slave-pen had disappeared from the District of Columbia forever, and with it had gone the great iniquity it fostered. With it, too, had disappeared the burning questions of debate that raged when we made our first trip to Washington, while the lips of the orators of those days were forever silenced. Where were Webster and Clay and Calhoun, who were in their prime then? Where was John Quincy Adams, the old man eloquent? Where was John P. Hale and Levi Woodbury? Where was John Tyler and his cabinet minister, Postmaster-General Wyckliffe? They had all passed off the stage where they were playing so prominent parts in the early months of 1844, and after them had gone too, men whom we had known as leaders in succeeding decades, Fillmore, Giddings, Lincoln, Chase, Greeley, Wilson, and a host of others. And we three gray-haired little people, with hearts as young as ever, were permitted to revisit these historic scenes, view the Capitol in its increased magnificence, meet the successors of the mighty men of those other days, and ponder on the moral of it all. A few months and Asa was gone; a few years, and Abby, too, had passed away. With them passed over the men who were even then largely occupying the public mind, Blaine, Arthur, Sherman, and the rest; and still I remain to tell the tale, and record these reflections, feeling, with good old Tom Moore —

"Like one who treads alone, some banquet hall deserted,
Whose lights are fled, whose garlands dead, and all but he departed."

We visited many scenes of interest and met old friends everywhere. On one evening we had our hands full. We were given a reception at Miss Ransom's and later went to the Unity Club, and sung, being elected honorary members. On another evening we had a reception at the Riggs House by woman-suffrage sympathizers. Susan B. Anthony, Mrs. Jane H. Spofford and others were present. We had pleasant interviews with Dr. George B. Loring, commissioner of agriculture.

On Wednesday, February 6th, I arrived in Boston on

my way home, just in time to attend the funeral of Wendell Phillips, our friend and co-laborer for so many years of anti-slavery struggle. Two days later there was a memorial meeting at Faneuil Hall, at which I sang "Lay Him Low," a song we afterwards sang at the funeral of Whittier. We had seen the words, or a part of them, in some stray place, and after the death of Phillips, before leaving for Boston, Abby and I had added several verses. The song, as we have often since sung it, is as follows:

> "Close his eyes, his work is done
>   What to him is friend or foeman,
> Rise of moon or set of sun,
>   Hand of man or kiss of woman?
> Lay him low, — lay him low,
> Under the clover or under the snow,
> What cares he, he cannot know,
>   Lay him low."

[By Abby.]

As man may, he fought his fight,
  Proved his truth by his endeavor;
Let his name in golden light
  Live forever and forever.

[By Abby and John.]

Great his love for human kind,
  Strong his faith in truth's promotion,
In his teaching gems we find,
  Beacon lights along life's ocean.

"Wreaths we bring that ne'er shall fade,
  Greener with the passing years,
Brighter for our error's shade,
  Jewelled with our falling tears."

[By John.]

Pure the radiant path he trod,
  Conscious of the fount 'twas given,
His allotted years from God —
  Are triumphs emphasized from Heaven.

HENRY J. HUTCHINSON

"Bend in love, O azure sky!
  Shine, O stars at evening time!
Watch our hero calmly lie
  Clothed in faith and hope sublime

"Lay him low,—lay him low,
  Under the clover, under the snow
How we loved him none can know,
  Lay him low."

Then followed days of exacting cares, with Henry too sick to help, and nights of weary watching by his bedside. One morning he awoke, looked at me, lying on the lounge in the room, and remarked, " Well, father, I've got to go." On the 12th of April he died. "Katie,' was his last word, spoken as he saw his cousin, Kate Dearborn, enter the room, having just arrived from Milford. A few days later he was buried in the family lot in the Eastern Burial Ground. Rev. V. A. Cooper, who had often been at his bedside during his sickness, spoke at the funeral words of hope and consolation. The dear form lay in the casket, clothed in his concert suit and we all gathered about it and sang " No Night There," " Jesus, Lover of my Soul," " Sweet By and By," and " We Are Almost Home." The *Lynn Item* spoke of the funeral as follows:

"The funeral of the late Henry J. Hutchinson, of the well-known Hutchinson Family, occurred Monday afternoon from the residence at High Rock. Mr. Hutchinson passed away on Saturday last, after an illness of three months with consumption. He was born at Milford, N. H., on the Hutchinson Family estate, and was thirty-nine years, five months of age. He sang in the family all over the country during their campaigns and assisted in the temperance cause. He first came to Lynn twenty-eight years ago, and this city has been his residence nearly all of the time since. The funeral services were conducted by Rev. V. A. Cooper, of the First Methodist Church. Mr. Hutchinson's life and character were dwelt upon by Mr. Cooper, who was personally acquainted with the deceased. The service consisted of Scripture reading and a general conversation by the minister. The family sang 'No

Night There,' and 'Jesus, Lover of my Soul.' Little Jack, his five-year-old son, sang, 'The Sweet By and By,' the family joining in the chorus. The floral decorations were a lyre and harp. The body was interred in the Eastern Burial Ground. Mr. Hutchinson will be remembered as a pleasant and agreeable gentleman, possessed of many noble characteristics."

The *New York Tribune* spoke kindly of Henry, making the mistake, however, in its editorial, of confounding my niece Abby, with my sister:

"One by one the historic Hutchinson family is passing away. It was reported a few weeks ago that Abby Hutchinson, the sweetest of the elder singers, had died. And now comes the announcement of the death of Henry J. Hutchinson, from consumption, at his home on High Rock, Lynn, Mass., where he kept a government signal station. A few years ago he was a handsome young man, erect and robust as an athlete. His long yellow hair was like the mane of a lion and he seemed destined to live many years. Unlike his father, John, and Abby, his aunt, he could sing opera music with fine effect, and his bearing on the stage reminded one of the adored Capoul. Alas, the sweet singer now sleeps in the lovely cemetery of Lynn, in full sight of the ocean breakers, and almost under the cliffs of the famous Hutchinson mansion, which looks far out on the sea. He was born in Milford, N. H., on the Hutchinson family estate, and was thirty-nine years and five months of age. He sang in the family all over the country during their political, temperance and social campaigns. Henry Hutchinson was generous, impulsive and fearless. About eight years ago he married a charming woman, and their first babe was born in the valley of the Yosemite."

The Lynn Assembly passed appropriate resolutions, offered by the Hon. E. B. Hayes, and many were the words of comfort and sympathy that came to High Rock from loving friends all over the country. And the invalid mother and burdened father, with the broken-hearted wife, left alone with her little ones, sorely needed these consolations. Lillie bravely took up the work of supporting her boys, continuing to sing in church, and opening a studio for piano pupils on Market Street. She was a successful teacher as well as a fine singer, and soon became engrossed in her work. The boys inherited the musical talents of both parents, and have each been before the public as singers almost from infancy. It was a privilege for me to assist their mother in bringing them out, at intervals during the months that followed.

The work of directing the completion of Terrace Lodge engrossed most of my time through the spring. On July 4th the day was ushered in by a big bonfire on the rock. Five thousand people were present. During the day there was a celebration on the lawn by the Stone Cottage. Hon. Arthur B Breed read the Declaration of Independence; several prominent men made speeches. J. P. Hayes, whom I have mentioned as singing with us in Philadelphia in 1879, with his wife, assisted us in the singing.

As is often the case on Independence Day, by night it rained. In the middle of the night I awoke with a sudden thought that the conductors on Terrace Lodge were probably carrying the water into the cellar. Hastily dressing, I went out to the Lodge to find my fears realized. The conductors were trying their best to carry off the flood falling on that fifty by eighty roof, but as they were not completed, it was all going into the cellar. The force of the stream of water had turned a valve in the pipe just the way it ought not to go. Hastily seizing the pipe, I turned it the other way. Then I realized that there was nothing more I could do until morning but stand and hold it there, for I was alone. I yelled for help. I called "Fire!" and "Water!" There was a man sleeping within a rod of me, but he did not arouse Meanwhile, I was getting drenched with water. Suddenly a form appeared on the scene. It was Mr. Hatch, the man in charge of the construction of the building. He had waked with precisely the thought in mind that had troubled me, and had hurried from his home down in the city to the rescue.

During the summer there were temperance meetings on the grounds by the Stone Cottage nearly every Sunday afternoon. We usually sung to the people. In August we gave several concerts in Swampscott to the summer residents. During this month also, we were visited by our life-long friend, Rebecca Moore, the well-known philanthropist and writer from England. With Mrs. Brown and her daughter, also from England, she came to Lynn, and it was pleasant, indeed, to entertain her. She also went to New Hampshire visiting Sister Abby at the old homestead in Milford. The friends of woman suffrage gave her many receptions, and her stay in this country was made as pleasant as possible.

On August 2d I, too, went to Milford, and on the following day assisted in celebrating the birthday of that dear, precious soul, my sister. For fifty-five years she had lived to bless me and humanity in general, for no person ever felt the sunshine of Abby's presence without being glad they had met her. It was pleasant to be in the old homestead again; though the brothers and sisters were missed, there were nephews and nieces and grand-nephews and grand-nieces in abundance, to show an old gentleman kindly courtesies and make him feel happy. Walter Kittredge happened in Milford just in time to join in the birthday festivities. I stayed several days, called on John Ramsdell, my poet-friend, back in the town after an absence of thirty-five years, went fishing, viewed my old farm, where Viola was born, and had a general good time. On the last night of my stay many old friends gathered at the homestead to hear us sing

This was the year of the presidential election when Grover Cleveland was chosen over James G. Blaine. I espoused the cause of St. John, the Prohibition candidate, and flung out on High Rock, September 4th, the first Prohibition flag in the State.

On September 16th there was an anti-slavery reunion at the woman-suffrage headquarters in Boston. Among those present were Theodore D. Weld, Mrs. C. C. Burleigh, William Lloyd Garrison, Jr., and Francis Jackson Garrison (sons of the great emancipator), Lucy Stone, James N. Buffum, and many others. I composed an original song, Lillie and my wife singing it with me.

I rather enjoyed the Prohibition campaign this year. My old friend William Daniel came up from Baltimore and participated. I sung at the rallies in many places. We had a funny time one night in Boston. Hon. Henry W. Blair, United States senator from New Hampshire, spoke and eulogized the work of the Republicans for temperance. Without other comment, I took my place at the piano and sung, "Which way is your musket a-p'intin' to-day?"

On November 25th the sad intelligence came that my brother Asa had died, at his home in Hutchinson, of nervous prostration. "I shall soon follow him," is the record in my diary. He was sixty-two years of age and left one son, Oliver Dennett, and six grandchildren. A New York paper recorded the fact that on the occasion of his last visit to that city — which I have mentioned — he wrote in a birthday book the following lines:

> "One by one we fade away,
> But there blooms another day,
> When we shall be in bright array
> In Summer Land."

In December I gave a few concerts in and about Lynn, with the assistance of Lillie, Fanny, Jack and Theodore Chute, a young Lynn tenor of painstaking nature and some prominence. The year closed with many hours spent in reflections concerning the brevity and sadness of life. But I felt, with Job, notwithstanding the bereavements of the year, that God was good to me and I would trust in Him, "though He slay me."

Through the early months of 1885 we gave a number of family concerts. One notice of them will suffice to show what they were like. A local publication said:

"The audience having got together — the evening was wet, dark and dreary — were well paid for the inconvenience in coming. The old veteran, John W. Hutchinson, is a host in himself, despite his years. His voice is as clear as a silver bell, and he is thoroughly 'at home' before an audience, while Mrs. Hutchinson and her little boys won rounds of applause. Mrs. H. is a beautiful singer with a strong, yet sweet voice. Although little Jack, a boy of five years of age, showed great natural ability and skill, yet it remained for Richard, a little tot of three summers — a mere babe as it were — to more than astonish his hearers. No one can conceive of the marvellous voice possessed by that child and his ability to carry a tune to its close, until he has heard him sing. We never heard such singing by one so young. The concert was a success. In the language of J. W., 'Those who were not present do not know how much they saved.'"

On Memorial Day I drove into the Lynn Forest, near Dungeon Rock, with my friends Mr. and Mrs. Hopkins, of Wellington, and Fanny. The "Poet's Dell" was consecrated, in honor of Maria Augusta Fuller, by several choice spirits of the Lynn Exploring Circle, Cyrus Mason Tracy being at the head of the affair. The *Lynn Item* referred to our presence as follows:

"A very pleasant little episode took place soon after the close of the exercises in the grove. Miss Barrelle (the singer of the consecration hymn), and Messrs. Barker and Tanner (of the Barker Family of singers) were among the first to start homeward, and while waiting at the roadside for the barge that connects with the car-station, two or

JOE AND HIS GRAND CHILDREN

three carriages suddenly approached. The foremost contained Mr. John W. Hutchinson, while in the other two were a number of ladies and gentlemen, among the former Mrs. J. W. Hutchinson. Mr. Hutchinson and party were on the way to the forest, but hearing that the exercises were over, he concluded that the next best thing to do was to request Miss Barrelle to favor the company with a song. The lady in question gracefully complied, and accompanied by instrumental music furnished by Messrs. Barker and Tanner, did her utmost to please her auditors, and their hearty applause at the close showed how happily she had succeeded. Mr. Hutchinson now took a hand, and favored the company with that inspiring song, "Which way is your musket a-p'intin to-day?" This roused the entire party, putting them on their taps, so to speak, and Uncle John was just getting ready to give them another, for he was evidently full of the spirit of song, when a gentle voice called out from the carriage, 'John, John.' 'Oh, don't stop him, Mrs Hutchinson! don't, please don't,' shouted a chorus of voices. 'I don't wish to stop him,' responded Mrs Hutchinson, 'but I do wish that Mr Barker would also sing.' The famous old singer promptly joined his wife in requesting Mr Barker to sing, and that gentleman complied by giving the time-honored 'Ben Bolt,' Miss Barrelle, Uncle John and Mr Tanner joining in the chorus, and with bass viol and violin accompaniment the effect was highly pleasing. The 'Roadside Minstrels' next favored the company with 'Home, Sweet Home,' and this touching old melody was rendered in a manner that evoked the warmest appreciation. At the close of this the barge hove in sight, and the concert was over, a pleasant finale to a merry day in the forest."

On June 22d there was a great parade of the Grand Army in Portland. I went down with Post 5 of Lynn. We celebrated the Fourth as usual that year, with Independence Day exercises at Old High Rock. A couple of years before I had sold a small strip of land from the easterly side of my premises, and the purchaser had built a retaining wall on the line. On this I had had built another wall. My wall stood all right, but his did not; one day it gave way, falling in on the basement of a big house he had erected, breaking a window, and frightening and hurting a woman, one of his tenants. My wall remained suspended in air. The man who had bought the land denied that he had given me a right to build on his wall, and brought suit for damages. After months of worry, the case was compromised. Then the woman who was hurt sued me for damages, and I paid her rather than fight it. I confess that I do not relish litigation.

In August I made a two days' trip to Milford, to bid farewell to Sister Abby, who started with her husband on a trip to Idaho. We went to the depot together, going different ways. I bought a ticket to Boston, placing it in my hat. As my train left the depot I stood on the car platform, lustily swinging my hat as a parting signal. Of course that was the last I saw of the ticket, and I had to make up the loss by paying my fare from my pocket.

In September I went to Maushacum Lake with Lillie and Jack to sing at a temperance gathering; Rev. Dr. A. A. Miner, Rev. J. W. Hamilton, T. A. Smith and Joshua Everett were among the speakers. A little later in the same month Fanny and I went to Philadelphia, where we spent two days singing in mass temperance meetings. We sang in several halls and churches, the last meeting being in the Academy of Music, six thousand being present. It was an inspiring occasion. We stayed with Mr. Phillips and wife, on Baring Street. They treated us with the utmost kindness. While there we sang "Countrymen, hear me," for the first time in the city. It made a great impression. A day or two after our return we went to Brockton, singing in temperance gatherings there.

In October a man named Mudgett came to me and promulgated the opinion that there were stores of lead and silver in High Rock. He had examined the rock in a cursory manner and seen unmistakable outcroppings of lead. Of course I was not averse to the development of lead and silver mines on my property, and at once we set out on a prospecting tour. We soon satisfied ourselves that the lead was simply spent balls, fired into the rock by sportsmen or others.

The boy hoodlums of Lynn made life miserable on High Rock that year. They not only disturbed our meetings on the Sabbath, but took advantage of my desire to keep the summit open to the public by making free with all parts of the property. When we picked our apples there were only two barrels, the rest having been stolen. The nuisance finally became so great that my janitor was appointed a special policeman. That solved the difficulty and the trouble ceased.

On October 21st there was a great meeting in the colored Baptist Church on Charles Street in Boston, to celebrate the semi-centennial of the attempt to hang William Lloyd Garrison, by a mob of the Hub's citizens. Many of the old-time Abolitionists participated. I sang "Get off the Track." A man from Chelsea, named George Haskell, told me later that fifty years before, when the excitement was at its height, he stood on the sidewalk, saw Garrison with a rope about him, and anxious to preserve the life of the great agitator if possible, resorted to strategy, and shouted, "He's a Democrat?" This seemed to raise a doubt in the minds of the mob, and its passion perceptibly cooled. Haskell was seventy-seven at the time he told me the story.

In November the history of Hillsboro County, N. H., was published. In the Milford section a steel portrait and biographical sketch of several pages appeared, covering some forty years of my busy life. During that month I sang in Wenham with Lillie, in Dover,

N. H., and also at Durham and Northwood, in the same State. On Thanksgiving Day all my descendants were gathered around the board in Daisy Cottage, we singing our Thanksgiving hymn. In December there were concerts in New Hampshire at Bow Lake, Centre Strafford, Barrington, East Rochester and Rochester, and then I came home from these pleasant experiences, as my diary says, to "Law, law, lawyers, frozen pipes and disaffected tenants." These and succeeding years were what the world would call years of "retirement and leisure." If the world wishes to see what this sort of leisure is like, each inhabitant should have some forty tenements on his hands, as I have, and try to preserve peace and harmony among a community of some one hundred and fifty to two hundred people, like that on High Rock, especially on some dreary morning after a "cold snap," when a complicated system of water and sewer pipes refuses to work.

During 1886 my wife's health became alarming. Consumption had fastened upon her, and it was evident that she could not hope for permanent recovery. Yet, as is so often the case, she kept about most of the time, visited friends and received their visits, and hoped for the best.

Early in the year I learned that a man was making money from my reputation in the West. He had allowed his hair to grow, dressed like the brothers and was giving "Hutchinson Family" concerts. It was a difficult matter to stop such an imposition upon the public, and I could only hope that his concerts were satisfactory to the audiences before whom he appeared.

On Washington's Birthday I sung in the State Prison at Charlestown to the convicts, on invitation of Colonel Roland G. Usher of Lynn, the warden. On the

24th I went to Worcester to attend the funeral of my tried and true friend, John B. Gough. It was a sad day indeed. In the course of the fortnight following I sang at several memorial services to the great orator. One was in Boston Music Hall on a Sunday afternoon. The great auditorium was packed. I sang "A Brother is Dead." In the evening of the same day I sang at the First Methodist-Episcopal Church in Lynn, at a similar service. The pastor, Rev. V. A. Cooper, was obliged to go to Boston soon after the service opened, and left the meeting in my charge. A few days later there was another at the Y. M. C. A., and I sang and made a short speech referring to my experiences with Gough.

Meanwhile my home affairs were giving me trouble enough. Between summonses to court, and conferences with lawyers, and the care of the lesser affairs, many of which had in previous years been looked after by Henry, anxiety concerning Fanny and Judson, I was almost distracted. In the midst of my terrible anguish came a sweet oasis in the desert of discord. The old-time anti-slavery people met in Melrose, at the home of Mary A. Livermore on April 22d. The principal meeting was in the Universalist Church. I sang "Over the Mountains, over the Moor." Among the speakers was William Lloyd Garrison, Jr., who paid a most interesting tribute to the memory of Maria W. Chapman, one of the most faithful workers in the anti-slavery cause. She deserved it. She was the handsomest, most faithful and active woman who espoused the cause of the slave. I can see her beaming countenance now, as she would sit in a prominent place at the conventions. We would go home, and recalling her presence, the many committees she was placed upon and her general air of activity, would say, "Well, Maria Chapman did speak, didn't she?" As a matter of fact she never spoke. She was a prolific writer, published fine reports of the conventions, and her initials are signed to an immense amount of matter in the files of the *Liberator* — especially in such times as Mr. Garrison was indisposed and unable to do much — but speaking was entirely out of her line. She dressed in perfect taste, and was one of the most attractive of all those at the meetings during those stormy times. We often enjoyed the hospitality of her home.

On May 2d, Lillie, Fanny, Jack and I sang at a meeting in Tremont Temple, Boston, a temperance "chalk talk" being a feature.

During the year two railroads were built to Hutchinson. Both of them took land belonging to Henry and myself for their terminals.

On May 31st Lillie and her boys left for the West, going to her old home in Chicago. On the night before they went I took Jack and Richie to the Reform Club, where they sang with me. I let them go with my blessing, but my heart went after them, and during the years that have passed since I have lost no opportunity of seeing them in whatever part of the land they happened to be.

On June 14th I went to Hutchinson. My wife was comfortable when I left, and I tried not to worry about her during my absence. On my way I stopped at New York for a day with Sister Abby. We spent the evening in company with Mr. and Mrs. F. B. Carpenter, David Hutchinson and wife, Lucius Hutchinson, wife and daughter, and Ludlow, of course. I remember that among other things done to amuse the company, I recited "The Raven," at Abby's suggestion. Carpenter rose to his feet and said, "Why didn't I know you could render that piece like that? I should have had you say it at the recent celebration of Poe's birthday, at which I presided." On June 17th I arrived at Chicago late at night, took quarters at the Brevoort, and the next morning hastened to Millard Avenue to see Lillie and the boys. After a good play with them, I took the train for St. Paul. On the 19th I arrived at Hutchinson, going at once to the home of Dennett, Asa's son. On the next day I visited the grave of my lamented brother. The day following we were treated to a cyclone, having to seek safety in the cellar. The big wind-tunnel, reaching a half-mile into the clouds, went by without doing much damage.

As usual when visiting Hutchinson, I was soon immersed in business affairs, but found time for an occasional fishing trip with Asa's grandchildren The Fourth of July came on Sunday, and there being no preacher at the Congregational Church, I occupied the pulpit, singing and speaking to the people. I took up the matter of improving the park in the south half of Hutchinson while there, and held meetings and also devoted a part of my time to "grubbing" on the property.

During my stay it became necessary for Lillie to come to Minnesota on probate matters connected with Henry's estate. She brought the boys with her and we gave some concerts. Of one of them the *Glencoe Register* said:

"The concert by the Hutchinson Family at the court-house hall last week Wednesday evening was not nearly so largely attended as it deserved to be The programme from first to last was replete with rich musical and elocutionary gems and was listened to with deep interest by the audience Several of the old familiar songs of the original Hutchinson Family were sung by Mr John W Hutchinson and Mrs

Lillie Phillips Hutchinson. The latter's rendition of the beautiful ballad of 'Mrs. Lofty and I' met with especial favor. The lady possesses a voice, the equal of which is seldom heard anywhere off of the highest operatic stage. Her two sons, Jack and Richard, aged seven and three years respectively, added immeasurably to the pleasure of the evening by their vocal efforts. The youngest has a most marvellous voice and enunciates as distinctly as a child of four times his years. Seldom, if ever was Poe's 'Raven' recited with such power and pathos as it was by J. W. Hutchinson, it certainly was never better handled in Glencoe. The universal verdict of all present is that it was the most satisfactory entertainment we have had for years."

After my return to Lynn the experiences for the remainder of the year were uneventful.

The close of the year was celebrated by a meeting of the Lynn Assembly at Oxford Street Chapel. James N. Buffum, who in the course of years had become the owner of the chapel — which the Hutchinson's songs helped to build and within whose walls the Rev. Samuel Johnson preached for so many years — in the course of his remarks took occasion to refer to himself as the "owner" of High Rock. This made my blood boil, and at the close of his speech I took the floor and reminded the audience that it was the Hutchinson family which had for years owned the rock and kept it open to the public. Buffum's statement reminded me of the remark of Amos Dorman, who gave me a deed of that portion of the rock in dispute — there has never been a question about my being the owner of the summit — after the court's decision that the deed given to Brother Jesse was only a life-lease, though Jesse had purchased and paid for the land in good faith: "Jim Buffum don't own a single inch of that land; it belongs to Jesse Hutchinson." After this encounter I visited the Coliseum, where the Grand Army was having a camp-fire, then went to a watch-meeting at one of the Methodist churches and finally to the home of a tenant on

High Rock, where the old year was being bid farewell in a social gathering. The result of these experiences was a decided disposition to drop into rhyme, which resulted as follows:

> I've started on another year
> With strong resolves for all good cheer;
> Its future, judging by the past,
> Some days of gloom will shadows cast.
> But time commenced in dread and fear
> At last may close in brighter cheer
> So jump aboard, put on the steam—
> Through fogs of doubt hope's light will gleam
> Our faithful guide we'll trust for aye,
> And when old '87 is gray
> And like his brothers passed away
> For, good or ill, he must resign—
> We'll sing once more our "Old Lang Syne"
> His service closed, we'll never fear,
> But welcome in the glad new year

Warwick Palfray and his aged bride celebrated their golden wedding on the first day of the year. I attended at his home on Essex Street, and during the evening, besides singing, told the story of my sickness, many years before, when Mr. Palfray acted as my nurse, and brought me through.

A few days later I found my poetic afflatus had again attacked me. I began a poem, but was interrupted ere the close.

> Oh, could I fill these lines with sense,
>   I'd gladly spend the time
> To labor hard both night and day,
>   And make it plain in rhyme.
>
> I'd have a thought of home and friends,
>   Of God, of heaven, and hell,—
> Eternity, its past and present
>   Its future I would tell
>
> I'd speak of joys that mortals have,
>   Encircling our sphere—
>   [Will see you later.]

"Later" never has come, and the poem remains a fragment.

On Thursday, March 10th, I went to New York, and with Sister Abby attended the funeral of Henry Ward Beecher at Plymouth Church. It seemed the breaking of another tie that bound us with such tender cords to our busy and happy past. Pleasant as have been the experiences of the past decade for me, and strong as is my hold upon life to-day, it seems as I look back upon it as though a large part of the time has been spent in the house of mourning. I have either been at a funeral or else lamenting the loss of some old and cherished friend or brother nearly every week of the time. Two days later, in New York, Abby and I attended the funeral of the wife of Hiram Hutchinson, a millionaire connection of the family, who originated in Danvers.

On April 7th, Fast Day, the Prohibitionists had a convention in Lawrence. I was appointed on a committee to arrange for a temperance camp-meeting, which was held at Asbury Grove, Hamilton, in August. During this year I find by my diary that I developed quite a passion for attending auctions. It made little difference to me whether the auction was of a house, a hotel, household goods or a store. The excitement of the affair, the manners of the auctioneer, the uncertainty as to whether I should get a thing after becoming a bidder, all fascinated me. However, I do not find among the treasures secured on such occasions many things which indicate that I paid too dear for my whistle.

I made two trips to Hutchinson this year, and built four houses. One was Cliff Cottage, under the lee of High Rock, and another was Tower Cottage, in which I now reside. The other two were on Park Place, fronting the park, in Hutchinson. I made my first start for Hutchinson on May 24th, stopping for a call on Abby in New York, as usual. I also stopped at Painesville, O., to see my old friend and agent, E. E. Johnson. Lillie had meanwhile married Rev. Henry Morgan, an evangelist. I found on reaching Chicago that they were in Minneapolis. Arriving there, I went to the Baptist mission with them. Morgan spoke, and I sang with Lillie "The Stranger on the Sill." They accompanied me to Hutchinson. On Sunday, the day after our arrival, Mr. Morgan preached in the Congregational church, and Lillie and I sang. On the following day they left for St. Paul. Immediately I became immersed in business, surveying and selling lots, and making arrangements to build my cottages. After getting the cellars pretty well started I left for Lynn, stopping on the way at Springfield, Wis., and at Chicago. At the first-named place I gave a concert with Lillie and my grandchildren. Then, after the concert, we drove eight miles in a carriage to overtake a freight train, in which slow-moving conveyance we spent the night. There was an educational exhibit in Chicago the next day, and then I bid my grandsons good-by, and left for the East, in an excursion party consisting of some thirty people. Three days later I was in Lynn, as my diary says, "Looking up my cares." While I was absent James N. Buffum had died, and whatever title he claimed in High Rock property had passed into the hands of Charles O. Beede, an enterprising citizen. What the "cares" I have mentioned were like can best be illustrated by some random quotations from my diary:

"July 25th. McF. on No. 4, Terrace Lodge, papering. Pike (painter) in stone house. C. paid five dollars on rent, owes four dollars

"July 26th. Pike all day, McFarlan all day; Pat 2d, one-half a day; Pat 1st, nine hours. Rode out with wife. Looking at house to build. Digging of cellar (Cliff Cottage).

"August 15th. Laid out front lot and commenced to dig cellar (Lower Cottage), paved John's Avenue, repaired Stone Cottage piazza. To the tent (temperance meeting) in the evening.

"August 17th. Commenced blasting to-day. Had twelve people working regular, and three masons.

"August 27th. Herne, Regan and three Irishmen worked for me to-day. Picked apples and pears. Moved plan of cellar two feet north.

"August 28th. Leave for New York.

"August 29th. Abby's birthday. Poor night's rest (on boat), breakfast with Abby. Coney Island, Gilmore's band, Lucius, David and wife, Ludlow, met, dined together. To Lucius's house on my way. Left N. Y. at 10.30 o'clock.

"August 30th. Arrived in Lynn to breakfast.

"September 3d. To Portland and home — 180 miles, seven hours. Returned in season to settle with help. Got ticket reduced to Minn.

"September 5th. Left for the West.

"September 7th. Chicago. Dined with Jonas Hutchinson.

"September 8th. Minneapolis. Arrived at 7.30. Left for Hutchinson at 4.05 P. M.

"September 9th. Hutchinson. Hard at work. Settling up. Houses not yet done.

"September 10th. Worked on house. Sold a lot to —— $25 down and $300 in three years. Carpenter built stairs.

Before I left Hutchinson I had built both houses, and they were tenanted. Then I returned to Lynn, caught up the loose ends there, and went on with the construction of my new home. Fanny was very interested in this, selecting the plans, specifying the style of finish, and arranging for the furnishing. In October Charles Dickens, son of the distinguished novelist, gave readings in Lynn, and I was glad to renew an acquaintance made in his father's parlors in 1846, when he was a boy.

On November 7th I went over to Melrose to hear General George W. Sheridan speak on Ingersollism. He accompanied me to Boston after the lecture, and we spent the night at a hotel, he going to Lynn with me the next day. Many years before he had acted as our advance agent in New York State. He was an earnest reformer and I rejoiced in his work and his success. His daughter, Emma Sheridan Frye, the actress, has been for years a friend we delighted to meet, both professionally and in our family circle.

On November 21st, my brother Andrew's widow, Elizabeth Ann, died at her home in Dorchester. She was a daughter of Jacob and Catherine Todd, of Rowley, and had survived her husband many years.

On November 27th I visited my lifelong friend, T. C. Severance, at Arlington Heights. He died soon after. I met his widow, who now resides on the Pacific coast, at the World's Fair in 1893, discussing with her the many stirring scenes we had witnessed together.

On December 9th I had a visit from Rev. Mr. Fisher, formerly of Lawrence, Kan., Omaha and Salt Lake City. He stayed in the vicinity of Boston some weeks, and on December 31st preached at the watch-night service at the First Methodist Episcopal Church in Lynn. During his remarks he spoke tenderly of our family, and of the loss of Henry. A love feast followed. Near the close of the vigil I sung, "No Night There." Then we all knelt around the altar, while the bell tolled the solemn hour of midnight.

In January, 1888, I called on Charles Hoag, at the residence of his brother Alvan Hoag, on Nahant Street, in Lynn, and found him to be in many ways an interesting and remarkable man. He gave the name to the city of Minneapolis, the first part for the Indian Minnehaha, and "polis," the Greek word for city.

On February 2d there was a woman-suffrage sociable at Horticultural Hall, in Boston, at which I both sung and spoke. Rebecca Moore, who had come over from England again, was among the speakers. I never saw her without recalling a conversation I had with Parker Pillsbury after his return from a trip to Europe. He said to me, "I have seen the most intellectual woman in England." "Well," said I, "I guess I can tell you who she is. Her name is Rebecca Moore." "Right," said he. Mrs. Lucy Stone Blackwell, Julia Ward Howe, and other friends of the cause participated in the sociable. The close of the week is thus summarized in my diary:

"This has been a busy week. Some trouble with men, carpenters finishing up Tower Cottage, my pipes are bursting and the plumbers are very busy. Wife has had a hard week; thinks she must go. The joy of the suffrage sociable is put in store for me."

On the 18th there was an auction sale by the government of its material at the High Rock signal station. I bought the flagstaff and steps (into the granite of which Henry's name is cut as the builder) to retain as a memorial of him.

About this time I record my conviction that looking over one's right shoulder at the moon proves a failure, for I had quite bad luck all the week. This is my one superstition.

During this year, as for a number of years before and since, I attended the important hearings before committees of the Massachusetts Legislature, usually in the Green Room at the State-house. The subjects that drew me were generally temperance and woman suffrage. On February 22d I attended the Wendell Phillips memorial service at Tremont Temple, Boston. On the 28th of February we moved into Tower Cottage. Fanny was at this time so weak that I took her in my arms from Daisy Cottage to the new home. On the 24th of March I went to Washington to attend the fortieth anniversary of the inauguration of the woman-suffrage movement. Practically all of the survivors of that famous first convention were at this gathering, together with many strong and faithful workers in the cause who espoused it later. The meetings continued several days, among those attending and speaking being Susan B. Anthony, Elizabeth Cady Stanton, Lucy Stone Blackwell, Julia Ward Howe, Mary A. Livermore, Dr. Mary E. Walker (the first to speak for woman suffrage in Washington, and the first American woman to attempt to vote), Frances E. Willard, Henry B. Blackwell, Mrs. Belva A. Lockwood, Phœbe Cozzins, Clara Barton, and some two thousand others, more or less famous. There were conferences of the pioneers, lectures, a reception by President Cleveland, and many other interesting features. At one large gathering — Pioneer Day, the 31st — I sung an original song, which I had prepared for the occasion. The bust of my dear old friend Lucretia Mott was at my right hand as I spoke and sung, and the event was inspiring to me. The song was as follows:

> All hail, ye brave and noble band,
>   We greet with cheer and song, —
> Most honored queens of all the land —
>   Who struggle 'gainst the wrong
> Bright hopes we bring from East and West,
>   Each sister's heart to cheer ;
> Though oft dismayed, your cause is blest,
>   Your crown of triumph near.
>
> For two-score years, through doubts and fears,
>   And conflicts fierce and long,
> We've battled 'gainst the host of sin
>   And fortresses of wrong
> With our great leader pressing on —
>   Whose spirit ne'er could yield,
> "Lucretia" waved the moral sword
>   That conquered every field.

Nor can our hearts to-day forget
　　The trio brave and free —
Our "Stanton" bold and Lucy Stone,
　　And earnest "Susan B."
With hope renewed again we come,
　　In love and joy to greet —
Throughout our ranks no feuds exist,
　　Our unity's complete.

From fields of conquest and renown
　　Our trophies rich we bring,
This council will rejoice to hear
　　The victor's song we sing.
Press forward then, our cause is just,
　　Our triumph all shall hail;
From sea to sea let all be free —
　　"There's no such word as fail."

After the anniversary days were over I lingered in Washington a few days, renewing acquaintances with old friends, dining with Congressman Springer and wife, attending various receptions and other gatherings. On March 4th I started on my return home, but got no farther than New York, when sickness delayed me. Dear Abby watched over me, and by aid of her tender ministrations I was soon able to go on to Lynn. The days that followed were full of care and anxiety. Fanny was failing. Jerusha, Brother Judson's widow and other relatives, including, of course, her children, joined me in caring for her comfort, but the end rapidly approached. Rev. V. A. Cooper, who had been at Henry's bedside during his last days, with his excellent wife came to our home to pray with the sufferer, and comfort us all. On May 4th, at 8.40 in the evening, Fanny died. One of her parting requests was that the inscription on her gravestone should be "She hath done what she could." I pass over the days of mourning and funeral service which followed. Every heart knows its own bitterness, and the reader will not expect me to detail scenes of sorrow that are sacred.

Fanny B. Patch was born in Antrim, N. H., June 27, 1823. She was the daughter of David A. and Susanna (Parker) Patch. Her father was a master carpenter. When she was quite young, a piece of timber fell across his chest, wounding him in such a way as to affect his lungs and produce consumption, from which he suffered thirteen years, being for most of that time confined to his house. He died in 1839, aged fifty-seven years. The home of the family was near the Contocook River. He had many children, most of whom grew to manhood and womanhood, and themselves raised large families. The musical faculty was very strongly developed in the family. Fanny, as I have already said, was a choir singer in Lowell at the time I met her. She had had good musical instruction, and about that time sang with Braham, the great English tenor, in concert at Lowell. I sang with him myself while in London. Maud Porter, who was with me on one of the most successful tours of my life, was a daughter of one of the sisters. J. Al. Sawtelle, grandson of another, has been before the public as a singer for many years. A brother, Burnam, sang with me for a while. He was a fine bass. I first met Fanny in Lowell. A young lady who had taught school in Milford came to our hotel to call on us, bringing Fanny with her. They were friends, having lived, one at Antrim and the other at Hillsboro Bridge, near by. As they came in, Fanny was leading a pretty little child by the hand, and her manner towards the child at once prepossessed me in her favor and she won my heart. We were married at Milford, by Rev. Abner Warner, February 21, 1843. Of her brothers and sisters, one only survives, Susan, who was married to Philemon Chandler, in 1824. She is now within a few months of ninety years of age. Her brother William married Catherine L. Lyon in 1834, and died in 1842. Mary Jane, a sister, married James M. Hopkins in 1836. She died in 1863. Caroline married Charles C. P. Porter in 1836 and died in 1879. Burnam Patch married twice, first to Susan H. Whittemore, and second to Sarah F. Pottle. He lived for a while in Sacramento, and died in 1852, at that place. David was a sea-captain. He married Mary Ann Dix in 1840, and died in 1848. William H. Hebard, who married Elizabeth, now lives on High Rock. Elizabeth died in 1887, aged seventy-four. Martha married Joseph C. Durkee in 1849. She died in 1865. Louisa married Samuel Gould in 1851, and died in 1869.

This family in the course of time nearly all settled in Lowell. Susanna, the mother, died in 1865, aged eighty. She was of good Revolutionary stock. Her grandfather was in the battle of Bunker Hill. On the night before June 17, 1775, her father and uncle, then boys, started from their home in Groton, Mass., with a tub full of eatables, designed for the patriot sire and his comrades. It was a long tramp to Charlestown, and the contest was hot when they reached the scene of the battle. They bore their burden suspended by the handles from a pole across their shoulders. They began to scale the height of Breed's Hill, when a shot from the *Somerset*, British man-of-war, struck the tub, demolishing it. "There goes daddy's dinner!" ruefully exclaimed one of the faithful boys.

Of Fanny's work with me in our professional tours it is hardly necessary for me to speak. The story has already been told. For years she shared the cares and discomforts with me that are inseparable from a life of concert-giving. She witnessed many of the most exciting experiences of our life before the public. For nearly a half-century we travelled through life together. Her scrap-books and mine are full of tributes from the press to her personal and professional qualities. She was a good mother to her children, and a warm friend to thousands of those she met in all parts of the land through her musical career. Her latter days, as I have already intimated, were largely given up to preparations for living in the new home, Tower Cottage. She lived there only two months before called to occupy one of those promised mansions in the better country.

> "Her's the city pure and golden,
>   Ours the earth-lite stained with sin;
> Her's the green fields and the gardens
>   Where the angels enter in.
> Her's the white robes ever shining
>   In the love that made them so,
> Her's the glory and the rapture
>   Which the angels only know.
> Her's the crown wreath never fading,—
>   Her's the music of the skies;
> Our's the eyes all dimmed with weeping,—
>   Her's the ever tearless eyes."

CHAPTER III.

LOOKING TOWARD SUNSET.

"I've lived so many years,
 But I'm growing old, you see,
Of all my early friendships
 But few are left to me
Yet my soul shall never grieve
 At the loss of friends below —
We'll gather up the jewels
 In the land to which we go"

THE year 1888, after the death of my wife, was largely taken up with home cares Before winter came I had erected another cottage, "Prospect," on High Rock, besides busying myself with many minor improvements. In May Rev. Edwin Thompson, the noted temperance advocate, with whom we had labored in Rhode Island and elsewhere, died at his home in Norwood. I attended his funeral and a month later, at Tremont Temple, Boston, spoke and sung at a memorial service held in his honor. In June, also, I was visited by my nephew, Lucius B. Hutchinson, with his wife and daughter Alice. The latter took a photographic view of Tower Cottage, which I hope to reproduce in this volume Abby, with my grand-niece, Marion, visited me later in the season. During the last of August I went to Milford, to see Abby and the other friends. During my stay I slept in my old room, the northeast chamber in the homestead, where Benny and father died This room Benny and Judson, Asa and I occupied for years, it being large and airy, with plenty of room for two double beds. After celebrating Abby's birthday quietly, I returned home, gladly, for my reflections were sad while there.

In September I went to Milford again, to attend the funeral of Irene, Joshua's widow. With Kate Dearborn, Abby and Ludlow, Viola and Lucius and wife, I sung at the grave the song we had sung over the biers of Joshua, David and Rhoda, "Our days are gliding swiftly by." I realized my loneliness keenly when called upon to ride in the first carriage to the grave, as the only survivor of Joshua's ten brothers. On the 28th of December Jerusha, Judson's widow, died, and on New Year's Day of 1889 I was at Milford again to attend her funeral. Her brother Jonas, whom I have heretofore mentioned, came on from Chicago with his family, and her brother Fordyce, from Waltham, and other relatives were there. During the service word came to me from my niece, Kate, Judson and Jerusha's only child, that she was particular that I should sing I sung "No night there."

On the 20th of January I went to Boston and lunched at the Parker House with Parker Pillsbury, one of the few survivors of the anti-slavery times. There was a reunion of Abolitionists at Berkeley Hall that evening, and Viola and I sung the "Slave's Appeal" and "Furnace Blast," amid much enthusiasm. Two days later I had a visit from Pillsbury, at Tower Cottage. On the 28th, with Judson and my granddaughter Kate, I went to the meeting of the Farmers' Club at Marblehead. Benj. P. Ware introduced us, praising the work of the Abolitionists. We sung to them and Kate gave several recitations. Later in the same week the woman suffragists had a hearing in the State-house, Viola attending with me. We sung an appropriate selection.

In February I made a trip to New York and Washington. While at New York I stayed with David, my nephew. David is one of the brightest and shrewdest of my brother Noah's sons; his letters are a continual feast. At Washington I stopped with General B. F. Hawkes and Elias S. Hutchinson. Of course my principal design was to witness the inauguration of Harrison and Morton. I attended the inauguration ball and other events. Later I was guest of Frederick Douglass at his home in Washington. With Douglass I attended the first reception by the new president. We arrived late. There had been a great crowd, which still continued, and Harrison, becoming weary, had ceased shaking hands, and was simply bowing to each one as he passed. When we came, however, he spied us before we reached him, stepped out, and shook hands with each of us heartily. As he spoke to me, Douglass said: "Mr. Hutchinson sung 'Tippecanoe and Tyler too' songs for your Grandfather Harrison in 1840." This remark, in various forms, got into the papers. For a day or two after I was rather surprised and a little amused to have the small boys inquire as I passed along the street, "Are you Harrison's grandfather?"

During my stay in Washington I sung for Elias's Sunday-school. He was an Episcopalian. On another occasion I went to William Hutchinson's church, Unitarian, to a sociable, singing to the people and reciting Poe's "Raven." I arrived in Lynn March 17th, after an absence of a month. The canvass to secure constitutional prohibition in Massachusetts was on, and I threw myself into it with all my spirit, attending meetings and singing wherever opportunity offered. On April 28th I went on to New York to atttend the centennial celebration. My good friend S. T. Pickard of the *Portland Transcript*, whose wife is a cousin to John G. Whittier, went on with me. While there Sister Abby, Ludlow and I sung to the President and Postmaster-General Wanamaker. Pickard came back home with me, and we made an effort to see Whittier at Oak Knoll, Danvers, his winter home, but he was away. We therefore resolved to try again later.

I was making, all these months, unsuccessful efforts to secure a housekeeper who would take good care of me and my premises. At one time I hired a steady old lady, who had had experience in the family before, but found it was quite a different matter for her to be at work for Fanny to what it was for her to be her own mistress. Then I tried a young girl — I considered myself lucky to get out of this transaction whole, financially or physically. She thought it a part of her duty to see that I had a daily ride, and would go to a stable and secure a horse — on my account, of course — and placing me on the back seat, would drive out. Once or twice I had misgivings as to whether she knew as much about driving as she claimed, but was not entirely satisfied until one day she took a girl companion on the front seat with her. One held the reins, the other the whip, and they drove far out on the Salem and Boston turnpike, until I began to fear abduction. I begged them to stop overdriving the horse and to go home. Finally my persuasions prevailed, and we returned. That was the end of her rides, and soon after I replaced her with a girl of more steady proclivities.

Before this year closed I had built two more cottages on High Rock, "Lookout" and "Whittier," the last of course named for the good Quaker poet. I made it in my way to call on another aged poet, the author of

"America," whom Dr. Holmes once remarked "fate tried to conceal by naming him Smith." A ride round the circuit road from Boston brought me to Rev. S. F. Smith's delightful home in Newton. We had a pleasant talk together and the genial dominie gave me the history of his song, which was written originally for a children's entertainment in the Park Street Church, Boston, he, of course, having not the slightest idea it would ever become so popular and useful. The world, and especially our America, owes a good deal to Dr. Lowell Mason, not only for his work in the interest of church music, but for interesting Dr. Smith in that little chorus at Park Street Church, and so securing to posterity this and other songs. Alas! Dr. Smith, too, has now joined the noble band of New England poets and singers on the other side.

In October I endeavored to put into operation a scheme to improve the social and mental condition of my tenants by establishing a literary club, to meet frequently in the spacious laundry of Terrace Lodge. This scheme promised good results, but the fulfilment was a disappointment. In the course of a short time the rank and file of the tenants gave up the club to the boys and young men among them, and the latter overlooked the idea of mental improvement and devoted themselves to social enjoyment of rather too boisterous a character for so quiet a neighborhood. I was therefore forced to adjourn the sessions of the body *sine die*.

The Nationalist movement took form this year. A club was formed in Lynn, and I immediately joined, for the principles of the movement were in accord with my convictions. For years I have worked and talked, sung and voted with these reformers.

On September 23d there was a reunion of anti-slavery workers in Boston, there being two sessions, continuing until eleven o'clock at night. I sang three times during the exercises. My anti-Masonic friend, Rev. Mr. Blanchard, of Wheaton, Ill., was present. A day or two later Sister Abby and Ludlow, who were stopping at Portland, came down as far as Newburyport, with our friend S. T. Pickard, and I met them there. We visited the Old South Church, and viewed the bones of George Whitefield, the great preacher, called on James Parton, the historian, and then went to Oak Knoll, Danvers, to see Whittier. As we rode up to the house, we could see the straight figure of the aged poet, clad in his light coat and Quaker hat, among the shrubbery. He was viewing the autumn foliage, and presented a picture indeed. As we approached, he cautiously turned, and glanced in our direction. Recognizing us, he hastened to the carriage, helped Abby out, and gallantly escorted her into the house. A wood fire was burning on the hearth, making an agreeable impression of homelikeness as we came in from the chilly September air. In the course of our call, members of his family, who for years had ministered to his comfort, asked us to sing. I suggested that as Mr. Whittier had never heard us in the "Furnace Blast," he might like to hear us sing it. Abby and Ludlow joined their voices with mine, in the poet's trumpet appeal to the conscience of the nation:

> "What gives the wheat-fields blades of steel?
> What points the rebel cannon?
> What sets the roaring rabble's heel
> On the old star-spangled pennon?
> What breaks the oath
> Of the men of the South?
> What whets the knife
> For the Union's life? —
> Hark to the answer: Slavery!"

Whittier listened attentively until we had finished. Then he said: "Well, if thee sang that song to the soldiers and pro-slavery generals with the unction and spirit that thee has just sung it, I do not wonder that thee had thy expulsion."

Abby and Ludlow came home with me and spent a day or two.

On November 26th Lynn's great fire occurred, nearly the entire manufacturing district being destroyed at a loss of some five million dollars, and many families being rendered homeless. The burned district was directly in front of my house, and the view of the conflagration from the summit of High Rock was simply magnificent, especially after the darkness had come on. It was an immense smoking, seething, blazing mass of fire, the smoke streaming miles out to sea, a veritable pillar of cloud by day and of fire by night. It seemed a death-blow to the city, but proved to be far otherwise. Two days later, within sight of Tower Cottage, the scenes were repeated in the great Thanksgiving fire in Boston, where there was an equal loss of property, though confined to a much smaller district, and several lives were lost, a calamity that did not mark the Lynn fire. Of course, the throwing of so many thousands out of work made the Lynn fire far more wide-reaching in its consequences.

On the 19th of December the Nationalists held their first anniversary in Tremont Temple, Boston. Edward Bellamy, the author of "Looking Backward," was present and spoke. I sang the "People's Advent," creating a great furore. This great poem of Gerald Massy's I had in conjunction with Henry set to music many years before. It never failed to make an impression.

"'Tis coming up the steep of time,
    And this old world is growing brighter,
We may not see its dawn sublime,
    Yet high hopes make the heart throb lighter.
We may be sleeping under ground
    When it awakes the world in wonder,
But we have felt its gathering round
    And heard its voice of living thunder,
'Tis coming, coming, O yes, 'tis coming!

"'Tis coming now, the glorious time
    Foretold by seers and sung in story,
For which, when thinking was a crime,
    Souls leaped to Heaven from scaffolds gory:
They passed, nor saw the work they wrought —
    Nor the crowning hopes of centuries blossom —
But the living lightning of their thought
    And daring deeds doth pulse earth's bosom.

"Creeds, empires, systems, rot with age
    But the great people's ever youthful,
And it shall write the future's page,
    To our humanity more truthful
There's a divinity within
    That makes men great when'er they will it;
God works with all who dare to will
    And the time cometh to reveal it

"Freedom! the tyrants killed thy braves,
    Yet in our memories live the sleepers
And though the millions fill their graves
    Dug by Death's fierce, red-handed reapers —
The world shall not forever bow
    To things that mock God's own endeavor,
'Tis nearer than they dream of now
    When flowers shall wreathe the sword forever

"Oh, it must come! The oppressor's throne
    Is crumbling by our hot tears crushed,
The sword that tyrant's hands have drawn
    Is cankered by our heart's blood rust
Room for the men of mind! make way,
    Ye robber traitors, strive no longer,
Ye cannot stay the opening day —
    The world rolls on, the light grows stronger
'Tis coming, coming, O yes, 'tis coming!"

A short time after Massy was the guest of Theodore D. Weld, at Hyde Park, and I was pleased to go and talk with the reformer-poet.

I did not celebrate watch night this year. My diary remarks: "Begin to think I will not attempt to rupture the laws of eternity; nor will I try to divide what God has joined together." The line between the years is largely artificial. In February of 1890 I went to Milford and meeting Abby, Ludlow and Lucius, went with them to visit Mrs. Jonathan Towne, who was celebrating her one hundredth birthday. Abby gave her an Oxford edition of the Bible, Lucius making the presentation speech, to which the centenarian responded in sweetly accented sentences. Then we sang.

"My sister I wish you well,
When our Lord calls, I trust we shall be mentioned
In the promised land."

She softly said "Amen," and we breathed another strain.

"We are almost home, to join the heavenly band."

Mrs. Towne was a youngish woman when I joined the Baptist Church, of which she was a member, sixty-four years ago.

Two days later Susan B. Anthony celebrated her seventieth birthday anniversary at Washington. Of course I, with suffragists generally, went to the capital to felicitate "Susan." I kissed the cheek of the intrepid agitator, and wished her all possible happiness for the rest of her days. The banquet was in the Riggs House. There were some two hundred around the tables. Mrs. Stone, Mrs. Stanton, Henry B. Blackwell and others made addresses. Susan made a neat reference to me in her remarks, that was of course appreciated. A convention followed for a few days in Lincoln Hall in which I participated, giving the new song "I may not be a Prophet." On my way back through New York I sat for my portrait with Frank B. Carpenter, and viewed his great arbitration picture, now the property of Queen Victoria. Abby had a party on the evening of Washington's Birthday, attended by the Carpenters, and family connections. On the trip from New York to Boston I stopped over at New Haven and visited Graziella Ridgway Robertson, singing with her some of the songs we sung together in the days when she commenced her concert career with the Hutchinson Family. Another very dear friend I visited was Anna Teresa Collins, now the wife of a New Haven druggist.

On the 2d of March I sang for the Father Mathew Total Abstinence Society in Lynn, interesting the members very much by telling them that I had shaken the hand of the founder of the society in the old country nearly a half-century before.

In the early summer of this year George W. Putnam, a literary friend of mine, interested me in a patent fire-escape of his invention, in the form of a non-inflammable shute. I invited him to attach it to one of the front windows of Tower Cottage, running it down into Highland Square. It remained a week, many persons meanwhile descending it in safety, through a hot fire burning around it. The exhibition was very successful, being witnessed by fire-experts and the public generally. Putnam died in 1895, widely lamented.

In August of this year the Grand Army of the Republic held its national encampment in Boston. From the grand-stand on Copley Square I watched forty thousand veterans pass in parade. President Harrison, Secretary Tracy, General Sherman, General Banks and a host of notables were present. The boys in blue had a very happy time for several days. Many of them visited Lynn, and I enjoyed grasping them by the hand. On one day the Fifteenth Maine Association met at the G. A. R. Hall. On another day two regimental associations came to High Rock and had their photographs taken. With my daughter I sang them war songs.

In August I went to Milford, and with Sister Abby, the cousins and nephews and nieces, enjoyed a day at the Purgatory picnic at Mont Vernon. From a contemporaneous publication I quote a few words which illustrate the spirit of the occasion:

"Milford's matrons and maidens, gents, gentlemen and children, early Thursday morning were turning Purgatoryward. The morning was warm, but heads were cool and hearts were happy. At noon two belated men, one a retired merchant, the other a newspaper man, neared the hill below which were the multitude. As they descended into Purgatory they met a double quartette coming up the incline in a carriage. They were sweetly singing that grand old hymn 'Maggie Murphy's Home.' Down into the gorge the two men dropped and they were soon lost in the surging mass, twenty-five hundred strong and more to come later. The picnic-ground contains sixty acres, owned in the same family for half a century. That family is the Hutchinson, some of whose sweet voices have been heard throughout America and in the Old World. 'Twas in the valley there that these same Hutchinsons went to mill in the 'Days of Auld Lang Syne.' The present owner is Henry Appleton Hutchinson. Thursday was the twelfth annual assembly at this popular resort, where the best people come and the best of order is maintained. The tourists are about in white suits, black suits, or whatever suits suit their fancy. Here the farmer talks potatoes and hay, swaps cows, discusses hens and meets and greets old friends.

"Such is life! Purgatory derived its name from the idea that the 'old arch lawyer' once passed through there, leaving his footprint in the rock, his heel pointing toward Alaska and his toes toward the Old Bay State — where is he now? The natural gulf there is seventy feet long, eighteen feet deep, twelve feet wide through the solid rock, with towering trees, sentinel-like, guarding around. An overhanging rock juts out thirty feet in mid-air at the gorge. A 'bean pot' so-called, is there, thirteen feet deep, five feet across the top, where the water used to surge, till it wore to its present shape. A small cave is to be seen, also a giant face, and in 'Hog Rock' an 'old boy's profile,' and a solemn baboon's phiz are visible. The devil's foot spoken of is seven feet long. Through the day the Milford Band, Frank Gregg, leader, did its duty well, and the grand orchestra, L. W. Dotch, of Boston, leader, furnished fine dancing music. An illusionist entertained all, and Edison's phonograph was there too. Rifle practice, bowling, a swing and ring-throwing made up the amusements. Ice-cream, pie and peanuts slipped down the small boy's mouth at a two-minute clip. The older folks ate, but took more time.

"No zig-zag liquor was on the grounds, but fine water from a natural spring was in abundance. John W. Hutchinson of Lynn was present and sang 'We're a band of brothers from the Old Granite State.'

"It was a red-letter day. May its like come again."

After this, with Abby and Ludlow, I went to the Isles of Shoals, where we stayed several days. We had some good times singing together and for the benefit of friends who were there. I gave a concert and visited Celia Thaxter, the poet of the Island. In November I went to New York, and spent many days with Sister Abby, looking over manuscript in preparation for this book, and also having many pleasant hours in social gatherings with the Carpenters, the various tribes of Hutchinson, the Mathersons, Andersons, and others. Lucius's daughter Mary was married during my stay to Edward F. Wendelstat. I sung at the wedding, "Thou art wooed and won."

The latter days of 1890 were spent in sending out invitations to the birthday party with which I had resolved to celebrate my seventieth anniversary. The date was January 4, 1891, but as that came on Sunday, the celebration was held on the day following. For several days previous to the notable event floods of letters, acknowledging invitations, were coming to Tower Cottage. It happened that the day when it arrived was stormy, and so many who would otherwise have attended were kept away. But as it was, there was a houseful.

and though I live to be twice seventy years old, I can never forget that day. What a gathering was that! First of all and best of all, came Sister Abby, bringing Ludlow with her. Then my daughter Viola, with her husband and three children, Cleveland, Harry and Kate. My son Judson is always with me. Lucius, son of Brother Noah, came on from New York, with Alice Hutchinson Wallace, his daughter. H. Appleton Hutchinson, of Mont Vernon, N. H., another son of Noah, was there. Kate Hutchinson Dearborn, only survivor of Judson's family, came from Milford with her four boys. Andrew's tribe was represented by his sons Jacob T. Hutchinson and wife, Marcus Morton Hutchinson and wife, and by his daughter Kate Hutchinson Elms with her husband, Joseph D. Elms, and their son. Added to these were old friends from everywhere. It was a happy, happy day and evening.

A short time after, I published a full account of the event in pamphlet form, and as it was written by the same hand which has assisted me in the preparation of this volume, it is perhaps well to quote from it the following account of the gathering.

"We're the friends of Emancipation,
And we sing the proclamation,
Till it echoes through the nation
From the old Granite State."

Such songs as this echoed through the parlors of Tower Cottage at Lynn, on Monday, January 5, 1891. They were sung by the Hutchinson Family — not all of the "Tribe of John," whose seventieth birthday was the cause of the gathering — but they were all, either by the ties of blood or matrimony, of the "Tribe of Jesse," and the songs were sung as only the Hutchinsons could sing them, bringing unbidden tears of mingled recollection and triumph to the eyes of the notable group who listened, for they were songs of a past generation, to be recalled only as treasured reminiscences. But to those who heard them ring again, they suggested the truth of that peculiarly family song: "There's no song like the old song."

What a group was that! First, its centre, John, gladhearted, soul-stirring, prophet-like, angel-voiced John, the last of thirteen brothers, the inspirer and strength of the most remarkable family of vocalists which ever travelled in this or any other land. Strong in the strength of years of right living; rich in the memory of continued successes in his singing missions; cultured by constant contact with the progressive minds of two continents; happy in the love of an innumerable host of admirers and friends. Sitting at his cherished organ, his hands drawing from the keys the full chords which marked the harmony of the stirring air he was singing, glancing first into the dear faces which surrounded him, and then into those that listened, his eyes alternately shining with joy and moistened with tears, he sung the songs of "Auld Lang Syne," with all the old expression and tenderness. By his side stood Sister Abby, Mrs. Ludlow Patton, of New York City, with heart brimful of love for all of the family group, but with a special tenderness for her only brother, with whom she had shared so many moral and melodious triumphs. "Do you want to hear 'The Old Granite State' again?" "Don't you want to hear 'Old High Rock?'" she would say, and then would take Brother John by the sleeve and go to the organ. A quick, nervous, care-taking woman, she would not sit, but stood by the organ, pressing the keys as she sung, and occasionally raising one hand to mark the time or gesticulate. Who can tell the thoughts in the hearts of these two, Abby and John — the crowding memories of the past — the scenes of other days when they lived, loved, talked and sung together? Once, under the spell of the eloquent words of a speaker, they bowed their heads together and closed their eyes as if communing, soul to soul, in a language too tender, too absorbing, too sacred for utterance.

In the line of singers stood Ludlow Patton, of New York City, the man for love of whom Abby suspended her great work forty years ago. He is a keen, substantial man of business, and blended his tenor voice with that of his wife and her talented brother, singing with a vim which indicated how completely he had caught the family abandon in song. By the great septuagenarian's side stood his daughter Viola, who has inherited so much of her father's musical talent, and who shared his professional triumphs so long. Her husband, Lewis A. Campbell, was there also, and with them was their vivacious daughter Kate, singing her pure, ringing contralto, and proud in the exceptional honor of being the host's only granddaughter; also her brothers, Cleveland J. and Henry D. There too, was Judson, quiet, but evidently enjoying the celebration as much as any one present, and always ready to come at the signal for the family to sing.

Lucius B. Hutchinson, of New York City, son of Noah, whose tuneful voice and accomplished air indicated that he shared both the family love of music and ability in affairs, was present. With him was his daughter, Mrs. Alice Hutchinson Wallace, also of New York. The tribe of Judson was ably represented by his daughter, Mrs. Kate L. Dearborn, and her four sons, T. Benton H., H. Hale, Jesse Judson, and Edmund S., all of Milford, N. H. There were also H. Appleton Hutchinson,

HENRY D. CAMPBELL   p. 16?

of Mont Vernon, N. H., brother to Lucius; Jacob T. Hutchinson and wife, Marcus Morton Hutchinson and wife, of Boston, and Mrs. Kate Hutchinson Elms, with her husband, Joseph D. Elms, and son, Paul Hutchinson Elms, of Dorchester, all representing the tribe of Andrew. The tribes of Noah, Andrew, Judson and John were there, and it was a touching as well as pleasing sight to see how quickly, when John or Abby pressed the keys of the organ, this remarkable group of gifted singers would gather.

And it was a remarkable gathering which listened, also. First, because of his great age and noble work, should be mentioned Theodore D. Weld, of Hyde Park, the co-worker of all the great Abolitionists, in personal appearance the prototype of Bryant, now eighty-seven years old. With him was his daughter-in-law, Anna H. Weld, and her son Louis. Rev. Alfred P. Putnam, D. D., of Concord, the historical writer, tall, scholarly and courtly, was there; also Rev. Jesse H. Jones, of Abington, the noted reformer; Abby Morton Diaz, the champion of woman suffrage, of nationalism and when it was the issue, of anti-slavery; Charles P. Birney, nephew of James G. Birney; Nathan E. Chase, of Boston, another well-known nationalist; William D. Thompson, brother of the lamented Edwin Thompson, apostle of temperance; George A. Thomas, of Portland, a noted basso of former days, now seventy-one years old, with Miss Charlotte J. Thomas; Hon. W. A. Clark, Jr., of Lynn, president of the Suffolk Trust Co., of Boston, with his son Alfred; J. Warren Newhall, formerly an editor of the *Lynn Reporter*, and an appreciative friend of the host; Chas. O. Beede, one of Lynn's most prominent citizens, with Mrs. Beede; Cyrus M. Tracy, poet and historian, of Lynn, and her orator at the celebration of her two hundred and fiftieth anniversary. David J. Lord, cashier of the National Security Bank, Lynn; Wm. G. S. Keene, an enterprising Lynn shoe manufacturer; Councilman W. Henry Hutchinson, with Mrs. Hutchinson; Benj. W. Currier; Quincy A. Towns, President of Belt Line Electric R R; David N. Johnson, Walter B. Allen, George D. Colcord, Samuel S. Ireson, George F. Lord, Jr, George T. Robinson, Dr. Charles Lloyd, George O. Fall, and many other prominent citizens of Lynn, with their families.

Adequate preparation had been made for the large gathering. The sightly piazza had been enclosed, and so transformed into an excellent music room, where through the evening Rhodes's Orchestra furnished appreciated music. George T Robinson, a friend of the host, received the guests, and assisted by Mr. and Mrs. Campbell and daughter did all possible for their comfort. A most bountiful repast was furnished by Bond, of the Winthrop Café.

At four o'clock in the afternoon the guests began to gather, and kept coming at intervals until late in the evening. Mr Hutchinson stood in his cozy parlor, and gave a warm grasp of the hand and a tender greeting to each of the guests upon their arrival He was assisted in receiving by Mrs. Patton. One of the odd occurrences was the occasional inquiry for "Sister Abby" by some one who failed to recognize the charming and youthful singer of long ago in the small, gray-haired and piquant lady with whom he was at that moment conversing.

A register was kept for the autographs of the guests. The most noticeable gift, because from his only living sister, was a gold-lined, sterling silver loving-cup, handsomely chased, bearing the inscription:

> 1821   JANUARY 4.   1891
>
> ### John W. Hutchinson.
>
> A LOVING-CUP
> FROM SISTER ABBY.
>
> ---
>
> FOR AULD LANG SYNE.

Other gifts were a handkerchief-box, decorated with hand-painted violets, given by his granddaughter, Miss Kate Campbell; a basket of beautiful flowers, presented by Etta and Marion, niece and grand-niece, of Orange, N. J.; a photograph album for one hundred cabinet pictures, given by John L. Robinson; a handsome book, entitled "Our New England," presented by Charles O. Beede and wife; a historical sketch of Swampscott, by Waldo Thompson; handkerchiefs with monogram "H" upon each, presented by Mrs. Susie Emerson. Mrs. S. E. Gardner gave him a birthday cake. A basket of flowers came from Mr. and Mrs. W. H. Hutchinson. Frank B. Carpenter, one of the country's best painters, who painted the great picture "Emancipation," partially finished a portrait of the host, but was unable to complete it in time. Many of the remembrances were in the form of letters and poems, which appear elsewhere.

For the first few hours of the reception, the time was mostly taken up with social converse, with songs interspersed informally. Mr. George Thomas rendered several bass solos with great gusto, among them "Simon, the Cellarer" and "Laugh, Boys, Laugh." His command of voice, considering his advanced age, was notable. One of the first songs called for from the family was "The Old Granite State," perhaps the most remarkable production, as a distinctively family song, that was ever written.

Another pleasant episode was the "Greeting Song," sung with much spirit by Judson's four grandsons, sons of Kate Hutchinson Dearborn of Milford, N. H. The mother had added a verse, as follows:

> We have come to-day from Milford,
>   The "Old Granite State" home,
> To celebrate the birthday
>   Of our dear Uncle John!
> May heaven's choicest blessings
>   Ever rest upon his head!
> And with the heavenly manna
>   May he be richly fed.
>
> CHORUS.
> Now God bless you!
> Now God bless you!
> And God keep you
>   In the hollow of His hand.
> May His angels guard you,
> And peace and love attend you
>   Till you join the heavenly band.

At 7.30 Charles E. Mann, editor of the *Lynn Daily Press*, who acted as master of ceremonies, called the company to order, and the more formal exercises began. He first introduced Theodore D. Weld, of Hyde Park, as a veteran of the abolition times, who had intimately known the host.

Mr. Weld spent several minutes in most interesting reminiscent talk, at Mrs. Patton's suggestion detailing some of his experiences as an advocate of abolition. "Some of the experiences I have had in the South," said he, "though long ago, are as plain in my mind as if they happened yesterday. I remember a three months that I spent in Ohio lecturing and talking on the slavery question. There was continually a mob wherever

I spoke, and I always spoke my mind as long as the mob lasted. I would talk, and the mob would howl and make as much noise as possible, but my determination to speak being known they would finally give me an opportunity. In one town I spoke in a court house, and the deputy sheriff who had charge of it told me beforehand that I would have trouble, and while I was talking I heard the tramp, tramp of horses, and finally the court house was surrounded by a mob. Then they began to blow horns and yell and ordered me out. I went out and then began talking in a school-house close by. They followed, keeping up the din, but as had oftentimes happened before, when they found out that I was determined to speak, like a defeated army they laid aside their weapons and meekly listened to what I had to say. I first saw the Hutchinson Family in Newark, New Jersey, in 1843. Then singing was a perfect feast, and a novelty in the campaign. The work that they have done for temperance, woman suffrage and other reforms is incalculable."

The family then gathered about the organ, and led by Sister Abby, sang a verse of "Auld Lang Syne." Mrs. Patton had prepared a surprise for the company, and added these verses:

TO JOHN W. HUTCHINSON ON HIS SEVENTIETH BIRTHDAY

BY MRS. ABBY H. PATTON

Dear brother, we have come to-day,
   To bring you words of cheer;
To join with you to celebrate
   The glad and opening year.
With wit and wisdom, art and song,
   We'll follow into line;
And sing the chorus, loud and clear,
   For auld lang syne.

Just seventy years have rolled away,
  Since first the light of heaven
Beamed in upon and brought the day
  Your life to earth was given;
What though your locks are silver now,
  Your heart is young as then,
The light of youth is on your brow,
  At threescore years and ten.

The loving-cup we'll pass around
  With water, not with wine;
Come, drink with us the cup that cheers,
  For auld lang syne.
Then fill it up again, dear friends,
  With Nature's oldest wine,
And take a cup of kindness yet,
  For auld lang syne.

Farewell, dear brother, ere ye go
  We give a parting hand,
May heaven send its blessings down
  Upon our native land.
From north and south, from east and west,
  May we again combine
To sing the song of brotherhood,
  For auld lang syne.

January 1, 1891.

Brother John was equal to this emergency, and read the following, written for him by his daughter, Mrs. Campbell.

THE ANSWER

"I never before knew how good it is to be seventy years old, and I advise you all to try it."—JAMES FREEMAN CLARKE.

Dear friends, for coming here to-day,
  I thank you from my heart,
Though looking in each kindly face,
  Sweet memory's tear will start;
Yet I'll not yield to sadness,
  For, rejoicing, I can say,
With health and love surrounded,
  I'm seven times ten to-day.

Threescore and ten of years have passed
  Since first I saw the light,
And though this world would call me old,
  I'm keeping youth in sight.
Still I am looking westward,
  And for another dawn,
Yet fancy travels backward
  To the year when I was born

Nine brothers and three sisters
  Had already come to share
The love of my dear mother's heart,
  Which was large enough to care
For me, the child of her riper years,
  And for all the Lord had given,
And for the three that followed me
  She still gave thanks to heaven

Now of all the sixteen children,
  Only two are left to stand
And greet you, friends, both young and old,
  And take you by the hand,
I cannot even yet feel old,
  Although I may be gray,
And can laugh with my grandchildren,
  Though seven times ten to-day

Mrs. Abby Morton Diaz was next introduced to the party. She said that she was an old Abolitionist of the truest blood, and that, said she, is why I am here with you. "The slavery cause was a good one. I am a Plymouth girl, descendant of the Pilgrims and born on the rock. I am therefore glad to greet those from the Old Granite State and High Rock. If I went out lecturing, I should talk on the economy of debate. In the anti-slavery movement, the question was asked: 'Would you have your daughter marry a negro?' That was not the question in that grand movement, which is what I mean by economy of debate. The old anti-slavery girls were always ready to attend a meeting of Abolitionists, and they were always first there and the last to depart. Why, they would put their gold watches in the contribution box and think nothing about it, not regretting their act." Mrs. Diaz continued at length, in a very interesting vein.

Then the family sang "The Old Granite State" again. The good old song could not be sung too often that night.

The next speaker to be introduced was J. Warren Newhall, who had come, notwithstanding his bodily infirmities and the severe storm, to read a poem he had prepared. He prefaced it with the following remarks:

LADIES AND GENTLEMEN:— I deem it a privilege to be numbered among those who have assembled to celebrate the seventieth anniversary of the birth of one of the renowned Hutchinson Family. The "Hutchinson Family"—what a wealth of pleasant memories that name recalls! How the hearts of many of these friends present thrill as retrospection brings to our mental vision the concerts given by that quartet of sweet-voiced brothers and their fair sister Abby in days gone by. What power they had to move us to mirth by their humor, touch us by their pathos, nerve us to effort by their inspiring earnestness and elevate us by their high moral and religious spirit! Theirs has been a grand and glorious mission and nobly have they fulfilled it. They have sung for freedom, they have sung for humanity, they have sung for temperance, they have sung for reform, they have sung for equality, they have sung for loyalty and union, they have sung for all that is pure and noble and true. All through the land and on foreign shores they have been recognized as the minstrels of Freedom and Right. But to-night all that are left of that wonderfully-gifted family are these two. All the rest have passed on before, and we feel they are joining in the songs of the celestial city. When I received the invitation, I sent in response a few lines of congratulation, not thinking I should be able to be one of the company, but our genial host insisted that I should be present and read my contribution, which I will do, feeling, however, that when compared with what you have listened to from the veteran Theodore Weld, and the true friend of progress, Mrs. Abby Morton Diaz, and what is to follow, my simple offering will be but a pebble on the seashore.

   Champion of freedom and humanity,
      Friend of poor, fallen and down-trodden men,
   We give thee joy, that thou hast lived to see
      Th' allotted years of man — threescore and ten

   Full well hast thou fulfilled thy mission grand,
      Whose echoes swell the shores of time along;
   Thy prophecies have sounded through the land,
      Borne on the pinions of impassioned song

   The captive, pining in his prison damp,
      The bondman, groaning, 'neath his galling chains,
   The weary soldier, in his guarded camp,
      Have listened to the soul-inspiring strains

   Thou'st seen Fulfilment's beaming star arise,
      The slaves no more the torturing fetter wear;
   Treason's dark cloud has vanished from our skies,
      And Freedom's flag greets the untainted air

   Last of that band of brothers who have wrought
      With thee such noble work in days of yore,
   What hallowed memories oft are brought
      Of those "passed on" to the shining shore

   Sing on, O minstrel of prophetic soul!
      Sing on, to cheer, to strengthen and redeem,
   Till thou shalt meet, where Heaven's grand anthems roll,
      The God whose "Fatherhood" has been thy theme

Mr. Mann here read the poetic contribution of Joseph Warren Nye, printed elsewhere in this volume, and a little later read the poem of Mrs. Bowles, and also bits of the letters which were received in such great abundance. After the letter of Rev. S. F. Smith was read, his great hymn "America" was sung by the entire company.

A violin solo was rendered at this point by Miss Bertha Lloyd, of Lynn, and a piano solo was performed by Miss Helen M. Cramm, of Haverhill. A fine poem followed, read by its author, David N. Johnson, author of "Sketches of Lynn."

>Brave, cheery friend of seventy years,
>　(For so time's dial tells the tale)
>　Kind hearts like thine keep young and hale,
>They take no counsel of their fears.
>
>For thou hast faith in God and man,
>　Built on this double arch, thy hope
>　Spans the wide world, and in its scope
>Thine eye sees His eternal plan.
>
>Born of a gifted race, thy voice
>　With brothers twain and sister's blent,
>　Was heard across the continent,
>And back the answer came — rejoice.
>
>The hills of the Old Granite State
>　Joined voices with the household choir,
>　And mightier than Orphean lyre,
>Men listened at the Golden Gate.
>
>From pen and tongue the cry was hurled,
>　And lightning couriers bore it on,
>　And lo! the slave's great champion
>Stood forth, the idol of the world!
>
>Beside the noble Garrison
>　Stood one serene, of classic mould,
>　And charm of speech, as Greece of old
>Had set within her Pantheon.

With these, ye sang your simple lays,
  Your theme, the equal rights of all
  One brotherhood of great and small,
And One who marks man's devious ways

Like minstrel band which legends tell,
  Ye sang old Freedom's keynote grand;
  "No slave must tread our native land."
No slave, no slave, the echoes swell

The poet's fire and music's charm,
  Ye summoned from their ancient throne;
  Where'er our eagle flag had flown,
Oppression shook, in dread alarm

And some are with us here to-day
  Who knew the greeting England gave
  When first they crossed the stormy wave,
And heard her gentle poet's lay —

"O band of young apostles, ye
  Who in your glorious youth have come
  To give winged utterance to the dumb
And sound the trump of liberty.

"Sing of the good time coming, when
  Old hate shall die, and passion's reign,
  And all earth's progeny of pain
Be banished the abodes of men

"Thrice welcome to the fatherland —
  One blood, one speech, one hope we own,
  And neither stands or falls alone —
Love gives to both her great command."

Sing, minstrel band, of coming peace,
  When olive wreaths shall crown the throne
  Of kings, and mail-clad warriors own
The spell that bids earth's tumults cease

The vision old the Hebrew saw,
  Whose lips, touched with the sacred fire,
  Foretold the suffering world's desire,
The Master's beatific law

Old England sent her welcome out,
   To hear the band of brothers sing.
   Through lordly halls their echoes ring,
And thousands answer, shout on shout

The miner in his living tomb
   Heard something stir the upper air;
   In thronging marts and gardens fair,
Where robins sing and roses bloom.

The toiling millions caught the strain,
   And bore it over land and sea,
   And millions joined the jubilee —
The slave shall be a man again

And so we gather here to-night
   Around the spot ye cherish most,
   From far and near, your friends, a host,
Give token of some mem'ry bright.

How glow the scenes our eyes behold!
   What visions waken as we gaze!
   The same sun with the ocean plays,
The old Rock gleams with sunset's gold!

The hills still hear the notes sublime,
   That Jesse, bard and minstrel, sung —
   The grand old hymns the ages strung
Like jewels on the brow of time

Long stand the dear old home where played
   The children of thy earlier years,
   Recalling scenes of joy and tears,
Sweet memories tinged with light and shade.

Hail, old-time friend, but not farewell!
   As the swift years shall come and go,
   Borne on by time's resistless flow,
May age serene sweet mem'ries tell.

Though Hampshire's hills no longer hear
   The echoes of the household band,
   One clasp of that dear sister's hand
Shall bring to Faith's discerning eye

> Old voices from the shoreless sea,
>   And echoes from th' eternal hills,
>   A chorus that forever fills
> The spaces of eternity.
>
> As sunset gilds the "Cottage Tower"
>   And paints with gold the eastern sky,
>   Sure pledge the morrow shall not die,
> May Faith illume life's evening hour.
>
> As trailing clouds at eventide
>   The glory of to-morrow tell,
>   So may'st thou hear life's evening bell
> Call thee to an immortal clime.

Next to speak was Cyrus M. Tracy, his remarks being as follows:

LADIES AND GENTLEMEN: — When, within the last hour, it was mentioned to me that I might be asked to say something at this time, I could see no reason at all for such a request. Nor, indeed, for that matter, any reason, aside from common friendship, why I should be here at all. Neither is this doubt made any less, as I have looked on the faces, and heard the names, of the eminent company, present and absent, who are concerned, nearly or remotely, in the reunion of this evening — a company, I venture to say, such as could be nowhere assembled, save in the parlors of a Hutchinson.

But the reason for my presence has gradually taken shape, as I have listened to what has been said here in your hearing. For I, too, though not an old man, am yet an old Abolitionist. I was alive and attentive in that day. I knew enough of the early struggles of that divine enterprise. I well remember the day when came to me in the public journals, the account of that disgraceful mob "of men of property and standing" in

Boston, who could, forsooth, with no supposed loss of honor, violate the privacy of a women's prayer meeting in a retired chamber, break up its exercises, and scatter its members like frightened sheep. I read it, ten-year-old boy that I was, and I said to myself: "There is a vile outrage, no matter who says no!" For such it was, a hideous breach of individual liberty, of the freedom that no man should dare infringe, except so far as may be actually needed for the protection of society.

This does not, indeed, touch personally the Hutchinson family, yet I knew them — some of them, long before they knew me, and before they knew much, practically, of abolition. I recall a certain time when I saw the words "Family Concert" on a hand-bill about town, and read that the Hutchinson Family would sing at the old "Sagamore Hall." It was the same old hall that stood near the depot — poor old building, it burned down three times, and the last time finished it — but it was a popular place then, and I went there to hear the Hutchinsons' concert. Before that I only knew Jesse, and then only as a business man. He had some valuable inventions in stoves that he manufactured — air-tight stoves, they were called — you put your wooden logs onto the fire, and shut them up tight, and they keep you warm a long time. But now the musical side of the family was to come out, so I went to hear what that was. Where I got the dimes to go with I don't remember, but that was settled long ago. I cannot say how many performers there were, but there were Jesse, Judson, John, Asa and Joshua, and enough more to fill the platform as full as the house, and that was so full that the only place I could get was close beside a great, red-hot salamander stove. There I stayed and sweltered all the evening, well pleased to hear them ring out the sterling old glees, madrigals and songs that were then in use; and when I came away, it was with full conviction that there was as much in the heart of a Hutchinson to warm a man on the inside, as there was in his stove to warm the outside. This was just before they went into systematic singing for anti-slavery, and of their subsequent work you do not need me to tell you anything. But pardon me, my friends, if at this point there comes over me the recollection of another zealous worker for the cause of abolition — my own brother, next older than myself. He, too, gave his efforts to the grand enterprise from the earliest; indeed, perhaps I learned its first lessons from his lips. He toiled and wrought bravely while he could, but when his health failed and he could do no more, he went to Europe to recruit. Coming home, he said to me, "There are more workers in the field of anti-slavery than every one is aware. The Hutchinson Family are over there." "Yes," I said, "I know they are. Are they doing much?" "Not a doubt of it," he said. "They sing in those great halls in England, night after night, and the poor, half-fed, begrimed workmen and toilers from the mills and factories crowd the audience, and stand, dirty and ragged, charmed with their melodies till the tears stream down through the grime of their faces, and their sobs are only overcome by their applause. Certainly, the spirit of their songs is going down into the very hearts of the English people." Poor fellow, he did not live to see the victory of his great national faith; he died before the last conflict, but in his will it was found written: "I direct that my funeral rites shall only be attended by some minister that has *never* apologized for slavery." Such a one was found, and so it was done accordingly.

I feel that you will indeed excuse the gush of these memories, largely personal though they are. I feel also that you will see their close relation with the joyful cheer of this occasion. For the memories of that wonderful campaign against oppression arise most vividly to those who passed through it; and such, most eminently, is our friend and host of this evening. To him, in a peculiar sense, it belongs to say with Æneas, in his story of the Siege of Troy:

> "Quæque ipse miserrima vidi,
> Et quorum magna pars fui."

["All of those sorrowful things I saw, and a great part of them I was."]

Hence, I recognize, as you all do, the fitness of every congratulation that we pay to this, our worthy entertainer. Well deserving is he — in the ripeness of his years, a faithful co-worker in the grand enterprise of American freedom — well deserving of all the happiness that is left him, or can be brought him by those who share the good he helped to work out; and standing no nearer than I do, I yet bespeak for him every pleasant fortune, and all comfort from sources human or divine.

E. K. Emerson, chairman of the Prohibitory City Committee, of Lynn, was introduced as representing one of the reforms which the family advocated, and one for which he announced himself ready to stand, through thick and thin. Walter B. Allen, a representative of the Friends' Society, so numerous in Lynn, also added words of congratulation.

Hon. W. A. Clark, Jr., said: — "It is certainly a very great pleasure to be present on an occasion like this, and pay my respects to one whose name and fame extends over the entire land. It is also a matter of gratification to me to have with me my son, so that when he grows up and fills the responsibilities of life, he may look back and find encouragement and strength from having known men whose lives were devoted unselfishly to a great cause. It was his fortune, too, to be with me on an occasion similar to this, to join with others observing the birthday of the poet Whittier, at Oak Knoll, who also was a co-worker with these distinguished men and women in the anti-slavery cause." [At this point, Mrs. Campbell, with that consummate eye to effect which always distinguished every member of the Hutchinson Family, gently pushed Mr. Clark's son Alfred to a position beside his father, while Brother John came up and laid his hand gently and affectionately on the lad's shoulder.] Mr. Clark referred felicitously to the pleasure of meeting one so perennially young as their honored host, and to the gratification it must give his family as well as all present.

The next speaker was Captain George T. Newhall, editor of the *Lynn Transcript*, who was introduced to speak for the press. His remarks follow.

MR. MASTER OF CEREMONIES: — We are assembled to hail our venerable fellow-citizen upon this event, the seventieth anniversary of his birthday. He and the family, of which I understand he is one of the two survivors, is of a long-time, artistic, unique and honorable fame — a fame with which the civilization of both continents is familiar. But, pleased as we are with that fame which links the name of Lynn with the Hutchinson family, and rejoicing with them, and especially with our host, that the cause to which in their chosen way they were untiringly devoted and faithful — that of anti-slavery — no more demands their aid, the peculiar satisfaction of this occasion is that we are assembled under his hospitable roof, which shelters us from this winter storm, to congratulate our fellow-citizen and each other upon "the day we celebrate," and to testify our unanimous good-will towards one whose ideal of humanity we warmly acknowledge and appreciate.

Later in the evening a ringing speech was made by Lucius B. Hutchinson, of New York, who took occasion to remark that he was nearer his birthday than his uncle, for while the latter reached his seventieth birthday the day before, Sunday, he, the speaker, would be fifty-two at midnight, which was fast approaching.

All notable events must have their end. The hour set for the close of the reception was past, when the band of noble singers gathered for a last song at the organ. It was "Old High Rock."

Then, hand-in-hand, the singers passed through the company, singing their parting song. There were other features, music by the orchestra and parting congratulations, but nothing could be more fitting, as a close to the story of that beautiful occasion, than this tender, pathetic, but hope-inspiring song, tearfully sung by that magnetic and patriotic family:

> Good-bye brothers, good-bye sisters,
>   If we don't see you more.
> May God bless you, may God bless you,
>   If we don't see you more.
>
> We part in the body, we meet in the spirit,
>   If we don't see you more
> We hope to meet in Heaven, in the blessed Kingdom,
>   If we don't see you more.
>
> Good-bye brothers, good-bye sisters,
>   If we don't see you more
> May God bless you, may God bless you,
>   Till we meet on the Heavenly shore.

For the next few days after the birthday gathering my mail was full of papers containing accounts of the affair and friendly notices, which indicated that they did not coincide with the views of the unreconstructed publication which a couple of decades before had said most of the family were dead, and I ought to die too.

A few days after the affair, I began to dictate new matter for my book, but soon discovered to my dismay that quite a large amount of the matter already prepared was missing. It has never been found, and the consequence of the loss was that I was compelled to reproduce hundreds of pages. A considerable portion of the year was spent in this pleasurable work. In January I sung two days at the woman-suffrage convention in Tremont Temple with Viola. On February 13th I sung for the Nationalists at Weymouth, E. S. Huntington accompanying me and speaking. In April I went several times to Boston to hear Annie Besant discourse upon Theosophy. I did not become very enthusiastic over the doctrine. In May, my good friend Joseph Warren Nye, the Lynn poet, with his wife, celebrated their golden wedding. I attended and sung an original song. Abby spent quite a portion of July in Lynn, and it is needless to say those were happy days for me. As the summer wore on, I visited Portland, Sebago Lake, Fabyan's, and finally spent a week at Bar Harbor, fully enjoying the sights at that great summer resort, enhanced as they were by the presence in the harbor of a squadron of the navy. In August occurred at Hartford the golden wedding of John and Isabella (Beecher) Hooker. It was one of the pleasantest events of that nature I ever attended.

In October I had a short visit from my old advance agent, E. E. Johnson, of Painesville, Ohio, in which we had a good time talking over old times. The convention of the World's Woman's Christian Temperance Union occurred in Tremont Temple, Boston, soon after. Lady Henry Somerset came over from England, and all the notable workers in this country were present. I attended each day's sessions. I sung "Clear the way" to them. They cheered me. The woman suffragists had a big fair in Boston in December, and I attended that. In January, 1892, James Warren Newhall, one of the poets who were with me on my birthday anniversary the year before, died, and on the 25th I attended his funeral. Mr. Newhall possessed one of the sweetest souls with which I have ever held communion, in a poor, crippled body which had been a burden to him for a lifetime. It was not possible to break his spirit, however, and he went through life singing and happy. A few days before his death I called at his home. He was suffering with typhoid fever. A brother lay dead from the same disease, and in the same house a sister, soon to be left alone in the world, was suffering from it also. I sung "What shall be my angel name?" to him. When I closed, he said, in a voice trembling with weakness, "Won't you go and sing that to Lyddy?" But a few months before, Cyrus Mason Tracy, who spoke so felicitously at my anniversary, had "crossed the great divide," and with a sad heart I now bade farewell to another of these choice spirits, happily not knowing how soon I must part with one far dearer than them all.

On Sunday, the 31st of January, Rev. A. A. Miner, D. D., spoke on the public school question at Odd Fellows' Hall in Lynn. I sung "The Prophet." In the course of his remarks, Dr. Miner spoke of the difficulty he experienced in keeping the hair on his partially bald head, at the same time looking whimsically at me. In turn I warned him against the sin of covetousness, said fair exchange was no robbery, and expressed my entire willingness to swap a part of my hair for some of the doctor's brains. This brought down the house. On February 6th Hon. Charles Carleton Coffin, the famous war correspondent, called on me, and I gave him the story of our experience in the camps for his "Life of Lincoln," in preparation.

On March 7th my old anti-slavery friend, John Mills, died at his home in Milford. I attended his funeral a few days later. Parker Pillsbury, with whom Mills was a co-laborer in the days of the New Hampshire Antislavery Society — those days when Milford was alive to the great wrong of slavery as few Granite State towns were — spoke at the service, as did J. W. Pillsbury, Hon. Charles H. Burns, his son-in-law, and others. I sung and spoke.

During this year I built Belleview Cottage, between the Stone and Daisy cottages. In June I went to Minnesota. The Republican National Convention was to occur at Minneapolis, and I thought it a good opportunity to see how such gatherings were conducted, especially as I had a good deal of business to see to in Hutchinson. On June 2d I went to Worcester, where the Prohibitory State Convention was in session, as a delegate. I sung them "Ridden by the Rum Power," and was vociferously cheered. At one o'clock in the afternoon I left them and took the train for New York. I spent the night with Sister Abby, and was at breakfast with her the next morning when Ludlow read from his paper that the New York delegation to the Minneapolis convention would leave the Grand Central Depot at 10.30. "I'm going with them," I remarked. "I'll go and see you off," said Abby. So we went to the train together. I had no difficulty in finding friends among the delegates, and Abby introduced me to several whom I had not previously known, a bright New Yorker named Bryant being with them. There was no difficulty in securing a passage with them, and we had a grand time on the journey. My good friends, to whom Abby explained that I was a "Republican Prohibitionist," spent a considerable amount of time trying to convince me that I ought to vote the ticket of the "Grand Old Party." The New York *Commercial Advertiser* in noting the departure of the delegates' train, said: "The quaintest character of them all was John W. Hutchinson. His long gray hair and kindly face made him a conspicuous character. He is a great Harrison man, is seventy years of age, and is known as the 'convention singer.'" The delegates were largely for Blaine. I presume the reporter may have referred to Old Tippecanoe when he said I was a "Harrison man." It was a two days' trip to Minneapolis, even by special train. During the convention I slept each night in my berth in the sleeper. It was an exciting time indeed, Blaine men and Harrison men hurrahing all day. I was kept supplied with tickets by New York, Minnesota and Massachusetts delegates. O. D. Hutchinson, Asa's son, was at the convention, and I spent much of the time with him. At last Harrison was renominated, and after witnessing this ceremony I took the train for Hutchinson. Had a good time with my nephews and grand-nephews, though the thermometer stood at 98° some of the time. After a few days spent here, I started on my return, taking a look at the buildings of the coming World's Fair in Chicago, as I passed through the city. I arrived home June 26th. Within a week I had replaced the flagstaff on the rock, which had been injured, by mother

On Wednesday, August 3d, the statue of Hon. John Parker Hale, presented to the State of New Hampshire by his son-in-law, Senator William E. Chandler, was unveiled at Concord. The statue stands in the State-house yard, and the exercises occurred from a stand at its right. I was invited to participate, and it was an unmitigated pleasure to thus do honor to the memory of our old friend. To my gratification, Sister Abby and Ludlow surprised me by being present, and Frederick Douglass was also there. At one point in the exercises I sang the "Old Granite State," Abby, Ludlow and Douglass joining me. This was the first time in our long acquaintance that he had ever sung with me in public. The words to which we sung the song were from a draft in the handwriting of Hon. Mason W. Tappan, dated Bradford, N. H., September 13, 1845, and were as follows:

"WELCOME TO HON. JOHN P. HALE

"*Tune*, 'Old Granite State,' as sung by the Hutchinsons.

"From each mountain top and valley,
And from every street and alley,
Let the friends of freedom rally,
　　In the Old Granite State —
To sustain the friend of freedom,
To sustain the friend of freedom,
　　In his conflict for the right.

"Come and let us swell the chorus
While victory hovers o'er us —
Tyrants all shall quail before us,
　　In the Old Granite State
It shall ne'er be said by any
It shall ne'er be said by any,
　　That New Hampshire's sons are slaves!

"John Parker Hale of Dover,
John Parker Hale of Dover,
　　In the Old Granite State,

On the right of petition,
On the right of petition,
Like a true-hearted freeman,
　　Gave his vote against the 'Gag!'

"And now when others falter,
Burn strange fire on Freedom's altar,
Tamely creep, or meanly falter,
　　In the Old Granite State,
Still on justice firmly planted,
Still on justice firmly planted,
He will face the storm undaunted
　　In the Old Granite State."

But before this song was sung, I had sung my own tribute to the memory of Hale, and I also gave reminiscences of the distinguished statesman. The song composed for the occasion by Walter Kittredge and myself, was as follows:—

O son of New Hampshire, thy fame cannot fade,
In the hearts of our people thine image inlaid,
This statue in grandeur now points to the sky,
A lesson is teaching to each passer-by —
A lesson to battle with life day by day,
And courage to conquer its foes by the way.

We must stand like our granite, and moving, be strong;
Let our glory live ever in story and song.

In the hearts of our nation, as imbedded in gold,
Our Rogers and Hale, and hundreds untold
Of brave hearts who stood for justice and right,—
And in every reform its battle we'll fight
New Hampshire stands foremost and mighty in fame,
She has left a fair record and glorious name.

Gone are slavery's days, the oppressed ones are free,
Forever to rest under liberty's tree
The brave men who stood forth in martial array
Are falling, like leaves they are passing away.

But they stood like our granite, and in battle were strong,
Let their glory live ever in story and song.

> He whose statue to-day in honor we raise
> Bared his breast to the tempest in Freedom's dark days,
> And while through the whole world truth and justice prevail
> Shall be loved and be honored the memory of Hale
>
> Then be true to our banner and liberty strong,
> That our glory live ever in story and song

I also sang several verses composed for the event by that veteran free-soiler, George W. Putnam. The speaking on this occasion was as fine as is often heard — Rev. Dr. Alonzo H. Quint, Hon. George A. Ramsdell, Senator Chandler, Governor Tuttle, Colonel Daniel Hall, the orator of the day, Hon. Galusha A. Grow, Hon. George S. Boutwell, Frederick Douglass, and others. Douglass caused great merriment by saying he supposed he was only present to lend color to the occasion, and though entirely unprepared, made one of the great speeches of the day.

In August I attended the Purgatory picnic at Mont Vernon, the two hundred and fiftieth anniversary celebration at Gloucester, and visited Portland and vicinity.

On September 7, John G. Whittier died, at the home of his friend, Sarah Abby Gove, Hampton Falls, N. H. At once I wrote to Abby, and on Saturday, the 10th, with Ludlow, we attended his funeral at his old home in Amesbury. The day was pleasant, and in order to accommodate the large number who attended, the simple ceremonies of the Friends' Society were held in the garden of the estate, being conducted by William O. Newhall, of Lynn, a minister of the society. Of course the Friends do not usually have singing in their exercises, but it seemed to be the general desire that the Hutchinsons, old friends as they were of the Quaker poet, should sing, and we for our part deemed it a privilege beyond estimation. We sang "Lay Him

Low," and "We are almost home," songs that I had sung at the memorial of Phillips, the words of which were partly composed by Abby and myself. Ludlow sang on the choruses. It was the last appearance of Abby in public, and if I were to have chosen, I could not possibly have selected a more fitting place or song in which our voices should blend for the last time. We did not realize the deep significance of those words.

"We are almost home, to join the angel band"

We thought only of that brave, loving, gentle, pure and gifted singer lying cold in death. But we sang, as we always tried to sing, with feeling, harmony and deep meaning. There were many references to the incident, some of which I quote.

S. T. Pickard, a family connection of Whittier, and his executor, wrote the story in his paper, the *Portland Transcript*, as follows:

"It was a happy thought of Mr F J Garrison, son of Mr. Whittier's old friend, William Lloyd Garrison, to hold the funeral services of the poet in the garden at Amesbury which the windows of his study and chamber overlook. Seats were arranged around a myrtle-carpeted plat under the 'Garden room' windows, where a luxuriant hydrangea bush, heavy with richly tinted blossoms held a central place. There were seats for several hundreds under the fruit trees on three sides of this square, and standing room for thousands besides. Boys clambered into the branches of the trees, and their bare feet hanging over the heads of the assembled multitude could not fail to suggest that it was the author of the 'Barefoot Boy,' to whose memory they were paying tribute

"The casket was placed in the little parlor, the one room in the house that has remained unchanged during the entire occupancy of the Whittier family. The portraits of the poet's mother and sister Elizabeth look down with tender benignancy from the walls. Here also is a Longfellow portrait, and one painted for Whittier in his early manhood The Rogers group, presenting Garrison, Beecher and Whittier, with a slave girl, are on a stand in the corner. Here the loved and venerated face that was soon to be hidden forever from view, wearing the expression of heavenly peace that deeply impressed all who looked upon it, was upturned to the tearful gaze of neighbors and friends, for several hours preceding the services.

"The venerable William O. Newhall, of Lynn, who was for many years at the head of the New England Yearly Meeting of Friends, took charge of the services and made a few brief remarks in the way of eulogy and exhortation. He was followed by Asa C. Tuttle of Dover and Dr. Allen H. Thomas of Baltimore. The poem 'At Last' was recited by the poet's dearly loved cousin, Gertrude Whittier Cartland, of Newburyport. Mrs. James H. Chase, of Providence, recited the poem, 'The Eternal Goodness.' Judge Des Brisay, of Bridgewater, Nova Scotia, spoke briefly, and was followed by Rev. Dr. D. T. Fiske, of Newburyport, and Mrs. Caroline H. Dall, of Gloucester. The last speaker was the banker-poet, Edmund Clarence Stedman, of New York, whose tribute was a gem of oratory, uttered with deep feeling.

"As a fitting conclusion of the impressive ceremony there arose the sweet voices of the Hutchinsons, which always had a charm for Whittier. The only surviving members of the original quartet were present, John W. Hutchinson, of Lynn, and Abby Hutchinson Patton, of New York. Fifty years ago their voices thrilled the hearts of the North, as they sang the stirring lyrics of reform. They set Whittier's stirring verse to music and gave it wings. During the war John sang it in the camps of the Union army, and when military martinets would stop him, Lincoln overruled them and allowed Whittier's voice to be heard. Now they came with heads silvered by age, but with voices still full of the old melody, to sing at the grave of their friend. They were assisted by Mr. Ludlow Patton, who has the voice and feeling of the family with which he is allied. They sang 'Close his eyes, his work is done.'

"Mr. Whittier died at the early dawn of a lovely September day; it was at the close of a day equally perfect that his casket was lowered to a bed of roses in a grave lined with ferns and golden-rod."

Another paper said:

"Among the interesting and touching features of Whittier's funeral was the singing by Mr. John W. Hutchinson and his sister, Mrs. Abby Patton. In that great assemblage of earnest representative men and women there were many who could recall the days in the old anti-slavery conflict, when the Hutchinson family helped the cause along with their stirring music; and when the clear notes of John and Abby, all now left of sixteen brothers and sisters, sounded on the still air of the delightful autumnal day, it was easy to see how hearts all about were stirred with tenderest emotion. That scene will never be forgotten by those who listened, for the music seemed to come from the upper air, and the great audience was spell-bound. Those strains will be reproduced by the phonograph of the soul of those who heard it while life shall last, and rival the sweetest music that shall greet the ear in the world beyond. It was a fitting and beautiful tribute to the memory of the noble, departed poet."

A week after the Whittier funeral I went to Washington in company with Walter Kittredge, to attend the national encampment of the Grand Army. Kittredge had his song, "Tenting To-night," in a handsomely bound gift-book edition. We sang it together on several occasions. Many copies of the song were sold. It was well into October when we returned. The political campaign was on, and Mrs. Helen M. Gougar and Rev. Sam Small were doing valiant work for the Prohibitionists of the Bay State. I fell into line, attended rallies in Faneuil Hall and Tremont Temple in Boston, in Lynn and elsewhere, singing for temperance reform as opportunity offered. Mrs. Gougar was my guest at High Rock when she came to Lynn to speak.

During the latter part of October Abby and Ludlow came from New York to Boston, making their headquarters at the United States Hotel. On October 30th they came to High Rock, Abby's last visit. "Abby will not stay long in this world," my diary says. I little realized, however, how short the time was. On Wednesday, November 2d, I dined with them at their hotel, and before I left we sang our dear old English farewell:

"Come let us part with lightsome heart,
  Nor breath one chiding sigh,
To think that wing of rainbow plume
  So soon should learn to fly.

"Then why not we as merry, merry be
  Though the song be the last?
Believing other days will come

It was our last song, though we did not know it. On the 20th, word came to me that Abby had been stricken with paralysis. On the following day I left for New York, and as soon as I arrived, was admitted to her bedside. The poor tongue could not articulate, but she smiled upon me in recognition. Two days later, on Thanksgiving Day, she died. Asa had died on Thanksgiving Day, just six years before. On Saturday, November 26th, funeral services were held at the house of her nephew, Lucius B. Hutchinson, on West 57th Street, New York City. Her nephew by marriage, Rev. Cornelius Patton, conducted the ceremonies. Abby's friend, Mrs. Anderson, sang two selections, and at Abby's request a year or two previous, I made a few remarks and sang three songs, "The Lord is my Shepherd," "No Tear in Heaven," and "We are almost Home." When she wrote me, I responded that she would be more likely to sing at my funeral, but if I survived her, I would surely sing and speak. On the 29th, the body having been taken to Milford, N. H., final services were held there, in the Unitarian church. Rev. Messrs. Rich and Pendleton were in charge, and again I spoke and sang. There was a large attendance of the remnants of the once happy family, but of her father's family I was alone. A sense of loneliness came over me that I hope few of my readers will ever experience.

Over the grave we sang again

> "For O, we stand on Jordan's strand,
> Our friends are passing over."

I stayed that night with Kate Hutchinson Burney, Judson's daughter, returning to Lynn on the following day. In two days I received another summons. Abel

Fordyce Hutchinson, my old neighbor and friend of boyhood days, died in Waltham. He was a brother to Jerusha, Judson's wife. His funeral occurred at Milford the following Monday, at the house of his daughter, Mrs. Wallace. Again I sang, "No Tear in Heaven," and spoke to the assembly of my hope of a heavenly meeting. As I rode through the cemetery, I saw the grave of Sister Abby, covered with green hemlock boughs, and freshly came to me my overwhelming sense of loss, a sorrow that has returned with every thought of her in the months that have passed. The joyous early days, the charming experiences of our concert beginnings, the months spent in Europe, the stirring scenes of anti-slavery days, the hundreds of happy interviews scattered over the years since her marriage, when we met at the old homestead, in New York, at Orange, N. J., on High Rock, in Florida, California or Washington — all of these come back and are often reviewed in memory when I think of the dearest, most gifted, most helpful sister it is often an unworthy man's good fortune to have. But truly, my loss is her gain, and the gain of her brothers and sisters who have gone before. And I shall soon meet her "over there."

In the middle of December, within a week of each other, two memorial services were held for John G. Whittier. The first was in Amesbury, and I made a few remarks and sung an original song by Joseph W. Nye, of Lynn, a native of Salisbury Point, and a life-long friend of the poet. On the 21st, Haverhill held her memorial in the city hall. Elaborate preparations had been made, and a large number of invitations had been sent out. Hon. Thomas E. Burnham, mayor of the city, presided. The exercises included a fine original poem by Will M. Carleton and an eloquent eulogy by

Edwin D. Mead, editor of the *New England Magazine*. At the close of the eulogy I was introduced, and sung "The Furnace Blast." The memorial volume published by the city council, speaks of the incident as follows:

"After the oration the Mayor said: 'Before the "Auld Lang Syne" shall be sung that will close these exercises, let us pause that we may ask a question.

"'Who does not remember the trying days when slavery had fastened its fangs upon this free country, and the instrumentalities that contributed to the overthrow of the monster evil? Foremost in this work with voice and pen was Whittier. But let us not forget his co-laborers and personal friends, some of whom lend their presence here to-day, and when we welcome the venerable John W. Hutchinson, the last survivor of that matchless family whose patriotic songs did so much to hasten the glorious cause, we welcome them one and all. And for them he will briefly respond in song.'

"When Mr. Hutchinson rose to respond, the scene was touching in the extreme. A man he was on whom the hand of time had been laid, leaving its imprint in the snow-white locks that hung about his shoulders and the patriarchal beard that lay upon his breast. More than three-score and ten years had passed over his head; sisters and brothers, old friends and associates, all had sung their last songs, and he, old and alone, stood there. His heavy brows still held their dark, strong shade, as if to add lustre to the keen, sharp eyes that, brightened by the occasion, flashed with the old-time fire; his voice, weak with age, yet clear and sweet, fell upon his hearers as an echo from another age, a legacy handed down from a crisis when right was struggling close-matched against wrong.

"He had come here to tune once more his lyre in honor of the dear friend of his youth.

"After a few feeling remarks, in clear and melodious tones, he sung with wonderful effect, 'Ein feste burg ist unser Gott.'"

That evening I was a guest of the Haverhill Board of Trade, and sung "One Hundred Years Hence," by request. Thus the sad year ended, and I commenced on a new and in many respects happier one, 1893. It was less marked by losses of loved friends, and was also notable as the year of the World's Fair, which I enjoyed to the full.

On the second day of January, Hattie Dow, daughter of Brother Zephaniah, whose home was in Chicago, visited me at High Rock. On the 16th I attended the funeral of General Butler, at Lowell. On the 26th I went to the funeral of Bishop Phillips Brooks, in Boston. On the 9th of February there was a great camp-fire of the Grand Army at Faneuil Hall, in Boston. I made a five-minute speech, and sung "The Furnace Blast." On February 28th I gave a lecture and concert at Spencer, Mass. I gave the entertainment alone, singing a miscellaneous programme. I was somewhat disappointed not to have the Rev. Samuel May, of Leicester, my old anti-slavery co-laborer, present to preside. In his unavoidable absence, Rev. E. Stuart Best, pastor of the church in which the concert was given, presided.

Sitting by the open fire on the 5th of March, its genial warmth so filled me with satisfaction that I dropped into verse, as follows:

> My housekeeper has built a fire,
> Just to meet my fond desire;
> Such service crowns my waning life —
> Almost equal to a wife.
> The warmth of heart and burning wood
> Beats high and flashes for my good.
> My thoughts revert to boyhood days,
> We grouped around the cheerful blaze,
> And friendship glowed for one another
> Mingled with love for father and mother.

On March 10th I went to Lancaster, twenty-five miles north of the White Mountains, in New Hampshire, and gave a concert in the Congregational Church. I stopped several days with Mrs. Louisa Dow Benton, daughter of Neal Dow, in that place, and received many kind attentions which I recall with gratitude. On one day we rode in a sleigh across the Connecticut River and over the neighboring hills. The winter view of the White Mountains from this point was magnificent. Mrs. Benton had sent for me the previous autumn, but the concert was postponed owing to the accidental death of her husband, he having been the victim of a runaway accident.

On the 17th of April George M. Hutchinson was killed by the cars at Charlemont. He was the son of my brother Caleb. As the report first came to the papers, I was the victim, but it was soon corrected.

April 26th was a notable day. The Danvers Historical Society held a commemorative meeting, in the honor of old anti-slavery days, in the town hall. Of all the reunions of the Abolitionists in late years, this was the most interesting. The town was the birthplace and home of my ancestors; it had its full share of the heroes of anti-slavery days; it had as president of its historical society Rev. A. P. Putnam, a man of just the cast of mind to place the emphasis on every salient point made by the notable group of men and women who addressed the meeting. He had the tact to know just who to invite to speak, and just where to put him in. The proceedings of the meeting were published in an elaborate volume, of great historical value to every friend of the cause of the slave. Dr. Putnam arranged with a photographer to take views of the group on the stage and also of the audience. Among those present were Winthrop Andrews, Rev. Peter Randolph, Rev. D. S. Whitney, George T. Downing, Abner S. Mead, John M. Lennox, Rev. Samuel May, Hon. Parker Pillsbury, William Alley, Rev. Geo. W. Porter, D.D., Mrs. Abby Morton Diaz, Cornelius Wellington, J. M. W. Yerrinton (the former publisher of the *Liberator*), David Mead, Hon. M. M. Fisher, George W. Putnam, Rev.

William H. Fish, Lewis Ford, Miss Sarah E. Hunt, Mrs. Lucy Stone, William Lloyd Garrison, Jr., Rev. Aaron Porter, George B. Bartlett, Henry B. Blackwell, Miss Sarah H. Southwick, Mrs. Kate Tannatt Woods and others. The proceedings lasted from one to half-past six o'clock, and then speakers who were prepared had to be omitted from the programme. My daughter Viola and granddaughter Kate were with me and joined in singing the old emancipation melodies. In fact, my daughter, though still a young woman, was one of the veterans, for this history shows that for several years before the war she was singing these songs of freedom with me.

The proceedings opened with prayer by Rev. William H. Fish. President Putnam then said he had requested the Hutchinsons to repeat some of the very words and music that so thrilled the old anti-slavery meetings for so many years, and in so many places at home and abroad, but that first I would sing a song I had especially prepared for the occasion, adapted to a tune of my own. He hoped I would preface it with a few reminiscences. To quote the report:

"Mr. Hutchinson then came forward and made the following remarks, addressed particularly to his former associates, after which he sung 'Few, Faithful and True,' accompanied in the chorus by his daughter, Mrs. Viola Hutchinson Campbell, and his granddaughter, Miss Kate Campbell. He said

"'DEAR FRIENDS: This is an impressive occasion and a momentous review. We bid you all a hearty welcome. To the few veterans whose lives have dwindled to so short a span, let me say, we congratulate you that one more opportunity is offered that will yield sacred remembrance of joys we have tasted and of true friendships we have experienced throughout the many years during which we labored in the vineyard of good-will to all mankind.

"'Your joys are full and our hearts are made glad this day, even though it should chance to be the last. We meet here upon ground sacred to the memory of our ancestors, who, two hundred and fifty

KATE HUTCHINSON CAMPBELL — (p. 200)

years ago, settled and cultivated this soil, deriving title from the aborigines, who had so recently vacated their corn fields and hunting grounds. Here seven generations bearing the name of Hutchinson, have followed in due succession. From this place heroes of that and many another family went forth to the defence of liberty and were among the bravest at the battles of Lexington and Bunker Hill and in the struggles of the Revolution. We, who have lived since that day of sharp conflicts with the foes of freedom, have rejoiced to hear again the sound of emancipation. And now, in our old age, we assemble with our countrymen here and commemorate the events that established the fact that the nation could live with chattel slavery entirely eliminated, and right made triumphant.

"'Familiar as household words shall be the names of Garrison, Rogers, Thompson, Phillips, Douglass, Weld, Quincy, Jackson, Burleigh, Sumner, Chase, Wilson, Birney, Brown, Foster, Kelley, May, Pillsbury, Putnam, Mott, Purvis, Chapman, McKim, Whittier, Abraham Lincoln and Lucy Stone with the Tribe of Jesse and full many others.

"'The scenes and occurrences of anti-slavery days shall, in our social gatherings, be ever remembered. I cannot express, as I would, the sentiments I feel at such a gathering as this. The associations of half a century of experience mingle with these passing hours and fill me with delight, which I can only try to voice in song.'

"Mr. Hutchinson's spirited verses were sung with wonderful effect, and those who were present and who had heard him forty or fifty years before were kindled by him with the same enthusiasm as then and discovered no loss of his musical genius and electrifying power."

The original song was as follows:

> Hail, all hail! ye brave and true!
> Joyful tidings we bring to you
> Voices angelic we hear above
> Sweetly singing in strains of love
> Come, ye faithful ones, tried and true,
> Heaven is waiting for such as you,
> Your work on earth is faithfully done,
> Come up higher, your crown is won
>
> The combat fierce, the battle long,
> You bravely strove against the wrong
> A guilty nation for woe or weal
> Turned a deaf ear to your appeal
> Upon your warnings the church did frown,
> While cowardly mobs would put you down,

But true to God and human might
You firmly contended for the right

Those braves were fitted for the hour
No threats of vengeance made them cower;
They pitied the sorrows of the oppressed,
And said such wrongs should be redressed.
"Deal gently with the erring crowd,"
Cried doughface Yankees, long and loud.
"No union with slave-holding now,"
Dear Garrison spoke the righteous vow

The battered front of Sumter's wall
Crumbled before the rebel ball
The dogs of war were loosed at last
Spreading o'er all their withering blast —
O'er North and South. It seemed their fate
To wreck and strand our Ship of State
While yet the slave his fetters bore,
The white man bathed in brother's gore

"Let my people go" we sang,
Through loyal hearts the echoes rang,
And freedmen by Lincoln's proclamation
Bravely fought to save the nation
Crowned with success our glorious flag —
Victorious o'er the rebel rag
No taint of slavery the land infests
Our prosperous nation now attests

So, now, good friends, rejoice with me,
The day of promise we live to see;
With grateful hearts and strong desire
We wait the summons, "Come up higher"
Dear comrades, faithful, tried and true,
Heaven is waiting for such as you,
Your work on earth is fully done,
Receive the crown that you have won.
  Rejoice! Rejoice! Rejoice!
  The crown is won

President Putnam then made an address of welcome, after which there were remarks by William Lloyd Garrison, son of the great agitator, who argued that the direct language of the Abolitionists was their tower of strength, that they were reformers, not politicians; Rev. Samuel May, the old organized Society's agent, full of interesting reminiscences of the anti-slavery epoch, Hon. M. M. Fisher, one of the leaders of the Liberty Party; George B. Bartlett, who read an original poem. Then we sang "Get off the Track," prefacing it with a history of its composition by Brother Jesse. Then speaking followed by Hon. Parker Pillsbury, who said this was the proudest and happiest day of his life, and gave an interesting view of his life-work. We followed this with "There's no such word as fail," a song written by George W. Putnam, and set to music by Brother Asa, after which another song was called for. George T. Downing, of Newport, who represented the colored people in the meeting, arose and said

"In conversation with Mr. Hutchinson in the early stages of this meeting, we carried ourselves back to a building in the city of New York where the members and friends of the anti-slavery association used to assemble annually. At one of these gatherings a notorious man, by the name of Rynders, came there with his associates to break up the meeting. I was one of the number present. Mr. Hutchinson and his noble band sat in the gallery. The meeting became a complete scene of disorder, owing to the interruption of Rynders and his gang. Without any announcement the Hutchinsons arose in the audience, or rather in the gallery, and with their sweet voices completely tamed the wild beast as I recall him on that occasion. They are about to give us the song which they sang then."

Following Mr. Downing's remarks, I said:

"It was not always convenient for us to be announced from the stage. We would manage to get among the audience, and when opportunity came to do our duty, we would do it. We did it on that occasion. It makes me feel like shedding tears of joy that we were privileged to serve and even to suffer for the great cause of emancipation. We were once with William Lloyd Garrison at Portland, and when the mob was so noisy that nothing could be heard, he remained silent, as they would not allow him to speak, and turned and asked us to sing. We arose and sung this very song. I would state that, of the two members of my family who are with me to-day, my daughter takes the place of my dear sister who was with me singing recently at the burial of our beloved John G. Whittier, who has gone to his glorious home above; and her husband wrote me a letter which I received just before I came, in which he says, 'Abby and myself cannot be with you, yet we will be with you in spirit,' and I believe it is so. We will sing, friends, 'Over the Mountain and over the Moor,' or 'The Slave's Appeal.'"

Rev. George W. Porter, D.D., of Lexington, then told the story of the mobbing of Garrison by the kid-gloved pro-slavery men of Boston. Mrs. Lucy Stone then paid a glowing tribute to Abby Kelley Foster, and her efforts to talk for abolition in the face of the opposition to women on the platform and detailed some of her own experiences in the same direction; Abby Morton Diaz followed, giving her recollections of the devotion to the cause that made it such a delightful thing to be an anti-slavery girl. Rev. Aaron Porter, son of Hathorne Porter, one of the "Seven Stars" of the anti-slavery days in Danvers, told the story of their meetings. George W. Putnam, of Lynn, a cousin of Edwin Percy Whipple, the essayist, and a family connection of Joshua R. Giddings, for a while private secretary to Charles Dickens, a constant contributor of anti-slavery poems, articles and reports to the *Liberator*, and who once acted as business agent for the trio of brothers in the West, writing "pioneer" letters from Hutchinson, Minn., made a fine speech in eulogy of the leaders in the agitation, all of whom he knew intimately. George T. Downing spoke of the political phase of the reform and made a declaration of his own principles, which evoked loud applause. Rev. Peter Randolph, born a slave, made the closing address, remarking that the settlement of the race problem lay in applying the principle of the fatherhood of God and the brotherhood of man. We sang once or twice more and closed our part of the exercises with the "Old Granite State."

Within a week of the Danvers meeting, I had started for the West and the World's Fair. I went to Wheaton, Ill., where I had before spent many happy days with my old friends Rufus Blanchard and wife, and took quarters with them. May 1st I joined with the hundreds of thousands in the chorus at the opening of the great exposition in Chicago, heard the President in his speech and realized the beginning of important events so well inaugurated. After a few days there, and a few visits to friends and relatives, I took a trip to Minnesota to take care of business interests that demanded immediate attention. While there I appeared in concert in Hutchinson, and sold several lots, some of them on the main street, the papers speaking of them as the most important sale in a long time.

Early in June I returned to Wheaton and Chicago, and then commenced a pleasant experience, lasting for months. When the round of sight-seeing became wearisome, there was the temporary home to retire to, and the rest of a few days would refresh me for new experiences. It would be impossible to chronicle all the pleasant surprises caused by meeting the friends of bygone days. There were to be found on any day, and at almost every turn, men and women often whom I had not seen since the days of the family quartet, or of the trio of brothers which succeeded it. Some were from foreign lands, and renewed friendships formed in the '40's. Then many new friends were made, which will never be forgotten while memory lasts. Asa's son, Oliver Dennett Hutchinson, with his wife, were in the company on the trip from Hutchinson, and I met them often during their stay in Chicago. My first call after my arrival at the grounds was on Frederick Douglass, commissioner for Hayti. The 17th of June was Massachusetts Day. The handsome old Colonial State Building was dedicated, the Sons and Daughters of the Revolution assisting in the affair. The opening exercises were held in the music hall, Governor Russell of Massachusetts, Dr. Chauncey M. Depew, Judge H. M. Shepard, General Horace Porter and other notables being prominent in the assembly. At 10.30 the exercises opened. I being introduced to sing "The Sword of Bunker Hill," the well-known composition of my friend Covert. I prefaced the song by reciting a few appropriate lines:

"Hail to the land on which we tread —
    Our fondest boast,
The sepulchre of mighty dead —
The truest hearts that ever bled,
Who sleep on glory's brightest bed,
    A fearless host
No slave is here, our unchained feet
Walk freely as the waves that beat
    Our coast.

"Our fathers crossed the ocean wave
    To seek this shore,
They left behind the coward slave
To welter in his living grave
With hearts unbent, high, steady, brave,
    They sternly bore
Such toils as meaner souls had quelled,
But souls like these such toils impelled
    To soar.

"Hail to the morn on which they stood
    On Bunker's height,
And fearless stemmed the invading flood
And wrote our dearest rights in blood,
And mowed in ranks the hireling brood
    In desperate fight
Oh, 'twas a proud, exultant day

Rev. Dr. Parsons then offered prayer, and Dr. Depew, president of the New York Society of the Sons of the Revolution, was introduced as the orator. There was a great uproar as he stepped to the front. He said:

"I want to excuse myself for being late, but the fact is, I got lost in the crowd and hearing of your rapid transit decided to try some, and so took a wheeled chair. Well, that boy told me all about himself, his family and the War of the Revolution, till I thought I would have to use a phonograph and send my speech to the hall that way.

"It is peculiarly appropriate that to-day we listen to 'The Sword of Bunker Hill,' from the man whose father was in the Revolution. Most of us are either grandchildren, or great-grandchildren, or some other distant relative of those heroes. But here is a man who is distinctly connected with that period. One of my earliest recollections was going with my mother to a concert by the Hutchinson Family, and hearing that gentleman sing who has sung to-day, and I must say that he looks now as he did then.

"It is mighty appropriate that we meet to-day on the anniversary of the battle of Bunker Hill. This battle was one of the smallest of the war, in so far as the number of men engaged were concerned and the number slain, but it was fraught with more importance than any other battle of the Revolution.

"It was the most useless battle, yet most useful conflict ever fought. The little band of farmers knew they could not conquer Boston. There was a great issue at stake on both sides. The Continentals were determined to find out if they would stand together, the British were determined to prove that the colonists would not dare fight. When the British were routed three times and Washington heard the news, he said 'The liberty of America is assured.'

"The battle of Bunker Hill created the Republic. Patriotism is not a sentiment that is not to be used in every day life except in an emergency. In the hurry of everyday life we are apt to forget sentiment and patriotism. We, the descendants of the revolutionary soldiers, have been building States for a hundred years. The issues that existed when the battle of Bunker Hill was fought do not exist to-day, but there are issues, and there will be new ones to-morrow.

"There are no dudes among the Revolutionary stock; they are all workingmen, knowing that the gospel of work is the gospel of Christ. They built States with the corner-stone — the Bible. The 'Sword of Bunker Hill' has been turned into plow-shares, it has been turned into rails, cables and electric wires, into plates that protect our ships, and it has made the ribs of the structures that comprise this 'White City.'

"'The Sword of Bunker Hill' speaks by every rail that girds this country, by every wire across the prairies and under the waters, by every improvement in this great continent; let it be our cloud by day and our pillar of fire by night, leading us in that pathway marked out for us by the heroes of the Revolution."

I have quoted the *Chicago News'* report of the speech, which evoked tremendous enthusiasm. I need not say how much it pleased me to have been able to sing the song which proved to be the key-note for such an outburst of impromptu oratory. Later in the day, Commissioner Hovey, Gov. Russell and other notables held a reception in the John Hancock Building. The Daughters of the Revolution also gave a banquet to the invited guests. I was treated with the utmost courtesy.

The 19th of June was California Day, and I was invited to participate in the dedication of the State Building. "O. D.," as Asa's son is affectionately termed in the family, sang with me, and we gave the song the trio of brothers used to sing in the days of the Forty-niners, "Ho for California." I had a very pleasant conversation with General Miles, I remember. Two days later I saw the big Ferris wheel start. On the 24th the Hayti Building was opened. I quote a short description of the ceremonies from a Chicago paper:

"Hayti is for the first time represented as a nation in a World's Fair. Its building was formally opened on the 24th. The exercises were very appropriately opened with a song, 'The Millennium,' by dear old John Hutchinson, who has so often sung in the cause of the freedom of the black people as he now sung their triumph. Frederick Douglass and his fellow-commissioner, Mr. Preston, were assisted in receiving the guests by Mrs. Douglass. Mr. Douglass's address was received with frequent applause, and he was eloquent when he said of this Exposition, 'It stands at the topmost height to which science and Christianity have upborne the world. No such demonstration could have taken place in the presence of slavery and war. Its white walls speak of liberty and human brotherhood to all nations, kindreds, tongues and peoples.'"

I had only the intervening Sabbath in which to rest before New Hampshire day came, the 26th. The State Building was dedicated by a speech from Governor Smith, after which I was called upon to sing. Of course there was but one song with which I could respond — that one which so many of the Tribe of Jesse sang together at the dedication of the New Hampshire Building during the Philadelphia Centennial, "The Old Granite State." The applause was as warm as that given us all on that other notable day. There was a great handshaking after it was over. It was a very hot day, and singing was wearisome indeed.

I found Wheaton a little too far away from the Fair, and so early in July moved into the city, taking rooms on Michigan Avenue. On the 3d of July I sang in the buildings of four different States. The Fourth was a great day. I sat on the platform facing five hundred thousand people. Commissioner Davis presided, and Mayor Carter Harrison spoke. Rain interfered with the programme, and I did not sing "Yankee Doodle," as I had expected to. I sought refuge in the New York Building, and there found such old friends as Mrs. Isabella Beecher Hooker, Mrs. Carpenter, Mrs. Ives, and others, and sang to them. July 10th was Pennsylvania Day. Governor Pattison gave a reception in the State Building, and there was speaking. I sang "Uncle Sam's Farm." Several days of alternate rest and activity followed.

At about this time the *Chicago Opinion* kindly referred to me as follows:

"John Hutchinson, the only surviving member of the celebrated Hutchinson Family, is a guest at the Millard Avenue Hotel. Mr. Hutchinson is an aged man, and most patriarchal in appearance, but is one of the youngest men to be found in manners and conversation. His reminiscences of the old anti-slavery days, when the quartet, consisting of himself, his brothers Asa and Judson, and sister Abby, electrified the North with their songs of freedom, are most interesting and are well remembered by those who were living away back in the '40s and '50s. Mr. Hutchinson still finds himself in active demand upon public occasions, he having sung at World's Fair, New Hampshire, and also Bunker Hill Day, and more recently before the Single Tax Club. The son of Mr. Hutchinson was the first husband of Mrs. Rev. Henry Morgan, daughter of the late Isaac S. Phillips."

I had just made my headquarters at the Millard Avenue Hotel at the time this notice was written. I made this my stopping-place practically all the time after that, until I came East again. Early in August the Peace Congress was held, this, of course, attracting my sympathy and presence. On the 15th of August I sung the "People's Advent" for the Liberal Congress at the Art Memorial Palace. On the 18th I sung and spoke for the peace people in the same place. On the 19th Lillie, with her husband, Rev. Mr. Morgan, and my grandsons Jack and Richard, arrived. Cleveland Campbell, another grandson, came on from Lynn about this time, and Kate also came. I contracted the habit of spending a good deal of time in the California Building. The matron, Mrs. Smith, was a sister of my dear friend E. R. Brown, of Elmwood, Ill., and through her kindness I held many receptions in the building, Lillie, Jack and Rich singing with me. Lillie's brother, Fred Phillips, who has a fine bass voice, also sung with us sometimes. I think I have mentioned that Mr. Morgan was a travelling evangelist. He secured a large gospel wagon, with sufficient sleeping accommodations for the whole family, when occasion required, and so arranged that the organ could be set up at the rear end to serve both as a musical instrument and pulpit. His method in Chicago was to locate the wagon at some point of vantage, after which

CLEVELAND J. CAMPBELL.—(p. 210)

Jack would blow a fan-fare on his cornet, which would soon attract a congregation. Lillie and the boys would then sing, after which Mr. Morgan would preach. This method of work they have carried out in various sections of the country, spending much of their time in the South for some years.

August 25th was Colored People's Day. The following report, clipped from the *News*, will show what the exercises were:

"There was a big meeting of both white and colored people in Columbus Hall in the evening. A feature of the session was an essay by Rev. Joseph Cook on 'African Civilization,' read by Rev. Dr. F. A. Noble, of Chicago. Mr. Cook vigorously denounced the liquor traffic, which is thrust upon the native Africans by England, America, and other civilized nations. He ventured to prophesy that when the centennial anniversary of Abraham Lincoln's proclamation is being celebrated in 1963 the colored population in America will number 40,000,000, while the whites will number 100,000,000, and before that time comes, the negro's full rights as a citizen will have been conceded. John W. Hutchinson, the only surviving member of the famous Hutchinson family, whose songs of liberty thrilled the land thirty years ago, was introduced, and sung one of his inimitable songs. Miss Hallie J. Brown recited 'The Black Regiment,' and Mr. Talley, one of the Jubilee singers, sung 'The Huntsman's Horn.' A paper on 'The Congo State and the Redemption of Africa,' by Dr. J. A. Casson, was read."

On August 29th, I sang at the Memorial Hall, at a meeting in which Henry George and Dr. McGlynn were speakers.

Early in September, I went to Lafayette, Ind., to visit my friend, Helen M. Gougar, the temperance orator. My arrival was announced by the *Journal* of that place, under the flattering heading, "A Noted Visitor," as follows:

"Lafayette is honored by the presence of a noted man whose name was familiar to the American public when our parents were young. John W. Hutchinson, the last of the well-known Hutchinson family of singers, is the guest of Mr. and Mrs. John D. Gougar. The Hutchinsons, whose voices were first uplifted for liberty and universal freedom fully fifty years ago, need no introduction to the people who have honored them so long.

"Garrison, Phillips, May, Sumner and Hutchinson blend naturally together. 'There are four quartets of that family, each with three brothers and a sister in it,' wrote Mary Howitt. But to-day there sings but one. His voice is as mellow and strong as though no seventy-third milestone of life lay before him. In his home in Boston he is known as 'Father Hutchinson' and 'Uncle John,' and whenever his beautiful patriarchal face is seen it is met with reverence and love.

"The history of anti-slavery times is indelibly blent with the Hutchinson family, and how much their stirring songs did to educate anti-slavery sentiment cannot be estimated. It is a liberal education to listen to the conversation of the grand old patriarch, and time passes unnoticed when one is hearing his eloquently told memories of olden times. Lafayette bids welcome to the last remaining member of the famous Hutchinson family."

The days spent with Mr. and Mrs. Gougar were happy indeed. Receptions were arranged, and on one night there was a lawn party in my honor. To my great regret, I had taken a slight cold, which made me hoarse, so that I was unable to sing as well as I wished. I had an idea that in going to Indiana I should secure a few days of absolute rest, after the excitement of the preceding weeks. In this I was disappointed, but could not complain, after such a pleasant reception and the friendly attentions I received.

I returned to Chicago on the 8th of September, and on the following day participated in the reunion of the Forty-niners in the California Building. The great religious congress opened at the Art Institute two days later. I need not say how gratified I was with these meetings. There was but one common ground upon which all these diverse religions could have met, and that was that of my song, which we had sung for so many years, the "Fatherhood of God and the Brotherhood of Man." Rev. Dr. Lorimer, returning to Boston from the parliament of religions commented upon it by saying, "The parliament of religions is entitled to commendation for the prominence given in its sessions to the fatherhood of God, and the brotherhood of man. This doctrine seemed to be the key-note of its meetings. Humanity itself spoke in address, article and wild enthusiasm, and has thus for the first time openly and publicly avowed its belief in its own brotherhood. Two articles of the ultimate faith — the fatherhood of God, and the brotherhood of man — have been considered and passed on by humanity, and shall never be annulled." I sang my song several times at these meetings.

During this week I sang at a Universalist assembly "Which way is your musket a-pintin' to-day?" by request of my genial friend, Rev. Dr. Miner of Boston. On Sunday, the 17th, I sang at the Sixth Presbyterian church, two selections, Rev. George Washburn, D. D., president of Roberts College, Constantinople, being the speaker. On the 21st I spent the day in Jackson Park with Jack and Rich, securing a wheeled chair, in which my grandsons pushed me all over the park. A shower came up towards night, and it was a sight to see 200,000 people scurrying for shelter. We got wet, and I was pretty stiff the next day. On the Sunday following, in company with Rev. Mr. Morgan, I went to hear my old friend Moody preach. On the 29th Mr. Morgan held evangelistic meetings in a hall, and I joined him and sang a solo, and also "Mary at the Cross" with Lillie. On the same day I mounted — in an elevator — to the roof of the sightly Masonic Temple, twenty stories high. On Sunday, October 1st, I sang for the W. C. T. U. in their beautiful temple. On the 3d I sang in Evanston. The 5th was Rhode Island Day, and I sang "One Hundred Years Hence" in the State Building. On the same day I was happy to meet the widow of my nephew Hayward Hutchinson, with her daughter, from Washington. Such meetings were sorrowfully suggestive of loved ones gone, but nevertheless pleasant. "Chicago Day" came on the 9th. The gathering was immense, and the enthusiasm as great as the numbers. I was on the ground at 6.13 A. M., and did not reach home until 2 o'clock the next morning. Perhaps an old boy like myself may be excused for being rather weary the next day. The 13th was Minnesota Day. Of course I had to be there. Attended the governor's reception and other exercises, and sang four songs. On the following Sunday, the 15th, I sang to a Sunday-school of waifs at Washington Hall. On the 19th there was a memorial service at the Art Institute for Lucy Stone. I sang and addressed the meeting. On the same day I sang "Vote it right along" for another gathering of suffragists. Susan B. Anthony was among the speakers of the day. On the next day I had a number of joyful meetings with old friends. First, I met Mrs. T. C. Severance, now of Los Angeles, Cal., and had an hour of precious conversation, concerning old times and old friends. Then I ran across Lucius B. Hutchinson with his wife and daughter. On the way home in the car, a lad of twelve politely arose, the conveyance being crowded, and gave me his seat. At once I entered into conversation with his father, sitting by my side, and soon discovered him to be the son of Rev. Mr. Stearns, pastor of the Baptist church in Milford during my young manhood. His mother died, and the heart-broken husband was compelled to give up house-keeping, holding an auction of his household effects. I told the son that I was the possessor of the cradle in which he was rocked, which I bought at that sale, and also of a handsome cherry table, which stood in the parsonage parlor, and on which, by the way, I am now writing.

The next day was "Manhattan Day." Chauncey M. Depew was the orator and by invitation I sang two songs, and rang the Columbian Liberty Bell in honor of the anniversary of the discovery of America by Columbus. A tremendous crowd witnessed the ceremony. On the 25th W. O. McDonnell, the projector of the bell idea, lectured in the Children's Building, and I sang with him. During the two or three days after, there was a tremendous influx of visitors at the fair, for it was almost over. On the 28th Mayor Harrison spoke and rang the liberty bell with the mayors of fifteen cities, in honor of the anniversary of the unveiling of the Statue of Liberty in New York Harbor. After the bell ringing, I lent the mayor my knife, and he cut the bell-rope into small pieces for mementos of the occasion. I have one of them now. That very night Mayor Harrison was shot. A day or two later while the funeral preparations were going on, I sent to the *Chicago Times* the following letter, which it printed under the caption, "Tribute of a Friend":

To the Editor —This is one of the eventful days of the World's Fair and of my life. Most of the six months during the exposition I spent in visiting the park as often as I felt able. While among the million, who from day to day congregated there, I endeavored while at halls, State buildings, inaugurations, receptions of governors, and on other notable occasions to give what I could in speech and song to add to the pleasure and happiness of the wonderful throngs of honest seekers after truth. Drawing near the close I had the pleasure of an acquaintance with that very congenial and inspired brother, W. O. McDonnell, who requested me to join in the ceremony of ringing the Columbian Liberty Bell Saturday, October 28th, it being the anniversary of the unveiling of the statue of "Liberty Enlightening the World" in the harbor of New York. Promptly at noon the multitude gathered, encircling the grand bell. The scene was enthusiastically impressive, for in the arena were gathered the executive officers from many cities of the United States—including Carter H. Harrison—who were to participate in the exercises of the ringing. As I had been requested, I sang "The Fatherhood of God, and the Brotherhood of Man", at the conclusion of which the brother mayors unitedly and with great gusto began to "ring out the old, ring in the new, ring out the false, ring in the true." Ere the bell ceased its quivering vibrations, our own executive, Harrison, caught the spirit of inspiration until it seemed that his whole soul was imbued with love for all mankind. He sprang upon the frame that supported the bell and poured forth in his cheerful manner and his wonted eloquence spontaneous expressions from his inmost soul that thrilled all who heard his words, emphasizing the sentiment of the song just sung.

"Peace on earth, the hosts above proclaim the nation's free,
And all of every kin enjoy this boon of liberty
We claim no creed for class or clan, but cherish all the good,
So round the world there soon will be a glorious brotherhood."

He held the audience spell-bound. The utterances came forth like a benediction touching in humorous but loving strain the heart-strings of the loving maidens, who, as he said, "are beautiful, and some there are with gray heads, and they are all beautiful too." He said of Chicago, "She was bound to embrace the whole creation with its friendships and its fellowships, and the officials present had only to name the date and Chicago would embrace the world." Referring finally to the worthy projector of this preacher of peace (the bell), he bade it God-speed on its voyage of mercy around the world.

At an opportune moment I took for the first and last time the hand of the speaker and said "Thank God the World's Fair and Chicago has been blessed with such an executive during the exposition." Permission was granted the members of the company to take with them cuttings of the red, white and blue cord by which the bell was sounded. I opened my pocket-knife and handed it to the mayor, who cut from this line souvenirs that all will associate with the scene and keep as heirlooms for generations to come.

As it was with our beloved Lincoln, who passed away quickly from his useful and active life, giving to all sorrow, so we join to-day and weep with those that weep as in state at the city hall he lies.

Yours for the millennium, JOHN W. HUTCHINSON

On the last day but one of the fair I stood by the bell and sang "The Indian Hunter" just after an old chief of a tribe had made a speech. He sold most of the Cook County, Minn., lands for four cents an acre and told us he never got his pay, even at that price. When I gave the whoops that accompany the song, he opened his eyes very wide. On the following day the fair closed I sang the last song in the Woman's Building. Mrs. Potter Palmer held her last reception and at the close I was invited to sing "The Old Granite State." After a farewell hand-shake, I went to the New York State building, and sang. Then I went and delivered a final speech and song by the Columbian Liberty Bell. This bell, the result of contributions of precious metals and jewels from people all over the Union, has since gone on a tour around the world. Its tones were as sweet as those of any bell I have ever heard.

I lingered four weeks in Chicago after the fair closed. During my stay, I had had many propositions to re-enter the concert field for active work. I had been able to stand the wear and tear of six months of sight-seeing so well that the suggestions were attractive, and thinking it over, I came to the inevitable conclusion that if I were to make a tour of the country it must be with my own company. Plates of many of my songs were in the hands of Chicago music publishers, and I made an effort to get them together in the hands of one house. "Old Hutch"—B. P. Hutchinson—out of good fellowship, gave freely of his time to assist me in this, as did Fred Phillips, whom I planned to have with me in my company. I also met Mrs. James Boyle, a lady of fine musical culture, with a soprano voice of pleasing quality, and engaged her to join me in concerts. We began rehearsals, but in an unfortunate hour I had taken a severe cold, and now pneumonia was threatened, and when I had become convinced that I had escaped that, indications of hemorrhages appeared, and I feared consumption. The concert plans were given up, and I began to long for home. I started the last of November, and reached home the day before Thanksgiving. My daughter Viola had come to High Rock during my absence, and had a fine Thanksgiving dinner for me.

Two days after my arrival in Lynn a parting salute appeared in the *Chicago Opinion*, C. C. Roberts, editor, in the form of a portrait-cut and a handsome and appreciative biographical notice.

The rest and regularity of home life soon restored me to my wonted good health.

On January 4, 1894, I celebrated my birthday by attending the inauguration of Governor Greenhalge, at the State-house. The *Boston Journal* made a note of my presence and gave me a pleasant felicitation on reaching my seventy-third milestone. In the evening many friends and family connections called to congratulate me. On the 10th there was a Prohibition banquet at the Quincy House, Boston, which I attended. On February 2d I went to Norwood, Mass., and sung at a temperance meeting, Mrs. S. Louise Barton being the speaker. On March 11th Mrs. Mary E. Lease spoke at the Lynn Theatre. I sang three appropriate songs. April 19th was the first observance of Patriots' Day. I visited Lexington and Concord with my granddaughter Kate and joined the swarms of people, one hundred and fifty thousand or more, who attended the various events. On the 26th there was an interesting entertainment in Boston Music Hall. The subject was "Retrospective and Prospective America." I appeared on the stage with Mrs. Livermore, who acted in the rôle of historian, and others. Mrs. Eliza Trask Hill was the

THE DEARBORN QUARTET, TRIBE OF JUDSON (p. 219)

moving spirit of the affair. The scene represented the first woman-suffrage meeting. I sang three songs. On May 8th I assisted at a miscellaneous concert at Mattapan, with Kate L. Campbell, and several of the Elms family, grandchildren of my brother Andrew. On the 10th of the same month Frederick Douglass gave a lecture in the People's Church, Boston. I was invited to make a few opening remarks and sing, and in doing so told the thrilling story of the redemption of George W. Latimer from slavery. At the close I introduced Latimer, who accompanied me, to the audience. Viola and I then sang "Over the Mountain and over the Moor." On May 31st we sang together again at a concert in Boston. On June 10th my friend Mrs. Mary Sargent Hopkins gave me a reception at her home in Wellington. A number of notable people attended, and I felt pleased and grateful for their kindness.

During this month I made three trips to Milford. The centennial of the incorporation of the town occurred on the 26th, but prior to that I made visits to Kate Hutchinson Burney, to Ludlow Patton at the old homestead, now occupied by Nellie Gray Webster, Rhoda's granddaughter, and other family friends. The celebration began with a union religious service in the town hall on Sunday evening, the 24th. During the exercises I sang "I may not be a prophet." On the 26th there was the usual firing of guns and cannon, a parade, the dedication of a memorial fountain in honor of Colonel O. W. Lull, band concerts, a dinner to invited guests, and in the afternoon, historical, musical and literary exercises in the town hall. These were participated in by Judge R. M. Wallace, who presided; Rev. J. C. Foster, D.D.; Gov. John B. Smith of New

Hampshire; Edward D. Boylston, who brought Amherst's congratulations (he died in March of the year 1895), Hon. Charles H. Burns, who pronounced the oration; John W. Hutchinson, who sang "Home of My Boyhood," and gave a reminiscent address, much of it covering the scenes in old Milford referred to in the opening chapter of this book; Hon. George A. Ramsdell; Hon. Albert E. Pillsbury, for three years previous attorney-general of Massachusetts, and a son of my old friend, J. W. Pillsbury, who died the same year; Hon. John McLane; H. H. Barber, C. C. Shaw, David Heald and Rev. A. J. Rich. The day closed with fireworks and a centennial ball in the town hall. Of course the papers and magazines paid particular attention to this affair. An elaborate souvenir volume was printed telling the story of the day, and containing the speeches in full. For two or three days following the celebration I stayed in Milford visiting friends and going fishing. Then I returned to my cares at High Rock.

But there were a number of notable events during the year. One was a reunion of the "Old Boys of Lynn" at Nahant. I attended, made a historical speech and sang "Old High Rock" and "Should auld acquaintance be forgot," with original verses, appropriate to the occasion added. Late in July I went to Portland, and attended the eighty-sixth birthday anniversary of Prof. F. N. Crouch, the composer of "Kathleen Mavourneen," held at the home of my friends, the Thomases. Crouch sung his famous song, and I sang five pieces.

On August 16th, the centennial of the birth of William Cullen Bryant occurred in his native town, Cummington, Mass. My cherished friend, Edwin R. Brown, of Elmwood, Ill., gave the memorial address,

Parke Godwin, so long associated with Mr. Bryant in the conduct of the *New York Evening Post*, was chairman of the day, and John H. Bryant, himself a poet, and brother of the author of "Thanatopsis" read an original poem and also his monody on the two brothers, composed just after the great poet's death. I sang "After All," better known, perhaps, as "The old friends are the truest," and by request our family song, "The Old Granite State." New verses were added to the first song. It was, complete, as follows:

"Oh, the old friends are the truest,
    After all
Though the face be not the newest,
    After all
When the fever heat is highest,
And the chilling tide is nighest,
Over all we see a reaching,
Of a friendship whose sweet teaching
Brings us love and trust and rest,
For the weary soul the best,
    After all!

"What are all the stings of malice,
    After all?
There are joys deep in life's chalice,
    After all
Must the shadows then pursue us,
Or the sunbeams then come o'er us?
While our feet pass by the daisies
Shall our soul ne'er count his praises?
Oh, there is some joy, some rest—
For the weary soul the best,
    After all

"Character makes friendship brightest,
    After all
Real worth makes dark hours lightest,
    After all
Not the creed our friend's believing
Or the dogmas he's receiving,

But the noble life he's living —
Help to human hearts he's giving —
Makes us in his strong love rest —
For the weary soul the best,
    After all

"Most divine are those who love us,
    After all
Like the angel ones above us,
    After all
Said the holy Galilean,
When he kept the rite Judean
'I no longer servants call you,
But my friends, whate'er befall you'
And his followers there found rest —
For their weary souls the best,
    After all

"For better than the old or newest
    After all,
Is that loving friend the truest,
    After all
Over calms and storms He sees us,
And from danger, too, He frees us —
And amid our faithless serving
Keeps a watchfulness unswerving
Heaven shows us perfect rest —
There our weary souls will rest
    After all"

Perhaps as good a pen-picture of Cummington and the scenes of that notable day as was painted was that of Clifton Johnson, in *The Outlook*.

"Bryant's Cummington home lies far up the eastern slope of a great hill. It is nearly a three miles' climb of crooked, 'thank-you-marmed' road to it from the village in the hollow where the church is. The way is half-wooded and lonely, but on the morning of August 16, 1894, it was black with the upward toiling of more teams than perhaps will pass that way in all the hundred years to come before another Bryant centennial. People came in all sorts of ways. Market wagons and buggies were the common vehicles of the farm folks, though shiny-top carriages and gay-colored buck-boards were not lacking. But

places, or from the towns and cities of the Connecticut Valley, and they often brought people from the far-distant States, who were attracted by the importance of the occasion. Bicyclers came by the score [he should have said hundred] and people who had no other way of getting to the spot were willing to tramp long distances on foot.

"All along the roadways for a half-mile circuit about the Bryant house were the teams of the visitors hitched to trees and gateways in the stone walls. Other teams had driven into the fields and tied up to trees and bushes there.

"The weather was, to most minds, ideal. The sun was bright, but not too hot, only a few lazy clouds sailed the sky and the air was fresh and invigorating and crystal clear. The distant hills we looked on that lay eastward across the wide-wooded valley had all the greenness and sharp definition of the fields about. Near and far the earth was all a-glitter with warm sunlight and every shadow had a blotty denseness.

"The place of meeting was a grove of young maples, a short walk up the road from the Bryant homestead. This grove had several advantages. The ground there formed a natural amphitheatre and it was near enough to the house so that the audience could adjourn to shelter in case of rain. Besides, it is not improbable that the young Bryant wrote 'Thanatopsis' in that grove.

"A wide platform had been built in this wood, elevated two or three feet above the earth, and in a three-quarter circle about were many lines of board benches. The platform itself was set full of chairs and settees reserved for invited guests, except for a space at the front where were a small organ and a table, on which a grocer's box was propped bottom upwards in a position to serve for the speaker's desk. Just back of this, well up on a tree-trunk, hung a lithograph portrait of the poet decked with flowers. Beneath this portrait sat the group of men who were to make the addresses of the day.

"In an orchard below the grove were many long, white-spreaded tables and at one side was a stove with its pipe thrust up among the tree-branches, and on it some great boilers of coffee were steaming. At noon the invited guests had dinner served at the tables. The uninvited for the most part brought their own lunches, and when dinner-time came they scattered far and wide about the near fields, wherever there was a patch of shade and in little family groups had a basket picnic. Ten o'clock was the appointed time for the exercises to begin, but it was half-past ten when the meeting was called to order. Estimates of the number of people present varied from three to five thousand — a remarkable gathering when one considers that the population of the whole township was only eight hundred. The platform was crowded every backless board bench of the surrounding amphitheatre was filled, and a fringe of people gathered and stood among the gray tree-trunks beyond the seats. It was only the core of the assembly that was able to hear everything that was said, for the open air diffuses the voice everywhere, and here there were the wind and the rustling of the leaves besides. Nor was this all, when the out-lying people thought they could not hear the speaker, neighbor would remark to neighbor something in this tenor, 'He ain't got a mite of any voice,' and then they would begin to do some low-toned visiting. Among the listeners were many patriarchs who had passed threescore years and ten, but these were very much out-numbered by the babies who had come along with the rest of the family. Not many of the babies were in the audience, but from the sound, one would conclude that there were several hundred of them holding a convention somewhere in the neighborhood.

"But above all this in the main unavoidable or thoughtless background murmur, the favored ones heard the thoughtful and often inspiring words of the distinguished band of speakers who had gathered to do Bryant honor. Some voices were resonant and penetrating enough to be heard by all, and when they were not, the audience as a whole was patient. There was immense curiosity to know who was who among the group of famous men on the front of the platform and a good deal of questioning and guessing was done.

"Parke Godwin, Bryant's son-in-law, presided. He paid the poet a warm and eloquent tribute in his opening remarks, and he was very apt in his introductions of the speakers that followed. The concentrated vigor of Mr. Godwin's features and the uncommon bushiness of his white beard and hair made him a conspicuous figure among the others on the stage.

"Music was furnished by a chorus accompanied by an organ, a bass-viol, violin and clarionet and all led by an energetic young woman of the town. The most interesting musical feature of the day, however, was the singing of John W. Hutchinson, the only living member of the famous Hutchinson Family which did notable work all through the North before the war in their songs for freedom.

"'They wa'n't like the singers we have nowadays,' said an old lady behind me. 'They were natural singers.'

"Mr. Hutchinson's long gray beard and white hair that fell down about his shoulders made him a picturesque figure and proclaimed his age, yet he was full of vigor and his old-fashioned songs had a feeling and simplicity about them that touched his hearers and aroused their enthusiasm.

"The chief address of the day was made by Edwin R. Brown, a Cummington boy, who now lives in the West. What he said was excellent in thought, and was both seriously suggestive and entertaining.

"Probably the man of all others on the platform in whom interest centered was John Howard Bryant, the poet's only living brother. He had reached the age of eighty-seven, yet his figure was still upright and his voice was strong and sonorous, and he showed an enthusiasm in the exercises that was remarkably youthful. He read two musical and thoughtful poems of his own composition, one of which was written within a few weeks.

"Another guest whom the audience seemed to regard with much attention was Julia Ward Howe. She read an original poem and her 'Battle Hymn of the Republic' was sung as a solo, in which all the company present joined in the chorus.

"Among the afternoon addresses was one by John Bigelow, whose face and gray hair and tall, broad-shouldered figure reminded one of George William Curtis, one by Charles Dudley Warner, full of the charm of mingled sense and humor; one by the poet-preacher John White Chadwick, which was a particularly fine characterization of Bryant's genius, and the only address with this theme of the day that was delicately appreciative and at the same time judicial, one by Charles Eliot Norton that was felicitous and delightful, as what he says always is, and one by President G. Stanley Hall, of Clark University, which was an energetic plea for science and showed the close relation of science to both poetry and religion.

"It was nearly five o'clock when the last speech had been made and the last song had been sung. The crowd on the benches had already thinned, for some had to make long drives to the railroad towns in the valley, and some had heard enough, and some were farmers who must get home to milk the cows and attend to the other evening work. Now, the others dispersed, too, and one of the most notable gatherings these hills have ever known was brought to an end."

All the papers treated me very kindly on this occasion. The *Springfield Republican* said:

"Across, next to the Cummington chorus and the instruments, sat a striking old man, with his long white hair brushed straight back all around his brow, without a part, and his long white beard beneath keen and alert eyes — this was John W. Hutchinson, whose voice is as good as when the Hutchinsons sang anti-slavery and woman's-rights songs, long ago."

The *Daily Hampshire Gazette* remarked:

"He looked like some ancient man of genius, with long flowing white locks and countenance beaming with intelligence and manly vigor.

And when he raised his voice in song, he rose to heavenly heights and carried his audience with him. His voice is still wonderful, his uplifting power a marvel."

The *Hampshire County Journal* made this comment:

"Conspicuous among all were the figures of John W. Hutchinson, Parke Godwin, John Bigelow and the brother of the poet, John Howard Bryant. The former with his flowing white locks and beard, his deep, white collar turned down over his coat, and his expressive, kindly face, attracting the sympathy of all present, seemed the embodied spirit of the occasion. He seemed for all the world like an ancient Druid in his temple fashioned by nature.

"The hearts of many hundreds were often stirred to strange emotions during the day, but surely never more than during the singing of the 'Old Granite State' by Mr. Hutchinson. As though inspired by his theme, the venerable man lifted his clear, rich voice until the fine lines of the old song could be heard in the farthest corner of the auditorium, dominating even the desecrating screech of a peddler's squeaker. Eyes glistened as the old man sang and a tumult of applause followed him to his seat."

On my way home from Cummington I went to Providence, and on the following Sunday evening sang several songs at the vesper service in the Plymouth Congregational Church, of which my nephew and namesake, John W. Hutchinson, is an official member. A few weeks later I gave a concert in the same church.

Early in September I went to Saco and sang at a regimental reunion of two Maine organizations. Two days later I sang at "Greenacre," the summer assembly held in Eliot, Me., there being a reception to Gen. Neal Dow, the "father of prohibition" (now ninety years old) and myself. I sang several songs and was finely received. Charlotte J. Thomas, my philanthropic Portland friend, was also a speaker during the afternoon. I returned to Lynn just in time to sing at the Labor Day celebration. The remainder of the year was principally spent in attending to home cares and literary labors, with occasional concerts in Lynn and vicinity.

The year 1895 was very much like others of my later life. There were many pleasant experiences, with friends here and there, and more partings from the tried and true souls with whom the Hutchinsons have been closely affiliated in their life-work. On Thursday, January 3d, I attended the second inauguration of Governor Greenhalge in the magnificent new hall of representatives at the Massachusetts State House, many pleasant references to me appearing in the papers of that date.

On February 3d Theodore D. Weld died at his home in Hyde Park. This history contains many references to him, and it may be imagined that I took a melancholy pleasure in attending his funeral and singing, as he had requested I should do while on his death-bed. Mr. Weld was born in Hampton, Conn., in 1803, and was consequently in his ninety-second year. His father was an Orthodox minister, and the son, after studying in Andover Seminary and at Hamilton College, N. Y., in 1833, went to Lane Theological Seminary at Cincinnati with a view of entering the ministry. Lyman Beecher was its president. A debate on colonization and slavery resulted in making the entire class, some Southerners and sons of slaveholders, Abolitionists, largely through Weld's eloquence and reasoning power. The faculty, alarmed for the popularity of the seminary, forbade the formation of an anti-slavery society, whereupon the students withdrew *en masse*, many entering the field as anti-slavery agents and lecturers. For a time Mr. Weld bravely battled with the forces of slavery, receiving his full share of bad eggs and other indignities, when he boldly made converts in the enemy's country, but an affection of the throat put an end to his public speaking. In 1838 he married Miss Angelina Grimké, one of the famous South Carolina sisters, who were pioneers for reform. For many years he conducted a school at Perth Amboy, N. J., Henry and Viola, my children, being among his pupils. For thirty years he lived in Hyde Park. His funeral was held in the Unitarian church and was conducted by Rev. E. E. S. Osgood. Ednah D. Cheney and William Lloyd Garrison also spoke.

A little later in February, Frederick Douglass, who but a few weeks before had written the introduction to this book, died at his home in Washington. Immediately on receiving the intelligence, I went to the Capitol city, and on February 25th sang at his funeral — which was largely attended — at the request of Mrs. Douglass. It was one of the most impressive scenes of my life. Before singing I recounted many incidents in my experience with Douglass, all of which have found their proper place in this history. It was nearly fifty years since we had crossed the ocean together on our famous anti-slavery mission to England. I am now the only survivor of that singing and speaking band. Douglass was always my true friend, and I rejoice that I was allowed to be a participant with him in so many stirring scenes that are a part of American history.

Before returning North, I visited Howard University, and addressed the students. On March 10th in Music Hall, Boston, there was a representation of "Longfellow's Dream," in which I took the part of the aged priest from "Evangeline." On March 20th, at the Women's Press Club, Mrs. Kate Tannatt Woods gave a vivid paper on war days and at the close I sang the

"Blue and Gray." Previous to singing I gave a few reminiscences of my dead friend, Douglass.

During this spring, two long-cherished friends passed away near the old homestead. J. W. Pillsbury, a brother to Parker Pillsbury, and one of the most staunch friends of anti-slavery in New Hampshire, died at his home in Milford, and not long after, Edward D. Boylston, so long editor of the *Farmer's Cabinet*, died at Amherst. I have several selections from his pen scattered through this book.

The summer was spent quietly at High Rock, with occasional visits elsewhere, including another period at the summer congress at Greenacre, in Eliot, Me., which is an extension or continuation of the work of the great religious congress at the World's Fair.

Early in September I determined to take a trip to the great cotton and industrial exposition at Atlanta, visiting my grandchildren, then with their mother Lillie Hutchinson Morgan, and step-father, Rev. Henry Morgan, at Portsmouth, Va., on the way. It was a joy beyond expression to see the manly little fellows again. With their parents they had been campaigning for years in the Southwest and on the Pacific coast, and following my visit they went on for one hundred days and nights of revival work, rounding them out at Atlanta, where for weeks they attracted large audiences.

My stay in Portsmouth lasted ten days. Then I went on to Atlanta, arriving on the day of the opening of the exposition. I need not describe in detail an event so fresh in the minds of my readers. By invitation of the management I was present on "Blue and Gray" Day. Who can picture my thoughts on that notable occasion? To think that at last the man who had known what it was to be maligned and buffeted in the South, should be received with honor in its chief city, and witness the effects of reconstruction in the great cotton country! It was a "New South," indeed, that I saw. And there, to the great gathering of Union and Confederate soldiers, I sang the song that had so often in later years been a key to open the Southern heart to the Hutchinsons:

> "Tears and love for the Blue,
> Love and tears for the Gray!"

After visiting the exposition for several days I took the train for Hutchinson, as my final destination, but turned aside on the way to visit one of the few of the living Abolitionists, Cassius M. Clay, at Richmond, Ky. It has always been Clay's fortune to have a controversy waging about him, but I honored him for his early adherence to the cause I loved, among hostile associations. He gave me two big watermelons when I departed.

Pausing in Chicago for a brief meeting with old friends, I reached Hutchinson early in October, where I attended to a good deal of business which had accumulated in the two years that had passed since my last visit. I stopped with my nephew, S. G. Anderson.

By November I was in New York City. When Elizabeth Cady Stanton celebrated her eightieth birthday, I was proud to be one of the guests; and on the Sunday following I had the happiness of again meeting with the American Temperance Union. The story of its organization has already been told. I remained in New York for a long time, attending temperance meetings and similar gatherings and giving many old-time concerts. On January 5, 1896, my old friends of the American Temperance Union tendered me a reception in honor of my seventy-fifth birthday. From among many newspaper notices of the occasion, I quote the following, published in one of the city journals:

"It was a very large and sympathetic audience that gathered in Chickering Hall on Sunday afternoon to do honor to that veteran minstrel, John W. Hutchinson. The platform was filled with ladies and gentlemen, all anxious to remind their venerable friend that good deeds never die. The usual musical programme was interspersed with songs by Mr. Hutchinson, who sings with as much vim and music as many a man half his age.

"In appearance the hero of the day is spare but healthy, a ruddy hue on his face being a fitting offset to his long white locks and beard. Mr. Hutchinson is full of anecdote of the past, and treated the large audience in his talks to snatches of song illustrative of what he was saying.

"The meeting was called to order by President Bogardus, of the American Temperance Union, who said he had received many letters of regret from old friends of Mr. Hutchinson, who would have been glad to have been present on this occasion. He did not intend to read all these communications, as the time would not allow. He, however, would read one or two. The first was from Elizabeth Cady Stanton, who regretted her inability to be present, but who said many pleasant and inspiring things about the cause she was engaged in, and the great help John W. Hutchinson had been to that cause. A letter was also read from Susan B. Anthony with similar regrets. The chairman called upon Mr. Hutchinson for a song. He generally had a short talk before singing, and the audience seemed pleased to hear both his speaking and singing.

"Among the speakers who addressed the audience none was more eloquent and forcible than Rev. W. B. Derrick, D.D., Missionary Secretary of the American Methodist-Episcopal Church.

"Dr. Derrick said, in part, 'We are gathered here to-day to do honor to one among the last remaining links that bind us to the past. If we could draw back the curtain that hides the spirit world to mortal gaze, it would reveal those noble friends of the anti-slavery movement, who would say, "The world moves." But let the past be buried. We live in the present. Four and one-half millions of my people live in freedom as the result of the efforts of Brother Hutchinson and his colleagues. We are to-day battling with another and worse form of slavery — the slavery to strong drink. But having subdued one we will overcome the other. This distinguished gentleman who took active part in ridding the country of the disgrace of slavery stands as a beacon light of the world. The black man may not be fully in possession of his political rights, but we expect these will come slowly but surely. To get linen clean it must pass through two washings. During the last thirty years the American linen had been passing through the first. It has now got to go through the second to come out perfectly clean. Abraham Lincoln was not only a benefit to the negro, but to the white man as well, because he fired the American pulpit and unshackled the American press, giving them courage to attack the monster. The American Judiciary also received backbone and impetus, and to-day the black man has a status in our courts, receiving justice the same as a white man. The spirit of abolition shall march on until 'Freedom forever and ever' is the watchword of the American Republic. The American conscience is all right when properly touched. The negro will always be found sustaining his end in a reform movement. In those counties where he is allowed to vote upon the local option question they go dry. Every time he gets a chance he casts his vote against the liquor traffic.'

"Mrs. Lillie Devereaux Blake, President of the New York State Suffrage Association, was the next speaker.

"Mrs. Blake said: 'When I was a little girl I remember hearing the songs of the Hutchinsons and they made a deep impression on me. It was not given to me to take any part in the anti-slavery struggle, but I am glad that I have lived to see the day when that blot is washed out. We women are not as well off as the black man to-day. A colored man can go into a restaurant after dark and get something to eat, but we women cannot, and I think we white women ought to have equal rights with our colored brother. Our freedom is not yet won. We are still in the fight. In Massachusetts the women voted twenty-two to one in favor of equal suffrage, and the men voted two to one against it. The part that the singer plays is an important one. In olden time he taught the lessons of patriotism and liberty. Mr. Hutchinson sung for the freedom of the slave, and also for the freedom of our sex.' Mrs. Blake spoke of Wyoming, Colorado and Utah as being in advance on the woman-suffrage question, and expressed the wish that the other States would come up to their altitude.

"Apologies were given for the absence of Rev. Anna H. Shaw, Mrs. Mary T. Burt and Dr. Collyer.

"George T. Downing, a colored man, seventy-six years old, of Newport, R. I., lauded Mr. Hutchinson, and then said the colored people should receive more rights than are now accorded them. He did not ask for social recognition, because he thought that should be earned by the members of his own race individually, and wound up by saying: 'This great negro problem has been given by God to this country to solve. We are growing in numbers and in intelligence, and we want our rights.'

reminiscences of the past in which Mr. Hutchinson and his family had taken part. He was full of wit and anecdote and pathos, as he always is.

"Another speaker was one who in these times shows his face all too seldom at Chickering Hall. Who does not know Rev. Stephen Merritt? He thanked God that he had lived through that abolition period, and he would like to live on until he had seen the end of that curse, the open saloon. Mr. Merritt related experiences of abolition meetings, where he said sometimes dead cats were used as arguments against the movement, but that only made him more and more an Abolitionist than ever. He was glad to see his old friend. He remembered the family and the work they had accomplished; he hoped there would be others rise up to do as much for Prohibition as they had done for Abolition. He hoped men and churches would be inspired by the Holy Ghost to fight against all these evils, and was sure that through Him they would be abolished.

"Mr. Hutchinson sang "The Blue and the Gray," between the verses of which Miss Park played military calls on the cornet, which were very effective.

"A large number of those present pressed forward at the close to shake the hand of Mr. Hutchinson."

I find that I have carried the narrative of this history along until it has brought me to the three-quarters-of-a-century mark. This is certainly a fitting point at which to close this chapter, and with it the annals of the Hutchinsons.

CHAPTER IV.

AN OLD-TIME YANKEE FAMILY.

> "David, Noah, Andrew, Zephy,
> Caleb, Joshua, Jess and Benny,
> Judson, Rhoda, John and Asa
> And Abby are our names.
> We're the sons of Mary,
> Of the tribe of Jesse,
> And we now address you
> With our native mountain song."

I FEEL certain that in the chapters which have preceded this, the reader must have become quite well acquainted with the leading members of the family, and yet it would not be doing justice to the "Tribe of Jesse" if a chapter were not devoted to a brotherly reference to each of them, giving perhaps a better idea of their work and personal characteristics than could be secured in any other way. In doing this I shall make free use of Brother Joshua's "Brief Narrative" of the family. This was published in 1874, and in place of an introduction, contained a very appreciative letter from William Lloyd Garrison, a part of which it is appropriate to quote at this point. Mr. Garrison says:

"Sixteen children, of the same parents, constitute an exceptionally large number, especially in these less fruitful times, and on this ground alone is a notable one. But that they all should have been endowed with a decided musical talent, in some instances amounting to inspirational genius, is, indeed, extraordinary, and probably unparalleled. The most widely known to the public, by their singing in concerts as a quartet, are Judson, John, Asa and Abby, occasionally assisted by Jesse,

WILLIAM LLOYD GARRISON — (p. 234)

the gifted *improvisatore*—comprehensively bearing the title of 'The Hutchinson Family', and to these I desire to make special reference, not forgetful of what is due to the others, particularly to yourself, who have done so much good service to the cause of humanity and progress both by the matter and manner of your singing.

"If I mistake not, they made their first appearance in Boston, at the anniversary of the New England Anti-Slavery Convention, in 1843, taking that body by surprise, and carrying it to a high pitch of enthusiasm. Starting out as inexperienced minstrels on an untried experiment as to what their success might be, even under favorable auspices, they had every conceivable worldly and professional inducement either wholly to stand aloof from the maligned 'abolition agitation' and give themselves exclusively to the singing of sentimental and mirth-provoking songs, or else to cater to the overwhelming pro-slavery sentiment that everywhere prevailed; but they were proof against all temptations. Whether they should sing to thin or to crowded houses, to approving or deriding listeners, or whether they should evoke a hospitable or a mobocratic reception, as they travelled from 'down East' to the 'far West,' they never stopped to calculate consequences, but unflinchingly espoused the cause of a despised and down-trodden race—nobly remembering those in bonds as bound with them. Yes, it shall ever redound to their credit, that, at a most trying and convulsive period, they gave themselves to that cause with a zeal, an enthusiasm, an unselfishness, and a sympathetic and enrapturing melody surpassing all power of prosaic speech, which most effectively contributed to the regeneration of a corrupt public sentiment, and ultimately to the total abolition of slavery. By the softening of prejudices and the melting of hearts under their pathetic strains for the poor fettered bondmen, they did their full part toward making it possible for Abraham Lincoln to issue his grand Proclamation of Emancipation on January 1, 1863.

"At all times singing 'with the spirit of the understanding,' as well as with their marvellously sweet voices, how charming to the ear, how quickening to the soul, was their every performance, with its unique and varied programme! But they sang not only for freedom and equal rights, but with equal zest in behalf of peace, temperance, moral reform, woman's enfranchisement, and other kindred movements, making many thousands of converts, and exerting a salutary influence far and wide.

"Never before has the singing of ballads been made directly and purposely subservient to the freedom, welfare, happiness and moral elevation of the people. Let the example become contagious!"

Of the sixteen children, the oldest was named Jesse, for his father. He was a beautiful and loving child, and as soon as he was old enough, was taught to make himself useful. Before his death there were three other brothers and a sister. He took much of the care of them from mother's shoulders. He was also the family errand-boy. On one occasion he was sent to take the dinners for father and workmen at the old saw-mill. While they were eating he was amusing himself sitting near a stack of boards, when a gust of wind threw over the pile, and crushed him, but not killing him instantly. He was tenderly borne three-quarters of a mile to his home, and hopes were entertained for his recovery, but fever set in, and he died. He seemed to have had a premonition of death, for before starting on that fatal errand he said to his brother, "David, I don't want to go to the mill to-day." This was the first of many sorrows for his loving parents.

David was the next son, and during a long life he bore the responsibilities and enjoyed whatever distinction there is in being an elder brother. He learned to bear the yoke in his youth, and as he came up to active life, many duties were placed upon him. He was a hard-working boy, who in father's absence took charge of the farm. We always considered him fully master of the situation. The other boys learned to fear him and to tremble at his exacting words. He was very enterprising, and when not yet out of his teens, acquired property, and soon had many interests in his charge. For a while, as a young man, he taught school in the neighborhood. He had a good bass voice, which was never cultivated, as he was afflicted with asthma. There were periods when he would almost lose his life in the struggle for breath, yet he outlived nearly all his brothers and sisters. He was married at twenty-two, and raised a large family, many of whom became very successful in life. As soon as he was married, he bought a farm, which he subsequently sold and secured another near the old homestead. He always solicited help from the younger boys, and would work them so hard that they would never want to go on that stint again. I think I have already said that when the quartet had hitched up the old "John horse" and his mate to the ancient carryall, and started on our famous first trip to New York State, David suspended his work in the field, and leaning over the fence as we passed, singing together, said, "Boys, remember that noise is not music." Then he turned and went to raking again. David was very "close," as the saying is. Nevertheless, on one occasion Asa and I had gone to a caravan with only twenty-five cents, the price of one admission, between us. We were bound to get through the gate on it in some way, but alas! the gate-keeper was obdurate, and only said, "Stand back, stand back, can't let you in for the price of one ticket." At last we concluded to go in search of some one to lend us a quarter. Just then David came up. "Boys," said he, "what's the matter?" We told him we could not both get in without another quarter. To our gratification, he took out twenty-five cents and gave it to us.

David was married April 28, 1829, to Betsy, daughter of Nehemiah and Rebecca S. Hayward. She was born February 19, 1806. Their children were Georgianna, born January 23, 1830, married John N. Gatch, of Milford, Ohio; Hayward, born January 19, 1832; Jesse L., born February 5, 1834; Elias S., born December 24, 1835; John W., born March 24, 1838, Virginia, born June 16, 1840, Delia Florence, born August 4, 1845; Lucretia O., born August 12, 1848, and married Leander Ketcham in June, 1873. They live in Mount Pleasant,

Iowa. They have four children, Florence, Leander, Winfield and Benjamin Hutchinson. Florence married Lewis Spidel. They also live in Mount Pleasant, and have two children, Elias and Alice Virginia Hutchinson married Fielding A. Kendall, March 15, 1864 Children: Nathan, born April 8, 1867; Florence Alice, born June 7, 1868; Katherine Prescott, born June 20, 1870; Susan Elizabeth, born October 16, 1874; Hayward Hutchinson, born March 18, 1876. Florence Alice married Herman A. Kelly, September 3, 1889. Children: Virginia Chandler, born June 1, 1891; Alfred Kendall, born September 21, 1892.

Noah, the third son, was not as tall a man as David, but was athletic and spry. He had a tenor voice, but gave it little attention, for his early years were given to "helping father out of debt," and he was the first of the boys to marry. He had a family of eight children. He had a loving heart, and was an upright, honest man. His principle was to owe no man anything. He had a fine farm on the edge of Mont Vernon, which is still owned by his family.

Noah married, April 5, 1827, Mary, the daughter of James and Azubah Hopkins, of Mont Vernon, N. H., who died May 16, 1866. Noah died March 10, 1873 Their children were: Frances Jane, born May 21, 1828, died October 25, 1833; Andrew Buxton, born July 9, 1830; Matthew Bartlett, born April 16, 1832; Aaron Bruce, born August 4, 1834; Ann Jane E., born May 15, 1836, married Daniel Sargent of Goffstown, N. H., Lucius Bolles, born January 6, 1839, married Alice M. Rollins January 6, 1864; David Judson; Mary Victoria, born June 22, 1844, died May 14, 1864, while teaching school at Orange, N. J.; Chestena Augusta, born October 5, 1847; Henry Appleton, born August 16, 1850.

THE TRIBE OF NOAH (p. 28)

Mary was the next child. She died at the age of four years. This was the first of the four family quartets, each "a nest of brothers with a sister in it," as Willis put it.

The fifth child was Andrew. His voice was baritone, and he sang bass in the family choruses. Like most of the other children he began active life early, but not being so enamored of life on the farm as many of his brothers, went to Boston at the age of eighteen, and commenced to tend store. For years he was engaged in mercantile business on Purchase Street, being a well-to-do merchant. Misfortune came to him in the California years. He chartered a vessel and sent it full of goods to that country, and it was never heard from. He had a family of five children. He was a great lover of music, and his house was often a home for his younger brothers when in Boston, during their early artistic struggles. He made a present to Asa of the violoncello which he played in our concerts so many years, and which is still kept in the family.

Most of our brothers were members in good standing in the Baptist church in Milford. During the revival which swept over the section in 1831 Andrew was in Boston. He was interested in religious matters, and in the hall over his wholesale and retail grocery store he established a religious society which was presided over by Rev. Mr. Speer, who was a Universalist. This liberal doctrine was meeting with much opposition from the established orthodox persuasion, but nevertheless he favored it. Brother Judson led the choir. As time passed on, however, Brother Andrew desired to avail himself of the ordinance of baptism by immersion. He at once went to Milford and besought my father to baptize him. "I will be baptized by an honest man," said he. So they together visited the Souhegan River, our familiar stream, the "Jordan" of Milford Baptists, and the conscientious father baptized the son. They were filled with the Spirit as they returned to the farm-house, and after receiving this blessing the brother returned to his Boston home, satisfied that his duty was well done. This was considered an overt act by the orthodox sentiment of the neighborhood, and many words of censure were heard. At a convention of clergymen which soon followed, the case was called up, but no one present offered condemnation. No one dared to pursue a case against honest "Uncle Jesse," whose reputation was beyond reproach, and when it was discovered that he was the offender the matter was dropped.

Andrew was married June 22, 1834, to Elizabeth Ann, daughter of Jacob and Catherine Todd of Rowley, and had five children: Jacob Todd, born July 10, 1836; Andrew Leavitt, born June 11, 1838, died 1867; Marcus Morton, born October 24, 1844; Benjamin Pierce, born April 14, 1848; Katie, born November 15, 1850, married Joseph D. Elms.

Brother Zephaniah was a farmer like the older boys, but quite early he was a pioneer. He went to Illinois and settled at Greenville, Bond County. There he lived in his log cabin, cooked his own corn meal, and just subsisted. He took the ague, and finally, after some years, started home again, taking what stock of cattle he had on hand. Before he reached home he had absorbed them all on the route. All he had left was two old horses. In those old days it took twenty-five cents to get a letter out to him, and he used to beg us not to send them to him. He substituted a newspaper, making a dot over certain letters, so as to spell a communication, — a rather original idea. He was our agent during two of the most successful years of the original quartet. He had a great ambition to have the whole family united in a concert company. He died on his Illinois farm at the age of forty, leaving three children.

Zephaniah was twice married, first in August, 1836, to Abby, daughter of Mark Perkins, of Mont Vernon, their children being Harriet, born July, 1837, died April 17, 1842; Hettie, born July 26, 1841; Levi Woodbury, born March 19, 1845; Mark Perkins, born 1847, died 1848. He married, second, September 10, 1849, Elizabeth Nettleton, of Newport, N. H., their child being Mary Frances, born February 6, 1851.

Then came twin brothers, Caleb and Joshua. Caleb was gifted musically, with a high pure tenor voice, but he chose to sing bass, and usually sang on that part in the church choir. He was quite devoted to the Baptist church. One day while the minister was expatiating on the great importance of a Christian life Caleb noticed a nodding among the congregation. It grieved him to see the people napping when such high sentiments were being preached, and suddenly from his station in the choir came in a high pitched voice, the exhortation, "Wake up!" There were no more naps that day. He died at forty-two, leaving five children.

Caleb married February 18, 1835, Laura, daughter of Oliver and Susan (Smith) Wright. Their children were Laura Ann, born January 23, 1837; Mary Josephine, born November 26, 1839; Susan Maria, born July 24, 1842; Caleb George Mason, born May 20, 1844; Caroline Jennette, born September 24, 1850.

Caleb and Joshua were as children called "the twin buglers." One would take a tin tunnel and the other a comb, and imitate the clarionet and bugle-horn. Their services were sometimes engaged at trainings and pubhe festivities. At the age of twelve, it became Caleb's duty to drive the cows, help milk, ride the horse to plough, and perform other tasks. While in the absence of girls in the family, Joshua was stationed in the kitchen to help mother. One baking day mother sent him to grease the pans for the dough. He made thorough work by plastering them with lard inside and out. Father had just bought the new farm, and all hands were cheerfully working to pay the debt upon it. Joshua had a very useful voice, on the middle register, and a good knowledge of music, and as he had sung in the choir from early youth, it was not strange that at the age of eighteen he was invited to take the lead. Disposing of the temporary incumbent of the office of chorister by a frank letter telling him that as there could be but one such functionary, it would be necessary for him to retire, Joshua assumed the position, and held it fourteen years. As we younger members of the family came along we were encouraged to join him, until at one time there were ten of us in the chorus. It will thus be seen that at the very beginning of our musical experience, Joshua had much to do with our development.

In 1836, by advice of the pastor of the church, Rev. Mark Carpenter, Joshua got together forty dollars, and went to Boston with his youthful wife, joining the music teachers' class formed by Lowell Mason and George J. Webb. When he returned to Milford, he at once inaugurated a new era in music. A singing-school was started in the society, and others were established in the adjoining towns, and this was continued for six or seven winters. It was his habit frequently to take one of his younger brothers to the schools in these towns, where their songs and instrumental music were a great attraction. Joshua was very proud of the accomplishments of his three younger brothers, and was very urgent in his advice to father to give us a chance to do something to astonish the world. The younger brothers were natural singers. Joshua was excellent at transposition, and his adaptation of music to the sense of the poetry was good. He was a good leader. I remember on one occasion a tribe of Indians came to Milford, and a union meeting of the churches of the town was held in the woods near their camp. Joshua, in selecting his tune for the hymn, chose a long-metre tune for a common-metre hymn. We sweat it out.

Joshua married June 3, 1835, Irene, daughter of Nathan and Sarah Fisher, of Francestown, N. H. Their children were Justin Edwards, born December 21, 1837; Lowell Mason, born 1839, died 1843; Julia Ella, born 1847, died 1848.

On the famous Thanksgiving when the family of thirteen children of the "Tribe of Jesse" made its *début* in concert at the Baptist meeting-house, to Joshua was committed the responsible task of making out the programme. After we had commenced our concert career, Joshua also started out, and did a good deal of concerting "on his own hook," the reputation of the family and the intrinsic merit of his entertainments making them quite successful. He would occasionally act as business agent for us, and would also sing in concert with the brothers. It was always possible for us, when any member of the main concert company failed to respond to a call for service, on account of sickness or other cause, to get a substitute in Joshua or Jesse. For thirty years or more Joshua gave an average of fifty concerts annually, and in that time he taught some sixty singing-schools. He had considerable literary ability, and besides publishing in 1874 his narrative of the family, wrote many interesting newspaper letters that are preserved in the family scrap-books. He died January 21, 1883, his funeral occurring at the Congregational church in Milford a few days later. Mr. Tainter, the pastor, made an impressive address, and then I gave a parting tribute to my brother, after which with my son Henry I sang, "The Lord is my Shepherd." Mr. John Mills, his friend from childhood, then spoke, and following this Sister Abby sang with us "No Night There." When his family had taken their last look at the face of our dear brother, we all joined in singing, "We are almost home, to join the angel band."

It seems proper that I should speak at considerable length of my brother Jesse, for present or absent, he was for many years so closely connected with the history of the original quartet and the concert entertainments by the brothers which followed its career, that his history is almost inseparable from ours. He was enthusiastic, warm-hearted, generous, in some ways eccentric, sanguine, gifted with a poetic temperament, and with an insight that made it possible to adapt his gifts as a song-writer to occasions where they told immensely for the advancement of the cause he espoused and to his own credit. At the early age of twelve he was sent to learn the printing business in the office of the *Farmer's Cabinet*, at Amherst. In his "Sketch of a Busy Life" Edward D. Boylston, for a lifetime the editor of that paper, has published a tribute to Jesse, which will be interesting not only to the friends of his youth, but to those in Massachusetts who knew him in his maturer years:

"Happy is the apprentice who has a Jesse Hutchinson for his associate. The boy truly foreshadowed the man. He was simply personified music. With a long comb wrapped in a strip of an unprinted *Cabinet*, he would distance Orpheus, provoke Æolus. On the office green by moonlight he would awake all the game-cocks in the neighborhood, and have them all a-crowing, by his imitations. Many were the long and strong pulls had with 'Jes' at the old Wells hand-press, for the 'belt', but his extra muscle always won — time, thirty and thirty-five minutes to a token (ten quires). And, too, when the President's message reached us in thirty hours from Washington, and forty-five minutes from Nashua (by the *Cabinet* express), on the all-night stretch putting it in type, Jesse at 'the stand' was always so much ahead, that all were fairly distanced, ourselves being judges. And he was as full of sunshine as of music and muscle. We recall a happy illustration of this. One summer day, at work at his case by an open window, a sudden breeze took his slip of copy into the garden. With the bounce and whiz of a katydid Jesse went through the open casement, and returning with his copy in hand, coolly remarked — 'The undeviating law of this office is *to follow your copy*.' He was a member and clerk of Engine Co. No. 1, whose 'tub' from long use was decidedly leaky, and a 'strike' was imminent. The machine was tested, and the clerk's record was 'In perfect *dis*-order!'

"The old engine and the old *Cabinet* have more than renewed their youth; the old press is still friskily 'flying its frisket' to record its own and this autobiography; those old 'stands' are still in good standing, and his old 'stick' and companion still stick by; but Jesse's 'form' has become 'dead matter' while in spirit he goes singing on —

"In the land by us untrod,
Of the sweet fatherhood of God.'

"After a life of signal brilliancy, in which he won the wide world's applause by his musical genius, and unbounded philanthropy and ever-flowing geniality, his harp ceased its sounding — and a world wept 'because he was not.' Peace to his ashes! — and may every future apprentice-boy share as genial and happy associates as were those of this apprenticehood."

This history has already related the facts concerning Jesse's removal to Lynn and engagement in the stove business, as also his long service as director of the choir of the Universalist church there. He enlisted in the anti-slavery cause through the influence of George Thompson's eloquence, and at once began to write songs to be sung in the conventions of the friends of emancipation. I have sketched the thrilling circumstances under which many of these songs were written. With the exception of the years when Zephaniah was our business agent, and short periods when Joshua acted in that capacity, Jesse was always our business man. Though he infrequently appeared with us in concert, he always shared equally in our profits. It is unnecessary for me to refer to the particulars of his death, which occurred at the age of forty, as they have been already detailed. Jesse was the first of us to see the beauty and worth of High Rock, and to secure it for a home. He was a close friend of Horace Greeley, who was a native of Amherst, and enjoyed the friendship of all the leaders in the great anti-slavery struggle. It would be easy to fill the remainder of this volume with tributes to his life and character which have been published. He left no family, his wife and five children all dying before him.

Jesse was a good correspondent, but his circle of relatives and acquaintances was so large, that while in California he resorted to the expedient of a circular letter to his loved ones, which was printed and distributed among them. The following is a sample:

SAN FRANCISCO, CAL., May 31, 1852.

DEAR FRIENDS AT HOME — Having many dear friends in my far distant home to whom I wish to send a word of cheer, and who may be anxious to learn a word of my present fate and those who accompany me — and being too limited in time to write to all — I have, through the courtesy of a brother printer, jumped into the *Herald* office, and am now picking up these little "messengers of thought" for a general circular.

Through the newspapers you will doubtless learn much of our trials and dangers during our weary voyage of fifty-eight days from New York. I have enclosed also to a few friends my rhythmical description. It was hurriedly and imperfectly done, but truthful in every particular. Nor did I tell a half our grievances. When I say that up to the present time, we enumerate nearly forty persons (who so joyously and hopefully left the dock with us on the twentieth of March, and who joined in our songs of farewell) — as having so soon gone to the land "whence no traveller returns," yea, more than that number, whose bodies now rest in the "stranger's grave," some at San Juan, some at Acapulco, some at San Diego, and others here — besides those, more solemn still, who have been buried in the silent deep — it will be quickly perceived that our lot has been cast in "dangerous places."

Yet my heart has not failed me (save once) through all our weary pilgrimage. At Castello Falls arriving at mid-day, under a burning sun, a sudden illness befell me, and report coming that the hotel to which we were wending was full of sick and dying, my faith faltered, and for an hour I wished myself "back again," once more among the dear friends and "good old folks at home." On consultation, our fears were ungrounded, and again our band of wandering minstrels pushed on to the goal of our ambition. At San Juan (pronounced San Wan), one of our number (Mr. Goodenow) was very sick several days, but kind and careful nursing finally restored him to wonted buoyancy and robust health. Miss Goodenow was also much indisposed during most of the sea voyage, but she has now fully recovered her elasticity of spirits and voice, and "sings like a nightingale," as she is. Mr. Dunning is yet suffering from slight fever, incident to the sudden change of climate, but well enough to sing in concert, four of which we have given. Mr. Oakley is hale, hearty and hopeful, albeit upon the Isthmus he barely escaped being mule-tilated by one of the donkeys. The basket of provisions and hard crackers were sent "far aft," by the nimble heels of the mule, while Mr. O. went as fast forward and for a time took a low note, in the key of B *flat*. But after the dust had cleared away, a shout of laughter announced the safety of Mr. Oakley, almost as miraculously rescued as the fictitious exploits and hair-breadth escapes of the celebrated Obadiah Oldbuck. So we trudged along, minus the preserves and crackers. As for me, I am what I am, as hearty and well as ever, though too much pressed by cares incident to this exciting, changing and wandering life. Yet my hope and my heart is above all difficulties and dangers, and so are we all, happy, hopeful, and harmonious, winning the good and golden opinions of the Californians. In due time, we hope to return safely again to home and friends.

I am delighted with the country, and this city is yet to be the Jerusalem of our land. Here, already, do we see perambulating the streets men from every kingdom and tongue under heaven — the swarthy Chinese from the celestial world, the European, and the native American of every hue and color. Lastly, though in the great future not the least, can now and then be seen a scattered few of the remnant race of the Ethiopians, pitied and pelted as they long have been, and yet the willing waiters and servants of their more favored brethren the whites. All are here, Jews and Gentiles, bond and free. And to this land of Hope and Promise, are the millions of the earth yet to come. I am glad England finds a diversion in Australia, for the crowds in their wind are too overwhelming. Half the folks that start for California ought never to move from home till better transits are provided, and Congress, capitalists and captains improve their own consciences and the comfort and condition of travellers — aye, and I might most justly add, the common people cultivate common-sense, cleanliness and comfort. Half of our troubles arise from the morbid and maddened rush of the multitude on board our steamers, lured by the sordid lust for gold, which perishes with the using and they with it. Friends at home will learn bye-and-bye (aye thousands have already learned by the woful lessons of death that have gone back like spectres to haunt the happy homes all over the land) what is their duty in the premises.

Here, on the Pacific side, men fare the worst; the steamers are inadequate to bring half the passengers that crowd in from the Atlantic. It is cruel and criminal to load the steamers so at New York. Strange, indeed, that when the whole tide of humanity is setting this way, and the whole nation, almost, seems "bound for California," that New York does not possess wisdom enough to despatch the noble *Baltic* and *Pacific* round the horn, and save more lives and earn more money in a twelvemonth than they will gather in a half century in their present obsolete way (California speaking) to the Old World. *Here* is the Eldorado! Behold, here is the city whose streets are paved with gold. *Here* is the finest climate under heaven and the mountains and valleys teem with wealth — the animal, the vegetable and the mineral. "O come to the glorious West, and buy a *Golden Farm!*" This is what I say and what we sing. And what we say here in song, we say in seriousness to friends at home, "Come out to California the most glorious and glowing and gladdening nation of Earth, but when you do come, come *wisely*." Send the noble steamers round first — blow up the rocks in the Isthmus rivers — (or blow up Vanderbilt for not doing it) — and when all is comfortable, and some decent hotels and roads are built on the Isthmus, then take your wives and little ones, and come out here by thousands and tens of thousands, yea thousands of thousands, and settle on your golden farms, and thus fulfil the great law and the prophets, "increase and multiply, and replenish the earth." Men! don't come without your wives, and women, don't let them, for your lives. But I digress immeasurably. I couldn't help it, the subject opens so widely. The great mail soon closes and my duties are multitarious.

only say to one, I now gladly say to all. Take good care of my home, my dear old cottage home among the hills, and Old High Rock. O! how many thrilling emotions loom up from the soul, as I think of the past, the present, and the great future. God bless you all, dear, dear friends, and forget not in your pleasant memories the spirit of him who, tho' a wanderer far, far away, yet clings with undying affection to those who are near and dear in native land. We shall meet again. On the wings of *Love* I send this little messenger. Pardon the errors of haste. I have set it up from the printer's case, just as the Spirit hath prompted. Again farewell.

Affectionately and forever, your brother and friend,

JESSE HUTCHINSON.

Jesse's last poem was written after an absence of a year in the land of "Gold and Graves," at San Francisco. It was as follows:

> "Brothers, I hear your voices sweet,
>   Re-echoing o'er the plain,
> And calling me in gentle tones
>   'O brother, come home again.'
>
> "I hear your voices, and Oh! I yearn
>   To see you all once more;
> But Fate says, I may not return
>   Again to my native shore.
>
> "I have a mission to fulfil,
>   For thus I'm doom'd to roam;
> When that is done, if Heaven's will,
>   Again I'll hie me home;
>
> "For thoughts go back to other days,
>   The good old days of yore,
> Again I am in childhood's plays
>   Around the old homestead door.
>
> "My father's voice again I hear,
>   Commingled with my mother's;
> While sisters' voices charm mine ear,
>   With our own dear band of brothers."

Perhaps nothing will better illustrate the love felt for Jesse by those who came most in contact with him, than the description of "High Rock" the place our brother loved so dearly, published in the *Herald of Freedom* in 1845, by N. P. Rogers:

"'High Rock,' the name of a commanding eminence in the rear of the town of Lynn, Mass. It overlooks the town and ocean and a great distance up and down the coast — as well as far back in the country. The view from it is very extensive, varied and striking. I do not remember such a view, from any point so easy of ascent. I went to the top of the rock, the other day, when I was at Lynn, with my beloved friend, Jesse Hutchinson, Jr., to see the spot he has chosen, and the beginning he is making, for the site of a cottage. He has obtained the title to the summit of High Rock, and of the ground at the foot of it, where if he succeeds, he will have an unrivalled spot. The rock ascends nearly perpendicularly some forty or fifty feet. At the foot of it, on the southeast side, spreads a patch of good ground for a building and garden — of, I should judge, a quarter or third of an acre. It then pitches off precipitously in front, some hundreds of feet to the level of the town below. On the sides it is accessible by a carriage road, up one side of which, a road is already constructed. Jesse has dug a well and found abundance of living water, on a spot pointed out to him by a clairvoyant friend. This encouraged him to dig, when all the waking and seeing people told him it would be vain to hunt for water at such a height. On the right of his level plat, in front, rises a splendid round rock some ten or a dozen feet, on which to plant a little summer house. The cottage is intended to be of stone, of which there appears to be an abundant quarry, and of beautiful quality, on the very spot he wants to level for its site. Jesse is a poet — but he can build songs, he will find, easier than he can stone cottages, in this flinty, hard-money world and among the cliffs of High Rock. If he succeeds in this design, though, he will have a home there like a song. It will look off, over Lynn with her ten thousand people, on to the main ocean — unobstructed on either hand as far as eye can reach. Egg Rock lays in the midst of the sea-prospect — and the ragged cliffs of Nahant. And it is within roar as well as sight, of the sea-beaten beach, one of the finest on the ocean's margin — the beach stretching more than a mile, level and smooth as a house floor and solid as a pavement. A fine race-ground for horses and carriages, which swarm it like flies, certain times of day, in the hot season. It would be most magnificent to see a storm break upon it, from the cottage at High Rock. Jesse means to cover the whole precipice of the rock behind the cottage, with one mammoth grape vine. It would be as sunny there, for the grapes, as Italy or any of the vineyard slopes of France. Off south you can see Bunker Hill Monument — its great solemn shaft of gray towering in the haze and smoke of Boston, and the State House dome looming just beyond it and surmounting the city — all in plain sight from the cottage window, by and bye, when Jesse has one. To the northeast, the Ocean House and Marblehead and Cape Ann — and from the top of the rock, the high mountains of Western Massachusetts. And Jesse means in his heart, to pile a tower of rude stone on the summit of High Rock — some five and twenty or thirty feet high, with an observatory in the top, where he will have a telescope, and the poetical creature indulges his fancy so far as to whisper he will have a *chime of bells* there! I wish to heaven he had the means. He would make High Rock the tallest affair on New England's 'rock-bound coast.' And how sweet to sit on the cottage piazza of a summer night and hear those sweet bells chime in answer to the moaning sea below upon the beach. And the whole enhanced and surpassed, some might, by the song of 'the Hutchinsons' themselves — his matchless brother-band ('with a sister in it') there from their own rocks of 'the Old Granite State.' Apropos — I propose here, they give Jesse a benefit or two, to be laid out in completing and embellishing the cottage on High Rock, in a manner that shall correspond with his genius, and be worthy their own peerless song. It wouldn't be the first time, at least in fable — that architecture has sprung into existence at the sound of Music.

"I say this much of High Rock and its contemplated cottage. The reader will indulge me in it, in tribute of respect to our Anti-Slavery Choir, and to their gifted brother who has given us the finest songs of the anti-slavery movement, as well as being one of the most devoted Abolitionists and most eloquent advocates of free speech."

The following poem was published by Jesse in a New York paper, under the caption "Welcome to the Hutchinsons, by a native of the Granite State," in the early '50's, just before the advent of the brothers for a series of concerts:

> Welcome, minstrels from the mountains,
>   To the Empire State again!
> Thousands of old friends in Gotham
>   Long to hear your warbling strain.
>
> Welcome from your home in Milford,
>   Skirting old Souhegan's shore;
> Sing to us of "teaming cattle,
>   And the good old plough" once more.

Come and tell us how you've made it,
   Raising pumpkins, wheat and corn,
And how many sheep and cattle
   Graze upon the old home farm

Thousands went to hear "Excelsior,"
   In our Metropolitan Hall,
And to catch those thrilling echoes
   As from Alpine heights they fall

O, to hear those songs of Freedom
   Which you sung in days of yore,
When our thousands shouted "bravo"
   And prolonged the loud "encore"

Some then thought you rather hasty,
   And of judgment seemed to lack
When you screamed, despite the hisses,
   "Church and statesmen, clear the track"

Even then we loved your boldness,
   Though we could not all approve,
Now what change! instead of coldness,
   Liberty songs are what we love

Come then, with your songs of gladness,
   Breathing through melodious strains,
Sing us of the good time coming
   When the slave shall burst his chains.

Help us cheer earth's stricken daughters,
   And the prisoner in his cell,
Sing, O sing of healing waters,
   Bubbling up from spring and well

Tell us if the fires of freedom
   Gleam upon your mountain high?
Will your sons rouse when we need them,
   When the storms are gathering nigh?

He who pens this homely welcome
   Once lived near your father's door,
And could many things recount you

Could sing of the generation
  Who lived there ere you were born,
When folks lived on plain bean-porridge,
  Spun their wool and cracked their corn

Those are days we love to "read of,"
  Even now, in modern times,
When the folks all wore plain homespun,
  Like your good old Uncle Grimes.[1]

Is the good old church yet standing,
  On Mont Vernon's lofty hill?
We could see it from the school-house,
  And from Deacon Wallace's mill

In the range of that old steeple
  Many a Yankee boy has grown,
Who has ris'n among the people
  To fame and fortune rarely known

Underneath its very shadow
  Came forth "George" of *Picayune*,
Three miles eastward, clear as sunshine,
  Our own "Horace," of the *Tribune*.

I might sing of many others
  Whom I knew in bygone days,
Last, not least, O Band of Brothers,
  You've obtained a world-wide praise.

Welcome, then, ye Band of Brothers,
  Lo, the multitudes await —
Long to welcome you with others,
  Warblers from the Granite State

In the early years of Brother Jesse's occupancy of the Stone Cottage on High Rock, he kept boarders, and it is rare indeed that such a company of choice spirits assemble in one household as Jesse and his guests. One of these was Capt. William Henry Merritt, afterwards a brave officer in the War of the Rebellion Another was Charles M. Merritt, then an apprentice in the *Lynn News* office and now one of the county officials.

[1] Mother's uncle, Milford's first settler.

Josiah F. Kimball, the editor and proprietor of the *News* and the "Tom Hood" of Lynn literature, was also there, with his brother, Rufus Kimball, then a journeyman printer, now one of the editors of the *Lynn Daily Item*, and prominent in political life. Still another was Edward Payson Weston, since of world-wide fame as a pedestrian, who was sometimes prevailed upon to take Jesse's place as business manager for the singing brothers. Many were the pranks these members of Jesse's family played upon him and each other, and the survivors still love to recall their experiences. Rufus Kimball says that on the night before the Minot's Ledge Lighthouse was washed away, he went into Jesse's observatory on the rock, and by the aid of the powerful telescope there, saw that the structure was still standing. Early the next morning he went up and looked again. The fears of the populace were realized; it was gone. He immediately went to the *News* office, got out an extra and announced the catastrophe before the intelligence reached Boston, by way of the harbor.

Jesse married June 8, 1836, Susanna W. Hartshorn, of Amherst. Their children, all of whom died in infancy, were James, Garrison, Charles Follen, Andrew Edward, Jesse Herbert, James, Susan Mary Emma.

In preceding chapters I have related the story of the death and burial of Brother Benjamin. He was a member of the "home guard," bore the burden of caring for the farm with Sister Rhoda when the remaining brothers and sister were in the concert field, and held himself in readiness to respond to the call whenever his voice was demanded in family chorus in the village or at the great conventions. His death at twenty-nine, was the first break in the ties that bound the children who grew up together. He was unmarried.

JUDSON J. HUTCHINSON — p. 255

Judson, "the dear, confiding, generous, loving, humorous, gifted Judson," as Joshua called him, was the eleventh child. The latter relates that while an infant upon the floor, he was heard to hum distinctly the melody of old Greenville,

"Gently, Lord, O gently lead us"

He was in the nursery alone with his mother, greatly surprising her, for she heard the music, but did not know whence it originated. I have told much of his musical history, for it was inseparable with my own, up to the time of his death. His voice was in many respects wonderful. It was high-pitched, expressive, sympathetic and of great beauty in every sense. He had great ventriloqual powers, and made good use of them in his concert work, especially in such songs as "Excelsior." He sang many comic songs in our entertainments, for he was a humorist, but as is the case with many men gifted with a great sense of humor, he had a very high-strung, sensitive organization that quickly dropped from a spirit of cheerfulness to one of the deepest gloom. Nothing could have more of pathos than his rendering of some of the songs he loved to sing. He was a master of satire, his song "Jordan" being a good illustration of this quality. Words are weak indeed when I would do justice to my brother, who was my closest companion during my boyhood and manhood. His best monument is in the love that was always so richly lavished upon him by his family, his friends, and the great public that has kept his memory green all these years. It is useless to go into the controversies that raged at the time of his death. It is a comfort to be able to quote from the many tributes to his life and character. Of him, Harriet McEwen Kimball wrote as follows in a metropolitan paper:

"To say he was a good man, in the ordinary acceptation of those words, is no more than might be said of many, and therefore conveys no acceptable idea of those peculiar characteristics which distinguished him from all others. He was manly in zeal and integrity, but womanly in refinement and sensibility. He was too sensitive to endure the rough life which must needs fall to the lot of man; and though his high sense of duty, when reason held sway over his faculties forbade him to forsake it, his inner nature secretly revolted alike from the battles and victories of earth. I remember on one occasion, when he came to our house in advance of his brothers' arrival to make preparations for a concert to be given by them, one of our household, surprised at seeing him unaccompanied, exclaimed: 'What! *alone?* and in such a storm?' He smiled a smile, which, like his nature, was feminine in sweetness and tenderness, and answered playfully, 'Yes! and it is quite time I *learned* to brave the elements!' The literal signification of his reply was a mere skeleton of words, but we, who knew him well, could penetrate to the soul of deeper meaning shrined in the form of speech. The brothers, John and Asa, who made up the delightful trio that for so many years have charmed the public with their unrivalled mountain melodies, were unwearying in their patient and affectionate care over Judson, whose delicate constitution and proclivity to nervous disease rendered him an object of their continual solicitude. I believe the world never produced a more beautiful example of fraternal devotedness than existed between the brothers, whose sympathies were as harmonious as their voices.

"In temperament, Judson was inclined to pensiveness and melancholy, and even in his gayest and most genial moods I never failed to observe the strong undercurrent of his thoughtfulness. In heart and manner he was as simple as a child. His reverence for all things good and beautiful was a childlike reverence. His love for woman in her purity and exaltation bordered on adoration; his sympathy for woman in her fetters of wrong and degradation was full of brotherly pity and distress. As he was naturally firm in his faith in God, so he was firm in his trustfulness of man; and any evidence of misplaced confidence in his fellow-creatures occasioned him deepest pain. I do not believe any other than a most 'righteous indignation' was possible to him. Charity and forgiveness he bestowed unstintingly on all who needed it. He was hopeful of '*the good time coming,*' but often depressed by the injustice and oppression which breed so many sorrows on the earth. Who that ever heard him sing, 'O had I wings like a dove,' can ever forget how the tones of his voice seemed to throb with the spirit of that desire which enabled him to render the thrilling song with such wonderful effect? Who that ever knew him can forget him? Not alone his rare vocal powers, of which I have no time to speak — not alone his eccentricities, which were unassumed and unostentatious — not alone his face, which, like his character, was a blending of manly and womanly beauty — not alone from his style of dress, which, though peculiar, was worn from his boyhood up and not assumed because of its becomingness — but his character, of which I have given a truthful though unworthy transcript, will make him dear to the memory of all who read it aright.

"In conclusion, I would add, that the simple doctrines of Jesus apparently engrossed his deeper thought and attention, and illumined his daily life with comfort and joy; and it is *our* comfort and *our* joy to believe that that Saviour has already welcomed to the heaven of the weary and heavy laden the spirit of him whose was one of the sweetest souls

"'That ever looked from human eyes.'"

A writer in a Milwaukee paper said:

"We visited the town of Hutchinson, Minnesota, a little more than a year ago, in company with Judson and his wife, and it was wonderful as well as beautiful, to see the affection with which he was received, especially by the poor, throughout all the region. They came to him with all their troubles and sorrows, as well as joys, and we were witness of many a little act of charity, whose recipients showered upon him in return, the most grateful love.

"One morning we stepped with him outside the door into the woods, by which his house was surrounded; all was silent and still in the dreamy flush of an Indian summer, not a bird was chirping in the branches. He said, 'Now we will have a concert,' and he poured forth such a flood of melodious sound as we never dreamed it in the power of mortal to produce. Then there was a rush of wings overhead, and an answering gush of song from the throats of a thousand birds. From whence they came, we could not discern. His bird-like, beautiful nature was in unison with theirs, and their little hearts beat responsive to his gentle heart, and recognizing their lover they welcomed him with a flood of rapturous melody, wonderful as divine.

"The Indian summer shall come again, and the little birds will listen among the rustling branches, and cry out with a painful twitter, but the song of their beloved will come not to them in the wail of the murmuring wind, yet in the gush of the morning gladness there shall descend upon them from out the auroral silence the spirit of his inspiration, whose song, mingling with theirs, went up through the hush of the Indian summer to gladden the souls of the angels."

Another newspaper correspondent wrote touchingly of the parting of the band of brothers, and then said:

"Three of the brothers were under our roof when the noble Lloyd Mills was wasting with consumption. The genial wit of the eccentric Judson, or the kindling enthusiasm of the impulsive John, could not dispel the shadow which rested damply on the soul of Mills. As they rose to leave, the three gathered fraternally around the invalid, and with hands upon his head, sang 'Where shall the soul find rest?' The scene has never passed from memory. It was joyous to weep under the influences of such an hour and such a song. The very light of bliss seemed to rest upon the half-sad and half-smiling countenance of Judson, as his eyes were upturned, and the harmonies of their voices seemed to die out among the angels. Mills and Judson are both over the river!

"A little over a year since, two of the brothers, Judson and John, were again under our roof, when the days of the writer seemed nearly numbered. We laughed and cried alternately at the quaint wit and touching pathos of Judson as the fulness of his child-like heart gushed out in chat and song. He spoke of terrible seasons of depression, which at times came over him, and shivered at the thought of some terrible fate which he was sure would some day be his. '*It will come,*' he said, and he looked dreamily and sadly into vacancy. As the brothers arose to go, they stood by the door, side by side, faces inclined kindly toward each other, and sang,

"'We live for those who love us,
For those who're kind and true,
For the heaven which glows above us,
And which we're hastening to.'

"The liquid eye of Judson was melting with that touching gentleness and trust which so endeared him to all who knew him, and as he clung to our hand, half-lightly said at parting, 'If we see you not again, we'll sing for you in heaven.'

"Some of our exchanges speak lightly of Judson — charge his death to his 'spiritualism.' Not a word of truth."

In 1843, while in New York City, the quartet bought a new scrap-book, and on the fly-leaf Judson inscribed the following lines:

The pages of this book are blank —
We may be so though now we're crank;
We'll fill it soon with music sweet,
And when our catalogue's complete

Each tune shall be of the highest order,
Or else I'm not a true recorder
It cost the buyer half a dollar
I wish he'd got one rather smaller—
Yet this will do quite well indeed,
For I'm a poet, and with speed
Will fill the title-page with rhyme
That won't look bad in after time
May future generations look
With pleasure on this old blank book,—
And think of seasons past and gone,
When Asa, Abby, Jud and John
Were giving concerts in old York—
Eating their food with knife and fork—
And had full stomachs and full houses,
Enough to buy three pair new "trouses"
I now submit these few blank pages
To be perused in after ages
Oh! may a better poet rise,
When this old critter's in the skies,
And if you ask who wrote these lines
It wasn't Shakespeare nor Old Grimes

Judson's most famous satirical song "Jordan," written during the Bell and Everett campaign, in 1856, is still often quoted. It was as follows:

JORDAN.

BY JUDSON J. HUTCHINSON.

I looked to the South, and I looked to the West,
  And I saw old slavery a comin'
With four Northern doughfaces hitched up in front,
  Driving Freedom to the other side of Jordan
    Then take off coats, boys, roll up sleeves,
    Slavery is a hard foe to battle, I believe

Slavery and Freedom they both had a fight,
  And the whole North came up behind 'em,
Hit Slavery a few knocks, with a free ballot box,
  Sent it staggering to the other side of Jordan
    Take off, etc.

If I was the Legislature of these United States,
   I'd settle this great question accordin',
I'd let every slave go free, over land and on the sea,
   Let 'em have a little hope this side of Jordan.
      Then rouse up, ye freeman, the sword unsheathe,
      Freedom is the best road to travel, I believe.

The South have their school, where the masters learn to rule,
   And they lord it o'er the Free States accordin',
But sure they'd better quit, ere they rouse the Yankee grit,
   And we tumble 'em over t'other side of Jordan.
      Take off, etc.

Pennsylvania and Vermont have surely come to want,
   To raise such scamps as Buck and Stephen,
And they'd better hire John Mitchell with shillalah, club and switchel,
   Drive 'em down to Alabama, and leave 'em.
      Take off, etc.

Edward Everett oped his mouth for the votes of the South,
   But his wishy-washy speech was so rotten,
That it struck to his spine, and he took a bee-line
   Lodged in State Street behind a bag of cotton.
      Take off coats, boys, roll up your sleeves,
      Cotton bags are hard things to battle, I believe.

But the day is drawing nigh that Slavery must die,
   And every one must do his part accordin',
Then let us all unite to give every man his right,
   And we'll get our pay the other side of Jordan.
      Rouse up, ye freemen, the sword unsheathe,
      Freedom is the best road to travel, I believe.

By his marriage with Jerusha Hutchinson, Judson had two daughters, only one of whom, Kate Hutchinson Burney, of Milford, is now living.

Rhoda was the twelfth child of our family, and coming, as she did, into a home where most of her brothers had never seen a sister, she was welcomed with exceeding joy. She possessed a high contralto, or mezzo-soprano voice, strong and melodious, with unusual flexibility. She always lived at the old homestead, and there her descendents remain. She was compelled from lack of physical and nervous strength to spend most of her life quietly, but nevertheless often in her younger days appeared with her brothers in convention work, and was the "sister" of the family quartet which sung through New England and New York State, while the other quartet was in Europe. She was twice married. Her first husband was Isaac A. Bartlett, and second, Matthew Gray, to whom she was married in 1855. Marietta Caroline Bartlett, her first child, was born March 17, 1844. Nellie Gray was born January 2, 1860. Two other children died in infancy.

It is unnecessary to give a further sketch of John and his tribe at this point, for our history is fully covered in this volume. As appropriate here, I will simply add a picture of the family group — John, Fanny, Henry and Viola — who sang together so many years after the "swarming."

Asa was the youngest son. I have spoken of my close relations with Judson, and it is true that we were nearer to one another in some senses than to the other brothers, but it is also true that for eighteen years I was always associated with Asa in concert enterprises, and meanwhile, as this volume has shown, we joined in many transactions of a business character. In fact, until the latter part of my life, there were few large business enterprises in which one was interested that did not also engage the interest of the other. As might have been expected, he was as a boy his father's favorite. Joshua records that while yet a child he would sit in church as the choir was singing, and indulge in moving his head against the old pew railing, producing a vibration so fine, that when the violoncello was in full blast, the feat, especially in the heavy cho-

262   THE HUTCHINSON FAMILY.

rals, was as effective as the sub-bass of a big organ, — guided entirely by his intuitive musical sense and innate love of harmony. Asa's voice, as he grew to man-

JOHN AND FAMILY.

hood, was a strong and heavy bass. While he had a good baritone register, he was able to descend to low C and double B flat with accuracy and ease, and his notes were a fine foundation for the harmony of the quartet.

AN OLD-TIME YANKEE FAMILY. 263

With the exception of myself, none of the family were so long and continuously in the concert-field as he. As long as his wife and children lived, the songs of Asa, Lizzie, Fred, Abby and little Dennett were as well known in the West as those of the tribe of John in the East, and each tribe often sang in the other's territory.

ASA AND FAMILY.

He died, at Hutchinson, Minn., November 25, 1884. During his later years, he made that town his permanent residence, and did much to develop it, temporally and in mental and religious lines. In the early '70's, he devoted the entire proceeds of an Eastern concert tour with my family to the erection of the Methodist church in his town. It was not strange that such a man died lamented. Under the caption, "His Music is Stilled," the *Hutchinson Leader*, which came out with turned rules, printed the following account of his death and funeral:

"Hardly had this little community recovered from the sad shock it experienced by the sudden taking away of the late Lewis Harrington and it is again plunged in grief over the death of Asa B. Hutchinson, one of the founders of the village. Although it was not unexpected, still many of us hoped against hope trusting that He who doeth all things well might see fit to delay the call that would take him home.

"For some weeks his condition has been such as to excite the anxiety of his friends, but it was not until about two weeks ago that any great fears were felt for the result. Then it was that alarming symptoms began to betray themselves, and he continued to grow worse until Death finally claimed its victim on the evening of the 25th.

"So widely was he known, and so universally beloved it hardly comes within our province, neither is it necessary for us to attempt eulogistic remarks concerning him. His life was like an open book — all might read — all might criticise. Yet so circumspect was he in all his dealings that criticism was completely disarmed. In earlier years he became one of that noble band of brothers and sisters that composed the celebrated family of vocalists that has made their name loved and revered in every household. Shortly after their organization they felt that they had been given a mission — fraught with danger, yet none the less inviting — the freeing of an enslaved race. Understanding and fully realizing their peril their voices were lifted up in sweet song in every hamlet and city in not only this but in foreign lands as well. Singing, praying, begging for the time when the dark blotch should be wiped from off our statute books. They lived to see their great work accomplished. Freedom reigned supreme throughout the land they loved so well.

"With this great mission performed the band virtually disbanded, but so strong was their love for music, also the desire to meet old friends, that the deceased, in company with members of his own family, still kept up occasional visits to different States, and during the memorable Centennial year one of the greatest attractions at Philadelphia was the sweet voicings of this honored family. Even now, within a few weeks of his death, he was planning a visit to New Orleans, there to meet and sing to those freedmen for whom he labored so long.

"In order that friends living at a distance might assist in the last sad rites the funeral did not take place until Friday at one o'clock. On this occasion it was fully attested how high in the public's affection and esteem he stood. The church was literally packed with sincere mourners and fully as many more lingered on the outside, all desiring to honor with their presence the one whom they all loved. At the appointed time, after a voluntary by the choir, Rev. J W Klepper delivered a brief prayer which was followed by a hymn. Hon Liberty Hall, by request of friends, then delivered the following short but beautiful eulogy:

"'This is the third time within the past few months that I have been called to aid you in conveying to their final rest the remains of our dear friends who have fallen by the way. First, Mrs Anderson, the beloved daughter of the kind and devoted father whose remains now lie enshrined before us. A few weeks later we conveyed from this house to that silent home prepared for all the living, all that was mortal of your distinguished fellow-citizen, Lewis Harrington, and now, before we have had time to recover from the shock of that sudden and untimely death, we are again summoned to perform the same sad duty for another old and dear friend, whose departure leaves a vacancy in our society that cannot and never will be filled. There was but one, there will never be another Asa B Hutchinson. Unique in character, one had to study him closely to know and appreciate his solid worth as a man and a citizen. Endowed with an excitable nature, his impulses were generous and noble. Quick to resent a wrong, he was equally quick to appreciate and reciprocate a kindness. Malice found no abiding place in the heart that for nearly sixty-five years sent the generous life-blood through the veins of that now inanimate body.

"'Thirty-five years ago, on the banks of the Merrimac, in New Hampshire, near the place of his birth, I first met Asa B Hutchinson. Older than myself by five years, he had already entered on that career that was to make his name familiar at every fireside in this broad land, possessed of that rare gift of song, that subsequently made him and his gifted family famous throughout the world. I remember as distinctly as if it were but yesterday, the impression that the ardent and enthusiastic natured young man made upon me. The bright world was then all before him, resplendent under a cloudless sky, and so full of joy and hope that it did not seem possible to him that clouds and tempests could ever arise. I see him now, as I saw him then, standing with four of his brothers, and that favorite sister, who still survives him — and by telegram requesting the reading of that beautiful psalm to which you have just listened — before an audience that filled the great hall, over the depot in Concord. I had never before been perfectly charmed with the melody and harmony of human voices, and from that day to this, there has been to me no music like the music of the Hutchinson Family.

"'The songs that Asa loved and sang were songs of sentiment, applicable to the times in which he lived. The anti-slavery sentiment that was destined in a few years to fuse the thought of New England in the white heat of indignant protest against that gigantic crime of the nation, human slavery, was just beginning to be fanned into a blaze, and nothing that was said or done contributed more to the final conflagration than the anti-slavery songs of the Hutchinson family, as they were sung in every town and hamlet from the Kennebec to the Mississippi. The influence for good that our friend has exerted upon the age in which he has lived, will never be known or appreciated, but the silent yet persuasive influence of his life will be felt long after his name is forgotten; for the songs that a people sing make a deep and abiding impression, and are potent influences in the formation of the character of society. If they are light and trivial they lead to triviality and folly; if they are imbued with a deep moral sentiment, their influence tends to develop and strengthen a healthy moral tone in society. We all know the general character of the songs sung by the Hutchinsons; their echoes have partially died away during the last decade, but not before they had accomplished the mission whereunto they were sent.

"'For ten or fifteen years before the war, the Hutchinsons furnished the music to which the great anti-slavery army marched to its wonderful conquests. It was their songs that inspired the hearts of the great anti-slavery leaders with the courage of hope. They were constant companions and co-laborers of Garrison, Phillips, Parker, Douglass, Gerritt Smith, and scores of other scarcely less distinguished leaders, and while these great reformers and orators appealed to the intellect and reason of the people, the songs of the Hutchinsons stirred the hearts of the great public and aroused the sentiment of sympathy for the slave. It may well be questioned whether the song was not more potent in the great effort that resulted in the emancipation of four million of slaves, than the cold argument addressed to the reason of man. Who of us that listened twenty-five years ago to that pathetic wail of Topsy, as rendered by the Hutchinsons, can ever forget the mingled feelings of indignation and pity that it inspired? Topsy stood out before us as a real character, the natural product of a system that made chattels of human beings.

"'But human slavery, with all its horrors, was too firmly rooted and grounded on our government to be either talked or sung out of its place, and when finally, in its desperation, it sought to rend in twain the government it could no longer control, and the friends of liberty and union were marshalled in its defence, there at the very front, beside the camp-fires beyond the Potomac, were the songs of the Hutchinsons heard, cheering the hearts of the despondent and inspiring the timid and wavering to deeds of honor and glory.

"'We have no standard by which we can measure the influence for good upon the generation so rapidly passing away, that our friend has exerted. For more than forty years he has stood here as a prominently in the public gaze, and, in his way, has made the most of life, and has faithfully used the gifts with which nature endowed him to make the world happier and better. That his efforts have been crowned with more than the average measure of success, those of us, who have for years known him intimately and felt the kindly influence of his genial nature, believe. And now that he has gone from us forever, we begin to feel how much of real, positive good and how very little of bad, we have lost. We are so constituted as to find a sort of pleasure in criticising the conduct of our best friends while they are living, but, when they die, the blemishes that we flattered ourselves we had discovered, all disappear, and only their virtues and good deeds are remembered.

"'I have thus far spoken of the deceased in his relation to the world through his profession. I should not do his memory justice did I fail to speak of him as a citizen, neighbor and friend. Asa B. Hutchinson was something more than a singer. He was a man of positive character, with broad views of life and its duties, a man who found his greatest pleasure in the prosperity and happiness of his fellow-men. He was devotedly attached to his home, and it was his oft-expressed desire to be buried here in the "Valley of the Hassan," that he made almost as famous throughout the United States as have the Hutchinsons the "Valley of the Merrimac," from whence they came. He was among the very first to make a home here, and the town that bears his name will forever remain a fitting monument to his memory. We are here to-day to fulfil his oft-repeated desire to lay his weary body away beneath the sod of the valley that loved him so well.

"'You, who for more than a quarter of a century have been accustomed to meet him in your places of business, in the church and at your firesides, will miss him. You will miss him in your social circles. You will miss the stimulating influence of his earnest and enthusiastic spirit that never quailed before any obstacle, however formidable, provided the object to be attained was one of public utility. If a church or a school-house was to be built, it was his quick and fertile brain that suggested the means to be used for raising the funds. It will be hard for you to think of any enterprise that has had for its object the moral, intellectual, or physical good of this people that has not received his hearty support. But his earthly work is done, and he has gone to that "mysterious bourne from which no traveller returns." Let us think of him as we knew him at his best estate, before the clouds of disease had closed in around him and obscured his mental vision.

"'Our friend was a firm believer in the immortality of the soul, and regarded death as but the door to another and better state of existence. With religious creeds, formulated by men, he had little to do. Religion with him was a practical, not a theoretical affair, and the spirit of true religion as displayed in the character and life of honest and good men, was always recognized by him whether exhibited in Protestant Catholic or Agnostic. It was a remark often made by him within the last few months, "My family and friends have nearly all passed over the dark river, and are beckoning me from the other shore." We can follow him no farther than the hither shore, and, having gone thus far and given back his body to the embrace of mother earth, our sad duty is done. Let us cherish his memory, and profit by the valuable lessons that his life has taught us.'

'He was followed by Rev. J. W. Klepper in a few pertinent remarks, in the course of which he alluded with much warmth to the time he had first met the deceased, the great love he had for him then, and how he had since met him, and always found him working for the right. He also alluded briefly to the life services of one who had always been to the departed friend a shield and guide, spurring him on to nobler deeds. He was pleased that God had called him to assist in placing all that was mortal beside the remains of her whom he had so fondly cherished. While it was a painful duty, still it was pleasant to think that now they would sleep side by side until the grand and glorious awakening.

"Miss Lizzie Pendergast then read a selection entitled 'Not Changed, but Glorified.' At first her friends feared she would not be equal to the task, so great was her love for the dear friend departed, but rallying, she seemed to throw her whole soul into the mournful duty, as if speaking to the silent one, reading better than we have ever heard her before.

"The singing of another hymn closed the exercises at the church and the solemn cortege slowly filed out of the edifice, following all that was mortal of Asa B. Hutchinson to the village cemetery, where the remains were deposited by the side of his honored wife and loved sons and daughters.

"In conclusion we would add, Mr. Hutchinson was indeed a remarkable man in many respects. In his business dealings he was thought to be close, yet he was generous to a fault when the hand of the truly needy was extended toward him. As a citizen of this place he was public-spirited in all that would redound to the general good. But for his efforts it is quite probable the Vineyard Methodist-Episcopal Church would never have been built. All remember his utter disregard of self in his efforts for the High School building. With children grown up he seemed to forget that he was burdening himself with unnecessary cares and taxes. He was in his sixty-third year, and leaves one son, Mr. O. D. Hutchinson, and a brother and sister, to mourn his

Asa and I looked very much alike. Our friend "Noggs" once said that one of us went to bed Asa and got up John. We were at the Marlboro Hotel at one time. A gentleman came in and engaged me in conversation on a matter of business. He wanted us to sing for an out-of-town concert. Before arriving at any decision, he happened to glance away from me for a moment, and caught sight of Asa coming down the stairs, some two rods away. With a look of surprise overspreading his features, and evidently chagrined to think I had got away from him so quickly, he left me and started after Asa, to stop him until he had decided the question.

Asa married Elizabeth B., daughter of Frederick B. and Phœbe B. Chase, of Nantucket, Mass. Their children were Abby, born March 14, 1849; Frederick Chase, born February 4, 1851; Oliver Dennett, born January 15, 1856; Ellen Chase, born May 22, 1861, died January 24, 1867.

Elizabeth, the fifteenth child and third daughter, lived but four years, and then left us. Her coming brought joy, her death the deepest sorrow, for a little child of four twines its affections in unbreakable cords around the loved ones in its home.

The fourth sister and sixteenth child was Abby, destined to become in many respects the most notable of the group. Her brother Joshua says: "A peculiar charm hung about her existence. Her gifts and development were watched with the greatest assiduity by the fond parents, while twelve brothers and sisters were guarding her childish steps on to virtue and excellence. She had scarcely entered upon her teens before she was brought into public life. Even at the age of eleven she was initiated into the quartet, and had given many public concerts. Possessing a large share of the 'gift,' and blending with her genial nature a smiling face radiant with the joys of conscious innocence, she modulated her voice in the harmony perfected by her own sweet contralto, or chanted her little '*Spider and the Fly*' so naturally that it gave the highest emotions of pleasure to the multitudes that heard it; as also her '*Jamie's on the Stormy Sea*,' with the finale, '*Home returned to Love and Thee*,' given with that touching naturalness peculiar to those bewitching sounds."

Abby died November 24, 1892. On December 7th, of the same year, in the New York *Home Journal*, Frank B. Carpenter wrote a tribute to her memory of several columns, from which I quote:

"The death of one so widely known throughout the United States and Great Britain as the sweet-voiced sister of the famous 'Hutchinson Family' quartet, who created a sensation when she first appeared before the public fifty years ago, almost as great as that of Jenny Lind, and her successors in the world of song afterward, justifies a brief biography in the *Home Journal*, with whose founders, Morris and Willis, she was a special favorite. Mr. Willis, writing of the Hutchinson family, with that felicity of expression so characteristic of him, coined the phrase which accompanied the singers ever afterward, 'A nest of brothers with a sister in it,' and to General Morris's exquisite poem 'My Mother's Bible,' they wedded their own music, and this song became one of the great favorites of their concerts.

"The whole family were singers, but the quartet was composed of Judson, John, Asa and Abby. The death of Abby leaves John the sole survivor of the family. This brother last year celebrated his seventieth birthday at High Rock, his home in Lynn, Mass. His voice is wonderfully preserved, retaining all of its original sweetness.

"Abby was a born musician. As soon as she could talk she began to sing. The first songs she learned were the hymns taught her by her mother while singing at her spinning-wheel. At the early age of four years she displayed such musical talent that people would come from afar to hear her childish songs. A little later she went to the district school, with her sister and young brothers. Her studies were pursued with avidity and she readily memorized pieces to speak or sing. A

ABBY HUTCHINSON PATTON 1892 (p. 270)

was when she and a rival schoolmate were allowed to choose sides in a 'spelling match,' when Abby triumphantly 'spelled down' the whole school.

"As the father had a large farm there was much outdoor work to do. While the brothers worked they sang. Rhoda and Abby would sing also with the mother, over their work, and when the father and the boys would come in to their meals, all voices would join in a song that would make the house ring. The evenings were usually spent in musical practice. Abby had an alto voice, and could make her own part, no matter how intricate the melody might be. To test her abilities, her brother Judson would sing the scales, and difficult improvised melodies, bringing in chromatic runs and changes. Abby would never falter, but would match him every time with her harmonious notes. Her ear was extremely sensitive to sound, and she always sang in perfect tune. Musical by inheritance, her childhood surroundings were all of music, melody and harmony.

"In 1839, when only ten years old, Abby made her first public appearance as a singer. This was at a concert given in the Baptist church in Milford, which was built by her father. On this occasion the parents and their thirteen children all took part, Abby singing with her sister, Rhoda, the evening song to the Virgin, 'Ave Sanctissima.'

"In 1841, Judson, John and Asa commenced their public concert career, with their Sister Abby as their chief attraction. For two years they made New England their chosen field, and went from town to town and from city to city, with varying success. Their habit for several years was to sing in the autumn and winter. Spring and summer were devoted by the brothers to the management of their farms, and by Abby to her studies at the academy in Hancock, N. H., and at the Edes Female Seminary, Plymouth, Mass.

"Early in May, 1843, the Hutchinson Family made their first visit to New York. They took the public by storm. One enthusiastic editor, who was a great lover of music, wrote of them: 'The harmony of this band was never surpassed by human throats. It moved to tears, it reached into the solemn depths of the soul, it was God-given and Heaven-inspired.' The press published extended accounts of their concerts, which were given in the old Broadway Tabernacle.

"The Hutchinsons were never mercenary; they aimed to make their music serve the cause of humanity. They were Abolitionists from principle, and in singing anti-slavery songs, they would sometimes be hissed and threatened with personal injury, but the presence of Abby held the pro-slavery audience of that day in check. With her marvellous voice and captivating manners, and a certain undefinable, magnetic power, she would look directly into the eyes of the mob leaders, invariably with the effect of subduing the unruly spirits. There was a charm about her that was irresistible. The anti-slavery conventions were often disturbed by mobs, but when the Hutchinsons began to sing, the uproar was hushed as by magic. Abby's voice would ring out with 'The Slave's Appeal,' and in the hush that followed, Garrison and Wendell Phillips would get a hearing. The songs she loved best were those which inspired the hearts of the great anti-slavery leaders, and other reformers, with courage and hope. Together with her brothers her voice was often heard in the lowly cottages of the poor, in the gloom of the prison, within the joyless almshouse, and at the gatherings of the people when they were called together in behalf of suffering humanity.

"Jesse Hutchinson was a gifted song writer, and the words of many of the Hutchinsons' songs were written by this brother. He wrote 'The Good old Days of Yore,' 'The Slave Mother,' 'Get off the Track,' 'Cottage of my Mother,' and other songs applicable to the times, which have become famous.

"In August, 1845, the Hutchinsons visited Great Britain, where a year was spent with great success in concert and social life. In the genial homes of Charles Dickens and Macready, of Harriet Martineau, Alexander Ireland, William and Mary Howitt and many others, they were welcome guests. They found warm friends in Douglas Jerrold, Mark Lemon, editor of London *Punch*, Hartley Coleridge, Eliza Cook, Mrs. Tom Hood, Samuel Rogers, Hogarth, the historian of music, Hon. Mrs. Norton, and such members of Parliament as George Thompson, Richard Cobden, W. J. Fox and John Bright. Charles Dickens gave a 'Hutchinson Reception' at his home just before their opening concert in London. Mr. Hogarth, the father of Mrs. Dickens, and the critic of the Italian Opera, after hearing the family sing, took them by the hand and said that he never before had heard such harmony. When the evening came for the opening concert the Hanover Square Rooms were crowded by a gathering of prominent literary and musical people. Abby, modestly attired in white, was radiant with happiness and intelligence. It was something new to behold one so modest, so artless, commanding the attention of English audiences. She won the hearts of all. Her voice was full and clear, and her execution faultless. Her singing of Tennyson's 'May Queen' had a heavenly charm. The first part was sung with such exuberance of youthful joy and hope as to win the instant uncontrolled applause of the audience. The second part in sad and mournful strains carried home the words of this pathetic song to every heart. It seemed an angel's voice whispering to the dying May Queen peace and resignation. It was the passing of a spirit to that heaven where the sun of righteousness forever shines. She lifted the audience to a state of unparalleled exaltation. The next day the press of London rang with the praises of the American singers.

"Mr. Alexander Ireland, editor of the *Manchester Guardian*, wrote:

"'Abby, the sister, is sixteen years old, with a bright intelligent face, speaking dark eyes, and exquisite complexion. Had Wordsworth known her, he would have immortalized her. She is totally unspoiled by the admiration and applause which her singing everywhere calls forth. Her grace of manner is natural; she is perfectly unconscious and unstudied. Her moral qualities are equally beautiful and winning. No one can converse with her without feeling himself to be in the presence of an artless, pure and simple nature, which no applause, or success, can divest of its original freshness.'

"'Throughout Scotland and Ireland the family had uninterrupted success. The inexpressible sweetness of Abby's voice seemed, as one Dublin editor expressed it 'like the subdued and distant voice of an angel from the upper deep.' Of 'The Pauper's Drive,' an Edinburgh editor wrote: 'I feel I would like to be the pauper whom nobody owns, if *such* a voice would sing my requiem.' A great favorite with the public was Abby's rendering of the popular ballad 'Jamie's on the Stormy Sea,' which always roused the audiences to the highest pitch of enthusiasm. The Hutchinsons' last concert was given in the great Free Trade Hall in Manchester. There were present between six and seven thousand people. It was sublime to see that ocean of human faces respond to every motion evoked by the thrilling strains of these simple children of the 'Old Granite State.' The genius of man's better nature seemed to be rejoicing, weeping, or prophesying in tones that caught their sweetness from the fountain of all harmonies. There was a magic cadence in each silvery note, which acted upon the heart like the refiner's fire, but to purify.

"In August, 1846, the Hutchinsons returned to the United States. After a brief rest, they visited the principal northern cities, their English success adding much to their reputation and popularity. During the next two years Abby introduced many new and beautiful songs. They breathed the spirit of freedom, of love, of hope, of joy and of sorrow, which find a response in every bosom.

"On February 28, 1849, Abby Hutchinson was married to Mr. Ludlow Patton of New York, a member of the New York Stock Exchange, and a son of the late Dr. William Patton of New York, one of the founders of the Union Theological Seminary, and the founder of the Evangelical Alliance.

"After her marriage Mrs. Patton sang occasionally with her brothers on special occasions. In 1850 she brought out 'If I were a Voice.' It seemed truly an 'immortal voice.'

"'To speak to men with a gentle might,
And tell them to be true.'

"Her next song was Mrs. Gildersleeve Longstreet's 'Mrs. Lofty and I.' In rendering this music composed by her brother Judson, her sympathetic voice seemed to reach the very soul of her listeners. The song still lingers in our ears.

"At the outbreak of the War of the Rebellion in 1861 Mrs. Patton again appeared in public, believing it to be her duty to do what she could to rouse the people of the North and bring about the abolition of human slavery. She sang for a year, with her brothers, the songs of freedom and patriotism.

"In April, 1873, Mr. Patton retired from business. For the next ten years Mr. and Mrs. Patton travelled for pleasure through Europe, Asia, Africa, and all portions of their own country. While in Rome, Italy, they saw much of William and Mary Howitt, who were then residing there. On their departure they received from Mary Howitt the following tribute:

"'TO MR. AND MRS. LUDLOW PATTON ON THEIR DEPARTURE FROM ROME FOR PALESTINE.

"'They are, dear friends, Christ's chosen ones who bring
  The sweet accords of peace to silence strife;
Who cast the fragrance and the flowers of spring
  Over the dark and desert wastes of life.
Who lift up the down-trodden, or who go
  As He did, to the sinful souls in prison;
Who love the poor and humble, yet who know
  Him, not the ever crucified, but risen.
Thus have you sought, dear friends, to serve him truly;
  Now, fare-ye-well, and may His love divine
Send a commissioned band of angels holy,
  To lead you through His land of Palestine.'

"On their return from their Egyptian and Palestine trip, Mr. and Mrs. Patton renewed their travels through Europe, visiting every country therein, except Portugal and Lapland. In the summer of 1879 they visited Sitka, Alaska, and then made the tour of Washington, Oregon and California, visiting all points of interest. They were so much pleased with San Diego, California, then a small town of two thousand people, that they afterward spent three different winters there, and watched with interest the growth of the city to its present size and importance.

"During her travels, Mrs. Patton was a frequent contributor to the American newspapers, describing many scenes and persons, and giving her own views on the questions of the day, more especially affecting the welfare of women.

"Mrs. Patton had not sung in public for many years, but her voice lost none of its sweetness, nor did she lose that winning vivacity of manner which characterized her in earlier days. Her husband was always a great lover of music, with a good tenor voice, and together they often entertained their many friends at their own home, or during their

LUDLOW PATTON — p. 274

"Among Mrs. Patton's musical compositions the best known are 'Kind Words can Never Die,' and Tennyson's 'Ring Out Wild Bells.' In 1891 she published a little volume entitled, 'A Handful of Pebbles,' consisting of her poems, interspersed with paragraphs and proverbs, containing the essence of her happy philosophy. Many of these 'Pebbles,' both in prose and verse, are gems of wise and happy expression.

"Mrs. Patton was closely identified with nearly every reformatory enterprise for benefiting the human race. She was interested in the education of women, and was an earnest believer in woman suffrage, which movement she aided by tongue and pen. Her hand was ever ready to help the needy, and her words to give courage to the weary and hopeless. Religious creeds had no interest for her. She fellowshipped all good people, whether Protestants, Catholics or Agnostics.

"In her last years Mrs. Patton will be remembered as a lovely, silver-haired woman, retaining all the charm of manner, and the attractiveness which marked her golden youth. Time touched her very gently. Her sweet face lost none of its charms. Her friendships were many, both with men and women. Alice and Phœbe Cary, Whittier and Greeley, Theodore Parker, Beecher and Wendell Phillips, Garrison and Frederick Douglass, Charles Sumner, Elizabeth Thompson, Grace Greenwood and Mrs. Stowe, all loved and honored Abby Hutchinson.

"Her last public appearance was at the funeral of Whittier, on which occasion her brother John and herself sang the requiem

"'Lay him low, lay him low,
Under the clover or under the snow.'

The funeral services of Mrs. Patton were held at the residence of Mr. Lucius B. Hutchinson, 314 West Fifty-seventh Street, Saturday afternoon, November 25th. Rev. Cornelius Patton, of Westfield, N. J., a nephew of Mr. Patton, made a most appropriate and touching address. Mrs. Sarah Barron Anderson, long connected with the choir of Rev. Dr. Paxton's church, rendered exquisitely Bonar's hymn, 'Beyond the Smiling and the Weeping,' and 'Some Sweet Day, By and By,' and the brother, John W. Hutchinson, in compliance with the desire of Abby, sang 'There is no night there,' and 'The Lord is my Shepherd.'"

The above sketch was written by the artist who painted the portrait of Abby which is described in another chapter. It shows plainly that when he made the picture he had the advantage of an intimate friendship with his subject. Many points of her life history are so told in Mr. Carpenter's biography, that it is unnecessary to go into them further. The literary instinct was developed in Abby more fully than in any other member of the family, as is evidenced by the large number of letters of travel, poems, and other contributions in the leading publications of the country for many years past, some of which will find a place in this volume. Abby's personality was charming, indeed. She had very decided convictions in regard, not only to the great problems of the day, but as to the way the Hutchinson family should meet them. She was not one who tamely acquiesced in the views of others, without at least expressing her opinion, but in a family composed without exception of members who also had convictions, and were not averse to expressing them, sometimes to the point of practical rupture, it was notable that Abby never aroused animosity. She was loved, adored, almost worshipped by all her brothers and sisters. In the days of the quartet, it was the highest privilege of each of her brothers to see that she was well cared for, comfortable and happy. Whatever hardships they had to undergo, she must not bear them if it was possible to prevent it. In return, she soothed them when in trouble or sick, and in the infrequent cases where there must be night journeys to meet engagements, or it was simply impossible to provide as comfortably for her as we felt she deserved, she did not complain, but made herself the light of the party, helping us to forget our trials. Her husband's business success made a continuance in the concert field quite unnecessary for her, and it was only the conviction that she could do good to causes that she loved, that persuaded her to sing during her married life. But she never forgot her art, and always rejoiced in the success of her brothers. She possessed the rare faculty of seeing just what was the proper manner of celebrating particular events, which is only an outgrowth of the genius of always doing the right thing at the right time. This was shown in innumerable ways. If she was returning from a transatlantic journey she timed it so as to get home and have a reunion with the family on mother's birthday. Anniversaries of this character

THE MOTHER OF THE HUTCHINSONS.

were never forgotten in our family, by-the-way. At the celebration of my own seventieth birthday, she was everywhere present, seeing just who ought to put in a word here, and what song should be sung there. She was the life of the occasion. For one of us to go to New York without finding time for a side trip to Orange, N. J., to see Abby, would have been not only a deep grief to her, but a matter that would have troubled our consciences, caused an irremediable regret, and spoiled the trip.

Abby, with all my brothers and sisters, has passed on before me to the better life. She "rests from her labors and her works do follow her.' In her earth-life she placed the emphasis upon deeds of kindness, lives of mutual helpfulness. Perhaps her view might be expressed in the words of another:

>"Character makes friendship brightest,
>   After all
> *Real worth* makes dark hours lightest,
>   After all
> Not the creed our friend's believing,
> Or the dogmas he's receiving,
> But the noble life he's living —
> Help to human hearts he's giving —
> Makes us in his strong love rest,
> For the weary soul the best,
>   After all
>
> "Most divine are those who love us,
>   After all
> Like the angel ones above us,
>   After all
> Said the holy Galilean
> When he kept the rite Judean:
> 'I no longer servants call you,
> But my friends, what'er befall you,'
> And his followers there found rest —
> For their weary souls the best —
>   After all"

Abby exalted friendship, and believed it her high privilege to make her friendship a prize worth having. As a result, her memory will be cherished, and every word of her letters to hosts of correspondents preserved as priceless mementos, until a generation has passed away.

Abby's own literary sense would hardly reckon the following lines as worthy specimens of her poetry, but they are of value as showing her warm, generous heart, and her vivacity of spirit. The poem was a letter, sent us in the early '50's, and would of course, if intended for publication, have been written with more care:

IMPROMPTU LINES FROM SISTER ABBY, ORANGE, N J, TO JUDSON, JOHN AND ASA, IN NEW HAMPSHIRE.

White-Washed Cottage, July 27

Dear Boys, good morning,
It has left off storming
And my heart is beating
To send you a greeting
So list to the story,
Not of "Old Mother Cory,"
But of Ludlow and wife,
Who are happy in life
Yesterday came to hand,
From my brave brother band,
Some lines of good cheer,
To our hearts ever dear,
How our hearts did bound
At the welcome old sound,
"They're coming again! They're coming again!"
Let hill and vale repeat the strain,
"We'll see them again! we'll see them again!"
How I love you all,
Short brothers and *tall*,
And my heart will rejoice
To again hear the voice
Of your wild notes ringing,
With your wild mountain singing

Dear Jesse has gone, and he's happier far
In his home beyond the bright morning star,
He longed for a world full of life, full of light;
There he drinks of the sunshine — there's to him no more night
He has with dear *Benny* a love-song begun,—
We'll all sing the chorus, when our work here is done
Mother says that father is beck'ning us on,
And that soon her children, *all, all* will be gone,

But she too will go with us, and then our band
Will be joined never to part in the Heavenly Land;
Oh, we must not shudder to think of old Death,
Though he cuts away all with his keen icy breath
He is but a messenger, God has given
To call his poor wanderers all home to Heaven
Our duty is plain — do good while we can,
Help elevate all, child, woman and man

Sing on my dear brothers, sing songs that endure,
Songs of *Freedom*, of *Temperance*, the *good* and the *pure*
So that *God* may say, " Children, your work is well done,
Enter in, faithful servants, sit down on My Throne !"

. . . . . .

I think while we can we should do a good turn,
So I ran out a minute to help Katy churn,—
You see that my thoughts soon leave the sublime
And come down to earth with poor, simple rhyme
I believe our kitty is more blest with the mews (muse)
Than I am, the thought almost gives me the blues
But this morning I feel just foolish enough
To bother you with my nonsensical stuff,—
I know you boys won't care if I do,
But if you expose me, woe, woe unto you
And now I want you all to remember
To come on here by the first of September,
For the World's Temperance Meeting is then in the City,
And if you're not there, it will be a great pity.
Then come, stay with us, and cut up your pranks,
Until the great party at the N. A. Phalanx.
I want you to come and see our old house,
And we'll tuck you away as snug as a mouse
If the girls come too, we'll make beds on the floor,
Such sleeping as that you've all had before
But where there is *heart room*, the *house-room* is plenty,
And I *guess* on a pinch we'd accommodate twenty
Give regards to all the good friends you meet,
To see them once more would be a great treat.
I am happy now wherever I be,
If I only can feel the dear Lord loveth me

. . . .

Now do what you think best for you to do,
And I'll love you, dear brothers, and bid you adieu

Abby

AN OLD-TIME YANKEE FAMILY. 281

The following tribute to Abby's singing, from Elizabeth Cady Stanton, deserves to be quoted. It was published at the time of her death:

"All through our fierce anti-slavery conflict there were youthful voices heard that could still the wildest storms From the White Mountain tops of New Hampshire came the songs of freedom that have echoed round the globe, making the Hutchinson Family and our Quaker poet immortal in verse and song. To many of Whittier's stirring sentiments these singers gave a new power and significance that the reader never had felt before. He was to them an inspiration, making a rare combination of harmonious influences, alike pleasing to all classes in all latitudes, to the rough pioneer on the far-off prairies, as well as to the nobility of the Old World in the palaces of kings, for music is the one universal language that speaks to every heart. This band of sweet singers has passed away, one brother only remains, now 'Sister Abby's' sweet voice is silenced forever. But she will not be forgotten by the generation that felt the inspiration of her song. The first time I saw 'charming little Abby,' as she was familiarly called, was on the platform with her four stalwart brothers in old Faneuil Hall. It was in a crowded anti-slavery meeting presided over by a howling mob. Neither the fiery eloquence of Garrison nor the persuasive, silvery tones of Phillips could command a moment's hearing, but the Hutchinsons' sweet songs of freedom were listened to in breathless silence. The very sentiments the mob applauded in the songs they would not let the orators in plain English say. Abby, with her youth and beauty and her sweet, unaffected manners, won all hearts. There was a pathos in her voice, high and clear above the deep bass and tenor of her brothers, that brought tears to many eyes. Indeed, their simple ballads, touching all earthly sorrows, and their glad prophecies of the good time coming moved their audiences alternately to smiles and to tears. The widespread influence of the Hutchinson family in the war for freedom cannot be overestimated."

Another of Abby's contributions to the press appeared in the *Portland Transcript*, and is as follows:

Naples, March 7, 1894

Many Americans have visited Naples this winter with the hope of seeing some unusual demonstrations from Vesuvius, and though Professor Palmieri still declares the mountain to be "in a state of eruption," it has not yet reached the boiling point. It is a mere question of time, however, or rather of the thickness of the crust which surrounds the molten mass, whether it gives way to-morrow or six months hence. Those who have been up "the cone" this season give wonderful accounts of strange rumbling, roaring and hissing sounds coming from the mouth of the crater. It is as though Macbeth's witches with all their fraternity were busy stirring the great cauldron to the song of "bubble, bubble, toil and trouble."

The brilliant color which is now often seen against the white smoke of Vesuvius being a reflection of the flames within, is another proof that the fire is getting very near the surface. Professor Palmieri has invented a wonderful electric instrument which is constantly *en-rapport* with the volcano, so that daily communications are telegraphed to the papers, what movements the great Mountain of Fire is about to make, or whether it will soon change its base; the seismograph will also at the first approach of danger, give timely warning to those dwelling under the shadow of the mountain, so that they may escape the horrible fate of those who were lost at Pompeii and Herculaneum.

I last wrote you of the carnival. People are now trying to get back to their usual way of living, but it is a difficult matter to get on a long face when one has been laughing steadily for a week. One noticeable fact which strikes Americans as peculiar in Europe, is that here Sunday is most religiously kept as a holiday, if kept at all. In many places, people go about their usual week-day vocations, treating all days alike; though now it is generally known that by one or another nation each day of the week is observed sacredly. Sunday, by the Christians; Monday, by the Grecians; Tuesday, by the Persians; Wednesday, by the Assyrians; Thursday, by the Egyptians; Friday, by the Mohammedan nations; Saturday, by the Jews and Seventh-day Baptists. Thus, while some hold sacred one day of the week, there are others who esteem all days alike, and who believe it lawful to do good on any day.

On the evening of the 22d of February, the birthday of Washington was celebrated by Americans in a manner worthy of the day. Our American consul, B. O. Duncan, Esq., with his accomplished wife, both hospitable and loyal South Carolinians, gave a charming reception at their pleasant rooms on the Corso Victor Emmanuel. Eleven States were represented in Mrs. Lippincott (Grace Greenwood) of the *New York Times*, Col. T. W. Knox, known by his contributions to the *New York Tribune*, also by James Cooley Fletcher, the Naples correspondent for the *American Register*, Paris. The Diplomatic and Consular Service had their representatives in Mr. Goodenow, of Maine, our late Charge and Consul-General at Constantinople; by Mr. Oscar Meuricoffre, Consul-General for Switzerland, and by our worthy host. The guests, after being presented to the lady of the house, walked to the

which the American colors were gracefully festooned and all paid respect to the well-known, genial face, after which conversation became general. The entertainment of the evening was enlivened by some really fine singing by Signora Barilli, who rendered the solo portion of the "Star-Spangled Banner" in a magnificent style, while, under the direction of her husband, Signor Barilli, the whole assembly joined in the chorus.

Professor Barilli is half-brother as well as teacher to the Patti family — Carlo, Adelina and Carlotta. He is a thorough musician, and for many years conducted the Italian opera in New York, where he became a naturalized citizen of the United States. Some other American songs were sung, and then Grace Greenwood, who was the "bright particular star" of the evening, recited "Barbara Frietchie" in thrilling tones, which reminiscence of our war brought with it "tears and love for the boys in blue," "love and tears for the boys in gray," as in that poem Whittier has immortalized Stonewall Jackson as well as good Dame Barbara. And so we celebrated the anniversary of the birth of our first American President on this the centennial year of the birth of American Independence.   A. H. P.

The poems here quoted are all from Abby's book, "A Handful of Pebbles," published a few months before her death.

THE COZY CORNER

In a cozy corner,
  Safe and snug and warm,
Lies a little birdling,
  Sheltered from the storm.

Little shining forehead,
  White and pure and fair,
Little wavy tresses
  Of bright silken hair.

Little pearly eyelids,
  Shading eyes of blue,
Little smiles and dimples,
  Little mouth so true.

Little rosy fingers
  Reaching for the light,
Catching at each shadow
  Passing out of sight.

And a mother singing
  Soft and low and sweet,
"Father, keep my darling,
  Guide his little feet.

"Many steps and weary,
  In his path may be
Lead him gently, Father,
  To his home and Thee."

In a cozy corner,
  Safe and snug and warm,
Lies a little birdling,
  Sheltered from the storm.

And this cozy corner
  Is a mother's heart,
Warm and pure and holy,
  Of God's love a part.

DAISIES AND CLOVER.

Oh, welcome me home, my dear daisies and clover,
  Give greeting to me;
Lift up your sweet heads and welcome your lover
  From over the sea.

I love your dear faces, my daisies, my clover,
  My long sorrows flee,
As near you in mist of the morning I hover,
  Just home from the sea.

My pure, honest daisies, my honey-bee clover,
  No welcome can be
More sweet or more warm to a world-weary rover,
  Than that you give me.

When I am sleeping, dear daisies and clover,
  Will you bend over me,
And say you are glad the long journey is over,
  The voyager free?

My own starry daisies, my pink and white clover,
  Oh, will you not know
The long-wearied heart which your fresh blossoms cover

Then welcome me, daisies and dew-dripping clover,
    As I bend low the knee,
I am sure you must know that your old-fashioned lover
    Is home from the sea.

    As the pebble on the sea,
    So, my love, my love to thee,
    Rings its circles far and free,
    Widening through eternity.

A little song, a little story,
A little fame, a little glory,
And man moves forward in the race,
To let another fill his place.

LOOKING TOWARD SUNSET.

Oh, when the long day's work is done,
And we clasp hand at set of sun,
    Loved friends we meet,
    In concourse sweet,
        At even.

So, when for us has passed away
The last bright hour of earthly day,
    Then may we meet,
    In converse sweet,
        In Heaven.

CHAPTER V.

AMERICAN SONGS AND THEIR INTERPRETATION.

"If I were a voice, a persuasive voice,
   That could travel the wide world through,
I would fly on the beams of the morning light
And speak to men with a gentle might,
   And tell them to be true.
I would fly — I would fly o'er land and sea,
Wherever a human heart might be,
Telling a tale, or singing a song,
In praise of the right, in blame of the wrong,
   If I were a voice."

As I look back on a half-century and more of service in song, the retrospect is at once pleasing and thought-compelling — happy and sad. I have tried to be honest with my readers, but freely as I have invited them into participation with my joys and sorrows; careful as I have been not to place in too favorable a light the acts of the brothers which have caused criticism, our mistakes and delinquencies; I confess that I have spared them many pages of details which might have been written, and have assumed that while the great reading public had a right to demand the full story of the public life of the Hutchinsons, many particulars belonging to their private and domestic history belonged to them alone. This has been for us a half-century of earnest, honest labor for reform as we understood it; never heeding the comments of the press when duty was in-

weaker and needed it; predicting the downfall of slavery and the upbuilding of humanity; travelling at all hours of the day and night, feeding at indifferent cafés and resting often at uninviting hotels and boarding places; still upholding the banner of equal rights, with "malice toward none and charity for all." We went hopefully through all crises, ready to utter a sentiment or approve a righteous act; going from town to town, from city to city, from State to State; here at a concert in behalf of the intemperate, there at a suffrage meeting, uttering the sentiments of the Fatherhood of God and the Brotherhood of Man. In the face of criticism, bigotry and suspicion the Hutchinsons boldly asserted their right to "life, liberty and the pursuit of happiness." Many grateful prayers have ascended to the Father of all, to watch over them in danger and bring them to eternal life. Never did our good brothers and sisters forget to mention the Hutchinsons in their devotions. We have often sung together "Thus far the Lord has led us on." Not dependent on a clique or clan or church or organization for our success, we followed the Yankee plan of taking a little from every one. As Rev. Dr. William Patton once said of us, "The difference between the Hutchinsons and the pesky mosquitoes is that they take their fees and then sing, while the insect first sings his song and then presents his bill." The bane of our existence was that amid our desire to do good by our sacred and pathetic songs, we were obliged to depend upon our own efforts to secure a living. It was my continual and earnest desire to so shape our finances as to eliminate the cares and responsibilities of gaining a livelihood, that they might not war against the spirit of free service.

Perhaps it is scarcely necessary to point out that not

only during our foreign tour were we recognized as in the strictest sense "American singers," but that during our long career, we were never anything else. It is a fact, that for a few years before his death, my son Henry, having a natural desire to try his powers in the operatic field essayed Italian music, and his wife, having been trained in that school, often sung music of that character in our entertainments; but it is also true that the public turned out *en masse* to hear our "old songs," and not the ballads and arias of the ordinary concert platform, which they could hear at any time. It was Henry's magnificent bass solo in "The People's Advent" and not his "Femina" that made his reputation. The experience of over a half-century has convinced me that what the people want — from the Hutchinsons, at any rate — is the old songs, sung in the old way. A recent writer expresses himself thus:

"Dvorak, the eminent composer and master, who came to this country a year or two since to direct Mrs. Thurber's great music school in New York, soon after his arrival delivered himself of the opinion that the real American school of music — which shall sometime be as distinctive as the German or Italian schools, must consist of compositions founded upon the negro plantation melodies. Musicians who were mischievously inclined were led to point out, that if the great man referred to such airs as 'Old Folks at Home,' or 'Massa's in the Cold, Cold Ground,' Stephen C. Foster was a long way from being an African. This, however, was hardly fair to Professor Dvorak, for he had been simply searching for the American folk-song, on which its music of the future should be founded, as has been the case with the music of every people since music began. Foster's songs represented this fundamental idea fully as well as 'Turn Back Pharaoh's Army,' 'Swing Low, Sweet Chariot,' or 'Don't Stay Away.' They were simple, singable, plain melodies, which found a lodgment in the memory, and took up their permanent abode. If the great investigator has pursued his inquiries, he has by this time found that in the same catalogue with Foster's melodies and the plantation songs, belonged what an old anti-slavery writer was pleased to term in a notice of the Hutchinsons, 'the music of the old advent time.' And this brings me to say that the

Hutchinsons have been pre-eminently the interpreters and disseminators of the American folk-song. For a half-century they have sung 'The Old Granite State' as distinctive a folk-song as was ever written in any country. By this means they have kept alive a 'Millerite' tune, which in the days of that great excitement was sung to the words:

> "'You shall see your Lord a-coming,
> You shall see your Lord a-coming,
> You shall see your Lord a-coming,
>   In the old church yard
>   With a band of music,
>   With a band of music,
>   With a band of music,
>   Hear it sounding through the air.
>
> "'There'll be Gabriel with his trumpet,
> There'll be Gabriel with his trumpet,
> There'll be Gabriel with his trumpet,
>   In the old church yard
>   With a band of music,'" etc.

"Jesse Hutchinson was an adept at adaptation, and it is but just that his service to his contemporaries and to posterity in saving for them some of the melodies of one of the strangest episodes in the social and religious history of the country should be recognized. Covert's 'Sword of Bunker Hill,' and 'Jamie's on the Stormy Sea,' the latter made immortal by Abby Hutchinson's incomparable voice, also deserve to be classified with Foster's as among the never-to-be-forgotten folk-songs. But the Hutchinsons very early in their career found that the *repertoire* of songs of this character, which the concert-going public was demanding of them, was limited indeed, and it was this fact, doubtless, that led Jesse to write and adapt so indefatigably. Very soon, also, they found that adaptation would not supply the demand, and so every member of the singing band set at work to supply the deficiency. Jesse wrote 'The Good Old Days of Yore,' and John instantly supplied the music to sing it into immortality. Lucy Larcom wrote 'Hannah's at the Window, Binding Shoes,' a perfect theme for a folk-song; Asa wedded it to typical music. 'Mrs. Lofty and I' is Judson's best folk-song; 'Kind Words can Never Die' is Abby's. John has been composing folk-songs all his days, 'The Old Friends are the Truest,' and 'The Blue and the Gray,' being typical illustrations. Many of his reform songs will hardly come under the designation.

"If we should ignore, then — though nobody will — the services to the various reforms rendered by the Hutchinsons, the fact will still remain that they, more than any other vocalists, for the entire latter part of the nineteenth century kept singing in the ears and minds and souls of the American and English public the home songs, the heart songs, of the Western continent. This service can no more be disregarded or forgotten than we can overlook and forget the service in depicting the home-life and heart-life of America rendered by Bryant, Longfellow, Whittier, Lowell, Holmes, and the distinguished galaxy of novelists whose works have become classic. The genesis of American music must include the Hutchinsons, who were the bards of every worthy cause in the most thrilling half-century in the history of the Western continent. Freedom never saw its full fruition until America, type of the highest civilization in the annals of the time, worked out her own salvation from the terrible curse, and made even serfdom impossible, here or anywhere else. The bards of this grand and awful epoch were the Hutchinsons, as much as Homer was the bard of Grecian mythology, or Virgil and Horace of Roman history. Macaulay has put in English for us the battle-songs of the classic ages; the Hutchinsons never gave utterance to a song that taught men to seek each other's lives in mortal conflict, but they sang the songs of a moral warfare, so grandly, so irresistibly, that the logic of the situation meant war, until the wrong was righted. Their courage was the courage of Elijah, going up single-handed against the priests of Baal, and trusting in God and the moral sense of a people whose eyes were to be opened to aid him. It was the courage of Jonah, prophesying against Ninevah. When Webster, and Clay, and Calhoun compromised, they but sung the louder the doom of the institution these blind statesmen were propping up. When Seward and Weed, and even Lincoln hesitated, and thought to save the Union by sparing slavery, they ceased not to cry out against it,—and it fell, as the walls of Jericho came down when the people shouted. There is a theory that every fabric has its key-note, and that if it can be made to vibrate, the structure must fall. The Hutchinsons sounded the gamut in their efforts to detect the weakness of the despicable oligarchy, and finally settled on one slogan, "Liberate the Bondman," which was sounded again and again until it became irresistible. All honor to them!"

President Charles Wesley Emerson, of the Emerson College of Oratory, lecturing before his pupils in Boston on November 17, 1894, used the following illustration in speaking of "Voice, the Natural Reporter of the Individual":

"Many of you have heard of the Hutchinson Family, that family of beautiful singers who advocated liberty and sang for it. They could sing as no other singers could. When the argument of a Phillips or a Garrison failed, the singing of the Hutchinson family could melt the hearts of the audience. Into their souls had entered truth, manhood, love for the human race, and worship for the government of God,— as opposed to the tyranny of men,— and these noble sentiments colored their voices. I remember attending a convention where grand orators had been speaking to an audience which was hostile to the cause of freedom. After the arguments had been made, the Hutchinson family sang. The audience listened, because there was no heresy in listening to a song. When they had finished, all present were not only temperance people, and Abolitionists for the time being, but even woman suffragists. Did the great John Hutchinson say, 'Lo! I will put benevolence into my tone'? No! In his heart he loved the human race, and lived to do it good, and his voice was an unconscious reporter of his life."

The Hutchinsons projected themselves into the concert field so suddenly that they had to learn by experience the wisest method of planning and carrying through their entertainments. Jesse and Joshua selected the programme for our first concert, in the Milford Baptist Church. It consisted of hymns and anthems from Kingsley's "Social Choir," and of popular songs. Abby and Rhoda sang the duet, "Ava Sanctissima," and we all sang a glee "Have you seen my Flora pass this way?" We later had all our selections with us, words and music, for a while, and I was kept busy distributing music. Asa was the programme maker, Judson, Abby and I did the solo work. In the course of time we found that we were distracted by looking at the music, and so committed all to memory and sung without notes, except when it happened that a new piece was sung, with which we were not familiar. It was many years before Asa sung solos, but finally he composed "Topsy Never was Born," and sung it. After that he always sang solos. "Topsy" was of course suggested by "Uncle Tom's Cabin." I remember that at one time before the war we sang it in

Alexandria, Va. The words were by Eliza Cook. The fashionable Southern audience listened with amusement to the first verses.

> "Topsy neber *was* born,
>   Neber had a moder;
> 'Specs I growed, a nigger brat,
>   Just like any oder
> Whip me till the blood pours down,
>   Ole Misses used to do it,
> She said she'd cut my heart right out,
>   But neber could get to it
> Got no heart, I don't believ,
>   Niggers do without 'em;
> Never heard of God or love,
>   So can't tell much about 'em

> "This is Topsy's savage song,
>   Topsy, cute and clever,
> Hurrah! then for the white man's right!
>   *Slavery forever!*

> "I 'spects I'se very wicked,
>   That's just what I am,
> On'y just give me a chance,
>   Won't I raise Ole Sam!
> 'Taint no use in being good,
>   Cos' I'se black, you see,
> I neber cared for nothin' yet,
>   And nothin' cares for me
> Ha' ha! ha! Miss Feely's hand
>   Dun know how to grip me,
> Neber likes to do no work,
>   And won't, widout they whip me"

> "This is Topsy's savage song
>   Topsy, cute and clever,
> Hurrah! then, for the white man's right!
>   Slavery forever!

> "Don't you die, Miss Evy,
>   I'se I go dead too,
> I knows I'se wicked, but I'll try,
>   And be all good to *you.*

You have taught me better things,
    Though I'se nigger skin,
You have found poor Topsy's heart,
    Spite of all its sin
Don't you die, Miss Eva, dear,
    Else I go deaf too,
Though I'se black, I'se sure that God,
    Will let me go with you

' This is Topsy's *human* song,
    Under love's endeavor;
Hurrah! then, for the white child's work!
    Humanity forever! '

The dialect pleased our pro-slavery audience, but soon those present began to realize that there was no fun in the moral sentiment of the song, and as we sang the last verse, they began to grow serious, a shadow passed over them and we inwardly said, "Ah, there's where the thing bites!" They looked at one another scornfully, and at the close of the concert took their departure without ceremony. Gangs of men seemed to linger around the door, but no violence was offered. Instead, the town clerk came and demanded a license fee. This was a favorite method with our pro-slavery friends of retaliation upon us for our anti-slavery sentiments.

For a number of years in the early history of our concerts we did not use printed programmes, but each song was announced.

We tried to do our rehearsing early in the day. Sometimes calling friends delayed us until after dinner. At about nine o'clock we would give an hour or two to practising. When we were so engaged, I never was quite satisfied. *Spero meliora*—"We hope for better things"—was my motto. We were not always agreed on this point. Judson, for instance, was usually satisfied when a thing was well done, without seeking for perfection, and when I suggested that we try it once more, would abruptly turn on his heel and leave the room.

For many years we sung to the music of two violins and a violoncello. We sought to have Abby use a guitar, and she did so to some extent. In my own company Henry often accompanied himself beautifully with this instrument. Sometimes in our carriage, as we rode along we would sing, she or he thrumming the chords on the guitar.

In playing, Judson always kept the air, and I played second violin to him. In early times we interspersed orchestral selections, but were advised to give it up, as it did not seem to really add to our concerts. In those days, one of our sterling selections was "The Maniac." It did a great deal to make a sensation and help us. I bought this song in Boston in 1841, as I have elsewhere said. It was a cantata, but I sung it alone to the accompaniment of the brothers. Judson and Asa would commence a prelude. Meanwhile, I would be in my chair behind them, with the fingers of each hand raising the hair on my head, and bringing it over in partial dishevelment. Then I would rise, with the expression of vacancy inseparable from mania, and commence:

"Hush! 'tis the night watch, he guards my lonely cell;
Hush! 'tis the night watch, he guards my lonely cell;—
'Tis the night watch,
    He comes, he comes this way,
    His glimmering lamp I see—
Softly!— he comes!
    Hush! Hush! Hush!"

This would be accompanied with appropriate gestures. Then, addressing the imaginary guard in most piteous tones, I would continue:

> 'No, by Heaven, I am not mad!
> Oh, release me! Oh, release me!
> No, by Heaven, I am not mad
>   I loved her sincerely,
>   I loved her too dearly,
>   In sorrow and pain
> Oh, this poor heart is broken
>
> Hush! I hear the music in the hall —
> I see her dancing — she heeds me not, —
> *No, by Heaven! I am not mad!*"

And so the song would go on, to the conclusion. I presume the critics were correct in saying it froze their blood.

In the course of time I introduced the melodeon which was for so long a familiar sight in all our concerts. I saw this Prince melodeon, made at Buffalo, in a music store in Springfield. I at once concluded it was just what I wanted. We had of course seen the ancient style of melodeon, made to rest on a table or in one's lap, with round keys, the size and general appearance of those of a typewriter. The bellows were worked like an accordian, pressing down on the keyboard, with a "Rock me to Sleep, Mother" motion. The Springfield melodeon had a keyboard of the regular pattern, and rested on legs with pedals. One miscreant paper called it a "washing machine." The boys thought this instrument an innovation, and gave it a cold welcome. Abby was sure she never could sing with it. She loved the accompaniment on the viols. Of course none of us knew how to play the new instrument. So I made no attempt to use it in any of our concerted pieces but at first brought it in for an accompaniment to my own song, "Man the Life-Boat," getting an imitation of the sinking of the vessel and the roaring of the waters that was very effective. In time, when I got used to playing it, the objections to the instrument on the part of the others ceased.

We made up our programme, a miscellaneous one, from the best songs from hymn books and song books, and utilized anything that came in our path. If we heard a song and liked it, we would find a way to get hold of it for ourselves. I was the only one of the family that ever heard the Ranier family sing. It was at a concert they gave in Lynn, and I was overwhelmed, though of course I could not understand their words. Ditson soon published their songs, with English words, and of course I remembered their Tyrolean style of singing, and taught the rest how to sing them as the Ramers did. We would give two of these songs in a programme. "The Grave of Bonaparte" was a song that became very popular. There was great good feeling toward France in this country, and the song was always well received. Then we had what was called "The Snow Storm," the words from one of our school reading books. Lyman Heath, a Nashua music teacher, contributed some songs. Once I let him have "Bingen on the Rhine," and in return he gave us "The Dying Child." Within two months of writing this, I have met his sister and niece here in Lynn. Then we had a humorous song, "A Trip to Cape Ann." One of our humorous pieces was "Matrimonial Sweets," which I usually sang alone, taking both parts alternately, one in falsetto. I taught Abby to sing one part, and it used to cause great merriment, sung as a duet. Then we sang "The Land of Our Fathers," and we opened our concerts for years with "The Cot where We were Born."

We found it better, in the course of time, to set songs to our own music. The first song that we published was one that we got out of an old school reader, "The Vulture of the Alps." This Judson set to music, and we published it in Albany, Luke F. Newland becoming our first publisher. I can remember just how it looked in his store window, the outside containing a picture of a vulture with a child in its talons. About two years from this time Jesse came up from Lynn to Milford. We had a family gathering at the old homestead. He had the words in manuscript of "The Old Granite State." This we sung together for the first time in the old southwest room of the house, which we called the bar-room. The house was once a hotel, and the bar was located in this place. In our early days teamsters coming from Peterboro continued their habit of stopping at the place, and father would put up their horses and care for their wants. Solely for their accommodation, he kept in a side cupboard some spirit, gin and rum. In the cellar we usually kept one hundred barrels or so of cider. Everybody drank cider then, and in those days hard liquors were considered indispensable in haying. I remember father made a contract at one time to pay a man a big silver dollar a day and furnish him a pint of rum daily, for haying. The rum was mixed with molasses, placed under a bush, and as the mowers came round the field to it, they would take a drink.

To return to the "Old Granite State." Jesse sang the solo and we came in on the refrain. The song seemed the essence of egotism to us, and we wondered that Jesse could have written it. We could not conceive that the public cared anything about the Hutchinson family names. But the fact was, Jesse saw better than we, that this song would make a hit, and we saw it too, after singing it once or twice. By the time we had sung it through Great Britain, we had ceased to think of it in the light of egotism. The song was somewhat changed by the addition of new verses on our trip to England, and as time wore on and conditions changed politically, other verses were modified and I added some to it. The song as it has been sung for many years is as follows:

>We have come from the mountains,
>We've come down from the mountains,
>Ho, we've come from the mountains,
> Of the Old Granite State.
> We're a band of brothers,
> We're a band of brothers,
> We're a band of brothers,
>   And we live among the hills.
>
>We have left our aged parents,
>We have left our aged parents,
>We have left our aged parents,
> In the Old Granite State.
> We obtained their blessing,
> We obtained their blessing,
> We obtained their blessing,
>   And we bless them in return.
>
>We had ten other brothers,
>And of sisters just another,
>Besides our father and our mother,
> In the Old Granite State.
> With our present number,
> With our present number,
> With our present number
>   There are thirteen in the tribe.

We're the tribe of Jesse,
We're the tribe of Jesse,
We're the tribe of Jesse,
  And our several names we'll sing

David, Noah, Andrew, Zephy, Caleb, Joshua, Jesse, Benny,
  Judson, Rhoda, John and Asa and Abby are our names;
We're the sons of Mary, of the tribe of Jesse,
  And we now address you in our native mountain song

Hail! ye noble sons and daughters,
Hail! ye noble sons and daughters,
Hail! ye noble sons and daughters,
  Of the Old Bay State,
    Here's a friendly greeting,
    Here's a friendly greeting,
    Here's a friendly greeting
      From New Hampshire's granite hills

We are all real Yankees,
We are all real Yankees,
Real native Hampshire Yankees,
  From the Old Granite State.
    And by prudent guessing,
    And by prudent guessing,
    And by prudent guessing,
      We shall whittle through the world.

We're the friends of emancipation,
And we'll sing the proclamation
Till it echoes through the nation
  From the old Granite State
    That the tribe of Jesse,
    That the tribe of Jesse,
    That the tribe of Jesse
      Are the friends of equal rights.

Party threats are not alarming,
For when music ceases charming,
We can earn our bread at farming
  In the Old Granite State
    We're a band of farmers,
    We're a band of farmers,
    We're a band of farmers,
      And we love to till the soil

Oh, we love the rocks and mountains,
Oh, we love the rocks and mountains,
Oh, we love the rocks and mountains
  Of the Old Granite State
    Pointing up to heaven,
    Pointing up to heaven,
    Pointing up to heaven,
      They are beacon lights to man.

And we love our glorious nation,
Holding firm its lofty station,
'Tis the pride of all creation
  And our banner is unfurled.
    Men should love each other,
    Nor let hatred smother,
    Every man's a brother,
      And our country is the world.

We have labored for our nation,
For its life and preservation,
And we've sung for emancipation
  Since the good old days of yore.
    But our warfare soon is ended,
    Human rights are well defended,
    And our voices, once more blended,
      Shout "Free Suffrage" evermore.

Yes, the good time's drawing nigher,
And our nation, tried by fire,
Shall proclaim the good Messiah,
  Second coming of the Lord.
    Heart and hand together,
    Every friend and neighbor,
    Let us live and labor
      For the good of all mankind.

Now, farewell, friends and brothers,
Fathers, sons, sisters, mothers,
Lynn people and all others,
  In the land we love the best,
    May the choicest blessings,
    May the choicest blessings,
    And may Heaven's blessings
      Ever rest upon you all.

While the song was written to be sung by the quartet, it was Jesse's ambition to have the whole family of children appear together. He wanted us all to be united in music. I sympathized with this, and deprecated anything suggesting trading or bickering between one another.

Whenever we found in the papers or had given us anything effective or beautiful in the way of poetry, we would pin it up on a bedpost or side of the house, and start in on a tune, each one making up his own part. Judson usually took the air, and so in a sense became the composer of the tune. We have often made our songs and sung them in public without ever having seen a note. In this way we composed "The Good Old Days of Yore," "The Bridge of Sighs," and other well-known songs, which were really composed by "The Hutchinsons" it being impossible to say that either of the quartet was the actual composer. Joshua wrote a tune for Caleb's song, "The Millennium," but in one of his hallucinations Judson wrote another to which it was ever afterwards sung. Caleb was in the field when this song came to him. He stopped his plough, took out his pencil, and wrote it out. Judson also wrote the tune of "If I were a Voice," "Mrs. Lofty and I," "Jordan," and other songs. Asa composed the music of many worthy songs, among them "Hannah's at the Window, Binding Shoes," "Creed of the Bells," "Stranger on the Sill," "Topsy," and others. He seemed to have no ability to put verses together, but perhaps this was simply because he never tried. "Necessity," "the mother of invention" led to my first efforts in this line. The necessity did not exist in Asa's case. Abby composed the music for "Ring Out Wild Bells," a favorite among the Hutchinson songs, and "Kind Words can Never Die." This latter she sold to me for ten dollars, not thinking much of it. I gave it to a music teacher for publication, and he without my knowledge put it into a **Sunday-School** singing-book. It therefore never brought me in much money, but it brought Abby fame, being in great demand for many years.

I have attempted nothing like a catalogue of the songs and music of my own composition. Incidentally I have given the history of some of them. To add that of the others would enlarge the volume beyond the scope originally contemplated and perhaps weary the reader. I have been publishing songs for fifty years and their continual production on the concert platform has given them a large sale.

During my fifty-three years of public life, I have given some eleven thousand concerts, and that, as the reader by this time has learned, does not by any means cover the measure of my public activity. Looking back over it all, I can see places where it would have been to my advantage to have varied my course, and thus have increased my wealth and perhaps my popularity. But take it all in all, there is little that I would have otherwise. My personal defeats have sometimes helped the cause for which I labored and so were not in vain.

A leading paper of Gotham, a short time before the death of Abby, printed a communication signed "J. F. D.," as the result of an interview with my sister, which is interesting as shedding light on some experiences I have mentioned in other portions of this history.

SOME OLD FRIENDS — What tender and stirring reflections of anti-slavery days must be awakened in the memories of the veterans of the struggle for human rights only by the mention of the "Hutchinson Family," that tuneful band whose sweet, natural harmonies were early inspired and strengthened by the abolition sentiment, and whose bold advocacy of the cause made their old-time concerts such interesting and even exciting occasions. They were genuine children of the rugged New Hampshire soil on which they were born, and endowed as they were by kindly Nature with sensitive musical organizations and strong, simple characters, they brought into the atmosphere of the concert room of their day a freshness and native sweetness of melody and motive which won a way for them, at once to the popular heart. They literally made and sang the ballads of a people — the anti-slavery people of the North, for, besides singing the fervent lyrics of Whittier and the impassioned words of Garrison, they composed, often, verses and songs of their own, and set everything to melodies that charmed, touched or roused their hearers to sympathy and action. No convention of "the faithful" in Boston, New York or Philadelphia was quite complete without the presence of the tuneful choir, four brothers and a sister, whose aid was always valuable, and sometimes indispensable. Their tour of Great Britain was so successful that, after a year spent in the necessary task of conquering English coldness and insular apathy, they were advised that another twelvemonth there would bring them lasting fame and a fortune. It is an indication of the simplicity of their tastes, and their love of home and country, that they turned their backs on the brilliant prospect, because they longed for a sight of their own land and the old, familiar faces.

Of the original singers there remain now but two survivors — Mr. John W. Hutchinson and the young girl of the family, once known as Abby Hutchinson, who retains in middle life all the charm of manner and the attractiveness which marked her golden youth. Time has touched her so lightly that it is easy to understand her former popularity, and to comprehend the determination of her brothers to add her presence to the attractions of the band, when, having won a reluctant consent from their parents that "Sis" should come to Boston and take part in one of their concerts, they kept her with them to the end of her professional career as the bright star of the company. Sitting in a circle of favored friends at her pleasant fireside, not long since, it was the privilege of the writer to hear from her own lips some of her experiences and those of her brothers in the United States and in England, and to examine the autograph letters and familiar epistles of Phillips, Garrison, Harriet Martineau and others, whose parts in the great struggle are now a portion of history. Sometimes the admirers of the Hutchinsons had reason to be concerned for the personal safety of their favorites. Once, in New York City, they were warned that to sing a certain song would cause a riot, and when the singers expressed their determination to sing it, riot or no riot, the friends felt it their duty to be on hand in goodly numbers for protective purposes, and a number of ladies stationed themselves in front of the audience to hustle "little Abby" out of harm's way if necessary. Happily, and to everybody's surprise, this particular selection was rapturously received by a large audience, and everything went on that night particularly well.

During the foreign tour of the family they won the admiration of many distinguished people. In London Mrs. Charles Dickens became their friend, and invited them on one occasion to make a morning call at her house for the express purpose of singing to her father, William Hogarth, who was a musical critic of considerable repute and influence. When the Hutchinsons arrived at the house on the appointed morning, and were introduced to a particularly cold and very serious old gentleman who seated himself stiffly at the farther end of the room, evidently prepared for the worst, their hearts quite misgave them. Without much reflection they struck up the "Ohio Boatman's Song," and went through it so successfully that the stern censor at the other end of the parlor literally flew to shake them, individually, by the hand, and to assure them he had never before listened to such delicious harmony. With John Bright and his sister, Esther, the Hutchinsons were on very cordial terms; and among their souvenirs of English friends hardly one is more interesting than a letter from him, written in the House of Commons, conveying to Esther, in words of simplest import, the fate of that great bill which every student of the history of English reform must identify with the life history of Richard Cobden and John Bright. He says "The corn bill has just received the royal assent," and goes on to suggest to this dear confidant, in words fit, though few, the meaning of this event to him.

It is to be hoped that the story of the travels and experiences of the Hutchinson family may be told some day in a form that shall be permanent. Certainly, it might be made a very interesting memorial of some stirring days now long past, while as a contribution to the history of the anti-slavery struggle it could hardly fail to possess great value.

Of the original quartet Judson had a naturally high voice, a pure tenor. My voice was a baritone, though I sang falsetto easily, and Asa had a deep bass. Abby had an old-fashioned "counter" or contralto voice. The result was an effect like that of a male quartet, Abby's part being first tenor, Judson's second tenor, mine first and Asa's second bass, respectively. But we practised an interchange of parts as we sang, and the blending of the voices was so perfect that it seemed quite impossible for the audience to distinguish the several parts. We were often told that such harmony had never been attained in a lifetime, if ever before.

Our concert manners were always a source of comment and sometimes of criticism. They interested our English friends particularly, and doubtless they thought characteristics peculiar to the family to be common to all Americans. At various times we wore concert suits of our own design, which were quite different from those ordinarily seen on the platform. I have endeavored to secure pictures of the group at various times which will illustrate this. In the course of time our costumes settled down to the conventional "swallow-tail," with only the wide Byron collar to specially distinguish us from the ordinary singer. I have already said that our long hair and beards were simply the result of a habit formed in the early '40's, when the style was fashionable. We never dropped it, that was all.

Some of our friends were troubled because we did not cover our hands in the concert room. To aid us in remedying the difficulty they purchased gloves and we obediently sought to accustom ourselves to the new departure by putting them on one bright day and going into the woods to see if they fitted and corresponded with Nature. We were so ashamed of them that we would take them off whenever we came in sight of any person. Gloves did not seem to be correct adornments to horny-handed sons of toil like ourselves, and we simply vetoed them. Then our friends tried to compromise by having Abby wear them, any way. We sternly refused.

Of course music was in no sense a novelty with us, for it was our natural atmosphere. But our love of the art was so great that we never tired of it. Early in our experience we were taught by the example of father and mother the value of a full chest tone, and whole-souled, hearty singing. Neither of our parents were what were termed ready readers of music by note. I have never placed much stress on the position of the mouth or facial organs in singing, but think the manner of producing the proper tone of great importance. I do not think any person should attempt to teach who has not the perfect mastery of the technique of the art of voice production and a good natural voice.

I do not think I have related an anecdote of the days of the trio of brothers which illustrates the enthusiasm always caused by our singing. We were at Homer, N. Y. Henry Ward Beecher had travelled with us all day. He was to lecture, and by invitation we were to sing. Asa was not there, but at the close of the lecture Judson and I, with melodeon accompaniment, shouted out Jesse's "Farmer's Song." The audience roared with delight and demanded a repetition. Then we sang the "Farmyard Chorus." In response to encores we sang one or two more selections. We stepped down and went to our hotel. Soon Beecher come in. "There," said he, in mock vexation, "you'll never see me appearing with the Hutchinsons again! As I came out of the church I heard a boy say 'I'd give more for one of those songs than forty of those lectures.'"

In 1858 the three brothers were at a big abolition meeting in New York, at which Sumner, Wilson, Theodore Parker and others spoke. We had sung a song which caused the greatest enthusiasm, and as we passed to our seats, Parker, who by the way was partially bald, said: "How do you manage to keep the hair on your heads?" "By singing other people's thoughts," was my reply.

In 1882, while Abby, Asa and I were in Washington, at the home of Miss Ransom, who gave us a reception, Dr. Bliss, one of President Garfield's physicians during his memorable struggle for life after his shooting by Guiteau, told me a story of our early days in the West. Judson and I were singing in Michigan. Dr. Bliss came to us on one occasion and engaged us to go to his town, Grand Rapids, some forty or fifty miles of stage-riding from Lansing, followed by a car ride. We had a concert that night, or supposed we had, at Lansing, but when we got there found a lecture going on, and the man who had hired us resting peacefully on the supposition that we could stay over and give our concert on the following evening. On the next day we started on our long jaunt, over the roughest corduroy road I have seen. The driver of the stage hurried his team, but when we had gone ten miles of our journey it became evident that we were not going to reach the train in time by that mode of conveyance. So we went to a livery stable and bargained with a man to drive us to the station. If he caught it we promised to give him eight dollars. If he failed we agreed to give him four dollars. Away we went, over that horrible corduroy road, bumping against one another, bounding from side to side, the man driving regardless of our comfort or possible danger, only intent on getting his eight dollars. When we were within three-quarters of a mile of our destination, we heard the whistle of the train. It was too late. It was moving out when we reached the station. Judson jumped out of the carriage and shouted, but it was useless to attempt to board it. We went no farther.

but finding it impossible to give a concert in the place, owing to the lateness of the hour, started on our return.

Some six years later, Dr. Bliss, who then kept a dry-goods store in Grand Rapids, was rummaging about his premises, when he came across a big bundle of bills. They were announcements of a concert by the Hutchinson Family, which we had given him, but which he had not put out owing to our non-arrival. The thought suggested itself that here was an opportunity to have some fun. He called in some lads and said: "Here, boys, put these bills out." They did so, and at the time stated in the bills a large audience gathered at the hall and waited patiently for the Hutchinsons to appear. Finally the indignation reached such a height that a meeting was organized, Dr. Bliss being chosen chairman, and there were free expressions of opinion concerning the shabby trick played by the innocent songsters, thousands of miles away, blissfully unconscious of the fact that their presence was so ardently desired. At ten o'clock the disgusted audience retired. The citizens do not know to this day why the Hutchinsons did not appear.

But this chapter, and this book, should close. Some years since, a Bay State paper said: "The Hutchinson Family, which has been giving concerts since the flood, and about one hundred of which have died, is singing away as though nothing had happened, up in New Hampshire." As I think of the few remnants of the family left to sing, it seems doubtful if there will be a need of such ill-natured comments longer. For myself, it is a satisfaction to reflect that I have been spared so long to sing. If I followed my inclination, I should be to-day actively before the public, for I had far rather die in the harness carrying on the work of reform by my songs than meet what the future has in any other way. I have only love and good wishes for the great public which has so kindly given me its hearing and its sympathy. I love all mankind, and with it would be

"Ever hopeful, never doubting, always working for the right,
Loving, waiting, watching, longing for the millennial day of light."

APPENDIX.

THE HUTCHINSONS IN EUROPE.

Of the singing of the family quartet, Judson, John, Asa and Abby, the *Birmingham Journal* said, early in 1846:

CONCERT OF THE HUTCHINSON FAMILY — The performances of this "Nest of brothers, with a sister in it," have come upon us with a novelty pleasing from its freshness, and exhilarating because of its inherent beauty. After the *staccatos* and runs of Italianized vocalism, which are all very well in their way, it is pleasant to hear music divested of its extraneous ornament and made subservient to the holy use of promoting good-will between man and man, and clothing the deep sympathy of the poet in the appropriate and winning garb of simple and unadorned harmony. How often have we longed for the quiet strain in which the untaught minstrel sung the airs which needed no ornament — "The Braes of Yarrow," "The Flowers of the Forest," and the kindred songs of Ireland! We never heard these themes attempted in the concert-room without dreading the coming embellishment, which drowns all appreciation of the sentiment of the song or the music, in surprise of the artist's mechanical skill. On Wednesday, Thursday and again last night, the real power of music was again displayed by this transatlantic family. Listening to their simple, yet vigorous songs, is like reading a poem of Herrick's and unconsciously following the eccentric measure with an air of Sebastian Bach. Our readers may be curious to know something of this talented family, so we shall gratify their feelings by a few introductory remarks. They are natives of New Hampshire State. Until they were prevailed upon to exchange their vocal notes for more standard currency, they formed a very happy and very harmonious family of fourteen. The father is a farmer in the Old Granite State, and he, as well as the mamma, who has been the principal tutor of the family, have fine voices, and the old lady continues to improve its power by singing about three hours every day. They were all accustomed to sing as soon as their voices were capable of modulation, and the fame of their abilities being spread, they were recommended to "run through the States" on speculation. Orpheuses in their own villages, they became "great guns" wherever they went, and if they failed to inspire inanimate objects with a desire to beat time to their warblings, their natural and simple songs animated in the minds of their hearers feelings that had slumbered before. Like Jonathan, however he may vapor, they had always a lurking kindness for their mother country, and without much preparation they found themselves in Liverpool one day lately, appearing in a concert there, and next morning awoke, and beho'd, they were famous through the medium of the tongues of every one who heard them and the opinions of the local press. The enthusiasm we can now understand and share in the admiration.

The portion of the family whose performances have attracted so much attention consists of three brothers and a sister. Their appearance and manners, like their songs, are characterized by great simplicity. The brothers are dressed with exceeding plainness. In sitting down, they cross their hands and form right angles with their arms; and in Yankee fashion, invariably rest their hands on their sides when they stand. In singing, their countenances evince little feeling, but their eyes often sparkle with unusual brightness, when the song is suggestive of pleasure, or the high imaginings embodied in the chant of "Excelsior." The sister is passing fair, and modest and retiring, reminding us of the Rose Bradwardine of Sir Walter Scott. She is dressed with great neatness, and her unpretending simplicity wins the hearts of the audience before she sings. Her voice is a superb mezzo-soprano, full and clear in tone and faultless in execution. It requires no discrimination to perceive that her singing is the inspiration of natural genius, uncurbed and unchecked, save by her own good taste. Her singing of a portion of Tennyson's celebrated poem, "The May Queen," is exquisitely beautiful. Her intonation is perfect and her expression so *naive* and artless as to gain at once the enthusiastic applause of the audience. Of the brothers, we should say that the tenor voice is the finest, rich and sonorous in tone, powerful in volume and of great compass. It may, perhaps, be hazardous to compare it with those of the florid Italian school, but its quality and power are not inferior to many of the finest tenors, and resembles, to a great degree, the rich and powerful organ of Signor Salvi. We have no English tenors to be compared with it. The baritone is a voice distinguished by great breadth and fulness of tone. In concerted pieces, such as the "Pauper's Funeral," it rolls along like the ground-swell of the sea before a storm. The voices are harmonized with the precision of a mechanical musical instrument, and blend, as it were, into one rich melody.

The songs selected by them seem to be chosen rather for their moral than their poetic beauty. In pathos, Judson, although the elder

of the band has a fine perception of the humorous. Occasionally they play a violin improvement, but this we consider to be no great improvement to the vocalism. It would swell this notice to an immoderate length, if we were to attempt to analyze all the pieces sung. A high tone of moral sentiment and a pure spirit of philanthropy breathes through them all.

If we might select from amongst the numerous songs they sung any for special approval, they would be poor Hood's "Bridge of Sighs," and Professor Longfellow's soul-stirring poem, "Excelsior." In the former the magnificent burst, "Leave in it, think of it!" was thrilling. "Excelsior" is a singular poem representing the aspirations of genius; the title, signifying "still higher," has a singularly dreamy and imaginative effect. The air, like almost all they sing, is merely a chant, which would be monotonous but for the varied expression and exquisite harmony. "The Snow Storm," "Westward Ho!" and "Get off the Track," are characteristic of the land of progress and were sung with dramatic power. The attendance on each night, though not so great as might have been expected, was most respectable, and the treat thus provided for the public is highly creditable to the managers of the Polytechnic Institute; we trust it has been productive of substantial benefit also.

The *London Morning Chronicle* of February 11, 1846, contained this flattering review:

A second party of American vocalists made their first appearance in London last night, at the Hanover Square rooms and was most cordially received by a numerous audience. English artists have met with such kindness and hospitality in their visits to the United States, that it would indeed be ungrateful if there were no reciprocity on our side; but the talents of the Hutchinsons would secure them a welcome from admirers of every clime.

There are four singers — a young lady and her three brothers. Miss Hutchinson is interesting in appearance, and her modest and unaffected deportment secured for her immediate sympathy. She reminded us in many respects of our charming vocalist, Miss Poole. Her brothers look like German students, with their flowing locks, turned-down collars and loose, black silk handkerchiefs round the neck. In the vocalization of this quartet, the attributes of the Teutonic minstrels seen at the great *tables d'hôte* in Germany, will be recognized — the lady without an instrument, the men having two violins and a violoncello, and the full and rich harmonies bear out the resemblance. But the Hutchinsons have distinctive qualities that give them the claim for the merit of originality — they sing from nature's impulses and produce an *ensemble* of remarkable charm. What care they for the musty laws of strict harmony? They despise all conventionalities. Their hearts are in their song, and like "music on the waters" are their sweet voices. The lady fair sometimes sings a fifth below the key — anon she will ascend to the first part — now the voices blend in unison, and then form a stream of harmonic combination enchanting to the ear and orthodox for the legitimates. The music of nature, is after all, the great secret, its elements are the chirpings of the feathered choristers and in things inanimate as well as animate, and why should not the children of the Old Granite State — for the Hutchinsons are from New Hampshire, which has given rise to the *sobriquet* — have music in their souls? We find music in the roar of the waves — in the hum of the multitude — we have heard music but recently from rocks, but here are breathing beings, setting at naught all scientific restrictions, and yet fixing the attention and exciting the imagination to an extraordinary degree. Right welcome is the Hutchinson Family.

The quartet party opened with the harmonized melody, "The Cot where We were Born," every word of which was distinctly heard — a rare merit, and the singers received a rapturous encore, and then gave a species of catch called "Good Morning," the speaking inflections of the voice being ludicrously intermingled with the singing portion. A pretty cantata, called "The May Queen," poetry by Alfred Tennyson and music by Dempster, was deliciously warbled in sweet contralto tones by Miss Hutchinson. On the demand for the repetition she substituted a comic piece, warning the ladies of the danger of "Little Men," so quaintly given as to elicit unbounded merriment. The "Lament of the Irish Emigrant" by the high tenor did not create so great a sensation; the melody, by the way, was essentially Scotch. It was admirably accompanied. The "Excelsior" quartet was a mystical exhibition, in which a curious effect was manifested by a distant voice on the mountain. Poor Hood's "Bridge of Sighs" was also rendered with almost appalling reality. Indeed, the expression of the gifted family is beyond all praise; its intensity is perfectly overwhelming. The American minstrels have opened a novel source of gratification to all lovers of sweet sounds.

THE "HOME BRANCH" IN 1846.

In the foregoing narrative reference is made to the fact that while the family quartet was in England, Zephaniah, Joshua, Caleb and Rhoda organized another, which travelled over the routes their brothers and sister had been in the habit of going in previous years. They met with good success, for the reason that they had voices much like the others and their sympathies and methods were the same. The following notice of them appeared in the *New York Tribune*, in April of that year:

SING SING, April 11, 1846.

HON. JOHN EDMONDS, *Chairman of the Executive Committee of the New York Prison Association*

MY DEAR SIR: — We had the "home branch" of the Hutchinson Family with us yesterday. They had been invited to sing in the prisons, and came up on Saturday for that purpose. Were you acquainted with them I should not have to tell you that the simplicity and genuineness of their characters add as much to the effect of the music as characters less beautiful derive from it. Such is the fact, and nowhere, as you are well aware, would the peculiar force of this be more keenly felt than among our unfortunate prisoners.

They took part in the Sabbath service of both prisons. In the chapel of the male prison, after a brief prayer, they sang the beautiful selection entitled "His love can never be told," and it would have delighted you to see how the sentiment lit up the hearts of that large congregation. This was followed by the announcement of three deaths that had recently occurred in the prison. One of these, as you already know, was a suicide. The victim was a young Englishman, about twenty-two, who had been laboring under depression of mind. He perpetrated the deed by hanging himself with his towel made fast to the hook by which his bed was suspended during the day.

The statement of these melancholy occurrences by the chaplain was followed by the very beautiful and appropriate piece "A Brother is Dead," sung by Mr. Joshua Hutchinson. The most perfect silence pervaded the audience, and as the tender low-breathed strains were uttered, every syllable, though whispered in the softest tone, was audible, and glistening eyes and flushed brows in many parts of the house testified that neither crime nor its consequences had utterly extinguished sympathy or sensibility.

An eloquent and appropriate sermon by Mr. Redfield of Brooklyn, was followed by the singing of the following hymn, written for the occasion by our excellent friend, Oliver Johnson.

LAY OF THE PRISONER.

The sigh of the prisoner is heard by the Lord,
　Though man in his pride turns coldly away;
The Saviour of man with compassion is stirred,
　When sinners in blindness his call disobey.
　　Pity kind gentlemen, friends of humanity,
　　Cold is the world to the cries of God's poor.

The tear of the prisoner is noted on high,
  And God, in his mercy, deals kindly with all;
Then why should proud man leave his brethren to die,
  Beneath the dark shade of the prison's cold wall?

The prayer of the prisoner is answered above,
  When humbly he pleads for forgiveness and grace;
The greatest transgressor — oh, wonderful love! —
  Repentent, may find even in Heaven his place.

You can better conceive than I describe the effect of these appropriate lines, sung as they were with a genuineness of feeling that rendered it difficult for the singers to suppress their emotions sufficiently to carry the performance through. We no longer looked upon glistening eyes and flushed faces, but the silent tears coursed down many a rugged and sin-stricken cheek, and the swelled veins of many a brow told of the deep and long-slumbering chord which these sounds had reawakened in their bosoms. I wish that those who regard their fallen brethren as brute animals, worthy only of such treatment as would be offensive to their Maker when uplifted even upon them, could have witnessed that scene and felt its sacred influences. If depraved and hardened criminals were not proof against them, surely such persons could not be.

After this the service closed in the male prison by singing "The Millennium" and the "Farewell."

In our prison the piece first mentioned was sung. Then followed the "Lay of the Prisoner" with an effect as touching as had been witnessed in the lower chapel.

Perhaps, after all, the most affecting scene occurred in the hospital of the male prison, when the unfortunate inmates of that place of sickness and death — some of them in a state of gloom bordering on despair, and others drawing near the grave — were permitted to listen to the heavenly strains of the charming minstrels. It was almost enough to "create a soul under the ribs of Death." The eye of the stricken invalid, moistened with tears, sparkled with unwonted brightness, and the pallid face seemed animated by a new hope. Such a scene, to have its full effect, must be witnessed; it cannot be described. The influence of this event upon the discipline of the prison can hardly be overestimated. I am confident it will be visible for months to come in the more cheerful obedience of the prisoners to the rules of the institution, in the diminution of that dulness and listlessness so observant in all prisoners, and a more serious attention to religious instruction.

Not one of our prisoners who was present at the visit of the other branch of this gentle and musical family had forgotten any of the pleasant incidents of that occasion, and I can scarcely tell you how grateful they are for this second blessing — for a blessing, indeed, it is
to   E. W. FARNHAM.

THE HENRY CLAY INCIDENT.

In March, 1848, the Hutchinsons sang to Henry Clay in New York City. This, as well as the adulation of the public generally, aroused the ire of Mr. Garrison, and on March 17th he published in the *Liberator* an article headed "Servile Homage of Henry Clay." He first spoke of Clay as "the slaveholder and defender of slavery — the advocate of the Missouri Compromise — the enemy of free speech and free discussion — the man covered with pollution and blood." "If he had been the deliverer of his country from the most galling servitude," remarks Mr. Garrison, "and the champion of universal humanity, his reception could not have been more triumphant." He then went on to copy an account of the banquet from a New York paper, which stated that during the dinner the Hutchinsons were invited and sang their songs to his intense delight, as well as every other listener. Among these songs was a new one, composed by the ever fruitful Jesse, which greatly affected Mr. Clay. "The following," says Mr. Garrison, "is the fulsome song alluded to, composed by Jesse Hutchinson, Jr." "Brave Harry of the West" is then quoted entire, and Mr. Garrison goes on to say:

"No wonder Mr Clay was gratified at the offering of incense of this kind from a reputedly anti-slavery quarter. The 'bravery' of 'Harry of the West' is to fight duels, scourge men, pollute women and sell children, and this the Hutchinsons well know. They have degraded themselves in the eyes of all who prize moral consistency and real uprightness. Great will be the astonishment of the friends of the slave across the Atlantic in receiving the intelligence. We are not surprised that Jesse should have written such a song — for there is no end to his inconsistencies and follies. His well-known 'Emancipation song' runs thus:

"'Railroads to emancipation
Cannot rest on *Clay* foundation'

but now the strain is 'Brave Harry of the West' — and 'garlands,' 'laurels' and 'honors' are recognized as justly showered upon this 'distinguished' pillar of the slave system. What makes all this still more disgusting is that politically Jesse is a rabid Loco-Foco, and was chosen at a Loco-Foco gathering in Lynn, at the last State election, as a vote distributor at the polls (in which capacity we are credibly informed he acted) to secure the election of Caleb Cushing, the lickspittle of the slave power, and the ambitious adventurer of the war with Mexico, for governor of Massachusetts! We deeply regret that the brothers and sisters should have been led into such a scrape by him."

This attack occasioned a good deal of surprise, and some papers took up the cudgels in defence of the Hutchinsons. Mr. Garrison therefore felt constrained to blaze away again. On March 31st, he said:

THE HUTCHINSONS. — In the statements of the *New York Eagle* respecting the laudatory interview of the Hutchinsons with Henry Clay, we do not find anything to modify the view that we took of their conduct; but we find a disposition to trifle with principle in the declaration "It was an honor (!) to which few humans would have been insensible," etc., and in the apologetic remark "consistency is a rare jewel." Instead of regarding it as an honor to be invited to visit Mr. Clay, the Hutchinsons should have looked upon it in a very different light. They knew his character — that he was the implacable opponent of the anti-slavery cause — that he was at the head of the American Colonization conspiracy — that he was a slaveholder and a slave-breeder — that he was the champion of the Missouri Compromise, by which every barrier to the unlimited extension of slavery was overthrown, and thus had done more than any other man to extend slavery on this continent. They knew, moreover, that the popular demonstrations in his favor in New York and elsewhere were made with a view to his election as the next President of the United States. What inducement, then, could they have had to seek his presence and sing a fulsome song about "Brave Harry of the West?" Were they not avowed Abolitionists, and was it not this belief that secured them so much sympathy and patronage on the other side of the Atlantic? But the *Eagle* says that, in addition to the Clay song they also sang, "There's a Good Time Coming," and "The Old Granite State," in which slavery is condemned and emancipation is advocated. It says, moreover, that "Mr. Clay bowed his head in token of assent, and was throughout the performance often affected to tears!" How pathetic! Mr. Clay is an adept at dissimulation, and knows well how to feign a virtue he does not possess. He would of course take no exception to the prophecy that at some remote period slavery will cease to exist. The value of the prediction was rendered worthless by the incense they had previously offered to him as a slaveholder.

We have no desire to sit too severely in judgment on this ill-advised step, but it was taken in so gross a manner — and under such circumstances that we should have been false to the Hutchinson Family, as well as untrue to our convictions of duty, if we had allowed it to pass without one word of condemnation.

The sentimental harlequin of the *Liberty Herald*, of Philadelphia, says the *Liberator* is particularly savage upon Jesse about that laudatory song to "Harry of the West." When we utter the language of reproof, we mean something by it and our testimony is effective. He thinks the abolitionism of the Hutchinsons has been a little of the strictest hitherto and he advises them to make it a little more liberal. This is all in character perfectly grotesque.

On April 28th Brother Jesse replied to some of Garrison's statements, though he offered no explanation or apology for the Clay incident. It was as follows:

PHILADELPHIA, April 5, 1848.

MR. GARRISON — Your personal attack on me some three weeks ago, charging me with having voted for Caleb Cushing is entirely unfounded and false. Immediately on seeing it, I sent word both to Boston and Lynn, to have it corrected, but late numbers of the *Liberator* evince that you have not been informed, or that you are determined on doing me a great wrong.

Though I will not deny even the charge of being a *rabid* Loco-Foco (if such an appellation be pleasing to you), yet I did not vote for Caleb Cushing, nor electioneer for him, neither was I chosen vote distributor, nor act in such "capacity" as you so insidiously stated. I was nominated as a member of the town committee and voted in, but never accepted, nor acted with the committee.

In view of these facts, inasmuch as my name has been so cruelly dragged before the public, common justice demands that this positive denial of the charges preferred against me should be published in the same channels where the misstatements have appeared.

Could my friends know that, instead of voting for Mr. Cushing, or the entire democratic ticket (which I have not done at any State election since 1840 — howsoever much I may have loved them — but on the contrary have refused to act with the party *solely* on account of the slavery question), they might be disposed to view with more charity my seeming "inconsistencies and follies."

That you have been misinformed and have most deeply wronged me, is most certain; and I trust you will cheerfully open your columns to this simple denial.
JESSE HUTCHINSON, JR.

Mr. Garrison was not in the habit of owning himself wrong in a controversy, and immediately replied to the letter with great severity as follows:

"In the 'personal attack,' alias reproof, alluded to by Mr. Hutchinson, we stated certain facts, in regard to his political course at the last general election in this Commonwealth, as we understand them. He denies that he voted for Caleb Cushing for governor, and if he did not we are glad to hear it. In denying, however, our statement that he was chosen by acclamation, at a democratic gathering in Lynn, to act as a vote distributor at the polls, and in representing himself to have been voted in as a 'town committee' as though he had been chosen on business pertaining to the town irrespective of party lines — he is amenable to the charge of equivocation."

This latter allegation is as ungenerous as the doubt implied as to whether Jesse voted for Cushing or did not, was unkind. His dense ignorance as to the meaning of the term "town committee," always used in connection with party organizations, shows conclusively how little Mr. Garrison knew of practical politics. He continues:

"The precise facts, we are assured on the authority of an eye-witness, are these — and we presume he will not attempt to contradict them, for our previous statement is only erroneous in regard to his appointment — Just before the election the democrats of Lynn made a strong rally at Lyceum Hall, for the purpose of promoting the election of that unscrupulous demagogue and most servile worshipper of the slave power, Caleb Cushing, who was then in Mexico, actively engaged in prosecuting the diabolical war against that ill-fated republic. The meeting was addressed by General Peaslee, of New Hampshire, who, in the course of his rabid harangue, expressed great satisfaction that the issue to be presented in the pending election, in the person of Caleb Cushing, was broadly and distinctly, on the part of the Democracy of Massachusetts, a hearty support of the Mexican war, and an entire approval of the course of the national administration, respecting that war. At that meeting Mr. Hutchinson was present, and in a somewhat prominent position, manifesting by his looks a partisan interest in the proceedings. Instead of being chosen a mere vote distributor, as we stated he was elected a member of the vigilance committee, to scour the town for voters, and the meeting greeted him with three cheers, with which he was evidently well pleased. This shows what his anti-slavery reputation is in Lynn. What greater opprobrium could be cast upon a professed Abolitionist, than an appointment, under such circumstances, with such manifestations of delight? Surely, the Democrats of Lynn thought they knew their man; surely, if he had done or said aught *against* the election of Caleb Cushing, they would not have put him on the vigilance committee, and surely, as he did not decline the appointment, but apparently accepted it in good faith, they had a right to expect he would be true to the party and zealous to secure the election of its candidate for governor. If he had no sympathy with them — if he held the nomination of Caleb Cushing in abhorrence — why did he not instantly rise in the meeting and avow his real sentiments, treat his appointment as an insult, and declare that instead of supporting Mr. Cushing, he should do everything in his power to defeat his election, as well as that of George N. Briggs. But he allows himself to be nominated, elected and cheered, with all seeming acquiescence, and now he says he did not vote for Mr. Cushing! Perhaps he did not, and why he did not, it is for his Democratic applauders to ascertain.

"It will be recollected that our allusion to the affair was only incidental, and simply to show the double inconsistency of Mr. Hutchinson, in writing a fulsome song in honor of Henry Clay, which was sung in the presence of that incorrigible slaveholder in New York by the 'family,' and the last verse of which runs thus:

"'Then hail, all hail! *thrice-honored* sage,
Our most distinguished guest,
We'll venerate thy good old age,
Brave Harry of the West.'

"Mr. Hutchinson makes no allusion to this song in his letter, and offers no apology for this highly censurable act. Hence we have a right to infer that he and the family feel neither shame nor regret that they have prostituted their fine vocal powers to the glorification of the author of the Missouri Compromise. 'The more's the pity!' Recently the 'family' have been giving several concerts in Washington city, and have been much patronized. In singing the passage in the song entitled 'There's a good time coming'—

"'War and slavery shall be
The monsters of iniquity
In the good time coming,'

some hissing took place, but the applause, it is said, was overwhelming. But that the anti-slavery testimony was of very little effect is apparent, from the following notice in the *Union*, the organ of the administration, and the most rabid pro-slavery paper in the country:

"'The Hutchinson Family announced for this evening their last vocal entertainment during the present season in Washington. We are gratified to perceive that the eminent abilities of these cultivated vocalists are appreciated by our citizens, and the large and respectable audiences at the concerts bear ample testimony to the pre-eminence which they have attained in their profession.'

"A correspondent of the *Chronotype* says: — 'It seems that the Hutchinson Family have broken caste with the dictators at No. 21 Cornhill.' To be a 'dictator' then is to object to professed Abolitionists making and singing ballads in praise of the man-stealer Henry Clay! The same writer calls this a 'bigoted and proscriptive spirit.' What next?

"It seems clear to us that what the friends of the slave have a right to expect of the Hutchinson Family is that they will, through some appropriate medium, frankly and unhesitatingly express their regret, that in the midst of the popular excitement at New York, on the arrival of Mr. Clay, they should have been led to have done an act so detrimental to the anti-slavery cause. Less than this they ought not to do, and in doing it, they will again commend themselves to the good wishes and liberal patronage of Abolitionists on both sides of the Atlantic. We dismiss the subject."

On May 19th Henry C. Wright, of Philadelphia, one of the most voluminous writers in the anti-slavery cause, who often seriously embarrassed Mr. Garrison by sending such an accumulation of letters to the *Liberator* that it was impossible to print them, published in that paper a long contribution, under the caption, "The Hutchinsons' Repentance." Here it is:

Minerva Rooms, New York
Wednesday, 12 o'clock, May 10, 1848

To Richard and Anne Allen, Dublin, Ireland.

Dear Friends: — I am in the Minerva Rooms, Broadway, in New York City, the commercial emporium of the Western continent. I am sitting by a table, in front of the platform, on which sit Wm. L. Garrison, as president of the American Anti-Slavery Society, Francis Jackson, Wendell Phillips, and others. The hall is full, and we are in the midst of a pleasant and exciting scene. I can term it nothing less than the "Hutchinsons' Repentance." Many, very many times, have we, sitting in your cheerful, happy parlor, talked on the Hutchinson Family. You have often alluded to the great happiness you felt in their song, and in having them at your home. Well do I know that they delighted many hearts with their sweet voices, in Ireland and in Britain. But to explain the scene that is passing around me.

You know well that Henry Clay is and has been the incarnation of American slavery. No other man in the nation has done so much to extend, perpetuate and strengthen slavery; none have been more subtle and untiring in efforts to make it a *national* crime. Principally by his means this damning sin of the land has extended its influence from 210,000 square miles of territory (its original limits in 1787), to over one million.

This is the man who now comes forward and offers himself as a candidate for the presidency of this Republic. He was, openly and unqualifiedly, on an electioneering tour through the non-slaveholding States. He was in this city. The false and craven-hearted Whigs gathered around the shrine of this their god, and were piling hecatombs of human victims upon his altar, and were moving heaven and earth to create political capital in his behalf. It was at that moment of time in this city, when the inhuman man-stealer was spreading his net to catch all sorts of game, and bowing and cooing to win golden opinions of all men, that the Hutchinsons appeared before him, and honored him with their melody. It sounded sweet and full of unction to him, and to his political sycophants, and they did what they could to make capital out of it for their idol; but in the ears of 3,000,000 of slaves and of their friends, this song sounded most harshly and unkindly. Anti-slavery felt that she had a right to the Hutchinsons. She fostered and cherished them in infancy. She stood over them and dropped the tear of pity as they knelt before the altar of Henry Clay, slaveholder, and her deadliest enemy. She uttered her most earnest, but kindly rebuke. Not a sign of sorrow had hitherto been given on their part.

Yesterday, in our anniversary meeting of the American Anti-Slavery Society in the Broadway Tabernacle, to the surprise of the president, Mr Garrison, and of all the friends of the society and of its enemies, the Hutchinsons arose and gave a song for emancipation and success in the struggle for human freedom. It was asked — "Do they wish us to take this as an evidence of their repentance?" "Are they sorry for what they have done? If so, should they not be heartily welcomed? If not, why do the devotees of Henry Clay — the personification of slavery — insult and outrage our anti-slavery meeting by singing of the triumphs of Liberty?" "Let us wait," it was said, "if they are sorry for the deed, we shall hear from them again."

We met in this room in the afternoon of yesterday. No voice of the Hutchinsons was heard among us, to cheer us on, nor did we wish to hear it, except on condition that it be given with the understanding on their part, that it was to be taken by the society as an evidence of their repentance. This morning we were early at our business again, and continued at it till eleven o'clock, with deep interest. The hall was quite full. Those around the platform knew not that the Hutchinsons were present. At a pause in the debate, their voices were raised again, in one of their finest strains, in favor of anti-slavery. As soon as the song was ended, Wendell Phillips took the stand, and said, in substance:—

"I am truly rejoiced to see the Hutchinsons here and to hear their sweet songs, and I believe this is the feeling of all of us, who have had such great cause to be pained by their eulogy of Henry Clay, our and the slaves' deadly enemy. It is especially grateful to our hearts at this time to hear them as we hail it as a sign of their repentance for having prostituted their extraordinary powers to utter sweet and inspiring music, to laud that hoary embodiment of tyranny. Such is the construction which the Anti-Slavery Society will put upon their presence and their song. If we are correct, they will signify it. Under this construction, and under none other, do we heartily welcome them."

Thus they were assured, that if they continued their presence, and sang again in our meeting, it would be received and published as the fruit of their sorrow for having for one moment given the power of their song to sustain slavery. They did continue present, and a few moments since arose and gave us two of their very sweetest and most soul-inspiring songs in favor of freedom, and against oppression in all lands, especially in this. Their strains thrilled every heart. Wendell Phillips arose on the platform, and moved to give three cheers for the Hutchinsons. The audience rose to their feet and gave three loud, hearty and joyful cheers. They never were cheered with more heartfelt and joyful sincerity. It was a shout of Anti-Slavery on their return to her side. Garrison, Jackson, Phillips, and others who had most deeply grieved on their treatment of Henry Clay, joined to welcome them, and to cheer them on in faithful allegiance to the cause of human freedom. I doubt if the Hutchinsons ever received a cheer that gave them happier or more grateful hearts. And sure I am, that you, the Haughtons, the Webbs, the Howitts, the Thompsons and their numerous other anti-slavery friends and admirers in Ireland and Britain, will receive this information with heartfelt delight. These songsters, with their wealth of most extraordinary melody, have great power for good and evil. Anti-Slavery claims them for her own, and should and will, I trust, have them to be *all* her own. Words of tender pity

agement and hope and triumph to Abolitionists sink deep into men's minds and stir their souls, when uttered by such voices in the strains of simple, affecting and original harmony.

HENRY C. WRIGHT.

The above remarkable production, as well as the incident that called it out, provoked a volume of comment, some adverse and some otherwise. That indefatigable reformer, Henry Clapp of Lynn, who seemed willing to say just what he thought whether he had to edit his paper from inside or outside a jail, wrote in his journal, the *Lynn Pioneer*, as follows:

"It was our good fortune to spend most of last week in the city of New York, in company with our dear friends, the Hutchinson Family and Christopher Robinson. We went there — all of us — in the hope, and with the express understanding that there was to be an open air anti-slavery meeting in the Park. The meetings of the respective anti-slavery *parties* one cares very little about. They have degenerated into mere sects, and are getting to be about as selfish and corrupt as the church. Looking on the anti-slavery organizations in this light, we of course rejoiced at the idea of having a free anti-slavery meeting, one beneath the broad blue sky, for we felt that such a meeting might be independent of all priest-craft. The Hutchinsons had entered into the idea of such a gathering with all the enthusiasm of their natures, and were ready to defray nearly all the expenses, but circumstances interfered with our plans, and the meeting was not held. The *people* would have been there; and though no word had been uttered except the words of song, though our anti-slavery minstrels had merely poured forth one of their matchless anti-slavery melodies, the meeting would have done better service for the slave than has been done at all the meetings at the Tabernacle for the last ten years. There is a prim passive kind of people that seem to enjoy them, after a fashion, but people of solid sense and stamina relish them about as much as a compilation of old almanacs. What did it amount to, in view of our great national emergency? If it be not profane to borrow a comparison of Mr. Garrison's, not 'two chips.' There were fine words there, fine as silk. But fine words — as the proverb goes — butter no parsnips.

"The best thing connected with the meeting was a spontaneous, unexpected song from the Hutchinsons in the gallery. This song, though received with great enthusiasm by the audience, was anything but welcome to the platform, the occupants of which, unmoved by the stirring strains, were for the time being the very picture of distress.   H. C."

The *Chronotype*, edited by Elizur Wright, was even more severe than Mr. Clapp, and in the course of a long editorial, said:

"The most thoroughly ecclesiastical of all organizations at present existing, not excepting Puseys or even the interior one which His Holiness has lately driven from Rome, the child of St. Ignatius Loyola, is what is called the 'old original' American Anti-Slavery Society. It has a sort of Shekinah, two High Priests and a great High Priestess. One of the High Priests is about altogether occupied in taking care of the dead,—cursing and excommunicating ghosts. At the late annual meeting at New York, the ecclesiastical machinery was more apparent than we recalled ever to have seen it before.

"The Hutchinsons, who are of the April shower and June sunshine school, thought proper to sing some of their sweet songs to Henry Clay on a recent occasion. Many of their friends, and we among the rest, thought it was a pity for them to waste so much sweetness on such carrion, but nobody except the Ecclesiastical Anti-Slavery Society thought it an apostacy to be atoned for only by kneeling, penitential tears, and affusion of holy-water. Last week, at New York, took place the solemn ceremony of the reconciliation of the Hutchinsons, with the most singularly doubtful *animus* on the part of the penitents.

'The circumstances are these.—The Hutchinsons, in their simplicity, attended the anti-slavery meeting as if nothing had happened. At a period in the debate, they broke forth into one of their fine songs. One of the High Priests immediately rose and said the Society would be glad to hear the song if it was to be regarded as a *sign of repentance*, but not otherwise. If he (the High Priest) was incorrect in so regarding it, he wished them (the Hutchinsons) to signify it. And if he was correct, he wished them to signify it. The simple-hearted Hutchinsons, whether they were so deeply penitent or so unconscious of guilt that they had nothing to repent of, were mute and signified nothing. But before the close of the meeting they sang another song, having really long ago earned the right to sing songs in all anti-slavery meetings, and not having forfeited it by singing anti-slavery songs to Henry Clay. Then rose again the High Priest, and pronounced solemn absolution by calling for three cheers for the Hutchinsons. They had repented and were pardoned. Whether any anti-slavery apostate who returns and *speaks* twice in an anti-slavery meeting will be pardoned as easily, we do not know.'

The Wright letter in the *Liberator* stirred up Henry Clapp even more than the incidents at New York, and inspired an editorial in the *Pioneer*, in which he said:

THE HENRY CLAY INCIDENT. 327

The Hutchinsons' Repentance.—Under this impudent caption, there is a letter in the last number of the *Liberator* from the prolific pen of Henry C. Wright, the baseness of which it would be difficult to exaggerate. We have no room to go at length into details, nor will any one at all familiar with Mr. Wright's habits require that we should. Suffice it to say, that when he states that at the call of Wendell Phillips, issued at a late meeting of the American Anti-Slavery Society, in New York, the Hutchinson Family manifested public repentance for having sung songs in honor of Henry Clay, he states what is *not true.* The fact of Mr. Phillips indelicately notifying them that having sung the song alluded to, then singing at the then meeting of the above-named society would be interpreted by its members as an act of repentance amounted, apparently, to just nothing at all. And the Hutchinsons acted accordingly. They had simply exercised the privilege accorded to all, of uttering their sentiments in their own way, and therefore considered that Mr. Phillips in singling them out in that professedly free meeting for the purpose of defining *the terms of their welcome,* had, to say the least, been guilty of great rudeness. But it being evident that there were not twenty persons in the hall who sympathized with the rudeness, our friends proceeded just as if nothing had happened; that is, in a few moments, the meeting being near to a close, they uttered themselves again — kindly forgiving, if at all remembering, Mr Phillips's pontifical speech — and creating, as usual, the most heart-stirring enthusiasm. Mr. Phillips, in a fit of vanity which would have done credit to Mr Garrison, construed this into an act of 'repentance' and proposed three cheers, as a sort of *quid pro quo.*

The *Chronotype* hits the matter off very well in the following fable:

"In a high latitude where sunshine is rather scarce and hardly sufficient to hatch tadpoles, there was a frog pond, with three or four bull-frogs and large numbers of peepers. The bull-frogs managed matters, you may depend. They not only solemnly reminded the peepers of their duty, but they remonstrated authoritatively with winds and clouds, and took care of the sun's conscience. If he went behind a cloud or rose in a haze, they denounced him. One forenoon, just in the most critical time for nascent tadpoles, the sun was eclipsed. The chief bull-frog immediately uttered a papal bull against him, which made the surrounding forests rebellow. They bade all the peepers dive into the deepest mud, and uttered a solemn anathema, that the sun should never again shine in the pond, till it made a humble and penitent apology. The pond was entirely silent for some days. At last the Batrachians, one cloudy morning, being all up in high conclave, the sun broke out clear. 'O hot sun!' exclaimed the chief bull-frog, 'glad I am to see you if this shine is a penitential sign, but on no other condition!' The sun directly went behind a black cloud, from which a copious shower pattered all over the pond. Then, after an hour or two he broke out again. 'Par-don,—full par-don!—Full pardon!' shouted the great ecclesiastical bull-frog, and all the rest chimed in."

H. C.

But there are other views of the incident. The *Pennsylvania Freeman* said:

'The Hutchinson Family, who were present, gave a voluntary and spontaneous song. At its close, Wendell Phillips arose and expressed his joy in hearing it, as he understood it to be a confession of their penitence for having baptized with the melody of their voices that old hoary offender, *Henry Clay*. This allusion caused some exhibition of rowdyism among the Whig gentry present, who hissed like wounded serpents. One of them called for three cheers for Henry Clay, and the rest shouted and swung their hats, all making as much noise as twenty or thirty rowdies could make, for a few minutes; when the poor creatures seemed to shrink into nothingness under a calm and scorching rebuke from Mr. Garrison. He reminded them that they had been invited to participate in the discussions, but instead of coming forward honorably and defending their own views, they had insulted the meeting and stamped themselves as rowdies. When the disturbance was still, Mr. Phillips added: 'Understanding this act as a confession of their error, I welcome the Hutchinsons to our anti-slavery meeting, but with no other interpretation of it.' Whether they would accept this explanation and manfully acknowledge their wrong seemed doubtful, as they sat silent for a few moments, and a painful suspense filled many hearts, as we waited and hoped and feared, but when they rose again, and poured out one of their sweetest melodies in deep and earnest tones, a new joy flashed like lightning through every heart, and at the close of the song, the gladness burst forth in a rapturous shout of cheers for the noble-hearted singers, who had thus publicly and honorably made amends for that sad inconsistency. They answered the cheers with another song which seemed to spontaneously speak out the joy of their unburdened hearts, and the unburdened hearts of the audience.

"We came from our meeting happier and more hopeful for this beautiful episode in its discussions."

The Newark N. J., *Reformer* told the story thus:

"On the morning of the 10th, toward the close of the meeting, the Hutchinsons, who seemed to be constantly present to cheer each heart

stitution supports this horrid institution, we go for revolution in the United States.' Immediately after the song, the silver-toned Wendell Phillips arose and remarked, that no one could be insensible to the charms of such music, but that he should give this interpretation to the presence of the Hutchinsons, namely, that it was designed as a confession for having condescended to sing for that old hoary offender, Henry Clay, while on his last visit to New York, that on the condition that this should be the interpretation they could be welcomed, *but on no other.* Mr. Phillips spoke not in anger, but in sorrow, and none but such a lion-heart as a Phillips, or such an uncompromising spirit as a Garrison could have hazarded so much as to deal frankly with the music and poetry of the talented singers. The noble-hearted Hutchinsons appreciated too well the high value of such disinterested frankness to be offended. Mr. Phillips was hissed by a few Clay men (rowdies) but the hisses were silenced by the generous clapping and expressions of approbation which followed. Soon order was restored, when the Hutchinsons arose and sung a most plaintive and affecting piece, expressing sympathy for the slave, and were received with great approbation. Mr. Phillips then arose and said it was the best song he ever heard and proposed three cheers for the Hutchinsons, which were given with a hearty good will. It was truly a pleasing sight to see the Garrisons and Phillipses and Burleighs and the Wrights swinging their arms above their heads, and hurrahing for the angel-hearted Abby and her brothers."

But Clapp's indiscreet support was yet to bring the heaviest avalanche of sarcasm from Mr. Garrison. On June 9th he gathered himself together and goaded by the remarks of his critics, said:

THE HUTCHINSONS — HENRY CLAY. — For several years past the Hutchinson Family have been considered as songsters of the anti-slavery cause, by the public generally, for their occasional attendance at anti-slavery meetings, and their remembrance of the slave in public concerts. In England, they were as much indebted to their *prestige* as Abolitionists for their success as to any other cause. When, therefore, that most guilty of slave-holders and slave-breeders, Henry Clay, received a formal visit from them in New York, and was by them lauded before the world as worthy of all reverence and honor in a fulsome song made by Jesse expressly for the occasion (and which has since been set to music), we deemed the act too grossly inconsistent and the dishonor cast upon the cause of the slave too great to be allowed to pass without reproof, and an expression of deep regret and surprise. In so doing, we merely gave utterance to the feelings of every sincere Abolitionist. Others united with us in deploring such a prostitution of the unusual talent and anti-slavery character of the Hutchinsons. Having regarded with lively interest and rejoiced in the success of this "family" ever since we became acquainted with them, we felt it wholly unnecessary to disclaim entertaining any unkind feelings toward them. Indeed, we know of no better way of testifying our friendship, or of manifesting our solicitude for their welfare than by rebuking them as publicly as they had erred. "Faithful are the wounds of a friend." It was not an occasion for private remonstrance, or private repentance; for the deed was perpetrated "before all Israel and the sun," and required to be as openly cancelled on their part. Personally, of course, we had no interest in the matter, except as one pledged to be true to the cause, let who would be treacherous. Several weeks elapsed, but they took no notice of the remarks upon their conduct, that appeared in this and other anti-slavery papers. Not a whisper was heard from any of them expressive of regret that they had been guilty of such folly. It was under these circumstances that at the anniversary of the American Anti-Slavery Society in the Broadway Tabernacle, New York, just at the close of the meeting they arose in the gallery and sang an anti-slavery song. It *looked* like wishing to retrace their steps — for they knew, or had good reason to know, that, unless they meant it to be so understood, their singing would not be heard with the pleasure and satisfaction that it had hitherto given. But that was no time to ascertain their real intention. When, however, on the subsequent day they again presented themselves and sang another song, it seemed to be a favorable opportunity to get them to undo the evil they had done, in a frank and manly way. Wendell Phillips arose, therefore, in behalf of the cause, and alluding to the fact that they had sung in the presence of that hoary champion of slavery, Henry Clay, but a short time previous, to the grief of their numerous anti-slavery friends, expressed the hope that by their presence and singing at this meeting, they wished to be understood as regretting that unfortunate step. They would be heartily welcome if we could put that interpretation upon their presence and voices, *but in no other view.* The manner of Mr. Phillips was unexceptionable, blending true delicacy of feeling with firmness of principle. It was a critical moment; the issue was fairly made, even in the presence of the partisans of Henry Clay, who insulted the meeting by their rowdyish conduct. Every friend of the slave then present felt the utmost solicitude as to the result. There was a brief pause — when the Hutchinsons sprang to their feet and made what every one present understood to be the *amende honorable,* by singing one of their loftiest and most thrilling strains. With genuine magnanimity, Mr. Phillips, after saying it was the

Hutchinsons. These were given in the most enthusiastic manner. Then again and again did the Hutchinsons renew their songs, as if to make "assurance doubly sure" that they were sincere — that they were clearly understood by the assembly — and that instead of offering incense to Henry Clay, they were ready to affirm

"Railroads to emancipation
Cannot rest on *Clay* foundation."

It was confession that exalted not degraded them, and great was the joy of all their real friends in the hall.

This interesting occurrence having been appropriately noticed in the *Liberator*, *Standard*, *Pennsylvania Freeman*, etc., forthwith the *Boston Chronotype* and *Lynn Pioneer* exhibited the deepest chagrin and anger with it. Elizur Wright in the former and Henry Clapp, Jr., in the latter (both the betrayers of the anti-slavery cause, unprincipled adventurers, wearing abolition masks, as wolves in sheep's clothing, actuated by a vulgar and malignant spirit towards the American Anti-Slavery Society, and incapable of appreciating a noble retraction of error or a magnanimous forgiveness of it, whom to touch is to be defiled) assailing Mr. Phillips in the coarsest language and declaring that the Hutchinsons were grossly misrepresented in the statement that they regretted having "bowed the knee to the dark spirit of slavery" in the person of Henry Clay. Their vituperative articles we consigned to their appropriate department [the "Refuge of Oppression," where Mr. Garrison took great delight in reprinting attacks on his course as a leader, caricatures of his appearance, and remarks and criticisms of his editorial utterances] in the *Liberator*, making no note or comment, because they were apocryphal so far as the Hutchinsons were concerned, and determined to wait a sufficient length of time for the latter to reply to the extraordinary assertions of the *Chronotype* and *Pioneer*, if they were falsely made. On this point all doubts are now removed. In last week's *Pioneer* is what purports to be an official announcement, as follows:

"MISREPRESENTATION. — *We have it from the Hutchinsons themselves,* that the representation of Henry C. Wright that they had taken the stool of repentance in New York *is not true,* they looking upon Mr. Phillips pointing them to that stool as just a grain too 'pontifical' for anti-slavery life. So did Frederick Douglass. So did we. So did nine-tenths of all the Abolitionists who were there (¹). So, without doubt, did Mr. Phillips himself (¹) before the meeting was over, for never in our life have we seen a person more embarrassed than he was on this occasion (¹).'

So then, "the Hutchinsons themselves" wish the public to understand that they acted the part of the basest dissemblers at New York, and extorted as hearty cheers as were ever given by a piece of low deception! Well, if they choose to glory in their shame, and add insult to injury, be it so! We feel more of pity than of indignation. The next time they make their appearance in an anti-slavery meeting they will be duly appreciated.

It is evident that their abolitionism is of a very superficial character, and Janus-faced. In New York, they sang as readily for the liberty party and a new organization as for the American Anti-Slavery Society. (This fact was not known at the time those cheers were elicited.) Why they did not attend the anniversary of the Colonization Society and sing in its behalf, we do not know, unless they felt that in singing the praises of Henry Clay, the president of the parent society in Washington, the act would be superfluous on their part, as the greater includes the less. We see it stated that they are to sing at the Liberty League Convention to be held in Buffalo in a few days — a league which scouts both the old organization and the Liberty party as unworthy of any countenance. And so they swing — first on one side, then on the other. Now it is "Good Lord," and anon "Good Devil." All this has a selfish and sordid look — like wishing to be all things to all men in a mercenary sense. At least, it indicates a lack of moral discernment, if not of principle. "The more's the pity."

N. B. In the last *Pioneer* "brave Harry of the West," as Jesse styles him, is called "the nasty Clay," who "delights to expatiate on the happiness of Kentucky slaves, and does it with a gusto that would do honor to the *Old* Harry." Yet that same paper indignantly denies that the Hutchinsons have repented of celebrating the praises of such a man in original verse!

Frederick Douglass seems to have had the last word in the controversy. In his *North Star* he said:

THE HUTCHINSON FAMILY. — The conduct of this talented family in singing a highly complimentary song to that notorious man-stealer, Henry Clay, when in New York two months ago, met at that time, as it does now, our most earnest and unqualified condemnation. Though we were disposed to make every allowance for them on the ground of their excitable and impulsive natures, we could but feel that they had fallen from anti-slavery grace. It was, therefore, with feelings of no ordinary pleasure that we witnessed their repentance at the recent meeting of the American Anti-Slavery Society in New York. We, in common with others, hailed their presence and noble songs on that occasion as an expression of regret that they had faltered and erred in singing complimentary songs to Henry Clay. In this view, it seems that we

seems to speak by authority says they meant no such thing, and couples our humble name with the declaration, in such a manner as to leave the impression that we sympathize with them in this view of the case. It therefore becomes our duty to speak of the matter again, though we had hoped it was settled to the satisfaction of all concerned, and we are quite sorry that any further reference to it is rendered necessary.

It is a little singular that papers like the *Pioneer* and *Chronotype* should be so anxious to make out a case of non-repentance for the Hutchinson Family. Their singing in honor of Henry Clay, if one may credit their former professions, is as much at variance with their idea of anti-slavery duty and testimony as with that of William Lloyd Garrison, Wendell Phillips, ourself, or any other friend of the anti-slavery cause. It seems to us that the course of these papers is to be understood in the light of their strong dislike of the American Anti-Slavery Society rather than in their regard for the honor, integrity and fidelity of the Hutchinsons.

The only point of difference between ourself and Wendell Phillips relates to the manner of receiving the Hutchinsons in our meetings. He thought it necessary to prescribe special terms, on which the presence and songs of the Hutchinson Family were welcomed at our meetings, whereas we think the constitution of the society settles that question, and leaves it without the power of any member of our society to say who are welcome and who are not welcome on its platform, either to sing, preach or pray. It leaves each member to decide for himself or herself his or her fitness to sing or speak in the meetings. We therefore thought and said at the time to some one near us, that we regretted the course pursued by our friend Phillips, and thought it would have been far better to have left each member of the meeting to draw what inference he pleased from the presence and songs of the Hutchinsons. We are free to say, however, that our inference was substantially the same as Mr. Phillips'. We took the songs as an evidence of their having ceased to do pro-slavery evil, and a resolve to devote their powers to the cause of the slave. We may also add, that we think so still; we cannot but believe it, when two of their number within the last ten days assured us personally that such was the case. How could it be otherwise? The attempt of the *Pioneer* and *Chronotype* to make the reverse appear, cannot but do that family great injury, and stamp them as popularity-seeking knaves, rather than high-minded, honest, and devoted friends of the slave. If the view we now take of the matter be not in accordance with the views of the Hutchinson Family, we hope they will do themselves and the public the justice of defining their position, and not leave it to Mr. Clapp or any one else to do it for them.

This ended the matter. A few days later the National Whig Convention, instead of taking Clay, nominated General Taylor, also a slaveholder and the embodiment of the Mexican war, for President. Mr. Garrison had enough to do to deliver his anathemas against Taylor and eulogize Wilson, Adams, Sumner and other Conscience Whigs for their protest, and soon forgot Clay and the Hutchinsons. The Free-Soil party soon came into being, and this placed an added responsibility upon Garrison and Phillips to preserve a neutral attitude while not discouraging a movement so clearly in the direction of freedom. At this distance the affair may look like a tempest in a teapot; it was a serious thing for the Hutchinsons and their critics. The author of this volume may be credited with some knowledge of the view of it taken by the members of the quartet, and places his story, as told in the main portion of the book, beside these here quoted, as the explanation. He may add, that the Hutchinsons had no thought of risking their abolition reputation in singing to Henry Clay. He was the choice of Horace Greeley and other friends of freedom for the presidency. We did not forget that he was a slaveholder, and much as we admired his ability, did not fail to sing our anti-slavery sentiments to him as we would have to a hissing mob in Baltimore or New York. We also bore our testimony to temperance. When we found the light in which the matter was regarded by Mr. Garrison and his friends, we felt it was far better to meet it by a continuation of our practice of attending and singing for anti-slavery gatherings, than by appearing in print. When Wendell Phillips uttered his remarkable words, we paused, not from hesitancy as to duty, but from surprise. We sang "Liberate the Bondman" as we would have sung it to Isaiah Rynders and his mob, because we had learned that music would melt where argument would only harden human hearts. By our song we meant "We are the friends of the slave, as we always have been." We believed Phillips heard and was convinced, and so called for the cheers, which made us happy. Douglass was right; we were sorry we hastened to set ourselves right in what would be the most appropriate fashion. It should be added that Brother Jesse was, as Garrison said, a life-long Democrat, but broke from the Loco-Focos simply for the reason that he could not conscientiously support slavery. Garrison's friendly and glowing tributes to the family in later years show that time convinced him that they were genuine in their advocacy of abolition.

LETTERS AND REMINISCENCES.

Many years ago the author first made known to friends his intention to write a history of the Hutchinson Family. From that time on he was frequently in receipt of letters of an encouraging character. Many of the writers will never see the book of which they wrote and for which they waited, but their letters are none the less interesting. It will not be possible to copy all in full, but copious extracts will be made:

JOHN G. WHITTIER.

John W. Hutchinson: Amesbury, 12 Month, 2, 1874.

My Dear Friend:—I have read with pleasure and deep interest thy brother Joshua's brief narrative of the Hutchinson family, and am glad to learn by a notice at its close that thee is to soon publish a fuller and more detailed account of your wonderful family. It will include, of course, the scenes and adventures of your remarkable career, especially as connected with the great Reform movements of the age, Freedom, Temperance, Peace, etc. A full history of your service of love in the anti-slavery cause alone would make a volume in itself of the deepest interest. You have run the gauntlet of mobs from Maine to Missouri. You have cheered the homesick soldiers of the Union, and made glad the heart of the slave. In overcoming evil with good and discord by harmony, you have realized the old fable of Orpheus, who soothed the mad heart of hell by his melodies. As one of the old pioneers of the cause, I am glad to acknowledge your service of song, and to wish you all the happiness which comes of duty done in your day and generation.   I am very truly thy friend,

           John G. Whittier.

GENERAL W. T. SHERMAN.

Headquarters Army of the United States,
       Washington, D. C., July 1, 1874.

John W. Hutchinson, Esq., High Rock, Lynn:

My Dear Sir:—I have received your note of June 27, and have read as much of the printed card as is given in plain English, but the

Recalling, however, the pleasant evening you passed at our house last spring, I doubt not the music is in perfect harmony with the generous sentiment which teaches peace on earth and good will to all men.

I was otherwise engaged during the long days and years when war's dread havoc bathed our land in blood and tears, and could not pause to hear the music or words that you uttered to cheer the afflicted, or to encourage the active; but I doubt not many a noble act of daring and of charity was inspired by your teaching.

That you should now aim to collect a history of the observations and experiences of your wonderful family during that period, as well as the equally interesting times which preceded and followed the Civil War, is proper and right.

I am glad you enjoyed the single evening with us. I know we did, and my family, one and all, join in the standing invitation to visit us wherever we may be, on any and all occasions when it may suit your pleasure. With great respect, etc.,

W. T. SHERMAN, *General*

THURLOW WEED

NEW YORK, January 23, 1881

MY DEAR SIR — Your most welcome letter was read to me yesterday. It recalls old and pleasant memories. My first acquaintance with the "Hutchinson Family" made a deep and lasting impression, and all that I saw, heard, or read of them during an ordinary lifetime, has increased my regard for their personal character and their patriotic services, and my admiration of their eminent vocal merits. I was reminded, half an hour since at church, of your sister while listening to Mrs. Wilson, whose voice was touchingly melodious. I have regretted every Sabbath for three or four years that the "Hutchinsons" were not here to sing the "Moody and Sankey" hymns.

Truly yours, THURLOW WEED

GENERAL O. O. HOWARD

UNITED STATES MILITARY ACADEMY,
WEST POINT, N. Y., January 25, 1881

JOHN W. HUTCHINSON, ESQ.

MY DEAR FRIEND — Your warm acknowledgments of kindness at my hands are noted. Certainly you and those with you have more than paid your way. The very thought of you is the embodiment of sentiment in song. Loyalty to man, loyalty to country, loyalty to God. These were the breathings — the still small voice, or the more enthusiastic outburst which your groupings, both small and great, for these many years have perennially issued. Memory takes me to the concert-room, to the home circle, and to your dear company on a passing steamer or in a departing carriage — in each place the appropriate sentiment was ever rendered impressively in song. God bless you, your brotherhood and sisterhood, for the uplifting effect of your hearty work. The poor and the rich, in fact, all people who dwell between, have been comforted in the hearing and in the remembrance.

Sincerely yours,
O. O. HOWARD, *Brigadier-General, U. S. Army*

GERRIT SMITH

JOHN W. HUTCHINSON   June 30, 1874

MY DEAR FRIEND — Your letter finds me an old man (77) and in broken health.

Your forthcoming history of the Hutchinson Family I shall read with great pleasure — for I love all the members of that remarkable family. I doubt whether any other family in the land has done so much to kindle brotherly love — and, may I add, the love of God also.

You have all sung sweetly on the earth. You will all sing sweetly and forever in Heaven.   Cordially yours,

GERRIT SMITH

PARKER PILLSBURY

[This letter should, perhaps, bear with it an explanation. Mr. Pillsbury refers to another letter written for the book. Into this letter he copied N. P. Rogers's graphic description of the singing of the brothers in their appearance in Faneuil Hall in 1844 and several other notices written by Mr. Rogers. These had already found their appropriate places in the volume before the letter of Mr. Pillsbury came into the hands of the compiler.]

CONCORD, N. H., January 17, 1885

MY DEAR OLD FRIEND — A newspaper came to me a day or two since from Elmwood, Ill., with a quite tragic letter from you, giving account of the bereavements in your family circle during the past year.

Of the young woman [Abby Hutchinson Anderson] departed, I had not before heard. Of the death of your noble son and super-excellent brother Asa I was aware, but to see their names grouped with a third, and all in so few months, appeared a tragedy indeed!

But, happily, for you and for those who knew them, we do not mourn them as gone far away.

> "There is no death; the stars go down
> To rise upon some fairer shore
> And bright in Heaven's jewelled crown
> They shine forevermore."

Or, as Bernard Barton, the English Quaker poet of a hundred years ago, puts forth the same thought

> "The dead are like the stars, by day
> Withdrawn from mortal eyes —
> But though unseen, they hold their way
> In glory through the skies."

Even good old John Milton, in his "Paradise Lost," dared declare

> "Millions of spiritual beings walk the earth,
> Both when we wake and when we sleep."

And, my dear John, we know who some of these "spiritual beings" are, and while we know, and know so well, let us ever try to make them more happy than they are, by being always glad and joyous in their continual presence, mindful continually, that we shall ere long rejoin them.

I hope you saw the *Glencoe Register* of the 18th of December. In it I said a few things on the beloved brother Asa, to which the editor, Mr. Hall, was pleased to add some words of kindness towards me and my book, the "Acts of the Anti-Slavery Apostles." I have some pleasant correspondence with another of Asa's western friends. You once asked me to write a little contribution to a Hutchinson Memorial. Subsequently Mrs. Patton renewed the reasonable request. At my first opportunity, I cheerfully responded, and the article is now in her hands. I read it over to a considerable number of her and your friends and all appeared highly to approve, and I do devoutly hope that the two hemispheres will at no distant day be made glad by a "Hutchinson Family Memorial" worthy in some degree of that remarkable eminence which they achieved.

Wondrous, is it not? that only two of you remain even now, to superintend so desirable and so truly important a work! How little you dreamed when you first visited Concord what was to come of it!

But I shall weary you all out with my many words. I hope you entered on the New Year with some good hopes and pleasant anticipations. The past has been dark and drear to you, I know. But O, to how many, many more it was darker and more dreary still! And yet, all will one day see that behind every cloud was the loving hand and all-seeing eye of that God whose very name and nature is Love.

A glorious reunion soon will be ours with all our darling ones, at least so ever confidently believes your own and Mrs. Hutchinson's affectionate elder brother.

PARKER PILLSBURY.

CONCORD N. H., January 21, 1893.

MY VERY DEAR FRIEND. — Since paralysis laid its dread hand upon me last summer, writing, except to limited extent, has been forbidden.

And my own sensations and feelings admonish me to heed all such counsels, especially seconded as they are, by more than eighty-five years of age.

The photograph is cheerfully sent you, since you so kindly propose to honor me with its insertion in your forthcoming book, which will certainly be impatiently waited for by the admirers of the "Hutchinson Family" in both the hemispheres.

I think the age is glad that you still live to so well represent that wondrous household! It seems to me that all the sterling virtues of the times, especially Anti-Slavery, Temperance, Peace and Woman Suffrage and Equality, found advocates and champions in you all. But I can write no more now, only that I am, my dear friend,

Faithfully and fondly your own, here, hereafter and forever,

PARKER PILLSBURY.

REV. BROOKE HERFORD.

CHURCH OF THE MESSIAH, CHICAGO, April 3, 1876.

MY DEAR MR. HUTCHINSON — Ever since the meeting at the "Refuge" the other day, I have been thinking I would write to you and tell you what a great pleasure it was to hear one whose voice had delighted and touched me, many years ago. It must be thirty years since, that I remember the Hutchinson Family coming to Manchester, where I was then living, and I can never forget the charm of their simple music, so beautifully given, and with such rare tenderness of feeling. The "May Queen," "Excelsior," and — I think — that very song, "The Bridge of Sighs," which you gave the other evening, are still among the cherished memories of many in England, and it was very delightful to me to hear once more of the "Hutchinson Family" as here in Chicago.

I am sure you will excuse my trespassing upon you with this little expression of respect from one who, though not gifted with any special musical power, feels deeply the beauty and worth of music as one of the higher influences of life. Believe me, dear sir,

Faithfully yours, BROOKE HERFORD.

[Of course Mr Herford was correct in thinking he had heard us sing the 'Bridge of Sighs' at Manchester. His words are a reminder of the letter of Dickens in his published correspondence with the Countess of Blessington. I must have some talk with you about those *American Singers*, the Hutchinson Family. They must now go back to their own country without your having heard them sing Hood's 'Bridge of Sighs.' My God, how sorrowful and pitiful it was!"]

MRS. REBECCA MOORE

BEDFORD PARK, LONDON, March 3, 1891.

MY DEAR JOHN,— You ask me for some recollections of your visit to England, with Abby and your brothers, in 1846. I recall vividly your first appearance in Manchester, at the Athenæum. America and anti-slavery were for me words to conjure with, from the time that Harriet Martineau had proclaimed the abolitionists the martyrs of our age, and I was still more interested in the cause when I became acquainted with Mr. Garrison and other anti-slavery leaders.

Naturally, a *Herald of Freedom* introduction attracted me to your concert, and soon afterwards I made your personal acquaintance. On the Athenæum platform I first saw the tall, nervous, highly strung Judson, who sang with marvellous skill, "Excelsior," in a voice that seemed to sound from a higher sphere; John, the dramatic personification of the "Maniac", Asa and Abby, sweet-toned twin singers, and Jesse, the stalwart man of business, who engineered the path to popularity and fame and to progress, if not to immediate fortune.

The simplicity and genuine worth and truth of character of these pioneers of temperance and anti-slavery,— "the nest of brothers with a sister in it,"— was as remarkable and as fascinating as the programme and the performance to the more sophisticated English public. The choice of songs was wholly new to the concert-going world. Instead of the usual romantic and sentimental songs, Italian and English, varied with glorifications of battle and slaughter, we had poems by Tennyson and Longfellow and Hood at their best, and, in the minor keys, Charles Mackay, Eliza Cook and Lady Dufferin in words touching and true, all these set to old and new melodies exquisitely adapted, as the Laureate himself says, 'Like perfect music unto noble words,' when he describes the harmony to be produced by the equal union of the sexes — a part of the "music of the future," of which we have not yet heard much

Other pieces that you gave, homely and simple in construction, with appropriate music, were relished for their autobiographical and humane interest which carried the audience along with you. I refer to such pieces as "The Cot where I was Born," "We're with you once again," "The Old Granite State," and still more emphatically, Hood's "Song of the Shirt," and "The Bridge of Sighs," the truth and pathos of which are not yet things of the past, like the "Slave's Appeal" and the spirited "Get off the Track!"

If you were to ask me which were the favorites with the public, I think I should say Abby's "May Queen," which enchanted every one, "Excelsior" and the "Maniac," which were always applauded, and Lady Dufferin's "Irish Emigrant" so beautifully given by Judson, touched the audience to the quick.

I think you stayed six or eight weeks in Manchester. I had frequently the pleasure of social intercourse with you at my own house, and at your temperance hotel, as well as at the houses of friends, for many of your admirers became personal friends. The concert-room of the Atheneum had soon to be abandoned for the more spacious Free Trade Hall, where Abby in her pretty white dress and neatly braided hair, was a universal favorite. Your visits extended to Liverpool, Rochdale, Bury and other Lancashire towns, before you went to Birmingham. Meanwhile, the local press echoed and re-echoed your praises. I can only allude to some of their verdicts.

The *Liverpool Mercury* spoke of the "never-tiring sweetness" of all that you sang, and declared that "the audience retired, unsated, ever more and more delighted with the repertory of the performance." Birmingham rejoiced in "the novelty, the freshness and the inherent beauty" of the concerts and awarded to the "young Americans the highest meed of praise."

But the most important opinions came from the London press. The *Times* reported, "The Hanover Square rooms were completely filled and every piece was followed by an *encore*. The performance was a perfect success, and when the quartet expressed the hope that there might be no war between their country and the old Fatherland there was a hearty burst of enthusiasm from the audience." The *Daily News* spoke of your music as "an adjunct and interpreter of poetry, enhancing its beauty and deepening its expression, and giving it the nameless charm which the sweetest tones and the purest harmony impart," and again, "The effect of the voices, in conjunction, which was so very beautiful and harmonious, was a distinct feature, and with the novelty and occasional oddity of the pieces ensured the popularity of the entertainments."

Abby's "fine contralto with the tenor and the two bass voices made the

Athenæum was rather picturesque. It ran thus: "The Hutchinsons' songs are airs, or scraps of airs, from every country — Old World and New World — so put together, however, and harmonized as to have an individual character. Nor do their serious part-songs fall less pleasantly on their ears, for the touch of psalmery, distinguishable in most of them, which carries the fancy far away to the rude meeting-house on the edge of some clearing or the camp-meeting in the open air. There is, in short, a color of nationality over the performance, which is gone through with a steady modesty, and withal conscious enjoyment, that enhanced the hearer's pleasure." To this I may add the final dictum of that sage journal, the *Nonconformist*: "Rarely have we seen audiences so completely fascinated by the power of music — never have we witnessed a more striking exhibition of its influence when made the vehicle of imparting moral sentiment and poetic feeling." This last point, the moral and philanthropic tone and teaching of your concerts, give them a missionary character that placed them higher than mere entertainments to charm the ear, and won for them sympathetic approval, that, I have no doubt, was your most heartfelt reward.

With kindest regards and remembrances, yours,

R. MOORE

REV. RODNEY H. HOWARD

TOWNSEND, MASS., May 10, 1888

JOHN W. HUTCHINSON, ESQ.

DEAR SIR — I feel prompted from a sense of the good you and yours have done me in other days to indite a word of condolence to you in view of your late unspeakable loss. In the days of my youth I heard you and your brothers sing several times in Burlington, Vt., and the memory of those concerts, and especially of your singing at that time one Sabbath in the Methodist church of that place, of "Tell me, ye winged winds," etc., has been an inspiration to me ever since.

Some twenty-five years ago I heard Asa, I think it was, and family sing in Johnson, Vt. Some ten years ago I heard you at a temperance convention at Hamilton Camp, and about the same time your brother in Boston. On the train once, near Danvers, I took the liberty of introducing myself to you. A few years ago I published an article in a Lynn paper giving some reminiscences of your earlier triumphs. Never did a singing family ever before win for itself so warm a place in its country's heart, and I venture to say, never will it happen again. "The Hutchinson Family," as it once was, can no more be duplicated than can John B. Gough, Wendell Phillips, or Henry Ward Beecher. The writer belongs to that generation with which all these alike were favorites. It makes one homesick to think he will never again hear any of these, nay, not even then like on earth again. Tens of thousands whom you and your gifted and generous "family" have delighted and blessed in days past and gone will pray that, in the days of your bereavement and sorrow you may all be comforted with at least somewhat of that great comfort which it has been your pleasure and privilege to confer upon them. Aye, you can scarcely imagine the extent to which, and the fervor with which, throughout the land, the elder people of the country will ever say, ' God bless the Hutchinson Family!"

I pity the rising generation chiefly — and all, as yet unborn, generations — because, though they will never know their loss, they will never hear the Hutchinsons.

With sentiments of the most earnest sympathy permit me, a stranger tho' I may be to you, to subscribe myself, ever yours,

R. H. HOWARD.

FREDERICK DOUGLASS.

BIDDEFORD, November 18, 1894.

MY DEAR JOHN: — I have only time while on the wing as I am, to tell you that you made me very much obliged to you for the little pamphlet you kindly put into my hands night before last in Lynn, containing biographical sketches of the several members of your remarkably musical family. No apology was needed for its publication. All who have listened as I have done, to the "concord of sweet sounds" from members of the "Tribe of Jesse" want more of the music and wish to know more of the persons from whom it comes. I especially have reason to feel a grateful interest in the whole Hutchinson family, for you have sung the yokes from the necks and the fetters from the limbs of my race, and dared to be true to humanity against all danger to worldly prosperity and reputation. You have dared to sing for a cause first and for cash afterward. I know of few instrumentalities which have done more for liberty and temperance than have your voices. But I only took this moment simply to thank you for the pamphlet and not to speak in the praise of the dear family.

Yours very truly, FRED'K DOUGLASS.

LIEUTENANT-GOVERNOR ROOT, OF KANSAS.

WASHINGTON, D. C., April 14, 1874.

JOHN W. HUTCHINSON, ESQ.:

MY VERY DEAR SIR: — I have taken the liberty of sending to you my

may find some thoughts in it of interest. I know that like myself, you have ideas peculiarly your own, and you have pleasant musical ways of bringing them before the public. Thus you have been and are, sowing rich seed, which must, sooner or later, bring forth plentiful harvests. Permit me to encourage you to press forward. Go on, singing your sweet, melodious songs through the world.

Pardon me for alluding to your great work for the glorious cause of woman's suffrage made several years ago, in the State of Kansas. Your vast labors of love—assisted by your noble son Henry and charming daughter Viola—will never be forgotten by the thousands upon thousands who listened to your persuasive arguments, poured forth in sweet silvery songs upon the fertile prairies in favor of a principle which must soon triumph and place woman on an equality before the law with man. Until which time, all our efforts—no matter how grand and arduous—in favor of temperance and universal reform will prove failures.

Permit me, while alluding to this subject, and in behalf of your multitude of hearty friends and well-wishers, to thank you and your co-workers for the great work you accomplished for the State of Kansas in the labor you there performed for woman's cause when we attempted to make that State—for whose interests I have labored so long, and within whose borders I have spent so many of the best years of my life—the banner State for woman's suffrage. That we were not successful, is not due to lack of earnest zeal or efficient labor on your part. The effort was grand, and though for the time an apparent failure, the good seed sown will ere long ripen into an abundant and victorious harvest, for which we shall ever bless you and yours for the noble part you performed in the work of placing society upon its true basis.

Go on, brother, in your God-like mission. Happiness here and hereafter awaits all who devote their lives to the great cause of humanity, and though an all-wise Providence may not often permit me the pleasure of meeting you in the flesh, I know that in the blessed land beyond—only by a thin veil hidden from our visions—we shall meet and still work happily on for the further advancement, elevation, and development of the race.

I shall always be glad to see or hear from you. Ever sincerely your friend,
J. P. Root.

WILLIAM LLOYD GARRISON

Boston, March 15, 1859.

DEAR FRIEND—Yours of yesterday is just received. I regret that you had the trouble of calling too at the Anti-Slavery Office without seeing me, especially on so kind and generous an errand. [Then follows a discussion of a matter relating to the tour of George Thompson.] I am to lecture in Fall River on Tuesday evening, and so shall be deprived of the pleasure of hearing and seeing you.

You may easily imagine how, in common with a great multitude of his friends and admirers, I was made sad, beyond expression, at the sudden termination of the earthly life of dear, impulsive, noble Judson, in the manner it happened. Of course, he knew not what he did. But he no longer sees "through a glass darkly"—every fetter is broken—his spirit is free—and *all is well!* I should like to hear the songs he is now singing in "Jerusalem, my happy home!"

In the great struggle which has been going on so long to deliver our land from the tyrannous dominion of the Slave Power and from the curse of slavery, and to make liberty the heritage and possession of every human being on our soil, the intelligent and impartial historian can never forget the disinterested and powerful aid rendered to it by the "Hutchinson Family." May you and yours, and Asa and family, long be preserved, to sing the songs of freedom and humanity in the ears of the people, and to see the triumph of the right!

Yours, for universal liberty, WM. LLOYD GARRISON.

W. AUGUSTUS FONDA.

"RAVENSCROFT," PATERSON, N. J., November 14, 1876.

MY DEAR BROTHER HUTCHINSON:—Some twenty or twenty-one years ago, you sang some of your sweet songs in the city—then the town—of Paterson, N. J. As you, in company with your brothers and sisters of the "Tribe of Jesse" were passing out of the audience-room after the concert was ended, you noticed me, then a boy of seven, in the audience, and placing your hand upon my head said kindly, "Well, sonny, how would you like to be a singer?"

Your words awoke in me a chord which neither I nor my relatives had never known to thrill before. I at once felt the spirit of song born in me, and nearly all my life since that time has been made glad with song, and it has gladdened the hearts of many of my friends, solely through your words. I have now spent nearly sixteen years in musical study here and elsewhere, all through your remarks to a little boy twenty years ago. I know not how better to thank you than by saying with all my heart, "God bless the Tribe of Jesse"—

> God bless the "Tribe of Jesse,"
> That band of singers sweet,
> Whose songs we've sung so often

And the soft notes of our evening hymn
   Float up toward the stars —
Rising to the gates of Heaven,
   Breaking on its golden bars.

God bless the "Tribe of Jesse,"
   They have charmed the weary hour
And soothed full many a troubled breast
   By music's magic power
And whether in the lordly hall
   Or in the lowly cot —
Those sweet, clear songs they love to sing
   Shall never be forgot

God bless the "Tribe of Jesse,"
   For they lifted up their voice
'Gainst wrong that bartered human life,
   And made the slave rejoice
They won the drunkard from the deep —
   The lowest deep — of shame,
So I sing the "Tribe of Jesse" —
   Their glory and their fame

God bless the "Tribe of Jesse,"
   When their earth song is o'er
May they sing the new song of the Lamb
   Upon the golden shore
Where our night is changed to morning,
   Where our weak notes shall grow strong —
With Heaven itself uniting
   In one universal song!

    Yours truly,   W. AUGUSTUS FONDA.

J. S. BLISS

    JANESVILLE, WIS., July 11, 1874.

MY DEAR HUTCHINSONS — Allow me by way of friendly utterances, to call you "*Emancipators,*" for when the bondman was still under the yoke, the sweet songs of your "Tribe" fell upon the ears of thousands of people throughout the Union, and our great and good Lincoln said, "Just the character of songs I wish the soldiers might hear." Thus song after song from you went forth on their missions of love and mercy, and ere long by the united efforts of a people who were being educated that it was right to do right, and wrong to do wrong, with the lamented Abraham Lincoln at the head, four million shackles fell to the ground like a thunderbolt from God.

"Emancipators," did I say? Yes — and still more are you to be recognized as such in the grand temperance reform. Speed the day when the evil of intemperance, that is tenfold more mighty than slavery was, will be eliminated from the land, and the toiling millions will be free from the sting of the whiskey scorpion. Sing on, dear friends, the Hutchinsons, and the victory you have sought to gain will be perched upon your sweet melodious banner. Once when I heard from you, "In the Old Church Tower hangs the Bell," it seemed to lift me far away from the terrestrial scenes, and the soft and mellow cadences were even *then* wafted down to me, filling the soul; the tones increase, then faint — slower — softer — gentler — yet lingering sounds hover near, and like the musical echo I have listened to in the celebrated Baptistery in Italy, they become more and more mellow as they ascend higher — softer — lighter, until the vibrations have ceased in a concave of beautiful amethyst. Ever faithfully yours,

J. S. BLISS.

REV. J. B. DAVIS.

HYDE PARK, MASS., July 4, 1876.

On this day of our national birth and independence — consecrated by the Declaration, embalmed as the date of Adams's and Jefferson's death, and now glorified by the fact that all beneath our flag and on our soil *are*, as well as are *called*, "free and equal" — I can but think of some of the agencies that brought this verity of the Declaration about. How easy to recall *other* days before the great military battles were fought, and when our whole civil and social fabric was shaken by the coming earthquake of God's recompense for our iniquity.

There is the tableaux of Garrison dragged by a halter to be hung by a mob to a Boston street lamp-post; Burns and Sims kidnapped, Lovejoy shot, and his printing-press emptied into a Western river — whereat God touched Brother Wendell's lips, and he, an aristocrat, became an apostle of the most Democratic type. On yonder cloud of leaves from the printing-press flies the world-awakening story of "Uncle Tom's Cabin," and right after comes the music of Emancipation, for the "Granite Hills" send down a band of freemen — a family of harps — born of one father and mother, to strike the key-note to which John Brown should march to execution and at the sound of which millions of slaves rejoiced, knowing that their own long-drawn lament should change from the minor key of prison dirge to the major key of jubilee praise.

When in the decade of 1850 the gate of Richmond was shut in the faces of this family, it was realized that the institution which could not suffer the strains of free melody to be sounded in the ears of its bond-

Civil War was finally crossed, like Miriam's timbrel rang out the voice of these "Larks of Liberty."

Let no pen or voice or name given in those years to that redemption of our people now be forgotten, and God bless the Hutchinson book for the memory of that cause. But other reforms enlisted the magic of their melody. What could Temperance have wrought without these Washingtonian singers? Pierpont's pen, and Gough's tears and speech were kindled to mightier enthusiasm, and a nation of drunkards dashed from their lips the enslaving cup, forgetting its fascinating kiss while harkening to their cold-water army music.

Oh! here is a lesson to American vocalist, instrumental or dramatic performer. From the example of this family and the history of the reforms it has promoted, let him learn that nothing short of "Devotional Hymns" can compare with "Reform Songs" in great and good results.

Reform songs! Let them again be constructed, and as the Hutchinson brothers once wrote and sung *their* wonderful choruses, so let every present abuse be held up by public song to public scorn, and let all sensuality and fraud and violence be swept from our beloved land, even as Jericho fell before the trumpet blasts of Israel's host. I shall never forget the first time I saw and heard these wonderful brothers and their sweet-voiced sister as they breathed out in glorious harmony the vital sentiments of social, civil and religious freedom; they were the first family of American bards, and they have never been equalled in vocalism or telling points in uttered verse.

Homer and Ossian sung in king's courts of the wars of the races — but these bands have also sung in the courts of foreign empires and before mighty peoples, but with a grander theme even — the overthrow of evil from every human heart — and their own peculiar chorus. "The Fatherhood of God, and the Brotherhood of Man." J. B. DAVIS.

J. N. STEARNS.

58 READE STREET, NEW YORK, July 14, 1874.

FRIEND HUTCHINSON — I am glad to notice that you are to publish a History of the Hutchinson Family — God bless them. I shall never forget the thrilling notes of the "family" as I first heard them in my own loved native Granite State and in later years as their songs of freedom and temperance have inspired the world. The song

"The teetotalers are coming,
The teetotalers are coming,
The teetotalers are coming."

was one of the first I ever heard on temperance and first turned my thoughts to teetotalism, and *I have been "coming"* ever since. Go on singing — don't stop. This world is to be reclaimed from the thraldom of rum — it shall "Blossom as the rose," for the Lord hath said it. "Wait a little longer." "'Tis coming up the steep of time," etc.

Yours, J. N. STEARNS.

GEORGE W. LATIMER

[An oldish man, looking perhaps sixty, with a face whiter than that of the average Caucasian (for his mother was half white, and his father own brother to his master when he was born), under the medium height, and carrying a cane (for besides being seventy-three years old he is paralyzed on one side), with as handsome a pair of gray side whiskers as those of any prosperous retired banker who might be mentioned, and gray hair, straight on the head and curling at the ends — George W. Latimer, whose thrilling escape from slavery, recapture and purchase did so much to arouse and solidify the sentiment of the North in favor of freedom, called at Tower Cottage to congratulate the author on the near completion of his family history. He, too, is writing his reminiscences. He gladly dictated the following contribution.]

LYNN, November 22, 1894.

I have known John W. Hutchinson since 1842. That was the year I came North. I started in September from my home in Norfolk, Va. With my wife, also a slave, I secreted myself under the fore-peak of the vessel, we lying on the stone ballast in the darkness for nine weary hours. As we lay concealed in the darkness we could look through the cracks of the partition into the bar-room of the vessel, where men who would have gladly captured us were drinking. When we went aboard the vessel at Frenchtown a man stood in the gangway who was a wholesaler of liquors. He knew me, for my master kept a saloon and was his customer. But I pulled my Quaker hat over my eyes and passed him unrecognized. I had purchased a first-class passage and at once went into the cabin and stayed there. Fortunately he did not enter. From Baltimore to Philadelphia I travelled as a gentleman, with my wife as a servant. After that, it being a presumably free country, we

days after leaving my home I was arrested as a fugitive slave in Boston. William Lloyd Garrison was living then, and took great interest in my case. I well remember the exciting scenes which finally culminated in the decision of Chief Justice Shaw that my master had a right to reclaim me. I recall with gratitude the generous act of Rev. Dr. Caldwell, of the Tremont Temple Baptist Society, who raised the money with which I was redeemed. My wife belonged to another master, Mr. DeLacy, and he sent a requisition to take her if I was taken. During my incarceration in Leverett Street jail she was secreted at the house of a friendly Abolitionist on High Street. Her whereabouts were never disclosed, and her master made no further trouble after I was released. A short time after this my first child was born, on Newhall Street, in Lynn.

Immediately after my release I began to attend anti-slavery conventions and appeal for signatures to the famous "Latimer" petitions, to be presented to the Legislature and to Congress. These asked the respective bodies to erase from the statute books every enactment making a distinction on account of complexion, and the enactment of laws to protect citizens from insult by alleged arrest. That to the Legislature bore 62,791 names and was borne into the Senate on inauguration day on the shoulders of four men. It was presented by Charles Francis Adams. That to Congress was presented by his father, John Quincy Adams, and bore 48,000 names. It was at this time I began to see a good deal of the Hutchinson Family. I not only knew John, but Jesse, Judson, Asa and Abby. For forty years I did not see Abby. Two years ago she called on me, a few months before her death. I did not know her, she had changed so much from the fresh young girl I knew in 1842. The family all did noble work for the cause of the slave. I am now in my seventy-fourth year. For forty-five years I pursued the trade of a paper-hanger in Lynn. My days in Virginia seem like a dream to me. I am glad to add these few words in recognition of the services to liberty of the Hutchinson Family, and to speak again my sense of gratitude to those who with them aroused the North in an agitation that made freedom possible for me and mine.

GEORGE W. LATIMER.

C. G. FOSTER

409 WEST RANDOLPH STREET,
CHICAGO, July 1, 1876.

JOHN W. HUTCHINSON.

DEAR BROTHER — Agreeably to your request, I send you a letter for your forthcoming autobiography. I desire to be numbered among your warm and true friends, as I have for many years been inspirited by the soul-stirring songs of yourself and other members of the "Tribe of Jesse." Your family have for many years been a fixture in the history of our country. The service they have rendered the anti-slavery cause, the temperance movement, and all the prominent reforms of their day, cannot be overestimated, and their well-earned fame will go down to the latest posterity. To my mind, never mortals sang like the Hutchinsons. Many of their songs seem like echoes from the blissful shores of the Beyond. If I cannot express it in mortal phrase, God and the good angels know what I both mean and feel. My acquaintance with the original "Hutchinson Family" has been almost exclusively confined to yourself. I have, however, some very pleasant memories of Henry and Viola, who have been "bright, particular stars" of your later organization. I have always considered you, dear John, "a man of cheerful yesterdays and confident to-morrows"—a man of the highest and noblest aspirations, with a heart overflowing with the most unselfish love.

I remember well the night when first I heard you sing. It was in Rand's Hall, Troy, N. Y., and must have been in 1842, soon after the commencement of your remarkably useful career. Since that time I have attended your concerts at regular intervals until last winter, when your songs seemed sweeter than ever — more soulful and pathetic, and gratefully do I acknowledge that they have, in all these years, largely contributed to my stock of reformatory ideas, and nerved me to strike for the right, believing that God would bless the blow.

In 1849, I left Troy and located at Beloit, Wis., where for a period of six years I was engaged in the publication of the *Journal*, and there had the pleasure of hearing you, time and again, and of speaking in my paper, in the most glowing terms, of your vocalization, and of the glorious reforms you were aiding with your inspirational songs. Again, in 1867, I had the pleasure of striking hands, and the honor of co-operating with you in Kansas during the campaign for woman's suffrage, which resulted in the largest vote ever given in the Union for the emancipation of woman, the total vote being 9,000 for the cause. I was then publishing the Kansas City *Daily Journal*, and had ample opportunities for working in the cause dear to my heart, as my paper circulated most largely in Kansas. During the struggle between Freedom and Slavery for the possession of the soil of Kansas, how well do I remember the stirring words of the Quaker poet, as sung by you, commencing

> "We'll cross the prairies as of old
> The Pilgrims crossed the sea,
> And make the West, as they the East,
> The homestead of the Free."

I claim the honor of first suggesting that you set to music Gerald Massey's immortal poem, entitled, "The People's Advent." You will remember that I met you, soon after our Civil War, on a railway train in Missouri. I was just then engaged in reading a volume of Massey's poems, when I called your attention to the poem in question, and I said I would present you with the volume if you would set the words to music. It is needless to add that I was more than gratified when I heard you sing it last winter for the first time. During all the years that I have known you, dear John, we have mutually yearned for a companionship with brothers and sisters who fully believed in and fully appreciated "The Fatherhood of God, and the Brotherhood of Man," and the very last hour's conversation I had with you, on the streets in Chicago, when I felt as if I could *not* let you go, we

"spake of love, such love as spirits feel
In worlds whose course is equable and pure;
No fears to beat away — no strife to heal —
The past unsighed for, and the future sure."

While I remain on the shores of Time, dear John, your song entitled, "What shall be my angel name?" will constantly be ringing in my ears, and as constantly lift me above all the trials and tribulations of earth; and when, at last, we are ready to graduate from this, the primary, to the secondary department of the Eternal School of Progress, I hope still to hear your ever-welcome and familiar songs on the "ever-green mountains of Life." Then, I doubt not, we shall more fully realize the truth of Tennyson's lines, that

"There are poems unwritten and poems unsung,
Sweeter than any that ever were heard;
Poems that wait for an angel tongue,
Songs that but long for a paradise bird!"

Truly and fraternally,   C. G. FOSTER.

GEORGE M. DUTCHER

BUENA VISTA COTTAGE,
LEOMINSTER, December 12, 1874.

JOHN W. HUTCHINSON.

MOST NOBLE BROTHER: — It gives me great pleasure to learn that you intend to give to the world the eventful and somewhat romantic history of the Hutchinson Family. I am satisfied that it will have a large sale and be the means of great good, as well as to enlighten the public in regard to the family of sweet singers who have for so many years charmed thousands in this and other lands by that great gift of song which God had so bountifully bestowed upon them. Well do I remember the first time I had the pleasure of listening to the Hutchinson Family. It was in East Hartford, Conn. Oh, how I enjoyed that afternoon! That sweet ministry of song still floats in my ear. It made my heart more warm for suffering humanity, and made me feel that it was not all of *life* to *live*, nor all of *death* to *die*, and I went on my way more than ever determined to do good, and lift up some poor, downtrodden brother. The next time I had the pleasure of seeing you was at my little cottage in Worcester, Mass., and you know, Brother John, how you sang to Mrs. D that most beautiful verse, "I love to tell the story." You remember how it brought the tears to our eyes, for Mrs. D was ill, and our hearts needed just such a healing balm — and when you left the room, some one whispered, "Shall not we name our little boy after him?" It was settled at once. He now stands at my side, wondering to whom I am writing. Then, do you remember how we went to John B. Gough's that very night, and how John talked and you sang, and Mrs. Gough smiled? Then do you recollect, John proposed to show us his new lecture, and when he came to look for it, it was lost! How long our faces were, and finally how bright they were when he found it! When we arrived in Worcester again you will remember we finished up the night by attending a convention at Mechanics' Hall, and what cheers went up when the successful candidate (Mr. Washburn) was announced. Since then I have spent many pleasant hours with you on "Old High Rock," and have often partaken of your generous hospitality.

Long may you live to sing the songs of temperance and humanity, and when called beyond the tide may you sing together, one unbroken family, as you walk through the leafy aisles of paradise, the song of redeeming love, with God's choirs who are washed in the blood of the Lamb! Soberly and cheerfully, Ever thine,

Geo. M. Dutcher.

BROTHER JOSHUA

New Boston, N. H., August 6, 1874.

Dear Brother John, — I learn with pleasure that you are to prepare a comprehensive history of our family for publication. I have long desired that some one having the ability and the disposition, as well as the pecuniary qualities would do so, and furnish a complete and meritorious work commensurate with the task. That desire was intensified in my own mind a few months ago, after the hasty scribbling during my concert engagements in Maine and Northern New Hampshire that resulted in the "Brief Narrative of the Hutchinson Family."

Since that has received words of approval from so many dear friends, I have a thousand times wished it could have answered a better purpose, which I hope to see fulfilled in your book. Most of the complaints made to me of the "Narrative" is its brevity, but with a host of material at your command, and a wider experience, somewhat, and with more leisure, I hope to see a book worthy of the name, and creditable to the author. I have ardently desired that the memory of the late N. P. Rogers, a devoted friend and adviser of the family, could receive the attention and kindly remembrance it so much deserves, for from his dashing pen, fired with the most disinterested love of humanity, did he couple the early history of the anti-slavery cause with the simple melodies of the Hutchinsons. Indeed, 'twas his persuasive power more than anything else that brought the family's influence as musicians to the aid of that cause.

Dear brother, I should be happy to express through your courtesy with you our mutual indebtedness to the many tried friends of the once traduced anti-slavery cause — most of whom have gone to their reward — and to the cause *itself*, as having done more for *us* than we possibly could have done for *it*.

I hope you will be able in your work to give that tribute to our beloved parents that only a child can utter, giving due prominence to their many virtues and labors of love for their numerous household all of whom, father used to say, were early dedicated to God. With what care and solicitude did they watch over the physical and musical interests of us all! and they always expressed the greatest joy when they found their children walking in the truth. I do hope that the sweet virtues with which we were inculcated will be more than demonstrated in the lives of the surviving members, and that a happy reunion may soon be consummated in the spirit life. JOSHUA

REV. SAMUEL MAY.

STRAWBERRY HILL, LANCASTER,
MEMORIAL DAY, 1893.

DEAR MR. HUTCHINSON: — I hope you suffered no ill consequences from your efforts at the Danvers commemoration. Fatigued you must have been, for you didn't spare yourself. I only hope that you didn't feel that the meeting, or its officers, urged you too hard. I was greatly interested by the contributions you made to the meeting. They were, as the Hutchinson singing has ever been, from the early times of the anti-slavery movement, a very striking and effective element, adding the clinching process, the riveting effect to every argument and appeal

It seemed to me really surprising that your voice continued so clear, so full and resonant and so like the old days. That most touching song — which, as I have heard you say, has quelled mobs and put violence to shame — the song "Over the Mountains and over the Moor," could hardly ever have been more beautifully rendered than it was at Danvers. There may well have been a tinge of sadness in your tones, with the remembrance of brothers and sister gone, — and yourself alone, of that so efficient and *eloquent* group.

I was one of the meeting in Faneuil Hall at that early day of the cause, when your brothers sang there for the first time, when, as it was said, your brother Jesse wrote some of the stanzas of that famous song

"Ho, the car Emancipation,
Rides triumphant through the nation,
Bearing in its train the story —
Liberty — the nation's glory," — etc,

while the meeting was going on. It was a new experience to me, as I guess it was to many more. The speaking had been most earnest and stirring, and the audience greatly affected. Then came *the song*, — I think by *four* Hutchinson brothers, you one of them doubtless. Were the others Jesse, Judson and Asa? [They were.] I think your sister was not at the meeting. The climax was certainly reached, the cap sheaf put on, by that song, and its spirited singing. It was a musical argument, harangue, appeal, call to arms, all in one. There was no escaping its power and effect, nor the conclusion that a mighty weapon had been added to the armory of the anti-slavery cause that day. Often and often did I hear them afterwards, and always with fresh pleasure and admiration. Their songs were always in a hopeful vein — always in a kindly, generous spirit — always cheering and animating, and immensely helpful. There was no need to specially eulogize it at Danvers, for it bore its own witness there. Your young ladies there did their part admirably, — filling well the vacant places and laying us all under deep obligation to them, as to yourself. Farewell for now. Always, with sincere regard,

SAMUEL MAY.

SEVENTIETH BIRTHDAY LETTERS

It would be impossible to print the hundreds of congratulatory letters received by the author on the attainment of his seventieth birthday. A few are selected:

CONCORD, MASS., December 27, 1890.

MY DEAR SIR — Thank you for the kind invitation to be present at the commemoration of your birthday, as you shall round your three-score years and ten. It is with great pleasure that I look forward to the privilege of meeting you on that happy anniversary day and extending to you my congratulations that you have lived thus long, and my thanks also, let me say, for all your beautiful service in the cause of liberty. A half a century ago I used to hear the "Hutchinson Family" sing the sweet and thrilling songs of freedom, and it has been a rare delight to hear again the voices of some of them in these passing weeks, just as fresh and melodious as ever. Who can tell how many chains have dissolved and how many slaves have been made free, under the influence of such potent, melting music? Thousands who have heard you have passed away, but thousands whom you have made glad are still among the living, and I trust many of them will tell you on the fifth, as they must have often done in the past, how they were cheered and inspired to more earnest service for the poor and oppressed by your heart-stirring words, and your faithful and unselfish work. Many a happy New Year to you still, dear friend of humanity, and I am,
Gratefully and cordially yours,
A. P. PUTNAM.

CONCORD, N. H., December 24, 1890.

DEAR FRIEND JOHN HUTCHINSON — You are so kind as to invite myself and Mrs. Pillsbury to be present at a reception tendered by you to your friends at the seventieth anniversary of your birthday. At this inclement season we can hardly expect in person to be there. In spirit and utterance it shall not be so. But how can it be that you are seventy years old?

I remember when you as a youth came to Concord to attend, in 1843, the annual meeting of the New Hampshire Anti-Slavery Society, with ten others of your brothers and sisters. Four of you were then known as the "Hutchinson Family Quartet." The editor of the *Home Journal* spoke of you as "a nest of brothers with a sister in it." Abby was then only a child, but you had already given many concerts and she had charmed thousands by her rendering "'Will you Walk into my Parlor?' said the Spider to the Fly," with a beauty and sweetness never before heard. I could give you more of these citations, but these suffice to show that you and your wondrous family were devout Abolitionists when it was a costly character to possess and sustain. It is not so now. When General McClellan refused your quartet within his lines with your songs of freedom, we all knew that it was out of respect to slavery and slave-holders. Those very melodies would now be good campaign literature in any of our political parties, for a presidential campaign. Your voice, whether in speech or song, has ever been on the side of justice, truth and right. What blissful memories must now be yours! May no shadow ever pass over them! Faithfully and fraternally yours,

PARKER PILLSBURY,
SARAH H. PILLSBURY.

BOSTON, December 29, 1890.

DEAR MR. HUTCHINSON — I have delayed reply to your kind invitation till I could know. It is not yet quite certain, but I fear I cannot be present. I would like to join my congratulations with your army of friends on your long and blessed life. May you have as many more birthdays as you desire. Your retrospect and your prospect both must be a delight to you. Respectfully,

M. J. SAVAGE.

NELSON, NEB., December 26, 1890.

JOHN W. HUTCHINSON.

DEAR SIR AND BROTHER — . It was really a great pleasure to hear from you. I have no doubt that you are still using your voice to the glory of the Master. . . . Many, many times my thoughts have turned to you, during the exciting campaign just past with us in Nebraska, especially in the selection of some of your songs, favorites of mine, such as "One Hundred Years Hence," and "Fifteen Dollars a Day," the rendering of which always created great applause. Now, my dear sir and brother, nothing would give me greater pleasure than to pay you a visit — the uncrowned king of song, of this our great and would be glorious country if the women had their just rights, the franchise — on the fifth of January, 1891. May the loving arms of our Heavenly Father ever surround you by night and by day in your declining years, is the prayer of,

Yours sincerely and fraternally,

JOHN H. HUNT.

PEORIA, ILL., December 26, 1890.

JOHN W. HUTCHINSON.

DEAR SIR — Your very kind letter and invitation received. It is with regret that I am not able to be with you. The receipt of your letter brings back many incidents of the past when all your brothers and sisters sang at the old Town Hall in Milford, the children arranged according to age, and the good old songs then sung can never be forgotten by me as long as my memory is retained... May health, happiness and prosperity attend you and yours.

Very affectionately,

JOHN J. WALLACE.

ELMWOOD, ILL., December 29, 1890.

JOHN W. HUTCHINSON, ESQ.

DEAR OLD FRIEND — Your kind invitation to go down to Lynn and help set up your seventieth milestone, is gratefully received. You will have a company such as it would be a delight to mingle with, and that it will be a memorable occasion, I cannot doubt. But it will be impossible for me to be there, except in spirit and warm remembrance.

I think history will be ransacked in vain to find another such band as that of which yourself and Abby alone remain. So numerous, all so rich in musical ability, and all so thoroughly devoted to liberty, equality and fraternity!

Hail to the remnant of the glorious band whose simple songs have made life richer, sweeter and holier to uncounted thousands! Don't fail to send me an account of the reception. All the Browns send warm regards.

Yours faithfully,

E. R. BROWN.

NEW YORK, December 31, 1890.

MR. JOHN W. HUTCHINSON.

MY DEAR FRIEND — I most sincerely regret that I cannot be with you and your dear family and many friends on the happy occasion of your birthday, January 5, 1891. Oh, how strange it seems! Your seventieth birthday! To me you always seem young, such a bright, youthful spirit as you have. May you keep it, my dear friend, to the last! . I hope you are well and facing the sunset as bravely as you faced the morning and noontide of life. May God bless you and give you many happy years. As ever and always,

  Your friend,   GRACE GREENWOOD

           ORANGE, N. J., January 1, 1891

DEAR MR. HUTCHINSON:—Accept my thanks for the remembrance which bids me to your festival on the fifth inst. With regret I must absent myself, but I am happy to join in the congratulations of your friends. It surprises me, indeed, to find you so young, for I have a very early recollection of you—about fifty years of conscious retrospect—and then, of course, you seemed very much my senior.

I hope the American people will never underrate the influence of the songs of the Hutchinson family. I wish we had another such, attuned to the times and needs of the present hour, when "the good time coming" seems still so remote. But now there is a dearth of poets and of singers. For this reason, if for no other, may your days be prolonged, that the tradition may be kept unbroken as possible. With a real sense of personal indebtedness,

  I am very cordially yours,
           WENDELL P. GARRISON

           NEW YORK, January 1, 1891.

MY DEAR FRIEND JOHN W. HUTCHINSON:—The first knowledge I had of the "Hutchinson Family" was derived from the song "The Old Granite State," so popular in my boyhood. The verse of this song

> "We're the friends of emancipation,
> And we sing the proclamation,
> Till it echoes through the nation
> From the Old Granite State,"

started in me the first anti-slavery sentiment and conviction that I can now recall. Little did I dream that it would be my privilege to paint the crowning act in the glory of our nation,—the picture of "The Proclamation," to be placed as an enduring memorial of Lincoln's immortal act, on the walls of the Nation's Capitol! . .

           FRANK B. CARPENTER

MILFORD, N. H., January 2, 1891.

DEAR JOHN:— My old anti-slavery jewel, I should indeed be pleased to be with you next Monday, but eighty-one years are scowling at me.

I remember the Hutchinson singers, and their songs are the sweetest recollections of my life. I hope that power that has kept your voice in tune so long will see that it does not fail for many years.

Very truly your friend, JOHN MILLS.

EVANSTON, ILL., December 24, 1890.

John W. Hutchinson.

KIND FRIEND:— Accept my thanks for the invitation to your seventieth birthday anniversary, and in return an invitation from me to my mother's eighty-sixth birthday anniversary, which occurs January 3, 1891. It is exceedingly likely that you will not be here, and that I will not be at your reception, but all the same we can have kind and friendly thoughts and best wishes, of which I assure you from us all here at Rest Cottage. Ever yours sincerely,

FRANCES E. WILLARD.

PAINESVILLE, O., December 22, 1890.

John W. Hutchinson.

MY DEAR AND MOST BELOVED BROTHER:— I wish I could tell you of the thousand incidents that, rapidly as thought, fill my mind, which transpired during our pioneering in the West over thirty years ago. No family of singers has ever given to the world such sentiments of freedom and humanity, in song of such harmonious and thrilling music as the "original Hutchinson Family." Notwithstanding the great victory that has been achieved in the progress of right over wrong, still there is a large class of the most worthy of our citizens (females) who are unjustly deprived of their vote and voice in making the laws by which they are governed. This is all wrong. May God speed the day when this class shall be free! Some say the times have changed, but I believe that your style of singing would be as popular with the masses of the people to-day as ever, if only some such harmonious voices could be found. Your true and sincere friends,

MR. AND MRS. E. E. JOHNSON.

CHICAGO, ILL., December 27, 1890.

J. W. Hutchinson.

MY DEAR FRIEND:— I thank you for your invitation, but geography forbids me to accept it. And have you indeed reached your grand climateric, and a heptade beyond it, on your way to the celestial city?—

APPENDIX.

singing all the way along your pilgrimage, and planting memories of song down all the ages, for your strains will not be lost. Methinks sometimes a bar will come back to the thought of some celestial worshipper, while he sings in heaven the new song of redeeming grace and dying love, and mingle with the harmony. I congratulate you on your happy old age, and the useful life which lies behind it. Sing on, dear pilgrim, you have aimed towards and attained the sentence, thus far, "Well done, good and faithful servant." For the melody to which you have devoted your life is an employment nearest akin to the employment of the blessed. God bless you, and give you many more years — and a song in them all. Cordially yours,

S. F. Smith.

John W. Hutchinson.   Boston, December 30, 1890.

Dear Friend — We thank you for remembering us by inviting us to your seventieth anniversary, but for several reasons we cannot come. You will not miss us, for you have been so long before the public that you have made only less than a legion of friends and acquaintances, and if those of them still living should half of them honor you with their presence, you would have to get the use of a half-dozen or dozen of the houses of your neighbors. As I make it out, it is fifty years since your family of brothers met for practice in the room over Oliver Porter's store, you occupying one part of the floor and we boys the other end, your first public concert being in the Old Sagamore Hall. You have been preserved, John, to come to the allotted age of man, threescore years and ten! How much a man can experience in that time! If your sister Abby is present, please pay her my kindest regards. Very truly yours,   Charles Butum.

Chicopee Falls, Mass., December 2, 1890.

Mr. John W. Hutchinson.

Dear Sir — I am very sorry not to be able to be present at the reception on the occasion of your seventieth birthday. I congratulate you not because you have lived long, but because you have lived to good effect. Most respectfully,   Edward Bellamy.

Commonwealth of Massachusetts,
Executive Department, Boston, January 1, 1891.

My dear Mr. Hutchinson — Your kind invitation to the reception of your seventieth birthday, on the fifth inst., has been received. I have delayed answering in the hope that I might see my way clear to accept. To-day, however, I find my engagements for Monday will be such as to prevent my attendance. I regret this very much, as it would afford me much pleasure to join with your other friends in offering hearty congratulations upon this event. I trust that the occasion may be a pleasant and memorable one, and that you may be permitted to enjoy, in health and happiness, many more anniversaries of your birth. Wishing you a Happy New Year, with kindest regards,

I am sincerely yours, J. Q. A. BRACKETT.

House of Representatives
Washington, January 1, 1891.

MY DEAR MR. HUTCHINSON — We have received your kind invitation to attend a reception tendered you by friends on the seventieth anniversary of your birthday, and regret exceedingly our inability to attend. But we desire to tender our earnest congratulations to you on this occasion and to express the wish that you may live many years yet to come in the enjoyment of good health and surrounded by hosts of friends and supplied with all the comforts of life. The songs you have sung have thrilled with joy the hearts of thousands of your hearers. And may the good you have done crown your mortal life with a halo of peace and win for you everlasting felicity in the life to come. Sincerely your friends,

WILLIAM M. SPRINGER.
REBECCA RUTER SPRINGER.

LYNN, January 5, 1891.

MY DEAR MR. HUTCHINSON — Mrs. Stewart unites with me in the regret that we cannot attend your reception this evening. But we wish to express our thanks for your very kind remembrance, and to wish, with the incoming year, many blessings for you. Your life has been one of noblest sympathies. You have always been on the right side. Your heart has been warm toward every movement of thought and love whose aim has been to make human hearts brighter and happier. Your heart-songs have cheered the patriot, the philanthropist, the reformer, the weary day-toiler, the sorrow-laden. Your cheerful spirit has been dampened by no failures. The hosts of wrong have never disheartened you. Hope has been ever at full tide with you. Seventy years! In them what happiness you have dispensed to your fellows in the world's most earnest endeavor for greater light and greater and true fraternity.

May God bless you and grant you many more years to love, to enjoy and to serve. Most truly, SAMUEL B. STEWART.

ROXBURY, January 3, 1891.

DEAR BROTHER JOHN — Though I cannot put in an appearance at High Rock, I shall yet be one of the goodly company who will congratulate you and give thanks to the Good Power for the coming of such a gracious anniversary. I am glad you were born, glad you drew breath in "The good old State, the brave old State", glad you were one of the Hutchinsons, glad you have lived in such a rich, historic period, glad your heart has inclined ever toward the struggling cause of justice and humanity, glad you have helped so greatly to sweeten the air of this continent and to make *right* things seem *fair*; glad, too, for all the domestic life of love and the wider circle of friendship and good-will which have been so large a part of your own varied experience.

Do you know it is over thirty-five years since we made that winter trip together — "Judson, John and Asa," with myself for supernumerary — across the thinly-settled new land from Minneapolis to Dubuque. We had never met till that year; we have met seldom since, but those few days spent together did the business. We have been friends and brothers as if we lived in one house; and I never meet with your name, nor catch a glimpse of your face without a warming of the cockles of my heart.

When James Freeman Clarke received the congratulations of his friends on just such an occasion, he said: "I never before knew how good it is to be seventy years old, and I advise you all to try it." Dear brother John, I trust you, too, find it good to be seventy. I know you have had many reasons for thinking well of this world, and for being grateful to the wise, all-including Providence. And my heart unites with the hearts of thousands in the earnest wish that your afternoon may be bright and useful, that your sunset may be serene and clear, and that when the shadow of twilight comes, the wider, deeper glory of the stars may break upon you like the Vision, the Infinite Love and the Endless Life. With affectionate respect,

CHARLES G. AMES.

SISTER ABBY'S LETTERS.

Sister Abby was an indefatigable correspondent. She found great pleasure in writing her friends. To no person was she more devoted in this particular than her brother John and her nephew Henry. Her letters, however, are so full of allusions to business and family matters of no possible interest to the average reader that a consecutive compilation of them seems hardly feasible. During her later years there were weeks when hardly a day would pass that did not bring a letter from her. It has been deemed advisable to quote from some of these as illustrative of her friendly and sisterly solicitude and affection, her cheerfulness even under suffering, and her mental characteristics.

TO HENRY

Hutchinson, October 16, 1870.

My dear Henry — Your very excellent and welcome letter sent from New London, Conn., reached me in Hutchinson, Minn., two days after my arrival. One from Uncle Ludlow came at the same time. This morning I have been to walk with Asa's two dogs. Found a few bright leaves which I will enclose to you, from your own woods. I am enjoying this great ocean of land, though it scares me when I look around, for I feel as though I was at the end of the world, and should never get back again. There is so much room that I feel as though I needed wings to get over the great country fast enough. I am glad you and your father are singing and doing well for yourselves and good for others. Just while I write Fred is playing the cornet, Abby pianoforte, and Asa bass viol. Music seems to belong to the Hutchinson family, wherever they may congregate. The sun is about setting, the autumn wind blowing, and I thank God for all his goodness. We have the very best of food here — cracked wheat, chickens, wild duck and goose, home-made bread, sweet butter and good cheese. Asa and Lizzy have done well here to get so much done; all they buy is sugar, tea and salt. I might be induced to go to farming out here, if your strong right arm was here to lend a little aid now and then. I am clearing out the brush from the woods near the house, and making paths through them. Henry, I know what dark hours are, and what bright ones are also, and I only hope to live and do somebody good as long as I stay. Give my love to your father and mother and Juddie. I hope you will sing every good sentiment you can, and help every sad and mournful soul to the light, either man or woman. God bless you. I may be in New York in two weeks. Call and see me when you come to town. I believe I love music best of everything. It covers all my friends and opens the way to Heaven. Try and save your money, Henry, and some day come and have a home near me somewhere, perhaps in Heaven.

Yours truly, AUNT ABBY.

NEW YORK, March 7, 1871.

MY DEAR HENRY — If you are my brother, nephew and son, and I your sister, aunty and mother, why, there is a large family of us to start with. I bless you for your words of comfort and cheer which came when I most needed them. I am better in body and mind than when I last saw you, though not all well. I suppose when the mortal puts on immortality, I may look for perfect health, but I don't know whether it will ever come to be my lot here, and yet, I have *so much* more than many people ever have — kindness and friends in every direction, and hardly a day passes but some one comes to give me a word of good cheer. I like to be well enough to give encouragement and help where it is most needed, to help those who are ready to perish, and to give strength to the weak and rest to the weary. I want to be a mother in Israel, and do good, and yet I cannot get to perfection. I can try for it though, and trust in God to help me. Well, life is not all of it to be spent here, yet it is good to begin to live right here to-day. I shall have times that I shall look for you through the eternities, and we will try to help each other forward forever. I am more glad you are devoting yourself to reading and books than I can tell you. I used to read a good deal with Asa. Our tastes in book knowledge were quite alike, and we were happy in one another's thought and company. I have always missed him in this respect. I wish you to read Huxley's Lay Sermons when you have time. It is a book which you ought to own. All Prescott's histories are good, I believe, and you will be glad to read scientific works also. As for me, I can only take up a little here and there as a bird picks up its crumbs, and though I may not make public use of what I learn, I hope to make use of it in my family circle. Dear Henry, pray for me as I do for you, and help me as I hope ever to help you, and most of all we must love one another as long as we stay. Uncle Ludlow is asleep, or he would send regards to you.

Yours, A. H. P.

[Abby and Henry were very fond of singing Scotch songs in character. A large photograph of them in their Highland plaids, when Henry was about eighteen, is still in existence. "Bonnie laddie" and "Bonnie lassie" were terms of affection they often used towards one another as long as Henry lived, the package of letters from which these selections are made being indorsed in Henry's hand, "From my dear bonnie lassie."]

NEW YORK, October 24, 1872.

MY DEARLY BELOVED HENRY — I read your letter to your father in which you speak of forming a new *male quartet,* and then you add that you would like to have "Aunt Abby" as "prima donna." Bless your heart, my dear nephew, Aunt Abby is old and at present too weak for public life. I made a vain attempt to sing with your father in Connecticut. I thought I should lose my voice altogether, I was so hoarse, and in fact I have just struggled against a fever, I think, for one whole month; one day up, the next day down, and so for a while it seemed as though my earthly existence was hanging on rather a slender thread. I would have been glad had God seen fit to clip the thread, as He did not, and as I wished to make myself strong against all work to come, I at once repaired to Dr. Taylor's Movement Cure, where at present I am stopping for treatment. How many times I have wished to sing, and all the time I feel that the spirit is willing, but the flesh is weak, and so I may have to wait for a new body, and to be clothed upon by the Father. If I was to make a suggestion, and it was a possible thing to carry it out, I would say — take Uncle Ludlow, your father, myself and you, for a quartet, and yet some younger people might do the work better. I think they would.

I am ever yours, dear Henry, AUNT ABBY.

CONGRESS HALL, SARATOGA SPRINGS,
August 17, 1873.

I want to be mad and say I will never write to you again. Ludlow says, "Not one of my friends think half as much of me as I do of them," and I shall pretty soon begin to think so. I wish to hear if you and Doctor Howe arrived alive in New York after that tremendous farewell, and all I have heard from either of you is a tremendous *big horn* which if I had now I would take to *blow you up* with, for your forgetfulness of your revered and respected though aged aunt. What is the matter? I want to tell you what a good visit we had at Lebanon Springs and to see the Shakers at Mt Lebanon, but I won't, neither will I tell you that we sang to them, and that they took us through the interesting parts of their houses and families, and treated us royally; and then I am not going to tell you one word about our being here at the biggest hotel in the United States, where we ride, walk, drink, sleep, eat, bowl and practise shooting at tin birds, and " that's what we do at the Springs." This house is full to overflowing, and it seems all the time like Vanity Fair or some other country Fair where things are brought to market — I mean men and women. If you were a good boy I might tell you that there are two or three young *millionairesses* here who are gotten up mightly regardless of expense, and one of them looks as though she was bored to death with her clothes, and being put up mightly for display. That is the only redeeming feature in her case. I wish to know if Frank and Augusta [Carpenter] are alive, and why they don't say so, and why in the world does not Frank answer such a wonderful correspondent. I cannot throw away such literary effusions every day. Are they going to Homer or are they going to Heaven, which? We expect to go to Lake George, from here. And now to prove to you that I have some method in my madness, I will say that we received a good letter from Viola at Put In Bay, inviting us there. We may go by-and-by, but not now. I hope you are well and happy, and you must give my love to " Abby Sage" and say to her that I saw her friend Miss —— at Overlook. Tell her that God lets us live through everything, but if we cannot have all our blessings here, we can have our treasures laid up in Heaven, and as God is merciful He will open the mystic gate for us some day into the land of the blessed spirits. Oh, Henry! sometimes I am too impatient to wait any longer. I want to be *all spirit* so I can hover around *all my beloved ones*. But that may be mental dyspepsia, and so I will go out and get a drink of Congress water and get over it. This crowd of people depresses one tearfully. Such aimless lives we lead here. I long for work and my friends, to have *my community* and plenty to do, and I am trying to live. Tell me if Doctor is well. *Pinch* him on both ears gently, kiss Augusta and shake Frank. Ludlow sends love.

Yours ever, ABBY.

MAGNOLIA, FLA., April 7, 1874.

BONNIE LADDIE.— " Will ye go, will ye go to the banks of Balquither?" And now I must tell you that your letter from Washington, March 26th, was received about one week ago. We have been away four weeks from Magnolia and returned yesterday. Have had a pretty sick time both of us, but we are better, and to-morrow or next day start on our way to New Orleans, thence up the Mississippi to St. Louis and home. Augusta and I had partly agreed to go to England the middle of May, our time is rather limited. I hope you will be in New York by the first of May so that we may get the light of your countenance before we go across the great waters. How I wish your business would take you across the ocean. Tell your father and mother I hope to see them before we go. Shall try to see the Milford friends, and wish we could have a *family* meeting. People at St. Augustine all remember you and your father's singing with great pleasure. I am glad you can make people so happy. Go on singing good words forever. A

Enclosed in this letter was the following, in Abby's handwriting:

  Here's to the year that's awa'
   We'll drink it in strong and in sma',
  And here's to th' bonnie young lassie we lo'ed
   While swift flew the year that's awa'
    (Repeat last two lines)

  Here's to the soger who bled
   And the sailor who bravely did fa',
  Their fame is alive though their spirits have fled
   On the wings of the year that's awa'

  Here's to the friends we can trust
   When the storms of adversity blaw,
  May they live in our song and be nearest our hearts—
   Nor depart like the year that's awa'

EDINBURGH, June 4, 1874.

MY DEAR BONNIE LADDIE,—I shall write you a wild, hasty scrawl, as we do not stay long enough anywhere to write sober, sedate letters. Old Ireland and the Shamrock gave my heart a great shaking, and we saw one of the prettiest green countries of the world while there. And then to come to Scotland and find its scenery grand and bold, though perhaps not on so gigantic a scale as America, adds more and more to our delight every day. We have seen Glasgow, the city second in size only in the kingdom. We went to old Sterling Castle, noted for its ancient history and for its being the home of kings of Scotland for hundreds of years. You will be delighted with Scottish history, and if you are ever going to cross the ocean I would advise you to become familiar with this history through the writings of Sir Walter Scott. We have seen a good many Highlanders in their real Highland costume since we came into the country, and yesterday a company of them marched past our hotel with a half-dozen bagpipes playing the same tune together, and the tune was "Auld Robin Gray." Tell your mother I shall always think of her when I hear that old music. I thought of you as we sailed on Loch Katrine and saw the 'Braes of Balquiddher' at our left. The same braes over which the beautiful Ellen Douglas used to roam. How too bad that you are not here! Henry, go right to the library in Frank's study and take down Scott's poems, and read every word of the "Lady of the Lake." Florence probably knows it by heart already. That will tell you just where we have been better than I can. At old Sterling Castle we saw the tower in which Roderick Dhu died. Saw, also, the room in which Ellen waited while she was trying to get her friend released. Do read it for my sake, and think how when you read

"Hail to the chief who in triumph advances!"

we have been over the very walk which Roderick Dhu and James Fitz James took together before they reached Coilantogle Ford. Oh Henry, life and death, love and hate, trust and jealousy went on then just as now; and the great human heart beats just as grandly to-day as ever. We are all kings and queens—ladies, lords, nobles and chiefs, now-a-days, instead of having a few men trying to lord it over us. The true noblemen and noble women are the poets, the singers, the artists, who keep alive the soul and the histories of all ages. Here we are in this beautiful city, Edinburgh. It is full of historical points of interest, and we cannot see them all in many days. It is a very picturesque city, and with its hills and valleys, noble castles and fine parks, very charming. We climbed to the top of Arthur's Seat yesterday. Saw Holyrood Castle and Chapel, Queen Mary's drawing-room and bedroom. You remember she was married to Darnley and she loved Riggio, an Italian. Darnley, being jealous, had him murdered. He was afterward murdered himself, and Mary Stuart married Bothwell. Strange, wild histories. Do write me. Uncle Ludlow is busy and happy and sends love. Tell Viola I wish for another picture of her and her babies. I think of her and her Scotch husband and boys over here. God bless them all and you, too, my dear bonnie laddie. Love to J. W. H. Yours ever, BONNIE LASSIE.

---

125 ABBEY ROAD, KILBURN,
LONDON, July 5, 1874.

By this time, bonnie laddie, you must have received some word from me. Your letter of June 18th came to 140 Abbey Road last night, and I cannot tell whether you are dreaming or whether my letter to you went astray. I am sure you must know something of our movements by this time. We reached London on Wednesday the 1st of July. Father Patton and Emily went to the station to meet us, but as we were late we reached Emily's house and found her two boys and her husband's father, Mr. Perkins, to receive us. Soon after, Father Patton and Emily came in, and we welcomed them to London. We take all our meals at their house, and have a bedroom and parlor at this house, which is but a short walk from them. I am now sitting in the little parlor, or as it is called in England — drawing-room. Ludlow is going with his father and sister to church, while I will try and hold communion with my transatlantic companions. I am glad you have heard Salvini and that you like him. It made me homesick to get your letter, in spite of all I could do, although I am glad to see the wonders and beauties of this land of Great Britain. Many, many times I have wished you and your father were with us. We have so far met with warm receptions from all the old Hutchinson friends and I have received notes from quite a number of those we were not able to see. They do not know me as a rule, for I was only sixteen when we were here before, and forty-four is a long way from sixteen, you know. Several friends have brought out our old daguerreotypes, and in mine is hardly the faintest look of the present countenance. It will be rather a sad affair it when we lay off the mortal coil those who have gone before us do not recognize us, will it not? Guess we will not borrow trouble, however. I must tell you how we spent the glorious Fourth. Lottus and Emily took us up the river Thames a long distance. We took railway as far as Teddington, and then went on board the launch "Emily," named for the wife of the inventor of the boat, Emily P. Perkins. You have heard before of Lottus' inventions. I thought of you all day for several reasons. First, the bright beautiful day, and next, the perfect little steam launch with its appointments I knew you would appreciate so much, and though the Thames is a narrow river, the banks are beautiful. Fine trees, and lovely lawns and handsome houses make a variety of scenery all the way up the river. And then the little boats of one kind or another keep you all the time on the lookout as they pass very close to your own boat. I thought we passed one hundred and fifty boats of different kinds, but Ludlow says that is a small number compared with what we saw. Parties of young people, parties of old people, some rowing, some sailing, some in small steam launches similar to that we were on. Whole crowds of young men in what I call a decided *undress*. Nothing on but undervests and white flannel pantaloons, their arms bared to the shoulder, their legs bare from the knee to near the ankle. Those were regular boating suits. We saw several of the outside riggers on Shelton boats, each with a man in, and in one were eight men, each with an oar

That is the number pulled by the Oxford and Cambridge regatta crews. Well, I guess I thought of you then, and we saw about the prettiest of English ladies in bright hats and dresses, and brighter faces. There is no doubt that these Europeans live more out of doors than do we Americans. Now I must tell you of our lunch. We had cake, biscuit and lemonade for lunch, and later in the day we had cold roast beef, delicious salad which no person can make better than Loftus himself, nice rolls, and what is indispensable on an English dinner-table, *cheese*. Do not faint at the word. I fear you would have to put on an extra hardening of the nerves over here, for you never see much less than half a cheese on the table, at any dinner. Then we had pine-apples, cherries, very fine, delicious large strawberries, and fresh figs — the first figs in this state I ever saw or tasted. They are very rich and sweet, and one cannot eat many of them. But the day was charming altogether, and one which you would have enjoyed to the full. There are many locks on the Thames, and when they are filled with small boats you seem to be sitting in a room with a great many people. We hope to hear Sims Reeves this week and also Adelina Patti in opera. We went into St. Paul's Church a few days ago, and it seems larger than ever. Went down into the crypt, and saw the stone tomb of the Duke of Wellington; also, the large funeral car, the iron of which all came from the cannon he took in various battles. Saw the tomb of Nelson, and of Landseer, the painter. The latter only died last year. Ludlow and I went up to the Whispering Gallery and though we stood one hundred and fifty feet apart, by putting our faces near the wall we could hear the slightest whisper. The dome is so perfectly constructed that sound is carried nearly around the circle. We saw the old clock that has not run down for one hundred and sixty-six years, so they say. I guess we will run down before we reach that age. I am tired and will walk before I finish this note.

Evening — Now that I have really written to you, *old fellow*, you will not find it necessary to send me a crest of such a terrible nature as His Satanic Majesty dangling his prisoner over a coal fire. I never saw such a design on an envelope, and I suppose I never shall be anxious to see another. I thank you and your father and mother for sending the photographs and music. They will be appreciated in the warm hearts and home of Thomas Webb, in Dublin. George Dawson, a radical clergyman of Birmingham, and an old friend of the Hutchinson Family is about to go to America to lecture. Ask your father to look out for him. I have given Mr. Dawson a note of introduction to Colonel Higginson, as he knows about everybody, and can help him in his way about Boston and New York. I am reading George Eliot's new book, "Jubal, and Other Poems." The legend of Jubal is very sweet, but very sad. There seems to be tragedy in all of George Eliot's writings. She knows what suffering is. How are you prospering in business? You must send me a new picture of yourself. I gave the one I had to Thomas Webb, and I wish to see your face daily.

      Yours,   ABBY

      LUCERNE, SWITZERLAND, September 25, 1874.

MY DEAR HENRY — Where shall I begin? You will say, where I left off. Where I left off I have not the faintest recollection. You know best, if you continue to carry about in your "left side pocket" such strange compositions as I send you. Your letter reached me on our arrival at this hotel. After I tell you how glad it made your old auntie's eyes and heart to see once more a word of cheer from home, you will know that your letters also are appreciated, though I have no "left side pocket" in which to carry them.

And so you, dear child, "thank God that He has spared me so long to scatter smiles and speak words of comfort like fountain's spray on everything around me." How I wish that could be true of me, but if you lived with me *daily* you would find the sweet words sometimes *very bitter*, sometimes *very acid*, I know. I am perfectly well aware of that fact, and yet I do like to have my dear friends as oblivious to it as possible.

Uncle Ludlow and I have had some good times since coming on the Continent, but we have recently had a pretty severe trial. We came into Switzerland the last of August, and were quite well at Zurich, and on to Como, where we took our first ride by diligence through the wonderful scenery of the Via Mala and the Splugen Pass. This we did on one day and the next day went on to Lake Como. Thence we started for St. Gothard route, but we could get no farther than Faido, a real Italian town, though in Switzerland. The sun and hard travel brought on a bilious attack to Uncle Ludlow. We called an Italian physician, who could not speak a word of English, and we had to get a young man who had been in America to come in to interpret for all of us. The doctor would not give Uncle L. the medicine which he asked for, and it seemed some of the time as though we should get desperate trying to make him understand what was needed. We were there seventeen days and when Uncle L. thought he was able to travel he was reduced to a mere shadow. You see we had so much sour bread and poor meats — that is, poorly cooked food — on the Continent, that we were both getting starved before Uncle L. was taken sick. Then he nearly had a sunstroke come upon him, and at last we were caught at Faido at a second rate hotel where it was next to impossible to get anything a sick man could eat. Well it was rather a blue time, but we lived through it, and are at a good hotel now, only I so longed for a friend to come in to whom I could say, "Give me some help." But sleep and hope kept me up, and we both were rejoiced when we could start again. We came over the St. Gothard, and on to Lucerne in three days from Faido. The scenery here is world-wide in its fame, and is considered as grand and fine as any in Switzerland. The lake is clear and a lovely emerald green. The mountains rise up in grandeur in every direction, some of them bare and rocky, some covered with verdure and green trees; others completely crowned with the eternal snows, which give them a still higher and more towering appearance, as though they really reached the heavens. The first snow mountains we saw we thought the clouds rested on them, but when we found the clouds did not move away, we then knew we were looking at the eternal Alps themselves. But I like them best at a respectful distance as they oppress me very much when we ride through the narrow passes or valleys, and these huge hills seem to be hanging right over our heads all the time. You must come and see them for yourself and then you will understand it all.

Heard a good band in front of the hotel play all last evening, and they closed the performance with the "Star-Spangled Banner" and "Yankee Doodle." The Americans staying here applauded well, and I am an American. Guess if I was half dead the national airs would arouse me again. To-day we have heard the wonderful organ in the Cathedral. It has a fine *vox humana* stop, and imitated nearly every instrument in the world. The wind and thunder were wonderful. The first night we reached the little town of Faido we asked the landlord for a room. He ran into the house and brought us a bottle of rum. The chambermaid could not understand either English or French, but spoke a German-Italian *patois*. She knew what hot water was, and always brought in "caldo" when asked. I had to learn enough Italian to make my wants known. Now I have a lovely *patois*, a mixture of English, French, German, Dutch and Italian. None of you will know us when we get home with our European accomplishments. Do study the languages before you come over.

  Yours, with continued affection, AUNT ABBY.

NAPLES, ITALY, January 25, 1875.
HOTEL DES STRANGERS.

MY DEAR BONNIE LADDIE — I want to send you my blessing and thanks for the noble thought you had of Aunty at Christmas time, and for getting all the good friends of Portland to write also. I have sent a letter to Mr. Pickard, asking him to thank everybody for me on his side the house, and now you must thank everybody on your Hutchinson side for me. What a good time you had with Mrs. Dennett, as we all have had so many years ago. Do you know that we have been here for three weeks to-morrow, and though we have seen much of Naples and its environs we have not seen all. It is so unlike home, and yet full of interest in its way. Pompeii, Herculaneum, Vesuvius, Capri, with its blue grotto, will ever be among the wonders of Southern Italy, and God grant that you may come over here to see for yourself. Study French and Italian if you ever expect to come abroad. You will find both languages useful. In Etty's letter to me of Christmas day she writes of the death of Aunt Lizzy very suddenly at Rushford, Minn., and since that time we have more of the particulars through the Western papers. Poor " A " has had a hard time, losing Nelly, Fred, and now Lizzy, whom he will miss most of all, and she has done so much work at Hutchinson that she will be missed there very much, in the church, and in the singing of the " Tribe of Asa." We are marching right along, dear Henry, and now we have as many relatives over the river, and almost more, than here. I hope God will let us all meet again where the "wicked cease from troubling and the weary are at rest." My dear child, it will not be Heaven to me unless I can have *all* my beloved with me. I want a great house not made with hands, eternal in the heavens.

We have seen Mr. Thomas Cook to-night, whose party we have joined for Egypt and Palestine, and find he is an old acquaintance, and knew the young Hutchinsons when they sang in England in 1846. Naples is all alive and the *noisiest* place, as far as whip-cracking and fast driving goes. We have music daily and nightly of all kinds. One sweet voice sang to us a few nights ago, with a good guitar and violin accompaniment, and it sounded like your voice, your father's, Uncle Judson's and Uncle Ludlow's all combined, so you can guess I was pretty happy with such a quartet. But the language was Italian, and not English, though very musical. We hope to go to Austria, Germany, Norway and Sweden next summer and see the sun that never sets, "away up North." Can't you all come? You and Dennett, Asa and John, would have great success in England, I believe. I long to hear some Hutchinson voices. Good-night. Good-by, and may the peace which passeth understanding be and abide with you all. Amen.

Tell John and Joshua I had a dream almost heavenly the other night. All of my brothers came home,— Judson, Jesse, John, Joshua, Caleb, Zephy, Andrew, Noah, David, Benny and Asa, and full as many of the children, and we sang old hymns together in great joy. God grant we shall all meet beyond the smiling and the weeping at our Heavenly Father's door. Yours, ABBY.

HOTEL VICTORIA, HANOVER, GERMANY,
October 4, 1875

MY DEAR HENRY — I must try and write you a small letter in answer to your long one, written at Martha's Vineyard, September 1st. We have seen the principal cities of Russia since I last wrote you,— St. Petersburg and Moscow. The former has magnificent churches, large palaces and picture galleries. We saw jewels enough in the homes of the different kings and emperors to set up several jeweller's shops in New York, and we came away without stealing even the smallest diamond or precious gem. We saw the little hut which was formerly the home of Peter the Great, and from whom St. Petersburg received its name. We saw very fine horses in St. Petersburg and even finer in Moscow. Some beautiful black steeds and others a very handsome iron-gray, and nearly all very fast in speed. They have true Arab blood, and were the delight of our eyes, for we never tired of looking at them, as they seemed to *fly* through the streets. The turrets, steeples and gilded domes of Moscow surpassed anything we have yet seen in Europe, Asia or Africa. We thought Rome and Constantinople could not be equalled in variety of churches, but Moscow is quite as wonderful as any place in the world. Many of the roofs of the houses are green, and the gilded domes which rise above them make a contrast very marked, and really beautiful. Our guide in Moscow said there were sixteen hundred churches in the city.

Here in Hanover many American and English people come to study, and the German language is spoken to perfection. What a sensation Moody and Sankey are creating. I think the sweet hymns make half the conversions, but none of them are better than "Coming up the Steep of Time," and the "Fatherhood of God and Brotherhood of Man." We have heard from Mary Howitt within a few weeks, and she has invited us to see them in their home in Austrian Tyrol. Good by. Love to all. We expect to leave for Paris to morrow *via* Holland. We love Germany, its music and literature. ABBY

HIGHLAND HOUSE, MILFORD, N. H.,
September 28, 1877

MY DEAR HENRY — If you had not written with your own pen the fact that I have *not written* you a word since my sickness and recovery, I would not have believed it true, but as I know you are the soul of truth, I now say forgive me, and I'll try to do better next time. The truth is, we two people have been pretty busy since coming to Milford, and I for one always feel as though my hands were more than full up here. I have never liked Milford so much as I do this summer in all my life, I believe. It may be because I seemed to have risen from the grave to come here, and I have been getting well ever since. We have here a railroad, telegraph office, three mails a day, coming into town, and three going out. We have a Congregational, a Baptist and a Methodist church, for those who are fond of attending church, also a Unitarian society, though that is small, and has no church. Then we have one of the best schools in the country in our high school. Besides all this, Milford has a free library, which has at present over two thousand books. Visitors to the town have the privilege of reading these books, as well as the residents. We have enjoyed this privilege in common with others, I can assure you. Uncle Ludlow has read several books of travel, and how to get around the world in eighty days, as well as in a longer time. We have travelled many miles around Milford, have seen Wilton, Mont Vernon, Amherst and Lyndeboro — have visited Milford Springs several times; have also found in Amherst a spring of iron and sulphur, also a soda spring, so we have been testing one after another. Then we have had a feast of grapes and peaches from the vineyard and orchard of Mr. Keyes. We have been there to-day and bought half a bushel of delicious peaches, and two boxes of grapes. We have seen a vineyard at Mason which has this year twelve tons of the handsomest Concord grapes I ever saw, nearly a pound in a bunch. It is really a treat to see such enterprise, and such good fruit right here in these rugged hills. I wish you could be here to enjoy it with us. On Monday last Asa came to Milford to be baptized in the river and to join the Methodist church, which was formerly the old Baptist. Your father and mother were in town for an hour or two. John and Asa are continually taken one for the other. Only last Monday the minister who was to baptize Asa walked up to John and apologized for being late. He was quite astonished when I told him this was John. The same day Asa was taken for John. So it goes.

Dear bonnie laddie, our lives any way hang on a thread, and "our hearts are beating funeral marches to the grave." Each heart-beat takes us nearer to the last, and we have not much to boast of at the best. Friendship and love, and every day a kind deed or word, are ours to give, and they don't cost much and pay in the end, only we have to be misunderstood, come what will. Good-night.

    Your friend,   Abby

TO FANNY

This letter was written just before Abby's trip to Alaska, and left in the hotel in Victoria, to which her brother with his company was coming in a day or two. It was written on odd paper, with representations of birds of passage flying in different directions upon it.

DRIARD HOUSE, VICTORIA, B C, July 10, 1879

MY DEAR FANNY — As we are again about to take our *flight* northward, I thought it would be eminently proper to write you upon a sheet which would represent the different directions we may make before we return. Oh, had I wings like a dove, I would fly — somewhere. It is said that "birds of a feather flock together." In this case I think the birds seem all to be flying apart just as your tribe and we seem to be doing. We have waited here one fortnight for our steamer, and just as your agent will arrive and announce that you are coming, off we go to Sitka. It would not do to have so many distinguished people at once in town. Remenyi has been and gone. He plays unlike any one we ever heard. I liked him when I was a little used to his style. Don't forget to see Beacon Hill and other pleasant places about this town. We have had two long drives. The roads are good as those at Lynn, and though they have no surf, they have great snow mountains in the distance. Good-by. I hope we shall see you before the swallows all get to their nests. Yours, ABBY

TO JOHN

NEW YORK, November 19, 1884

DEAR JOHN — I write to know how you are and how Fanny is in health. Dear "A" has overworked and over-worried, until he is quite broken down in health. Dennett writes that he is very anxious indeed about his father, and only wishes he could have joined you in singing in order to get his mind away from his bothers and cares in the West. I wish you would write to Asa and cheer him up all you can. I felt as though I must have you come right down and see us when I heard of Asa's health, for it seemed as though you and I might save him from despair. He is sick and needs a change. I fight away to keep out of bed myself and cannot keep well much of the time. I begin to think that no man is truly happy until he is dead, and yet we cling to life so hard. We had a great disappointment in not having Blaine elected. We are trying hard to swallow the bitter pill, but it may prove good for us. God bless us all. Write to Asa. Yours lovingly, ABBY.

NEW YORK, November 26, 1884

DEAR JOHN — The silver cord is loosed and the golden bowl is broken, and our beloved brother Asa has gone to his long home. He

ger bear the strain. His last letters to me showed how he had worked and worried all summer. Then the cold came and chilled his blood and brain. I am trying hard to be resigned, and at peace with God, but it is hard. Abby in January, Henry in April, Asa in November. You and I are alone. This has been a sad year for us all, but there is a haven of rest for the weary soul and we will soon be there. God pity us and keep us ready for the watch that may come in the night. Three of our treasures laid up in Heaven in one year, "We a little longer wait, but how little none can know."

Your sister,   ABBY.

New York, October 5, 1890.

My dear Brother:—I am aware as I sit in the rays of a blessed October sun, that time is fast winging us away to our eternal home. Ludlow and I went to Plymouth Church to hear Lyman Abbott preach this morning. How the memories flooded in upon me as I looked at that platform where once the great-hearted, stalwart man poured forth his eloquent unstudied discourses. There, in her pew sat Mrs. Beecher, white-haired and nearing the mystic river. The organ, the choir, the flowers, all were there, but the great crowd that rarely ever could all get seats did not appear. There was a fine congregation to hear a beautiful sermon by Lyman Abbott. He speaks without notes and is a fresh, free speaker and thinker, but the fire of Henry Ward Beecher and the tremendous personal magnetism has gone out from Plymouth Church. I pity any man who has to stand in Beecher's pulpit. No place in the world could be harder to fill. Mr. Abbott in any other place would be a star of the first magnitude. Our dear friend the great contralto Antoinette [Sterling] I miss also from the choir. I have not been to Plymouth Church since the funeral of Henry Ward Beecher, when you and I went to look at his face for the last time, you remember. Well, I hope he at last is happy, and not a martyr any more to the struggle for joy on earth. "We a little longer wait, but how little none can know." My only comfort is to do my little good daily, and trust in God for the future. Take all the comfort you can with your children and don't worry too much. You need not go to the dismal swamp but to Heaven for your mate, who will meet you at St. Peter's gate.   A. H. P.

New York, November 26, 1890.

Dear John and Family:—Lewis, Viola, Judson, Cleveland, Harry and Katy—This is to wish you all a Happy Thanksgiving. I hope you will have a feast of reason and music and flow of soul, without the sparkling bowl. Dinner is a good thing to have, but not too much. Better let the turkey do the *stuffing* and keep your heads clear for good singing of the grandfather's Thanksgiving song. Ludlow unites with me in wishing you good cheer this bright day of the year, at Old High Rock. Sing "The breaking waves dashed high." Wish everybody could have an open fire in a good room to-morrow, except our friends in Africa, who don't need fire or clothing to speak of. I am trying to invent a house to open and shut up for the future. Need George Putnam to help me teach the young ideas how to (chute) shoot. My regards to him. Toast for Thanksgiving dinner:

> The grandfather joins in the innocent mirth,
> And praises the boys at the family hearth;
> He sighs not for pleasure, he feels no decay,
> But thinks his whole life is a Thanksgiving day.

Keep up the family harmony, and *find* all the "Lost Chords," but be sure to *lose* the *discords*. This idea is purely original and I may get out a patten-t soon, so don't infringe, but keep it in the family.

A. H. P.

NEW YORK, April 16, 1891.

MY DEAR JOHN — Last evening the postman brought to our house the enclosed piece of paper which is probably a newspaper wrapper. I send it at once to let you know what it means. I guess the gum came off. Have been very busy of late. We went last week to the Greeley semi-centennial. Last Monday went to hear the great Englishwoman Annie Besant — pronounced like peasant. She spoke about the riches and poverty of London. She goes soon to Boston, and you will wish to see her. She is a Socialist, and I think a Theosophist, and is to attend some convention in Boston, I think. She has done, and is doing much for the poor of London. My religion is to educate people how to work — then give them work and pay them for it, and if they are too sick or won't work, send them to a hospital or a reform school for lazy folks. Some people are born tired, and no wonder, when their mothers were all tired out before they were born. My pen is dreadful, but I must tell you one thing more. We went to a concert night before last, the very finest of the year. The "Rubinstein Club," a society of women singers, about one hundred and fifty in all, who are picked singers of New York. Mrs. Raymond, who was Annie Louise Cary, sang with the altos, and the whole chorus was very fine. They sang the "Lost Chord" better than it was ever before sung. The organ started them, and then the voices took up the theme and the altos and t

voices you never heard anything to equal it. Ludlow nearly blistered his hands trying to make them sing it over. So did the whole audience, but the conductor was relentless, and would not repeat.

Yours, ever sincerely, ABBY.

NEW YORK, May 29, 1891.

MY DEAR BROTHER JOHN:—This is to let you know I have your letter of May 24th, and am glad you are pretty well. Glad you will have the oven ready for your picnic on Decoration Day. [Abby took great interest in this oven, and the plan to furnish the settlement on High Rock with Vienna rolls, though she expressed a mock horror lest it should set Bird's Nest and the contiguous cottages afire, and cremate the inhabitants.] Hope you received my song, of "Wild Bells." Hope also that the arrangement for orchestra which Ludlow sent reached you all right, and that your Lynn band will like it and play it. We went to a concert last evening where a lady sang the song very well indeed. Day before yesterday we sent to you my little book, "A Handful of Pebbles." I tell Ludlow I expect *this* and "Ring Out Wild Bells" will be my last will and testament to my relatives. He says no; that now I must go to work and make some more songs. Let me hear all about the oven and be sure and get a number one baker for bread and everything else. Give love to Juddy, Viola and family, and take for yourself the old-time affection from your little sister in the faith, ABBY.

NEW YORK, June 6, 1891.

DEAR JOHN:—Glad to hear from you so often. Our friends seem to like the book, and the song also. Glad you will play the song on the Fourth of July. Glad the oven is panning out well, and that your baker will say "*Well done*, thou good and faithful servant," as he passes out the loaves and fishes to the well bred (bread) people of Lynn, Saturday nights. We get plenty of change in these days, especially in the weather. One day we are in the melting mood; next day in the frigid zone, so that linen dusters and furs look well together. If all summer is like this, New York will be a good sea-side summer resort. I would like to plant a few trees before I die in the old town of Milford as well as in Lynn—but I guess my "Pebbles" will have to go as my last will and heirloom to my brothers' and sisters' children. Life is full of beauty when we are well. Yours ever, ABBY.

NEW YORK, July 1, 1891.

DEAR JOHN:—Providence, and the Providence boat, permitting, our little book will leave New York on Thursday for Boston. We will go to the United States Hotel, where we will stay until we decide whether we go North, East, South or West. Our hope is to lunch or dine with you on July 4th, returning to Boston the same evening. Don't have a crowd to meet us, only your own family, so we can sing, and dance, and wave the red, white and blue in earnest. Hoping to reach Boston safely on Friday, and see you Saturday morning,

I am yours ever truly, ABBY.

P. S. — Ludlow, Etty, Marion, Helen and Baba comprise our party, personally conducted by General Patton.

UNITED STATES HOTEL,
BOSTON, July 11, 1891.

DEAR JOHN — We saw Marblehead Neck, Swampscott and Lynn yesterday, and have decided on Lynn. Hope to be at 40 Tudor Street, Lynn, next Monday afternoon. The house is kept by Mrs. Kimball, and Miss Nellie Hutchinson boards with her. So we may have some music after all. After Sunday we will all be Forty Tudors, and you may have strength and fortitude to come to see us. We know how to get to the Lynn Woods now by electric car. We are close to the ocean and can get to the surf in five minutes. Come down and see us Monday afternoon or evening. Yours ever, ABBY

OLD HOMESTEAD (MILFORD),
August 31, 1891

MY DEAR JOHN. — We thought you would be with us on August 29th but were disappointed, and now the last day of summer is blooming alone. We have been at the Homestead one week. Have received many calls and have made some visits to relatives. Lhas sent me on my birthday a very handsome pair of brass andirons, which we have placed in mother's fireplace, and for two days we have had a nice open wood fire. Helen has seen the cradle that rocked sixteen children, and she enjoyed sitting in it, to hear the story about her great-great-grandmother Polly Leavitt Hutchinson. It seems very pleasant to be with the home friends at the old camping ground. Love to you and all the tribe of John. Yours faithfully, ABBY H. PATTON

HUTCHINSON HOMESTEAD,
MILFORD, September 8, 1891

DEAR JOHN. — Thank you for your letter, also for the kind invitation to be with you Wednesday evening to hear the band play "Wild

goes. We are having good times at the Homestead, playing, working, reading, singing, and the piano is going from morn till dewy eve. Already I call this great house a conservatory of music. It ought to be, for in no other house does music ring out as it does here. Ludlow is well and happy. We drive to the village daily for the morning paper and our mail. The country is looking very fresh and green after the rain, and to-day is very clear and lovely. We are glad, for we have had much wet weather, but the open wood fires make our rooms cosy and comfortable. This old house is worthy of being preserved for centuries after we are gone. Life is short. We can only make it long by doing good while we stay. Yours truly, ABBY

NEW YORK, November 5, 1891.

DEAR JOHN — Your letter of November 2d came safe to hand. The mind is ever more active than the body. If my hand would perform as fast as I think you would get a letter nearly every day. Now I must tell you, when I am out of pain I have a very full life, in reading and in music, when I can hear it. Last Saturday Cousin Mary Moorhouse sailed on the steamship *Gascogne* for France. I sent her your souvenir and your love before she sailed. Last Monday afternoon Ludlow and I went to call on Mrs. Sara Baron Anderson away up in East 50th Street. She and her three daughters sang to us solos, trios and quartets. They never get tired talking about you and your singing, and your wonderful power of entertaining. I told them you would be going to great meetings and I supposed you would sing as long as you could do anything. I have had numerous requests to sell my book or to place it where it could be bought; so far have preferred to give it away. Last night Ludlow and I saw the great poet of England, Sir Edwin Arnold. He wrote "The Light of Asia," a beautiful Eastern poem, and more recently the "Light of the World," which brings in the life of Jesus. The great Carnegie Music Hall will hold four or five thousand people, and it was filled to give Arnold a welcome. A host of poets and other literary people, all men, in full dress, sat on the large stage, and Chauncey M. Depew introduced Mr. Arnold to the audience in a most happy speech. Arnold looks somewhat like Dickens. His face is strong and remarkable. He is not quite used to speaking in public and has only read his poems once in public, but he did very well and was listened to with marked attention. I think he will go to Boston. Hope you will see him. His poems about women and children are very delicate and beautiful. I have had a beautiful letter from Frederick Douglass. Have read his vindication in September and October *North American Review*, and also his lecture given in Washington on Hayti and her good and evil. I cannot read fast enough, so much is to be read in these days. It is a great age to live in and yet we do not solve the mystery of birth and death. People have to believe in a future or lose their minds altogether. I suppose you know Fanny gave me the book "Who knoweth Life but questions Death?" and the first poem in it is by Edwin Arnold, beginning

> "He who died at Azan sends
> This to comfort faithful friends."

I think it was recited at William Lloyd Garrison's funeral. Will send you some books in a day or two.

Yours, ABBY.

NEW YORK, November 8, 1891.

DEAR JOHN — I send you by Monday's mail five "Handful of Pebbles," and I have put my autograph and compliments in each one, therefore I will be anxious to know to whom you will give them. I have sent my books to a number of your and our old friends, and on that account do not wish them duplicated. If I send them myself I get letters in return, so I know who receives them. Please let me know the names of your friends who receive them, as so far we have kept account of every book we have sent away and we like to know who has them. The weather is beautiful, and we have had a long walk in Central Park this morning and a row around the lake. It seems like September in mildness. Hope you keep well. There is so much to live for yet, when we are out of pain. Do read Edwin Arnold's lovely poems. I send you Rebecca Moore's last letter. Please return it soon so I can answer it. She is going to Egypt, to the wonderland Ludlow and I visited in 1875. It is the most wonderful country we have visited, but all are wonderful. Would you not like to live fifty years more to see what grand work will be done in the world? I wish you and I might be inspired to do a great work before we die. I look on Rebecca as one of my most interesting friends, and she never will grow old, because her mind is larger than her body. Her life is blessed by her son and grandchildren. Do let me hear soon from you, and do not overdo in worry about tenants as long as you can pay all your debts and have good food, clothes and an open fire. Ludlow joins me in love and I am thankful to be pretty well to-day.

Yours in truth — lovingly, ABBY.

NEW YORK, January 4, 1892.

MY DEAR BROTHER JOHN — I must not let your birthday pass without a loving word and many happy returns in this world, and more in short lives here. Have just had a call from Mary Sinclair, the daughter of Horace Greeley's cousin, our old friend Mrs. Charlotte Sinclair. The last named was born in Bedford near Horace Greeley's home. I hope you have no terrible colds such as are now prevailing in all parts of the country. I wanted to send you a little book to-day. If I cannot find it, will send it later. Do keep well. One year ago to-day we all were at your cosy Tower Cottage, celebrating. We must live fast and do our work in haste, to be ready for the next High School to which we go. God bless you, and keep you and your voice strong until you go to join the "choir invisible." Ludlow sends love to you and hopes you feel as young as when threescore years and ten had passed. Yours until we cross the silent river, and then I hope we will all sing together once more. Your loving sister, ABBY.

NEW YORK, February 16, 1892.

DEAR JOHN:— I had finished and sealed my letter to you [Another letter was enclosed in the envelope] and was about to mail it, when Ludlow brought me a package from England. On opening it, my heart bounded, you may well believe. What do you suppose came before my eyes? The *water-color painting* of the Hutchinson Family made by Margaret Gillies in her studio for our dear Mary Howitt in 1846. Some time ago I wrote Mary Howitt to know what had become of the painting, and now she has been so good as to send it to me. There we are, just as we stood in 1846, for our pictures. Our names are all written in our own handwriting, directly beneath the figures. The card is a little torn, but I think can be mended. I shall have it mounted at once, and put in complete order for framing. This will complete my list of pictures, which I am having prepared for printing. Cheer up; we will have a book yet. Lucius goes to San Diego Thursday with his wife. Wish we all might go. ABBY.

[In the letter accompanying this, Abby suggests that John and herself each have a chapter in the book, containing their epistles to the Americans, as Paul wrote his to the Ephesians.]

NEW YORK, May 27, 1892.

MY DEAR JOHN:—Heaps of things I would say to you, and I think every day I will tell you that you must come right down to stay a day or two. The next minute I think I will take my bag and go right to Lynn to see you—and the next minute the weather changes, I get tired out, and have to rest, therefore do not get started to carry out my plan. We have heard the most instructive lecture of the season, called "From Chaos to Man." The lecturer is very intelligent and speaks well, and the pictures are simply superb works of art. How I wish you could come down for a day or two. Lucius will be home June 1st, and he will have great stories about the West. He is in love with California — especially with San Diego. To-day has taken place the funeral of young W. H. Vanderbilt, son of a many times millionaire, and a millionaire himself. He could not be saved any more than a poor man's son. Death equalizes the rich and the poor. I do not believe in embalming bodies or preserving them after death, but rather to let them go back to nature and the sweet dust. I think cremation far better than all, when we have no farther use of our mortal bodies. I hope the mind lives on forevermore. Am glad you could plant trees on Arbor Day. I wanted to plant some in Milford. I believe my trees still live there at the homestead. David has gone to Appleton's. Katy Elms made us a little visit last week. She is a beauty and a sweet woman. She enjoys having visits from you very much. Ludlow is busy with down-town matters and at odd times he plays banjo and gets new songs. "Ring Out Wild Bells" is meeting with success, and orchestras are taking it up in several places. The chimes player in Washington, D. C., says he plays it every Sunday at present. Quite complimentary, is it not? Hope you will come before we go East or West. Have no plans yet for summer. Saturday noon — Your telegram just received. Can't go to Lynn to-night, so I beg you will come here on your way West by-and-by. I want to go there or away down East. Be sure to come, and do not disappoint me, for life is short, and time is fleeting. We soon will be beyond the river. So come. Answer me at once. Yours, ABBY

NEW YORK, June 6, 1892.

DEAR JOHN — Your two postals came in this morning to greet us at our breakfast table. We are very glad that your journey was so happy, and I am glad that you gave the red, white and blue to Mr. Bryant and Mr. Bellamy. We are still for Harrison and I am next for McKinley, who is a most deserving man. If Mr. Blaine is nominated I think he can make a good president, but I would rather keep Ben Harrison in the White House. We went to Orange yesterday to see our children. Hot and cold waves visit us, and the human body cannot resist all the changes. The country is very beautiful.

> "Oh, what is so rare as a day in June?
> Then, if ever come perfect days,
> Then Heaven tries the earth if it be in tune,
> And over it softly her warm ear lays."

God bless the poets, who keep our hearts warm, and the singers who keep us in harmony. Let us hear again from you soon. L. P. sends love.   Ever your sister,   ABBY.

SUNDAY, July 17, 1892.

DEAR JOHN:—I sent you a paper containing Miss Johnson's letter. She is an old friend of ours, and begged to "write me up." I said my life was so connected with my brother's, he would have to come in, too. So she called us "Two famous singers." The photographs I gave her were good, but the wood-cuts as usual were not flattering. I wish I could get some work done on the history. Have the notes but want some one to put them together in right form. We can't get away from New York. Something happens all the time to keep us here. Weather horrible all last week, but glorious to-day. There are only three or four things I wish to see accomplished before I drop off the mortal coil, and then I am ready to open my eyes on the "undiscovered country." We must not forget what we live for. Your grandsons, Cleve and Harry, gave us a call. We gave them a welcome. They are fine fellows. I am glad you will go to Concord and sing for our old-time friend, John P. Hale. He with so many others we have known has gone to join the great majority. How short life seems at the longest! God bless and keep you, and may we meet again some time soon.

Yours ever true,   ABBY.

Glad you raised the flag on High Rock, 4th of July. Keep it ever before the people.

EAGLE HOTEL, CONCORD, N. H.,
August 6, 1892.

DEAR JOHN:—We are getting rested after the burden and heat of the long day's celebration, August 3d. I hope you did not half kill yourself with your exertions on the occasion. I think you believe it is better to *labor* than to *wait*, at such times. We are getting acquainted with Concord and its interesting people. Saw Mr. Marshall Pierce of Oakland, the day after you left. He was the gentleman who gave up his seat near Hon. Frederick Douglass for me at the table. He is a driving, thriving, intelligent man. Went with him to the State-house to see the large topographical map of New Hampshire, which gives heights of all the mountains and names of all counties and towns in large letters. A most useful and instructive map. Yesterday we met Mr. Eastman, who keeps the book-store near the hotel. He gave me an old New England primer, like one I had when I was a child. At the beginning it says "In Adam's fall we sinned all." He also gave us a

Farmer's Almanac. Mr. J. B. Walker told us much about the forests of New Hampshire, and how he was trying to preserve them. I am proud of New Hampshire and its people. I suppose you have received all the papers giving account of the celebration on August 3d, and containing your original song. After all, the "Old Granite State" is the one that arouses the people to enthusiasm. Lots of people have told us so since the day we were with you. Everybody says your voice is a wonder, and does not sound old at all. Hope you found all well at High Rock. Called at the Pillsburys last evening. They have a cozy home, and a fine library. Write to us here for the next few days. Weather cooler.

Yours ever, ABBY

Love is the best thing in the world — and a generous heart.

[A slip of paper accompanied this letter, saying, "It seemed doleful to stay here after you and the others had gone. We still sit at the same table where all the notables sat that morning. How good to have Frederic at the head of the table. He goes to Chicago for six months."]

HOMESTEAD, August 30, 1892

MY DEAR BROTHER — We are once again in the house where I was born, and it is good to be with our own folks once more. I wished to write you yesterday, but was so busy I could not get at it. We called at Aunt Lucy's and took Anna to ride in the forenoon — called on Ann Jane, and Myrtie, on Bruce and Nelly. In the afternoon, Charles took us to Appleton's and on to Mont Vernon. Beautiful day, and the views fine. Ann Jane and Myrtie, with Edward and young Ben Wooster took another carriage, and rode with us for a birthday treat. I visited my mother's and sisters' graves, and put a few flowers on them, as well as on the graves of father, brothers and sisters-in-law. Only their dust remains there, their spirits have gone to the Creator who made them. Do not know how long we will stay. I miss the old voices and the singing brothers, and the sweet sister who could outsing us all, when about her household duties. If God is good to us, He will let us all meet and sing again "beyond the smiling and the weeping." Ludlow sends best wishes and hopes your cares will not break you down. I live mostly on oat-meal gruel. It is good for everybody.

Yours faithfully, ABBY

Don't sing in too many great meetings at your age. Too much strain and care in it, without somebody sings on the chorus.

A. H. P.

[Soon after this Abby went to Boston for a few days stay. She announced her arrival as follows:]

United States Hotel,
Boston, October 11, 1894.

Dear John Wallace H.:—We are making a visit in Boston. Send us a line when you will call to see us. I have a cold, but hope soon to conquer it. L. P. joins me in best wishes to you.

Yours, Abby.

Boston, October 18, 1892.

Dear John:—I forgot to tell you that the Boston papers of to-day announce the death of our dear old friend Theodore C. Severance, in Los Angeles, Cal. So one more of our friends and companions on the voyage of life has gone to join the great majority. "We a little longer wait, but how little none can know." Boston is getting ready for the Columbian celebration on Friday, and the decorations will be fine, we think, from present appearances. Let us know what time to look for you on Friday. I suppose we will be somewhere to see the parade if we are well enough to go out. Try to take tea or dinner with us. If Mr. Pickard is with us will let you know. I expect Katy Elms to dinner to-morrow and on Thursday expect Edith Abell and Fanny P. Hoyt. I am going to write to Mrs. Severance a few lines; you will of course do the same. Lucius went to call upon them at Los Angeles when he was there, at my request. He also saw Mrs. Fremont. I am yours, for truth and progress,

Abby H. P.

[A day or two later Abby was so severely afflicted by a cold, as to be confined to her room and bed for several days. Then she improved, and came to High Rock for a short time.]

Boston, November 1, 1894.

Dear John:—We go to New York Thursday morning, Providence permitting. Saw Denman Thompson this morning, at breakfast. Said all the house in Lynn was sold for last night, so they had a crowd. Hope if you can you will come in Wednesday, to-morrow, to say goodbye. I must get settled and get well to do any work. Hope you are all feeling comfortable, and that Juddie is holding his own.

With love I am yours ever, Abby.

NEW YORK, November 13, 1894.

MY DEAR JOHN — We have had quite a struggle to find a human place to live in and yet be near Dr. Taylor's "Improved Movement Cure." I think I wrote you from this address a few days ago. I have taken cold again, and have been in bed two days to pay for it. This reminds me that I beg of you to have a hole knocked in the chimney of your bedroom at once, so as to have an open fire for yourself in case of sickness. You must do it at once. We have been trying steam and furnace heat the past few weeks, both of which roast you but do not warm you. You know this, do you not? To-morrow, God willing, we will have a grate fire, and a cheerful blaze. We have fortunately a lovely, sunny room. When the sun shines we bask in its rays you may be sure. Another thing I wish to say is that in the November *Century*, in an article on "Brook Farm" by George P. Bradford, there is a very pretty and graceful note about the Hutchinsons. So you see we are remembered even if we forget ourselves. If I get better I promise to do some work, if very little. Hope you are well. New York seems more like home after all to us than Boston, though we miss the comfort of our Sixteenth Street home. However, the people are kind to us here, and we will get along I hope. Write to me what you are doing. Yours ever, ABBY.

[The above letter is priceless, for it was Abby's last. She died on the 24th.]

THE PORTLAND RIOT.

A few years since a correspondent of the *Portland* (Me.) *Transcript*, printed the following reminiscence of anti-slavery times:

"I wonder how many remember the four-days' meeting of anti-slavery folk, or Abolitionists, as they were then reproachfully called, that was held at Concert Hall on Union Street sometime in the forties? Most of the speakers were from Massachusetts, or at least did not live in Maine. The audiences were small in the day-time but larger in the evening. Among those who took part were William Lloyd Garrison, Henry Clapp, Jr., —— Rémond, a fine looking young colored man from Salem, the Hutchinson family of singers, Friend Buffum of Lynn, and others whose names are not remembered for the moment. The proceedings consisted of speeches, debates and discussions, for the speakers were not all of one mind. Not only was negro slavery held up for execration, but other social wrongs and customs were also bitterly assailed.

"Mr. Garrison was chairman. He was easily first in all that pertained to the presentation of the subjects which they had met to consider. His manner was calm, moderate and unimpassioned. The chief justice of the United States Court could not have stated, as a historical fact, in his Dred Scott opinion that when the Constitution was framed and adopted 'black men had no rights which white men were bound to respect,' with more judicial calmness than Mr. Garrison would show in calling the Constitution 'a covenant with death and an agreement with hell.' With Mr. Garrison there was no splattering nor frothing at the mouth.

"Mr. Clapp, fiery, caustic, satirical, made harangues of brilliant eloquence, witty, sharp and to the very point.

"Mr. Rémond was an orator by grace of nature, and having had a good education he appeared remarkably well in public speaking. The Hutchinson family, brothers and sister, the original choir, whose concerts were so popular in those days, sang some of their characteristic songs as interludes between the speeches. They were Abolitionists of the Garrison type, and doubtless gave gratuitous assistance.

"Friend Buffum, a plain, unpretending man, said he had left his planing mill and come to meet his anti-slavery friends in Portland, his heart was touched with the sorrows of the Southern negroes in their almost hopeless bondage; if they sought freedom in flight, they could find no safe refuge nearer than Canada, for even if they found their way to Pennsylvania, bloodhounds from Maryland would — 'It's a lie!' shouted a voice from the audience. Immediately a gentleman arose, and announced that he was born and lived in Maryland and that bloodhounds were never used there for the pursuit of fugitive slaves. Mr. Buffum tried to explain, but the impetuous speaker hardly gave him the chance to say that the bloodhounds he meant were white men pursuing the fugitives. After this interruption the Marylander resumed his discourse, inveighing against those Northerners who were slandering his people, and trying to deprive the South of its rights under the law. 'If you at the North,' the gentleman said, 'really wish to benefit our slaves, why not come among us, and try to help us correct our faults. Slaveholders are as humane as other people, and would kindly receive you, as well as profit by what you might say, if they found your complaints were reasonable.' The speaker went on in this same strain of remarks for a few minutes more, the chairman's gentle 'hear, hear,' having been occasionally heard meanwhile, and then took his seat.

"After a short pause, Mr. Garrison arose, and without any appearance of excitement on his part, made a most scathing answer, full of sarcasm and irony, to the charges and statements that had just been made. He had the advantage of thorough familiarity with the question, while his impulsive and impetuous opponent was new to the position, and had evidently spoken in heat of anger, so that he had laid himself open to attack at almost all points. 'The gentleman' said Mr. Garrison, in the course of his response, 'invites us, if we really have at heart the welfare of their slaves, to visit the South and labor there to that end, promising us kind treatment, if we shall deserve it. For one I shall not accept the invitation, as I have tasted the sweets of Southern hospitality in a Baltimore jail.'

"The last one of the meetings was held the following evening. Excitement had gradually arisen among some of the townspeople over reports of the proceedings at these meetings, and it was in the air that there was going to be trouble. The hall was crowded with men and boys that evening, and it was a noisy assembly. After some talking, partly by citizens of Portland, among whom was Mr. John Neal, tumult and confusion prevailed, settees were broken, and there was every sign of a riot impending. Mr. J. B. Brown, owner of the building, got up and requested that damage to his property should cease, disclaiming responsibility for any offence that might have been given by those who had hired the hall. This request was heeded by the not ill-natured crowd, which then contented itself with loud but harmless demonstrations, and dispersed peaceably soon after Not much damage was done to property, and no injury to persons so far as known"

[The scene described by our correspondent is fresh in the memory of the editor of the *Transcript*. One incident that afforded amusement at that time may be added Mr. Garrison's entire freedom from excitement contrasted strangely with the heat displayed by John Neal, who while avowing himself an Abolitionist, and one of the earliest of Abolitionists, was at odds with Garrison as to the best methods of carrying on the reform. The hall was not well ventilated, and the air was very close and warm. Neal had closed an impassioned speech, and Garrison rose to reply. As he did so, he asked the janitor of the hall to open the windows, as the air was too warm for comfort Neal jumped up excitedly and exclaimed, "*The heat is in the individual!*" This was so funny, considering the coolness always displayed by Garrison, that the audience enjoyed it greatly.]

SEVENTIETH BIRTHDAY POEMS

TO A SONG PROPHET

When Israel's prophetess, long years agone,
  Sounded her timbrel and rejoicing sung —
  When through the wilderness the triumph rung —
The Lord was praised because of victories won
When the bright chariot, flaming like the sun,
  With its celestial steeds from glory flung,
  For Carmel's prophet came, and quick among
The angels took him, 'twas for duty done.

But thou, O singing prophet, canst rejoice —
  Thine eye foresaw the strife would not be long,
And so, ere victory came, it was thy choice
  To sound the trump of right, the doom of wrong.
So, when thy chariot comes may thy glad voice
  Ring 'mid supernal music, in triumphant song.
                CHARLES EDWARD MANN.

To MY DEAR FRIEND, JOHN W. HUTCHINSON, on his Seventieth Birthday, with the added greetings of the season:

    Dear brother of the House of Song,
      That nest of brothers true,
    With one sweet sister in the midst,
      Our hearts go out to you.

    With loyal love in every throb,
      And gratitude and praise
    To Him who gave you to the world,
      And lengthened out your days.

    As steadfast as your granite hills,
      Sweet-voiced as winds that blow
    Around their heaven-pointing pines —
      We loved you long ago.

When joined with all your band you sang
    The songs that lift the heart
With pure desires, purpose strong,
    And bid the tears to start

What shining world of all the host
    Has gained those voices gone,
Those sons of Music, who, as you,
    Must still be singing on?

Ah! well, I ween it cannot be
    To you an unknown land,
With such a bridge of melody
    Uniting heart and hand

Sing on, dear Friend of Liberty,
    Of Brotherhood, of Peace,
Till on the air of heaven breaks
    The song of earth's release

Till on those higher heights of life
    The right shall find a wrong,
And you again to combat go,
    To sing its victor song

With many regrets that I cannot attend the reception,

    Faithfully yours,   ADA C BOWLES.

ABINGTON, December 24, 1890

To JOHN W. HUTCHINSON   *Greeting:*

The benison of seventy fruitful years upon thee lies;
The snows of seventy winters wrap thee softly round —
Safe keeping, in thy heart, the warmth of seventy summers

Many happy returns of the day.

     MRS. L J HITCHCOCK,
     Secretary Lynn Nationalist Club.

LYNN, 1891.

To Mr. John W. Hutchinson, on his Seventieth Birthday:

    I told my muse this morning
      It was your natal day,
    And bade her kindly give me
      Some fitting words to say

    To drape the thoughts unshapely
      A thronging in my mind,
    And bring them out in clearness
      All perfectly defined

    She tarried not a moment,
      But like an arrow sped
    To some mysterious region
      By strangest fancies led

    And though I rose in sadness
      And called her o'er and o'er,
    I feared her face of gladness
      Would cheer me never more

    I spoke in tones I fancied
      They heard at Heaven's Gate,
    Of a little Home in Milford
      In the dear Old Granite State

    Where the Tribes of John and Jesse
      First saw the light of earth,
    And learned the power of music
      Around the fireside hearth

    I recounted many journeys
      By land and by the sea,
    When "matchless songs" were ringing
      To set the captive free

    I mentioned that "sweet sister"
      Whose charming voice and air,
    Won loving admiration
      From people everywhere

    My muse heard not the stories,
      Loud tones were all in vain,
    Aweary with her absence
      I sang this bright refrain:

"O which way is your musket,
 Which way, which way, which way,
O which way is your musket
 A-pintin' to-day?"

The music brought the lost one—
 With brightly beaming face,
And radiant companions
 She glided to her place.

"We've been to Tower Cottage—
 The singer lured us long;
His children and their children
 Unite in sweetest song."

O send him happy greetings
 To honor his birthday,
For threescore years and ten have come,
 And gone like sprites away.

On Old High Rock, long may you live—
 So say this loving throng;
May all your life be full of joys
 That overflow in song.

H. MARIA PROCTOR.

LYNN, January 4, 1891.

Fraternally inscribed to JOHN W. HUTCHINSON on the Seventieth Anniversary of his Birthday.

Music, the heavenly maid, was born to wield
A power to which e'en savages will yield;
Through instruments and voices sweet expressed,
She gives to life its highest joy and zest,
Consoling hearts oppressed with grief most dire,
And nerving soldiers to withstand the fire,
Prompting devotion in the thoughtful mind,
And leading souls the way of peace to find.
Her voice the young creation joyful heard,
When God pronounced His first omnific word.
From chaos dark then order quick appeared,

And light, life-giving, all the prospect cheered
The "morning stars" were jubilant and sang,
Wide through the azure vault the chorus rang;
The "Sons of God" joined the harmonious strain,
To hail the hour when Time commenced his reign!
And ever since, that never-ending song
Hath o'er the earth and ocean rolled along,
Breezes and billows in accord rejoice
To hymn her praises with harmonious voice,
Heard in the tempest and the gentle breeze,
That strike the sweet Æolians of the trees,
And in the ocean's murmur and the roar
Of foam-plumed billows thundering to the shore!
The feathered choir on every leaf-clad spray,
Unite in chorus at the break of day
Down through the ages of resistless Time,
She still advances on her course sublime,
Still marching on till all will own her sway,
In the bright region of eternal day!
With hearts elate, dear friends, to-day we meet
One of her favorite sons with joy to greet
Who oft has cheered us with his music sweet,
Whose years have reached the full threescore and ten —
(The Scriptural bound allotted unto men),
Retaining still his wealth of heart and voice,
So often raised to make mankind rejoice
His voice for freedom rang from shore to shore,
Joined with the voices heard on earth no more —
His kindred dear of whom he is bereft,
Of whom alone he still to us is left
The clank of fetters and the bondman's cry,
His quick ear heard and, ringing through the sky,
Sped swiftly forth the soul-inspiring strain,
Like those the angels brought to Bethlehem's plain,
Which broke the stillness of the midnight air,
Where faithful shepherds watched their tender care
"Emancipation!" was his battle-cry,
And he has lived to see its victory!
May this his grand birthday auspicious be
Of happy years he yet on earth will see,
Till he is called to wing a joyful flight
To meet his kindred in the World of Light!

JOSEPH W. NYE.

ACROSTIC

Fraternally inscribed to JOHN W. HUTCHINSON

Joy fills my heart to hear thy strains once more,
   Of sweetest music to my raptured ear!
How mindful of the good old days of yore,
   Now held in sweet remembrance ever dear,
When thou with songs didst first in Lynn appear.
Here would my humble muse her tribute pay,
   Unfolding freely all the pleasure sweet
   That cheers my heart thy melody to greet
Charmed and inspired by thy potent lay,
Hath many souls been valiant made to fight
   In life's hard warfare with the powers of Wrong!
   Ne'er hath the sword done nobler work than song—
Sung for the truth and in defence of right!
O, sing thou on till all the world will hear
No dread alarm of war when Love has conquered Fear.

                              J. W. N.

A VETERAN'S TRIBUTE

   The Slave was dying in his chains,
      The feet of millions trod his neck,
   And to Oppression's curse there seemed
      To be no limit bound or check.

   God spake!—along a guilty land
      The trump of "Boanerges" rang!
   And to the rescue of the slave
      True hearts and arms to battle sprang!

   The star of Whittier flamed afar,
      Lighting up all the Northern sky;
   From Parker's lips came piercing tones,
      And Phillips' silver trump rang high!

   And Pillsbury's heart-awaking words,
      And songs from Pierpont's "snow-flake lyre,"
   And gentle May's persuasive voice,
      Great Sumner's scathing words of fire.

   Wilson and Alley, Giddings, Hale,
      And Burlingame the young and brave,
   Sent echoing through the council halls,
      Their words for freedom and the Slave!

And Woman, from her bowers of ease,
  Swift hastening to the scene of strife,
To her dark sisters reached her hands,
  To guide them up to Light and Life!

From farm and work-shop stalwart men
  Answered the cry — that ever thrills!
The "Hope Forlorn" of Liberty
  Rallied upon these Northern hills!

In that great "trial hour" of Time,
  Unheeding scorn, and threat and frown,
A band of youthful minstrels came
  From Hampshire's mountains trooping down.

By day and night with zeal unquenched,
  By hill and vale — along the shore,
They sang great freedom's glorious songs
  As they were never sung before.

They sang of scourges dripping blood,
  Of suffering Tyrants only mock,
The crush of souls beneath the chain,
  Hearts broken at the auction block.

And consciences — which long were seared,
  Aroused to see the boundless wrong,
And hearts which could withstand all else
  Melted beneath their tide of song.

Long, weary years the strife went on,
  And still their priceless aid was given
Free, constant and unstinted help,
  To the best cause of earth and Heaven.

When for the Nation's priceless life —
  The battle raged on Southern plains,
The Northern soldiers in their camp
  Listened with joy their thrilling strains.

And as they sang of Washington —
  And of our Revolution's band,
Their hearts responded — and they grasped
  Their weapons with a firmer hand.

And when the charging bugles rang,
  Sweeping along the plain and shore,
Their war-cry, "Freedom, God and Right!"
  Swelled high above the cannon's roar.

At last there came the triumph hour,
   And Freedom's glorious work was done;
No chains, no whips, no chattel slaves
   From rising to the setting sun!

But these — the minstrels of the free,
   That faithful, tireless mountain band —
Have won themselves a lasting name
   In the proud records of our land.

Brothers and sisters, child and wife,
   No longer sit beside the hearth,
Their voices so familiar once
   Are heard no more upon the earth;

But still their presence fills our hearts,
   And to the "spirit-ear" 'tis given
To hear their voices in the strains
   That sweep the empyrean of Heaven.

Two only now on earth remain
   Of all that youthful mountain band —
Brother and sister — down the vale
   They now are passing, hand in hand.

The children — and *their* children still
   Sing Freedom's songs on hill and shore,
And the gray minstrel's bugle tone
   Rings out as in the days of yore.

And so his seventy years have passed;
   Standing to-night with his loved ones
We join the unchained slaves, and pray
   God's blessing on the Hutchinsons!

                      GEORGE W. PUTNAM.

Lines respectfully dedicated to JOHN W. HUTCHINSON, on his Seventieth Birthday, January 4, 1891.

Down the long avenue you're looking to-day,
   The vista of seventy years,
While the lightning shadows lightly play
   With memories of joys and tears.
Perchance on your list'ning ear there steals
   Sweet voices of long ago,
Whose tones floated out on the summer air,
   Making heaven of all below.

Down the long avenue when the years were young,
    And life a page unread,
Did the spirit of Prophecy ever tell
    Of the work of the years now fled?
When the band of brothers sang their songs
    That echoed far and near,
"*Emancipation*" for the slave
    Rang out in voices clear

Down the long avenue stalked a fiend
    With pestilence in his breath,
The blighted lives he drove to their doom,
    Went down to hopeless death
The Brothers put on their armor of Love,
    And song-tipped arrows hurled,
"*Prohibition*" was their theme
    And their cry reached round the world

Down the long avenue in days now past,
    A whisper was heard on the air,
The daughters of men were asking that *they*
    The rights of their brothers might share
The whisper was heard by the Sons of Song,
    And their heavenly voices swelled
As they sang their hymns of liberty
    And "*Women's Rights*" upheld

Down the long avenue came a day
    When the sunlight seemed faint o'er the land,
And a requiem, such as angels might sing,
    Stole from that death-broken band
Down the long avenue they're lying at rest,
    The brothers you left by the way,
Their life-work done, their voices mute,
    While they wait for the dawning day

Down the long avenue the western sun
    With its crimson, slanting rays,
Foretells a morrow yet to come
    And promises glorious days;
When the silent ones shall sing again
    The wonderful songs of yore,
And in rapture list to harmonious strains
    From those who ne'er sang before.

When the Right shall appear clothed in garments of Grace,
   And the Wrong be buried from sight,
While Beauty and Love shall walk hand in hand,
   And Sin be banished with Night.

MARY SARGENT HOPKINS.

MY DEAR FRIEND JOHN W. HUTCHINSON:

   O yes, Friend John, with pleasure true,
   My wife and I will call on you;
   Accept your kindly invitation,
   And join in warm congratulation
   And as you pass threescore and ten,
   The years of time allotted men,
   And through your course of life in store,
   The short'ning span that lies before,
   I would with cheer to you extend
   The sincere greeting of a friend.

WALTER B. ALLEN.

LYNN, January 3, 1891.

TO MY FRIEND JOHN W. HUTCHINSON, on the Seventieth Anniversary of his Birthday.

Welcome this birthday, which makes you threescore and ten,
The limit of life given by Scripture to men;
Now I have arrived at nearly fourscore,
And hope we'll enjoy many birthdays more.
January first was the day I was born,
Whilst you was only three days behind me, friend John;
Although I am eight years your senior, my friend,
I hope many years on this earth to spend;
And when life's sunset comes, may its last golden ray,
But usher in the morn of the more perfect day.

E. H. THOMAS.

PORTLAND, ME., January 4, 1891.

1821 — HUTCHINSON — 1891

   Brave singer, whose sweet clarion voice
     Helped rend in twain the bondman's chains,
   This natal day his friends rejoice
     That perfect health with him remains.

Though many years have outward flown
   Since through the land his songs first rolled,
With gratitude to-day we own
   Their strains have never yet grown old.

Not in the stretch of this broad land
   Has all his wealth of song been spent,
His voice in measures strong and grand
   Has blessed another continent.

Though threescore years and ten have twined
   Some silvery threads about his head,
His heart beats warm for human kind,
   And for their good his prayers are said.

Long may his voice be heard in song,
   Whose holiest strains ne'er die away,
But help to put down human wrong
   And make December warm as May.

                  THOMAS F. PORTER.

LYNN, January 5, 1891.

INDEX.

A

Abbott, Francis Ellingwood, ii. 30
Abbott, Rev Lyman, ii 379
Adams, Capt J G B, ii 98
Adams, John Quincy, i 74, 103, 104, 235.
Æolian Vocalists, family's name, i. 45
 Name dropped, i 63
"After All," song, ii. 221
Albany, N. Y., Early concerts in, i. 59, 60, 61, 62, 230
Alcott, A. Bronson, i 82
Allen, Walter B , ii. 168, 403.
Alley, John B , ii 98, 101
Ames, Rev Charles G , i 343, ii 364
Ames, Mary Clemmer, ii 39.
Anderson, Sara Baron, ii 383.
Andrew, Mrs John A., i 404
Andrews, Winthrop, ii 199
Anthony, Susan B , i. 437, 451, 478, ii. 33, 125, 147, 160, 214
Anti-Slavery Standard, i 93
Arnold, Edwin, ii 383
Atherton, Charles, or "Gag," i. 105.
Atwood, George, i 181, ii 5
Atwood, George W , i 379

B

Babcock, Rev D C , ii 18
Bacon, Charles R , ii 79.
Baily, John, i 90
Baker, Prof Benj F , i. 65
Baker family, i 232.
Baker, George, ii 92
Bancroft, G F P , ii 12.
Barker, Charles N , ii 132
Barker, Nathan, ii. 123
Barnabee, Henry C , i 46
Barnum, P. T., i. 88, 264. 267.

Barre, Bells of, i 395.
Bartelle, May C , ii 132
Bartlett, Caroline, i 14
Bartlett, Isaac, Rhoda's husband, i. 134, 135
Bartlett, J. C., ii 55
Barton, Clara, ii 147
Barton, S Louise, ii 218
Baxter, Rev William, ii. 21.
Beach, Dr. William, i. 87.
Beecher, Rev. Henry Ward, i 94, 260, 271, 420, 488, 493, ii 15, 24, 53, 106
 Funeral of, ii 142, 306
Beecher, Rev. Lyman, i 86
Beecher, Rev Thos K , ii 16
Beede, Charles O , ii 143 167
Bell, Andrew J., i 339
Bellamy, Edward, ii 158, 362
Benjamin, Frank, i. 491, 495
Benjamin, Dr. J., i 350
Bennett, Dr S F , i. 441.
Benton, Laura Dow, ii 198.
Berry, John W , ii 19
Besant, Annie, ii 185, 381
Best, E. Stuart, ii 198
Bidwell, Gen John, ii 88
Birney, Charles P , ii 167
Birney, James S , i. 386
Bishop, Anna, i 307.
Blackwell, Henry B., i 490 ; ii 106, 147, 160
Blaine, James G , ii. 109
Blair, Gen Francis P , i 463
Blair, Henry W , ii 131
Blake, Lillie Devereaux, ii 232
Blanchard, President John, ii 68, 94, 157.
Blanchard, Judson, i 338
Blanchard, Rufus, ii 68, 94, 205
Blanchard, Stillman S. i. 338

Bliss, Prof. Howard S., ii 117
Bliss, J S, ii 347
"Blue and the Gray," song, ii 39
Bodwell, Rev Lewis, i. 455.
Boutwell, George S, i 404, ii 191.
Bowen, Henry C, i 111
Bowers, Wilder J, i 422
Bowles, Rev. Ada C., ii 81, 89, 176, 395
Boyle, Mrs James, ii 217
Boylston, Edward D., ii 220.
Boylston, Richard, i 12, 219
Brackett, J Q A., ii 362
Bradburn, George, i 120, 131
Bradford, George P, i 82, 85, ii 390
Bradley, Cyrus, i 251.
Bradley, F M., ii 38
Brainard Samuel, i 311
Breed, Arthur B, ii 129
Brett, Cyrus, i 415.
"Bridge of Sighs," song, i 163
Brier, Benjamin F, i 245
Briggs, George N, i 117 245
Bright, John, i 195
Broadway Tabernacle, i 111
Brook Farm Experiment, i. 80, 81
    Hutchinsons at, 83
Brooks, Phillips, ii 198
Brougham, Lord, i 185
Brown, D. L., i. 419.
Brown, E R, i 419, ii 93, 210, 220, 224, 359
Brown, Henry B, i 254.
Brown, John, i 364
Brown, Olympia, i 451, 461
Brown, Wm L, ii. 75
Brownson, O A, i 82
Bryant, John H, ii 221.
Buchanan James, i 371
Buffington J M., ii 79.
Bullum, Charles, ii 362.
Bullum, James N, i. 142, 164, 478, ii. 70, 95, 101, 140, 143, 391
Bull Ole i 134, 315, 458, 460, ii. 30
Bungay, George W., ii 15.
Burdett Family, i 232
Burleigh, Charles C, i 82, 100, 117, 316, 323, 461, 494, ii 49
Burleigh, George, i 405.
Burleigh Gertrude, i 100, ii. 131
Burleigh, Wm H, ii 1
Burney, Kate Hutchinson, tribe of Judson, i. 355, 359, 362, 367, 417, ii. 26, 28, 30, 51, 69, 104, 133, 166, 170, 195, 219, 261

Burnham, Col. Joshua, i 8, 9, 10
Burnham, Thomas E, ii 196
Burns, Charles H, ii. 187, 220
Burns, rendition of i. 338.
Butler, Gen B F, i. 381, 431, 491, ii 31, 49.
Butler, William, i 337
Buxton, Sarah, i 2

C.

Calhoun, John C, i. 237.
Cahill, John F, i 338
"Calomel,' song, i 87
Cameron, Simon, i 381.
Campbell, Cleveland J, tribe of John, i. 478; ii 58 166, 210
Campbell, Henry D, tribe of John, ii 13, 58, 110, 166
Campbell, John C, i 433
Campbell, Kate L tribe of John ii 58, 110, 122, 124, 153, 166, 200, 210, 219
Campbell, Lewis A, i 433, 434, 460, ii 26, 110, 166
Campbell, Viola Hutchinson, tribe of John, i 231, 241, 242, 308, 309 368, 389, 397, 401, 428, 431, 432 Marriage, i 460, ii 13 50, 21, 82, 91, 110, 121, 122, 123, 124, 153, 166, 183, 185, 200, 218
Carleton, Will M., ii. 196
Carpenter, Frank B., i. 6, 188, 223, 334, 420 438, ii 32, 107, 138, 161, 163, 169, 270, 300, 368
Carter, F W., ii. 117.
Cartland, Gertrude Whittier, ii. 193
Cary Annie Louise, ii 69
Casson, H. F., i. 250.
Caverly, J W, ii. 45.
Centennial at Philadelphia, ii 58-61.
Chadwick, Rev John W ii 225
Chamberlain, William P, i. 307
Chambers, Henry, i. 338.
Chandler, Philemon, ii 150
Chandler, William E, ii 189
Chandler, Mrs. William E, ii 46.
Chapin, Rev E H, i 313
Chapman W S, i 339
Chase, Elizabeth C. (See Elizabeth C. Hutchinson.)
Chase, James H, ii 193.
Chase, Nathan E, ii 167.
Chase, Salmon P, i. 298, 312, 379, 381, 390, 399, 402-405, 431 ii 34

INDEX.

Chickering, Jacob, i 65
Chidlaw, Rev. B W, i 432
Child, David Lee, i 131.
Child, Lydia Maria, i. 93.
Christian Commission, Closing of, i 431.
Chubb, I A, i. 338.
Churchill, Stillman, i. 459
Chute, Theodore, ii 132.
Claflin, William, i. 490, ii 101   [391.
Clapp, Henry, Jr, i 88, 121, 215; ii 325,
Clark, William A, ii. 167
Clark, W Milton, i 427, 431
Clay, Cassius M, ii 230   [334
Clay, Henry, i 232, 234, 235, 311, ii 317-
Cliff Dwellings, ii. 115
Cobden, Richard, i 198
Cochran John W, ii 84
Codding, Rev I P, i 469
Coffin, Charles Carleton, ii. 187.
Colcord, George D., ii. 168
Collyer, Rev Robert, i 478.
Coleridge, Hartley, i. 208.
Colfax, Schuyler, i. 431
Collins, Anna Teresa, ii 161.
Collins, John A., i 73, 74, 132
Community Block built, i. 116
Comstock, John, i 254, 493
"Come-Outers," i 119, 272
"Coming Right Along," song, i 372.
Conant, Rev H. W., i 493, ii 16, 19.
Congdon, Joseph, i 243.
Conger, Louisa T, i. 459
Cook, Eliza, i 175, 178
Cook, Joseph, ii 81, 211.
Cooper, Rev A, ii 127, 137, 148.
Chapman, Maria W, ii 137
Cousens, Phœbe, i 488, ii 33 147
Covert, Bernard, i. 418, 419, 441.
Cramm, Helen M, ii 176
Cranch, Christopher P., i 82
Crawford, John G., i. 365
Crouch, F N, ii 220
Currier, Benj W, ii 168
Curtis, George William, i 82
Cushing, Caleb, ii 318, 319, 321.
Cushman, Charlotte, i. 174, 178.

D.

Dainty, Laura E., ii 107.
Dall, Caroline Healey, ii. 193.
Dana, Charles A, i. 82.
Daniel, William, ii 26, 131.

Danvers, Emigration of Hutchinsons to,
   i 2   Pioneers, ii. 198
Dartmouth College, Singing at, i. 54.
Davis, Rev. J. L., ii 348
Davis, Paulina M, i 492
Dawson, George, i 171, 194, 197, ii. 372.
Dearborn, Edmund S, tribe of Judson,
   ii. 166.
Dearborn, H Hale, tribe of Judson, ii
   166
Dearborn, Jesse Judson, tribe of Judson,
   ii. 166.
Dearborn, T Benton H, tribe of Jud-
   son, ii 166
Degarmon, James M, ii. 22.
Dennett, Oliver, i 127
Dennison, Henry, i 138
Depew, Chauncey M, ii. 206, 207.
De Roode, Eugenie, ii 55
Derrick, Rev W B, ii 231.
Diaz, Abby Morton, ii. 167, 199
Dickens, Charles, i 176, 459 ii 341.
Dickens, Mrs. Charles, i 175, 177.
Dickens, Charles, Jr, ii. 144
Dickinson, Anna, i 420
Disston Family, i. 151
Dix, John Ross, i 178, 340.
Dodge, William E, ii 33
Donnelly, Ignatius, i 474.
Doolittle, I R, i. 432.
Dorman, Amos, ii 140
Doten, L W, ii 163
Douglas, Stephen A., i 374
Douglass, Frederick, i. 70, 74, 89, 115, 121,
   142, 145, 146, 157, 215, 221, 222, 240, 243,
   262, 275, 419, 461, 488; ii 35, 37, 49, 154,
   189, 206, 219, 228, 332, 344, 588
Dow, Hattie Hutchinson, tribe of Zepha-
   niah, ii 55, 198
Dow, Gen Neal, i. 313, ii 226
Downing, George T, ii 199.
Downs, Rev W W, ii 106
Drunkenness in Milford, i 27.
Dungeon Rock, Story of, i. 273
Durkee, Joseph O, ii. 150.
Dutcher, George M, ii 353.
Dwight, John S, i 82

E

East Wilton, first concert, i 44.
Edmunds, George F., ii 66.
Elder, Dr William, ii 49

Elms, Joseph D., ii. 167
Elms, Kate Hutchinson, tribe of Andrew, ii. 167, 386.
Elms, Paul Hutchinson, tribe of Andrew, ii. 167
Emery, George E., ii. 123
Emerson, Charles Wesley, ii. 290
Emerson, E. R., ii. 182.
Emerson, Ralph Waldo, i. 82, ii. 106
Emerson, Susie, ii. 169
Endicott, George, i. 111
Errett, Rev. Isaac, ii. 21
Evans, John O., ii. 34
Everett, Joshua, ii. 134
Everett, Rev. Samuel, i. 12, 14, ii. 93.

F

Fall, George O., ii. 168
Farnham, E. W., ii. 316
Farnsworth, Gen. John P., i. 389, 392, 471
"Fatherhood of God and Brotherhood of Man," song, i. 447.
Fillmore, Millard, i. 245, 311
Finch, Francis M., ii. 40.
Finch, John B., ii. 75
Fish, Rev. William H., ii. 200
Fisher, Rev. H. D., i. 465 ii. 75, 91, 145
Fisher, M. M., ii. 203
Fisk University Jubilee Singers, ii. 23
Fisk, James, Jr., i. 232
Fiske, Rev. D. T., ii. 193
Flandreau, Judge, i. 342
Florence Community, i. 80
Fonda, W. Augustus, ii. 346
Formes, Carl, i. 376.
Forrest, Edwin, i. 151
Foster, Abby Kelley, i. 120, 123, 332, ii. 49
Foster, C. G., ii. 341
Foster, Rev. J. C., ii. 219
Foster, Stephen S., i. 78, 123, 130, ii. 20, 45
Fowler, Prof. O. S., i. 132, 283, 315
Franklin, Gen. W. B., i. 381, 387, 389, 395, 396
Fremont, Gen. John C., i. 371, 400, 401
Fremont, Jessie Benton, i. 401
French, John R., i. 122, 140, 281
French, Rodney, ii. 19.
Frothingham, Rev. O. B., ii. 30
Frye, Emma Sheridan, ii. 145.
Fuller, John, i. 308

Fuller, Josiah, i. 55, 59
Fuller, Margaret, i. 82
"Furnace Blast," Whittier's anti-slavery song, i. 382-384.
Furness, Rev. Wm. H., ii. 49

G

Gage, Mrs. Frances D., i. 298
Garfield, James A., ii. 21, 102
Garrison, Francis Jackson, ii. 131, 192
Garrison, Wendell Phillips, ii. 360
Garrison, William Lloyd, i. 74 75, 87, 120, 129, 140, 224, 235, 242, 244, 262, 263, 272, 279, 294, 492 ii. 45 49, 234, 317-332, 345, 391.
Garrison William Lloyd, Jr., i. 246 ii. 131, 137, 200, 202, 228
"Get Off the Track," song, i. 113, 117, 128, 130, 138,
Gibbs, J., ii. 52
Giddings, Joshua R., i. 107, 237, 239, 298, 303, 312.
Gilmore, Patrick S., i. 489
Girard, Stephen, i. 98
Glover, Lloyd, i. 335
Godwin, Parke, ii. 221.
"Good Old Days of Yore," song, i. 260
Gougar, Helen M., ii. 194, 211
Gougar, John D., ii. 211
Gough, John B., i. 42, 116, 128, 230, 312, 426, 435, ii. 44, 71, 108 Funeral of, ii. 137
Gould, Samuel, i. 378.
Gould, Hannah F., i. 127, 281
Gove, Sarah Abby, ii. 191.
Grant, Gen. U. S., i. 431, ii. 29, 34, 88
"Grant, Our Great Commander," song. i. 474
Gray, Nellie, ii. 43, 60, 105, 219
Greeley, Horace, i. 80, 83, 91, 225, 263, 271, 285, 288, 394, 425; ii. 1, 3.
Greenwood, Grace, ii. 39, 282
Gregg, Frank, ii. 163
Gregg, Rev. J. B., ii. 117
Grinnell, James S., ii. 109
Grow, Galusha A., ii. 191
Guard, Rev. Thomas, ii. 81.

H

Hale, John P., i. 103, 104, 236, 239. Welcome to song, ii. 189.

INDEX.

Hall, D C, i. 485
Hall, Col Daniel, ii 191.
Hall, Rudolph, i. 485.
Hamilton, Rev J W, ii 134
Hanaford, Phebe A, i 492
Harper, Mrs F. E W, ii 49
Harriman, Jesse, ii. 96.
Harrington, Lewis, i 338, 317, ii 264
Harrington, Wm E, i 353
Harrison, Carter, ii 209, 215
"Harry of the West," song, i. 234
Haskell, George, ii 135
Hassan river, i 339, 342, 355
Hastings, William, i. 6
Hasty, Rose ii 92
Haughton, Richard, i 152
Hawkes, Adam, ii. 97.
Hawkes, Col B F, ii 98, 154
Hawkes, N Mortimer, ii. 98
Hawthorne, Nathaniel, i 82
Hay, Col John, ii 39.
Hayes, Elihu B, ii 128
Hayes, J P, ii. 72, 129
Hayes Rutherford B, ii 64, 67, 71.
Hayward Jonas, i 102, 103
Hayward, Nehemiah, i 103
Heath, Lyman, i 50
Hebard, William H., ii 150
Herald of Freedom, The, i 51, 75, 117, 123, 140
Herford, Rev Brooke, ii 340
Higginson, Thomas Wentworth, i 81, 82, 366, 492; ii. 30.
Hildreth, Mrs Richard, i. 315
Hill, Eliza Trask, ii. 218
Hill, George, i 229
Hingham, Excursion to, i 120
Hitchcock, L J, ii 395
Hoag, Alvan, ii. 145
Hoag, Charles, ii 145
Holt, George, i 475.
Home Journal, i. 91.
Hood, Mrs. Thomas, i 184
Hooker, Isabella Beecher, i 498, ii 185, 209.
Hopkins, James M, ii 150
Hopkins, Mary Sargent, ii 132, 219, 403
Hopper, Edward, i 226.
Hopper, Isaac T, i. 93.
Howard, Rev R B, ii 101
Howard, Rev Rodney H, ii 343
Howard, Gen O O, i. 431, ii 4, 84, 337
Howe, Julia Ward, ii. 146, 147.

Howitt, William and Mary, i 178, 181, 188, ii 274
Hunt, John H., ii 359.
Hunting, Rev A, i 452.
Huntington, E S, ii 185
Hutchinsons, The, ancestry, i 2 Coat-of-arms, i. 2. First concert, 1839, i 35. In Lynn, i 37, 241 Early tours, i 41, 54. First song published, i 64 First concert in Boston, i. 65. Early anti-slavery singing, i. 73 In New York, i 86, 111, 258, 259, 285 At Philadelphia, i 95 At Baltimore, i 100 In Liverpool, i 151 In Dublin, i 152. In Manchester, Eng , i 170 In London, i 178 At Ambleside, i 200-209 In Glasgow, i 209 And Spiritualism, i 271 In St Louis, i 292 In Ohio, i 298. In Potomac camps, 381 Tributes to, 510, 513 "Home Branch," ii 314.
"Hutchinsons' repentance," ii 317-334
Hutchinson, Aaron B , tribe of Noah, ii 238
Hutchinson, Sister Abby, i 6, 46, 67, 78, 133, 179, 201, 225 Marriage, i 250, 252-259, 284, 510, 323-328, 345 354, 355, 364, 366, 367, 371, 438, 459, 461, 489, 490, 494, ii 3, 11, 14, 41, 44, 57, 60, 70, 84, 99, 101, 104, 107, 124, 126, 134, 138, 142, 144, 148, 152, 155, 157, 160, 163, 164, 165, 187, 189, 192 Death of, ii 195 Sketch of, ii. 269. Letters, ii. 365-390
Hutchinson, Abby, tribe of Asa, i 356, 367 , ii. 53, 61, 122, 123, 124
Hutchinson, Andrew, i 4, 361
Hutchinson, Andrew B., tribe of Jesse, i. 6, 13, 39, 113 , ii. 239
Hutchinson, Andrew B , tribe of Noah, ii 238
Hutchinson, Ann J E , tribe of Noah, ii 238
Hutchinson, Asa B , tribe of Jesse, i. 6, 21, 40, 103, 108, 116, 135, 231, 258, 265, 274, 300, 320, 321, 329, 333, 337, 340, 345, 367, 416, 470, 490 , ii. 53, 60, 122, 124. Death of, ii 131 Sketch of, ii 261
Hutchinson, B. P ("Old Hutch"), ii 217
Hutchinson, Benj P , tribe of Andrew, ii 240.
Hutchinson, Benjamin P , tribe of Jesse, i 6, 49, 116, 134, 135 Sketch of, ii. 254
Hutchinson, Bernard, i. 2.

INDEX.

Hutchinson, Caleb, tribe of Jesse, i 6, 100, 119, 266, 319 Death, i 328 Sketch of, ii 241

Hutchinson, Caleb George M, tribe of Caleb, ii. 199, 241.

Hutchinson, C. C , i 456, 457

Hutchinson, David, tribe of Jesse, i 6, 19, 22, 23, 50, 119 ii 70, 99, 100 Death of, ii 102. Sketch of ii. 256 Descendants, ii 257

Hutchinson, David J , tribe of Noah, ii 107, 154, 238

Hutchinson, Delia Florence, tribe of David, ii 237

Hutchinson, Elias S , tribe of David, ii. 16, 109, 154, 237

Hutchinson, Elisha, i 2, 3

Hutchinson, Elizabeth A , tribe of Andrew, ii 115

Hutchinson, Elizabeth C , tribe of Asa, i 90, 231, 354, 356, 474 , ii 269

Hutchinson, Fanny B , tribe of John, i 100, 116, 137, 231 241, 255, 298, 312, 354, 367 , ii. 57, 68, 73, 76, 83, 103, 110, 132, 133, 134, 138, 144 Death of, ii 148

Hutchinson, Frederick C , tribe of Asa, i. 356, 367 , ii 32

Hutchinson, Fordyce, ii 153, 198

Hutchinson, Georgiana, tribe of David, ii. 237

Hutchinson, Hayward, tribe of David, i 317 , ii. 33, 88, 105, 109, 237

Hutchinson, Mrs Hayward, tribe of David, ii 214

Hutchinson, Henry John (Jack), tribe of John, ii. 81, 107, 124, 132, 140, 210

Hutchinson, H Appleton, tribe of Noah, ii. 100, 105, 166, 238.

Hutchinson, Henry J , tribe of John, birth i. 115 , 255, 353, 362, 368, 401, 421, 431, 433, 439, 445, 450, 461, 467, 478, 485, 492, 494 , ii. 8, 21, 24, 25, 30, 31, 36, 41, 43, 44, 52, 55, 56, 63, 76, 86, 90, 101, 106, 108, 123 Death, ii 127

Hutchinson, Hiram, ii. 142   [153.

Hutchinson, Irene, tribe of Joshua, ii

Hutchinson, Jacob F tribe of Andrew, ii 167, 210

Hutchinson, Jerusha, wife of Judson, i 231, 345, 354, 361 , ii 148, 153, 260

Hutchinson, "Uncle" Jesse, father of tribe, i 4, 48, 68, 125, 136 His death, i. 283.

Hutchinson, Jesse, oldest of tribe of Jesse, ii. 235

Hutchinson, Jesse, Jr tribe of Jesse, "Brother Jesse," i 6, 39, 70, 77, 78, 232, 239, 249, 289, 298, 302, 309, 310, 317 Buys High Rock, i 141. In Europe, i 179, 181, 201 In Lynn, i 231, 241, 264, 273 His death, i 318 ii 80 Sketch of , ii. 244, 317-334.

Hutchinson, Jesse, tribe of John, ii 106

Hutchinson, Jesse L , tribe of David, ii 56, 105, 237.

Hutchinson, John W , tribe of Jesse, i 6, 21 Marriage, i 72 ; 250, 253, 298-333, 338, 341, 368, 369, 388, 461, 475 , ii. 2, 17, 22, 28, 30, 40, 80, 113, 117, 152, 133, 159, 163, 165, 188, 193, 197, 200, 209, 211, 224, 231, 256, 266, 275, 291, 303

Hutchinson, John W , 2d , tribe of David, i 439, ii. 108, 226, 237.

Hutchinson, Jonas, ii. 28 55, 153

Hutchinson, Joshua B , tribe of Jesse, i 6, 8, 13, 100, 205, 216, 267, 311, 318, 363, 367, 417, 475, 490 ii 26, 27, 43, 53, 60, 70, 99, 104 Death of, ii 108, 234 Sketch of, ii 242

Hutchinson, Judson J , tribe of Jesse, i 6, 25, 45 49 68, 69 108, 113, 132, 133, 148, 180 184, 240, 236 247, 255, 258, 265, 275-278, 285, 289, 297, 317, 320 337, 340, 345, 356, 359 Death of, i 362 Sketch of, i 255

Hutchinson, Judson Whittier, tribe of John, i 415, 435 , ii. 47, 68, 69, 74, 75, 82, 91, 153, 166

Hutchinson, Kansas, i 456, 457 ii 113

Hutchinson Kate L (See Burney)

Hutchinson, Lillie Phillips, tribe of John, ii 69, 70, 74, 76, 92, 101, 123, 124, 128, 131, 132, 135, 138, 140, 143, 210, 229

Hutchinson, Lucius B., tribe of Noah, ii. 138, 144, 152, 153, 160, 166, 184, 195, 214 238, 275

Hutchinson, Lucretia O tribe of David, ii 237

Hutchinson, Mary, tribe of Jesse, ii. 239

Hutchinson, Mary tribe of Noah, ii 163

Hutchinson, Mary Leavitt, mother of tribe, i 4, 6, 67, 143, 319, 364. Death, i 470 Portrait, ii 277

Hutchinson, Matthew B., tribe of Noah, ii 238

Hutchinson, Marcus Morton, tribe of Andrew, ii 167, 240
Hutchinson, Minn, founded, i 340 Story of, i. 340-353, 424, 445, 447 ii 53, 122, 138, 139, 144 230, 257
Hutchinson, Nellie MacKay, ii 14
Hutchinson, Noah, i. 6, 119 Sketch of, ii 238
Hutchinson, Oliver Dennett, tribe of Asa, i. 367, ii. 60, 152, 188 205, 208
Hutchinson, Richard, tribe of John, ii 132, 138, 140, 210
Hutchinson, Rhoda, i 6, 43, 143, 319, ii 70 99, 104 Death, ii 105 Sketch of, ii 260
Hutchinson, Richard, emigrant ancestor, i. 2.
Hutchinson, Robert, i 435, ii 93
Hutchinson, Viola (See Campbell)
Hutchinson, Virginia tribe of David, ii 237
Hutchinson, William, ii 154
Hutchinson, William Henry, ii 168
Hutchinson, Zephaniah K, tribe of Jesse, i 6, 13, 100, 111, 113, 127, 231, 289, 290. His death, i 318 Sketch of, ii 240.

I

Ingersoll, Col R G, i 472, ii 109
Ives, Rev B 1 ii 3

J

Jackson, Francis, i 74, 87, 112, 119, 217
Jackson, Harriet, i 78, 143
Jackson, Joseph C, i 387, 388.
Jackson, Dr Sheldon, ii 81
Jennings, C C i 304
Jerrold, Douglas, i 176, 178, 215, 340
Johnson, Andrew, ii 3.
Johnson David N, ii 168
Johnson Clifton, ii 222
Johnson, E. E. i. 338, 339, ii 53, 143, 185, 361
Johnson Rev. Herrick, i 432
Johnson, Rev Samuel, i 460, ii 30
Johnson, Oliver, i. 131, 497
Jones, Rev. Jesse H, ii 167
"Jordan," Judson's song, ii 259
Judson, E. Z C, ii 2
Judson Lake, Minn, i. 340.

K

Kalloch, Rev J S, i 463, ii 79, 80, 89.
Kansas campaign, i 470
Kearney, Denis, ii 88
Kearney, Gen Philip H, i 385 388 408, 411.
Keene William G S, ii 94, 95, 168
Kellogg, Rev G N, ii 117.
Kendrick, Rev T F, ii 3
Keppler, Jonathan, i 467
Kimball, Josiah F, ii 254
Kimball, Harriet McEwen, ii 256
Kimball, Rufus, ii 254
Kirk, Rev E N, i 241
Kittredge, Walter, i 367. Composes "Tenting To night," i 417, ii 45, 61, 101, 130, 190, 194
Klepper, Rev J W, ii 261
Knight, "Master," i 31

L

Ladd, President H O, ii 117
"Land Beyond the Blue," song, ii 78
Latimer, George W, rescued from slavery, i 71 Anti-slavery addresses, i 78; ii 219, 350
"Lay Him Low," song, ii 126.
Lease, Mary E, ii 218
Leavitt, Andrew, "Old Grandfather," i 5, 36, 218, 220
Leavitt, Deacon John, i 5
Leavitt, Joshua, i 376.
Leavitt, Kendrick, i 220, 240, 317, 379
Leavitt, Mary, mother of Hutchinsons, i 4, 6 (See Hutchinson)
Leavitt, Col Nathaniel, i 64, 67
Leavitt, Sarah, i 7
LeBaron, Marie, ii 41.
Lee, Gen Robert E, i 364, ii 7
Leggett, M D, ii 38
Lerow, William A, ii 109
Leui, Frederick, ii 56
Lewis, Alonzo, i 320
Lewis, Dr Dio ii 37
Liberator, The i 73, 240, ii 317-334
Lincoln, Abraham, i 291, 370, 372, 373, 374, 380 427
Lincoln, "Tad," i 380.
Lind, Jenny, i. 267, 268 307, 308
Little Crow, Chief of Sioux, i 349, 351, 352.
Little, Dr. F. F, ii. 117.

Livermore, Mrs Mary A., i 479-483, 488;
 ii 45, 106, 137, 147
Lloyd, Bertha, ii. 176
Lloyd, Dr Charles, ii 168
Lockwood, Belva A , ii 33, 147
Logan, Gen. John A , i. 471
Logan, Olive, i 488
Longfellow, Henry W , i. 91, 252
Longfellow Rev Samuel, ii. 30
Longstreet, Mrs Gildersleeve, i 357 ii 86
Loomis, Martha, i 357
Lord, David J , ii 96, 108.
Lord, George T , ii. 168
Loring, George B., ii 125.
Loveridge, Marietta Bartlett ii 105, 108, 261
Lovejoy, Owen, i 420
Lowell, James Russell, i 79 82
Lull, Col. Oliver, i 319
Luscomb, Charles, i 428.
Lydston, Frank, i 42
Lynn, i 37, 40, 45

M.

MacKaye, Steele, ii 48.
Macready, Charles, i 176
"Maniac" song i 93; ii 294.
Mann, Charles L , ii 170, 176, 394
Mann, Horace, i. 62
Mann, S T , i 296
Mansfield, Rev L D , ii 88
Martha's Vineyard, i 321, ii 14, 18, 26
Marble, Hiram and Edwin, i 273
Martin, Frank, i 379
Martineau, Harriet i 200, 243
Marvel, Abby, i. 320
Marvel, Henry, i 249
Marvel, William, i 119
"Mary at the Cross" song, i 484
Mason, Dr. Lowell, i 38.
Massey, Gerald, ii 16
Mathew, Father i 159
May, Capt , ii 6
May, Rev Samuel, i 75 , ii 148,199, 357
May, Rev Samuel J i 127 132, 278
Maynard, Caroline B i 296
Maynard, John Q , ii 32
McClellan, Gen George B , i 387, 391, 394, 395.
McDonnell, W O , ii 215
McLane, John, ii 220.

McMartin, Duncan, i 257
Mead, Rev C H , ii. 232.
Mead, Edwin D., ii 197
Merritt, Charles M , ii 253.
Merritt, Rev Stephen, ii 1, 43.
Merritt, William H , ii 253
Merwin, Rev J B , i 381 386, 423, 462
Messer, B L , i 338
Miles, Gen. Nelson A , ii 208
Milford, N H Hutchinsons settle in, i 3 Description of i 7, 8
"Millennium," The, song, ii. 51
Mills, Ezekiel, i 36
Mills, John, ii. 187
Mills, Lloyd, ii 258.
Miner, Rev A A , ii. 109, 134 186, 213.
"Moll Pitcher " i 422, 423
Montgomery, Gen , i 390, 392
Mont Vernon, N H , i 4, 415
Moody, Dwight L , i. 483, 484
Moore, Rev Humphrey, i 11 12
Moore, Rebecca i 161 162, 194, 199, 450, ii 130 146, 341
Moore, Robert, i 161, 195
Morgan, Rev Henry, ii. 143, 210, 213 229
Morris, Gen George P , i 92
Morris, Robert, ii 92.
Morse, J F , i 303
Morse, S T B , i 332
Mosher, Minnie F , ii 106
Moss, Rev Lemuel, i 431
Mott, Lucretia i 226, 227, 246, 460 ; ii. 30, 49
"Mrs Lofty and I," song, i 357.
Muir, Dr John, ii. 81
Muzzey, Osgood, i 106, 249
Muzzey, R D , i 6
"My Jesus says there's Room Enough," song, ii 5.
"My Mother's Bible," song, i 139

N

Nast, Thomas, ii 23
Neal John i 129 ii 392 393
Neale, Jenniebelle, ii 103, 183
Newhall Capt George Thompson, ii
Newhall J Warren, ii 123 167, 189
Newhall, William O , ii 191
Newland, Luke P , i 61, 63, 131, 297
Newman Bishop John P , ii 63, 64
"Noggs' (Dr Kittredge), i. 164, 173, 177, 242

INDEX.

Norton, D S , i. 473.
Norton, Charles Eliot, ii 225.
Norton, Hon. Mrs , i 176.
North American Phalanx, i 80, 263
Nye, Joseph Warren, ii. 176, 185, 398, 399

O.

O Connell, Daniel, i 158, 159.
Oglesby, Richard, i 469, 471, 473.
"Old Granite State," family song, i 86, 160, ii 298
"Old High Rock,' song, i 323
"One Hundred Years Hence,' song, i. 161
Owen, Robert, i 85

P.

Painesville riot, i 301-303
Palfray, Warwick, i 44, ii 141
Palmer, Mrs. Potter, ii 217
Parker, Theodore, i 78, 231, 271, 378
Parton, James, ii 157
Patch, Burnam, ii. 150.
Patch, David, ii. 150.
Patch, David A , ii. 149
Patch, Fannie B , wife of John, i. 72 (See Hutchinson.)
Patch, Susanna (Parker), ii 149
Patton, Rev Cornelius, ii 195
Patton, Ludlow, i 230, 231, 248, 250, 258, 278, 432 ; ii. 84, 86, 104, 105, 108, 155, 157, 160, 163, 165, 189, 192, 219
Patton, Rev. William, D D , i. 86, 239, 265 , ii 44, 287.
Patton, Rev. Wm. W , i 229, 254
Patton (See Abby Hutchinson)
Payne, Bishop D A , ii 49
Peabody, Col. Stephen, i. 27
Pendergast, Lizzie, ii 268.
Pendergast, Roswell i 338.
Pendergast, W W , i. 350.
Pentecost, Rev Geo F , ii 107.
Phillips Fred , ii 210
Phillips Philip, i 431
Phillips, Wendell, i 74, 77, 120, 137, 240, 407, 452, 461 , ii 49 Funeral of, ii. 126, 317-334
Pickard, S T , ii 155, 157, 192
Pierpont, Rev. John, i 78, 113, 120, 230, 246, 260

Pierce, Franklin, i 336
Pilley, John H , ii 72
Pillsbury, Albert E , ii 220
Pillsbury, Gilbert P , ii. 4
Pillsbury, J W , ii. 187, 229
Pillsbury, Josiah H., i 451
Pillsbury, Parker, i 78, 88, 119, 126, 130, 140, 153; ii. 187, 199, 358, 358
Pinkham, Lydia F , ii. 110
Plug Uglies, i 375
Polk, James K , i 237
Pomeroy, S C., i. 451
Poole, Mrs Clara J , ii 55.
Pope, Gen John, i. 351
Porter, Rev. Aaron, ii 200
Porter, Charles C P , ii 150
Porter, Rev. George W., ii. 199.
Porter, Gen Horace, ii. 206
Porter, Morgiana M , "Cousin Maud," i 422 , ii 149
Porter, Linn B , i 143.
Porter, Thomas F , ii 404.
Portland, Me , i 127
Portland riot, ii. 391.
Portsmouth, N H , i 46, 66.
Potomac, Army of, i 381-398
Powell, A. M., ii. 33, 36
Pratt, Rev E H , ii 15, 19
Proctor, H. Maria, ii 397
Punshon, Rev. William Morely, ii 29
Purdy, Capt E S , i. 388.
Purvis, Robert, i 120, 223, 226 , ii 49
Putnam, Rev A P , ii 167, 199, 357
Putnam, George W , i. 268, 428 , ii. 161 191, 401

Q

Quincy, Edmund, i 74, 120, 459
Quint, Rev. Alonzo H , ii 191

R.

Ramsdell, Ella F , ii 61
Ramsdell, George A , ii 191, 220
Ramsdell, John, i 281, ii 130
Ramsey, Alexander, i. 319, 353
Randolph, Rev. Peter, ii. 204.
Ream, Vinnie, ii. 39.
Redpath, James, i 494
Remond, C L , i 74, 89 , ii. 391
Richardson, Rev. J G., i. 36, 135
Richmond, Va , ii 43
Richter, Carl, ii. 34.

Ridgway, Graziella, 1 460, 462, 489; 11 15 30 161
Ripley, Rev George, 1 40, 82.
Roberts, C C , 11 218
Roberts, James H , 11 106 [463
Robinson, Gov. Charles, of Kansas, 1.
Robinson, George T , 11 168
Robinson, John Lewis, 1 335, 11 169
Rochester, N Y , 1 271
Rogers, Nathaniel Peabody, 1 51, 74, 75, 87, 88, 100, 117, 123 126 140, 242, 272 , 11 250, 355
Rogers, Samuel, 1 176
Root, F W , 11 43
Root, George F , 1 417
Root, J P , 11 344
Russell, Constance, 1 450.
Russell, Henry, 1 93, 159, 196
Russell, William E , 11 208
Russell, Thomas, 1. 491
Rynders, Isaiah, 1 262, 263

S

Saco, Me , 1. 46
Sanderson, Rev Alonzo, 11 107.
Sankey, Ira D , 1 484
Santa Fé, N. M , 11 110
Saratoga, First visit to, 1 55
Sauret, Auguste, 11 55
Savage, Rev. M J , 11 358
Sawtelle, J M , 1 427, 11 149
Sawtell, John, 1 314
Sawyer, Mrs Estella, 1 465
Saxe, John G , 1. 56, 308
Saxton, C M , 1 91
Scott, Gen. Winfield, 1 374
Severence, Theodore C , 1. 277, 299, 312 11 12, 145, 389
Severence, Mrs. T C , 1 297, 298, 11 214
Seward, William H , 1 311, 451
Sharpe, Edmund, 1 148, 191, 196, 197
Sharp, Henry John, 1 19
Shepherd, Col Allen G , 1 477, 11 31 45
Sheridan, Gen Geo W , 11 144.
Sheridan, Gen P H , 1. 486
Sherman, John, 11 64
Sherman, Gen W T , 1 431, 11 38, 336
Shields, Gen James, 1 401, 424
"Ship on Fire," song, 1 329
Shurz, Carl, 1 401, 448
Sibley, Gen H A , 1 350
Sigourney, Lydia H , 1 115.

Simpson, Bishop Matthew, 1 432
Sing Sing, Singing at, 1 139, 225.
Slayton, H L , 11 68.
Small, Rev Sam , 11 194
Smith, Dexter, 1 485
Smith, Elias, 1 255
Smith, G P , 1 458, 462.
Smith, Gerrit, 1 428 , 11 338.
Smith, John D , 11 219.
Smith, Rev. J Hyatt, 11 26
Smith, Matthew Hale, 11 1
Smith, Rev. S F , 11 156, 362
Smith, T A , 11 134
Sioux Indians destroy Hutchinson, 1. 350
Sohier, Charles W , 11 32, 43, 61.
Somerset, Lady Henry, 11 186.
Spiritualism, 1. 271.
Spofford, Jane H , 11 125
Sprague, Kate Chase, 1 401, 403
Sprague, Seth, 1 73
Springer, Wm M , 11 113, 148, 363
"Standing Collar," song 1. 261, 287
Stanton, Elizabeth Cady, 1 457, 451, 461, 479, 482 , 11 33, 281.
Stanton, Edwin M , 1 381, 431.
Stark, Rev J W., 11. 117
Stearns, J N , 11 46, 349
Stebbins, George C , 11. 107.
Stedman, Edmund Clarence, 11. 193
St John, John P , 11 109.
Stephens, Alexander H , 11 40
Sterling, Antoinette, 11 23, 30
Stevens, George P , 1. 475
Stevens, John H , 1 338, 339.
Stewart, Rev Samuel B., 11. 363.
Still, William, 11 49
Stimpson, Phineas, 1 30
Stimpson, S B , 1 491, 495, 11 4
Stone, Rev. A L , 11. 91
Stone, Lucy, 1. 316, 456, 458, 461, 483, 490 ; 11 45, 146, 160, 2 0
Storrs, Emory A , 1. 471
Stowe, Harriet Beecher, 1 314 323 , 11. 4.
Stuart, George H , 1 431
Sumner, Charles, 1 312 , 11 37 [411.
"Sweet By and By," Story of song, 1.

T

Talmage, Rev T DeWitt, 11 17.
Tanner, T H , 11 132
Tappan, Mason W , 11 189

INDEX.

"Tenting To-night" song, i. 418
Thaxter, Celia, ii. 163.
Thayer, Adin, i. 337
Thomas, Allen H., ii. 193
Thomas, A. H., ii. 403
Thomas, Charlotte J., ii. 167, 226
Thomas, George A., ii. 167
Thompson, Rev. Edwin, ii. 19, 152
Thompson, George, i. 165, 166, 173, 178, 181, 183, 186, 278
Thompson, Waldo, ii. 169
Thompson, William D., ii. 167
Tiffany, Rev. O. H., ii. 19, 29.
Tilton, Theodore, i. 492
"'Tis Coming Up the Steep of Time," song, ii. 159
"Topsy," song, ii. 292
Tottingham, M. T., i. 307
Tourjee, Eben, i. 489.
Towne, Mrs. Jonathan, ii. 160.
Towns, Quincy A., ii. 168
Tracy, Cyrus Mason, ii. 123, 132, 167, 179, 186
Train, George Francis, i. 479.
Tribune, New York, i. 91, 235
Trumbull, Lyman, i. 473
Tuck, Amos, i. 294
Turner, Granville, i. 122, 125.
Tuttle, Asa C., ii. 193
Tyler, President John, i. 89, 105

U

"Under the Ice," song, ii. 90
Urso, Camilla, i. 485, 486, ii. 55
Usher, Col. Roland G., ii. 136

V

Van Buren, John, i. 243, 245
Vance, R. B., ii. 36
Vincent, Bishop John H., ii. 81.
"Vote it Right Along," song, i. 444.

W

Wade, Benjamin F., i. 491.
Waite, Charles B., i. 481, 482.
Walker, J. B., ii. 388
Walker, Dr. Mary E., ii. 42, 147
Wallace, Alice Hutchinson, tribe of Noah, ii. 152, 166
Wallace, John J., ii. 359.

Wallace, Luther, i. 99
Wallace, R. M., ii. 219
Wallace, William Vincent, i. 358, 359.
Wanamaker, John, ii. 62, 155
Ware, Benjamin P., ii. 153
Warner, Rev. Abner B., i. 48, ii. 149
Warner, Charles Dudley, ii. 225
Washington, D. C., i. 103, 236, 311, 374, 398, 431, ii. 34, 154, 194
"Wax Work," song, i. 269
Wayland, Rev. Francis, i. 130
Webb, Prof. Geo. James, i. 38, 65
Webb, Richard D., i. 163, 461
Webb, Thomas, i. 156
Webster, Charles, ii. 106
Webster, Daniel, in Harrison campaign, i. 26, 103, 116, 306
Webster, J. P., i. 440
Weed, Thurlow, i. 61; ii. 336
Weiss, Rev. John, ii. 30
Weld, Anna H., ii. 167
Weld, Theodore D., i. 377, ii. 131, 167, 170, 227
Welling, Col. E. L., i. 381, 396
Wellington, Duke of, i. 182, 183
Wendelstat, Edward F., ii. 163
Weston, Edward Payson, ii. 254
"Which Way is your Musket A-p'intin' To-day?" song, ii. 101
Whipple Zerah C., ii. 31
White, May, i. 300
White Mountains, Early trips to, i. 122
White, William A., i. 79
Whitcomb, Jack, i. 415
Whitmore, W. H., ii. 53
Whittier, John Greenleaf, i. 101, 315, 382, 384, 397, ii. 49, 157; Death of, ii. 191, 336
Whittier, Louisa L., i. 440
Widdows, F., i. 458, ii. 34.
Willard, Andrew L., i. 229, 243
Willard, Frances E., ii. 147, 361.
Willett, Rev. J. W., ii. 18
Williams, Moses, i. 466, 486
Willis, Nathaniel Parker, i. 46, 309, ii. 270
Wilson, Henry, i. 366, 378, 491, ii. 33, 50
Wilson, Gen. James, i. 26
Wilson, James M., i. 388
Winnebago Indians, i. 345
Wood, S. N., i. 451
Woodbury, Hon. Levi, i. 66, 105.
Woods, George, ii. 62

Woods, Kate Tannatt, ii. 200, 228
World's Fair, ii 205.
Wright, Edward N., i 148
Wright, Eliza, i 217, 240, ii 49, 326
Wright, Henry C, i 74, 240, 332, ii 322

Y

Yale College, i. 230
Yard, Rev R B, i. 379, 381, 386, 389, 420 ii 17.
Yates, Richard, i. 166–168, 173
Yerrinton, J M W, ii 199
Young, Edward, ii 33.
Young, Frank L, ii 72
Young, James R, ii 34
Young, John M., ii 34
Young, S G, ii 34

Z

Zerrahn, Carl, i 489.

CPSIA information can be obtained at www.ICGtesting.com
Printed in the USA
LVOW050606030212

266861LV00002B/489/P